C0-ARE-110

The Vision and the Reality

The Story of Home Missions in the General Conference Mennonite Church

By Lois Barrett

Commissioned by the Commission on Home Ministries
of the General Conference Mennonite Church

Faith and Life Press
Newton, Kansas

Library of Congress Catalog Card Number 83-80402
International Standard Book Number 0-87303-079-6
Printed in the United States of America
Copyright © 1983 by Faith and Life Press
718 Main Street, Newton, KS 67114

This publication may not be reproduced, stored in a retrieval system, or transmitted in whole or in part, in any form or by any means, electronic, mechanical, photocopying, recording, or otherwise, without the prior written permission of Faith and Life Press.

Design by John Hiebert
Printing by Mennonite Press, Inc.

MENNONITE HISTORICAL SERIES

To all those Mennonites who can't play the "Mennonite game" because they aren't related to anyone the other player knows

Foreword

This is the story of General Conference Mennonite Church (GCMC) outreach ministries in North America since the conference was founded in 1860. It is a dramatic story. A large cast of characters of very diverse social, ethnic, and economic backgrounds have been and are involved in the drama. At times it is a sobering story of mistakes and prejudices, personality conflicts, and failure. But it is also a story of significant achievements, sacrificial giving of time and talent, grace and faithfulness. Many people dreamed many dreams, and a good number of them came true.

The scope of material gathered by the author is impressive, but so is the broad responsibility of the Commission of Home Ministries (CHM), which is presently responsible for carrying on the work described here. The old pattern of itinerant ministers has been discontinued, but native ministries, peace activities, planting churches in the cities, voluntary service, and other programs have continued and grown in their challenge for today. The conference has grown in its skill in choosing significant points of involvement among a myriad of possibilities. In terms of personnel and budgets, it is truly amazing to see how much has been, and is, being done with so little. The GCMC needs to enlarge its vision and commitment to ministries in North America.

Is this volume primarily a description of the work which has been done in some 125 years of "home" mission? It is indeed that, but much more. It is biography in which the lives of countless persons open up to us as they struggle for faithfulness against great odds. It is the story of people who were being assimilated into the mainstream of North American life while trying to find the relevance of their sixteenth-century heritage for their own day. It is, in a particularly poignant way, also the story of non-ethnic Swiss-German-Dutch "new" Mennonites trying to find out what they had become and where they fitted into the larger conference family.

The author has done well indeed in gathering together a great deal of detailed information and organizing it into such a readable and interesting manuscript. Beyond that, she has succeeded in asking the critical question, probing the roots of seemingly insignificant events, thus creating not only an account of what happened, but helping the reader to think further about the origins and consequences of these events.

What does it mean to be a Mennonite? There are no neat and final answers to that question in this volume, but it does present a magnificent, down-to-earth interpretive account of what this has meant in specific situations and what it can increasingly come to mean for all those who are caught up in this vision of kingdom work.

Cornelius J. Dyck
Elkhart, Indiana

Preface

How does an ethnic church do home missions? Almost by definition, missions is to transcend ethnic barriers. So what kind of missions is established by an ethnic church? What effect does missions have on an ethnic church? Is it possible to be in mission and remain an ethnic church?

These are the questions that intrigued me as Dale Suderman and I set out to research a history of North American missions in the General Conference Mennonite Church. The questions had personal importance as well, since neither of us grew up in the General Conference. I had had no Mennonite background at all before becoming a Mennonite in 1971.

There are other questions that could have been asked of the conference's home missions history. Within the book, there are references to the rural-urban tension, race, the role of women, the relationship of mission and service, and the effects of neo-Anabaptism and fundamentalism on missions. But the primary focus is on ethnicity, because basic to being a people in mission is overcoming the "dividing walls of hostility" between groups within the church and becoming a new people of God.

Although I take full responsibility for the final form of the book, I owe a great debt to Dale Suderman, my colleague at the beginning of this project. His vision for the book sparked my own enthusiasm. His research and interviews—and in some cases, his first drafts—formed the basis of the chapters on missions among the Cheyenne and Hopi.

Many thanks also go to the Commission of Home Ministries, which has funded the project; to Palmer Becker and E. Stanley Bohn, successive executive secretaries of the commission, who supported, encouraged, and pushed Dale and me; to

Melanie Gingrich Mueller, who typed most of the manuscript twice; to Lawrence Hart, Larry Kehler, Ernest Neufeld, and Dale Schrag, who served as a reference committee for the North American Mission and Service History Project and made suggestions on the first draft of the manuscript; to all those who read individual chapters and offered suggestions for improvement; and to all those who gave interviews and sent us congregational records, histories, and photographs. My special thanks goes to Thomas Mierau, my husband, who babysat through two summers so that I could finish the project and spent many additional hours listening to my excitement and my depression concerning the project.

My hope is that this book will help General Conference Mennonites to understand their missions history, to learn from past successes and failures, and to continue building that new household of God, written of in Ephesians 2:19, which has no walls dividing Jew from Gentile, or German from English, Spanish, Chinese, Cheyenne, and Hopi.

Lois Barrett
Elkhart, Indiana

Contents

Introduction:
Acquiring the Mission Spirit

"The remarkable thing about the conference is that there is a strong bond of family relationships existing among us as well as a loyalty to a common faith. The same family names appear in the lists of membership in all our local conferences and churches. Perhaps no other Protestant body comes so near being a large family as well as being a united church. Yet, if it be true that our people are so much of one blood, it is also true that the home mission vision is a clear and compelling one."
Silas M. Grubb, The Mennonite, *June 18, 1931*

"Resolved, that home and foreign missions work be carried on in the future by our conference according to its strength, willingness, and discernment...." So decided the first session in 1860 at West Point, Iowa, of what was then known as the *General Conference of Mennonites in North America*. The decision for conference involvement in home as well as foreign missions was not controversial among the small group from Iowa and Pennsylvania assembled to found the new denomination. The idea of designating special people to win non-Christians to the Christian faith—the missionary movement—was sweeping across North America and Europe. With it came the ideas of church-sponsored schools, church periodicals, and the structuring of the denominations which multiplied in the United States particularly after the disestablishment of the state churches (the last state church being dissolved in Massachusetts in 1833).

A new era for churches in North America was under way in the midday of the Second Great Awakening. Disciples, Presbyterians, and others were setting up new denominational structures or centralizing old structures. Mission societies were being formed; the American Home Missionary Society was started in 1826 to establish churches on the frontier of white settlements. Sunday schools were springing up; the American Sunday School Union was formed in 1824. Colleges were established to train the workers for these activities. Periodicals, including "new" Mennonite John Oberholtzer's *Religioeser Botschafter* in Pennsylvania, spread the news of the Awakening.

The Mennonites who formed a General Conference in the 1860s were those who had been deeply influenced by the new religious movements around them, yet wanted to remain Mennonites. Some other Mennonites, like Christian Newcomer (1750-1830) in Pennsylvania, had left the Mennonite church to work in other, more revivalistic circles. But most Mennonites in North America were suspicious of the new movements, fearing erosion of traditional beliefs in church discipline and nonconformity to the world. One later writer labeled such traditional Mennonites in terms of "the dormant state, the exclusiveness and bigotry that was found among these people who wished to be aloof from the 'world.'"[1] But those who formed the General Conference were ready to try to combine what they thought was the best of the religious movements around them with their distinctive Mennonite beliefs.

The missionary convictions of the "new" Mennonites of eastern Pennsylvania, Ohio, and Ontario, mostly descendants of seventeenth- and eighteenth-century immigrants from Europe, had been influenced by the Protestants around them, including the Moravians, the Quakers, the Schwenkfelders, the Dunkards, and the German Baptists of the Ephrata Community. But the main force behind the new missionary movement among North American Mennonites in 1860 was South German Mennonitism of more recent immigration. Pennsylvania Mennonites had had contact with these South German Mennonites through their periodical *Mennonitische Blaetter*. Then in 1830 to 1860 many South German Mennonites, fleeing Napoleonic conscription into the military, immigrated to Summerfield, Illinois, and Lee County, Iowa, bringing with them the ideas of European Pietism, including the Christian's obligation to preach the gospel to those outside the church, particularly in other lands, and the importance of inner conversion. Some of the new immigrants had been educated in European theological or mission schools.

This emphasis on mission was attractive to the Russian-Dutch, Prussian-Dutch, and Russian-Swiss Mennonites who immigrated to North America in the 1870s and thereafter and who were to become a majority in the General Conference. Mennonites had already been involved in mission work in Russia after their exposure to German Lutheran Pietism through Eduard Wuest. In 1869 Heinrich Dirks and Agnes Schroeder Dirks from the Gnadenfeld Church in the Molotschna Colony had gone to Sumatra under the Amsterdam Mennonite Missionary Society, established in 1847.

Russian Mennonites had been helped financially in the immigration most by the "old" Mennonites, but that group had yet to organize denominationally (not until 1898) and had shown little interest in missions. Many Russian Mennonite congregations in the United States joined the General Conference of Mennonites because of its interest in missions, and they, in turn, added enthusiasm to the conference's missionary movement.[2]

The young General Conference of Mennonites, unique among Mennonite groupings in its weaving of various Mennonite ethnic strands into a coalition, tried also to weave together its Anabaptist heritage with its newfound missionary interest. Carl H. A. van der Smissen, whose father had been brought from Germany to Ohio by the conference in 1868 as theological professor in its new Wadsworth school, justified the current interest in missions, particularly the traveling ministry, in 1890 by pointing back to the missionary activity of the sixteenth-century Anabaptists in central and northern Europe, the religious forebears of Mennonites.[3] The General Conference leaders thought Mennonites could still retain their belief in nonparticipation in warfare or refusal to swear oaths while observing Jesus' commandment to preach the gospel to all nations, almost forgotten during centuries of persecution and then isolation. The early issues of *The Mennonite*, first the periodical of the Eastern District Conference, then the English paper of the whole General Conference of Mennonites, included many articles on peace as well as numerous reports of missionary activities by other denominations.

But there was a difference between the missions of the Anabaptists and new missionary movement as adopted by the Mennonites. The Anabaptists as evangelists had called their neighbors out of the Catholic and Protestant established churches around them into a disciplined community of believers. The Mennonite missionaries of the nineteenth century, on the other hand, focused not on their non-Mennonite neighbors nor on other German-speaking North Americans, but on those most like them—other Mennonites who had moved out of concentrated Mennonite communities or traditional Mennonites who had not yet adopted the new ways of Pietism and missions—and second, on those least like them, the "heathen"— those in foreign lands who had never heard the gospel, or the North American Indians—in short, "those of other races," as one missionary later put it.[4]

The choosing of these two groups as objects of mission satisfied both the old and the new parts of General Conference Mennonite theology: it allowed the sending of missionaries to spread the gospel, and it preserved the cultural and ethnic purity of the Mennonite churches at home. New Christians in India or China or even Oklahoma Territory were unlikely to ask for membership in Mennonite churches at home.

Not until after the turn of the century, influenced both by Moody revivals and, to a lesser extent, by the Social Gospel proponents, did General Conference Mennonites begin to think of a mission to Americans not of Mennonite heritage. Just as Mennonites fifty years earlier had had to be convinced of the need for foreign missions, now most General Conference Mennonites had to be convinced that missions to other Americans, especially urban Americans, was desirable, or even possible. New questions arose: Were the converts of Mennonite city missions Mennonites? Should the missions include the word *Mennonite* in their names? Should the missions emphasize Mennonite "peculiarities" such as nonresistance? How would the new mission churches be integrated into the larger conference if there were no family ties? Some General Conference Mennonites even asked, If people of Mennonite heritage move to the cities, can they still be Mennonites? At stake was a three-hundred-year-old definition of *Mennonite* in which theology, church, family, and culture were tangled.

What follows in this book is the story of how General Conference Mennonites, tangles and all, began reaching out in mission and service to others in North America: to their own wandering kin, to native Americans, and to other immigrants who came to these shores with different family names and different cultures.

J. B. and Jennie (Roberts) Baer

Mennonite Library and Archives

Chapter 1:
The Traveling Ministers

"The traveling ministry has the calling among us to clear the field and prepare the soil for a systematic and energetic carrying out of home missions by our fellowship." David Goerz[1]

The new General Conference inaugurated its home mission work at its second session May 20-23, 1861, with the appointment of its first home missionary, Daniel Hege of the South German Mennonite settlement near Summerfield, Illinois. As conference *Reiseprediger*, or traveling minister, his job was more than just visiting existing churches and holding revival meetings. He was to promote conference membership among the unaffiliated Mennonite churches (of which there were many) and to find support for the conference's plans in education, publication, and foreign missions. He was also to visit scattered individual Mennonites to encourage them and to organize them into congregations.[2]

Just as this establishing and building up of congregations was basic to the Methodist circuit riders on the American frontier, so it served a function among General Conference Mennonites and Mennonite Brethren in North America. The Mennonites of South Germany, Switzerland, France, and Russia also used traveling ministers, beginning in the late nineteenth century.[3]

Although Daniel Hege's term as traveling minister was cut short by his unexpected death in November 1862, he is credited with providing the impetus to start First Mennonite Church in Philadelphia, the conference's first church in a large city.[4] Upon his first visit there in 1862, he contacted a number of Mennonites who were living in Philadelphia but attending worship and holding membership in churches in the surrounding towns and countryside. The Philadelphia church, organized in 1865, was a "downtown" church. Under the thirty-nine-year pastoral leadership of Nathaniel B. Grubb it grew by 1920 to be the largest and perhaps the most influential congregation in the Eastern District Conference. Grubb also founded the periodical *The Mennonite* and organized at least four churches in the Eastern District. First Church, Philadelphia, was responsible for a number of innovations in the conference, including child consecration in 1884 and the use of a printed weekly bulletin in 1901.[5]

For the first twenty-five years of the General Conference's existence, most of the traveling ministers appointed by the conference spent only a few weeks or months going from church to church, spending a day or two here, a week there. A few were authorized to help part-time in specific locations. For example, M. S. Moyer served Clarence Center and Niagara Falls, New York.[6]

Before 1884, the sending of traveling evangelists for the conference was sporadic, almost haphazard. Between the 1878 and 1881 conferences, for example, Samuel F. Sprunger, M. S. Moyer, and Albert E. Funk visited Indiana, Ohio, and the area near Niagara Falls but "comparatively little was accomplished."[7] The 1881 conference decided to send one minister from the East to the western churches and one from the West to the eastern churches, but the exchange never took place. The early Home Mission Board was, in fact, so inactive that neither the president nor the secretary of the board was present at the 1884 conference, nor had they even sent reports. Disturbed by the lack of activity, the conference increased the size of the committee from three to five and decided to hire a full-time "permanent" home missionary.[8]

The person the Home Mission Board appointed was John B. Baer of Summerfield, Illionis, a student at Union Theological Seminary in New York City. Baer had worked as a colporteur for the American Tract Society in New York and in Canada and as a missionary in New York City. He began working for the General Conference in the summer of 1885 among Pennsylvania and New York churches and continued full time after his schooling was finished in 1887.

Home mission work for Baer was primarily the encouragement of independent Mennonite congregations to join the General Conference, stimulating them to new interest in the causes of missions, education, and publication. But he worked on an individual as well as a congregational level. When Baer went to an area, he not only preached in the churches, but he also called at homes, sometimes making as many as fifty calls a week. "In most cases," he reported, "I read a chapter from God's Word, prayed with the people, and spoke to them of the 'one thing needed.'"[9] In spite of his education at a seminary disliked by those who feared "higher criticism" of the Bible, Baer was evangelical in his approach to the congregations. At the Berne, Indiana, church, he asked: Are you a Christian? Will you become one? Why not tonight?[10] During Baer's eight-day stay at one church in Iowa, thirty conversions were reported. "Everywhere," commented historian H. P. Krehbiel, "[Baer] sought to awaken and stimulate spiritual life, as also to cultivate a sense of fellowship with other churches."[11]

The General Conference of Mennonites in which Baer worked had only forty-eight congregations in 1890. No member congregation was west of Kansas, and there was just one in all of Canada. The Ontario churches that had participated in the founding of the conference had become the Mennonite Brethren in Christ (now United Missionary Church). Baer, as traveling minister, set about to build up the size of the conference.

In 1890 Baer went to the Pacific Coast, encouraging new Mennonite immigrants in the area to organize churches, even if only a few families had yet settled there. He personally planned and arranged the first meeting of the Pacific District Conference on May 25, 1896, in Pratum, Oregon. Representatives of congregations near Irving, Polk Station, and Eugene, Oregon, and Colfax, Washington, were present, but conference leaders from farther east dominated the conference. Samuel F. Sprunger of Berne, Indiana, was chairman; Jacob J. Balzer of Mountain Lake, Minnesota, was secretary; also present were Baer; P. P. Steiner and J. A. Amstutz of Bluffton, Ohio; and Christian Kaufman of Childstown, South Dakota. At the second session, Baer was president and David Goerz of Newton, Kansas, was secretary of the Pacific District Conference.[12]

Baer also visited budding churches in North Dakota and Minnesota and was influential in the beginnings of the Northern District Conference, which met first in 1891 in Mountain Lake, Minnesota, with Baer as chairman.

In 1890, on the same trip in which he went to the Pacific

Coast, Baer stopped in Southern Manitoba for another visit to the Bergthaler Church (he had been there first in 1887). In general, the Russian Mennonites who had immigrated to Canada in the 1870s were more conservative than those who had gone to the United States from Russia. But the Bergthaler Church (with a number of meeting places presided over by a common group of clergy) was the most progressive of the Mennonite groups in Manitoba. Baer went to Manitoba to encourage the Bergthalers in developing a missions spirit and joining the General Conference of Mennonites.

H. H. Ewert, who came from Halstead, Kansas, in 1891, became an educational "missionary," heading the Gretna, Manitoba, school already started by the Bergthalers. Both he and his brother Benjamin remained in Manitoba and became ministers in the Bergthaler Church.

The General Conference Home Mission Board also sent Nicholai F. Toews of Mountain Lake, Minnesota, to the Gretna area as a traveling minister in 1890. Influenced by American evangelist Dwight L. Moody, Toews stressed a radical conversion experience. In this respect, he was little different from Mennonite Brethren evangelist Heinrich Voth, also from Mountain Lake, who had come to Manitoba in 1884. Both the General Conference Mennonites and the Mennonite Brethren considered the more traditional Mennonites in Manitoba, particularly the Reinlaender, or Old Colony group, as fertile ground for sowing the seeds of revival and fostering mission-minded churches that would want to join their respective conferences. Voth and Toews had similar messages. One difference between them was that Voth was baptizing converts immediately into a new Mennonite Brethren congregation, while Toews, working closely with the existing Bergthaler Church, had to tell his converts to wait until Pentecost for baptism, as was the custom among the Bergthalers. However, Elder H. H. Regier came from Mountain Lake for midyear baptisms of the new converts. The early baptisms kept the new converts from going to the Mennonite Brethren church, but they angered Bergthaler Elder Johann Funk and H. H. Ewert. Accusations soon began flying, including a charge that Toews had smuggled a pair of shoes over the border. The "smuggling" was soon explained, but because of the controversy Toews was recalled by the General Conference Home Mission Board and went back to Mountain Lake in 1894.[13]

During the time that Baer was traveling full time for the conference, others were being sent out for shorter periods. D. B.

Hirschler, at that time an appointed missionary among the Indians in Oklahoma, spent seven months in 1886-87 in Illinois, Kansas, Arkansas, Missouri, and Nebraska. William S. Gottschall of Pennsylvania spent most of a month in northwestern New York and Ontario. Levi O. Schimmel also of Pennsylvania worked with the Germantown Mennonite Church in Philadelphia to revive its sagging membership. Ephraim Hunsberger of Wadsworth, Ohio, visited scattered Mennonite families in Michigan. Christian Krehbiel of Halstead, Kansas, traveled for the conference in Missouri and Kansas.[14]

Stimulated by the General Conference's home missionaries, the district conferences were also sponsoring some work in the traveling ministry. The Eastern District, through the visits of its more established ministers, was organizing town and city congregations in Pennsylvania in the period from 1880 to 1900. Nathaniel B. Grubb also visited Dover, Delaware, on behalf of the Eastern District Conference.[15] The Middle District (Indiana, Ohio, Iowa, and New York) made some efforts to follow Mennonites to urban centers (see Chapter 5). But occasional visits from out-of-town ministers of rural churches failed to keep the city churches going. The Western District (centered in Kansas) had no traveling minister at first, but older congregations started daughter churches as their members moved, looking for more or better land.

The churches which were in 1908 to organize as the Central Illinois Mennonite Conference (which later merged with the General Conference and its Middle District) were starting daughter churches in both town and country under the leadership of Peter Schantz. Here, too, the method was one of sending in an established rural minister for a series of visits until the congregation was ready to function on its own.

The visits of district traveling ministers and of Baer were an important communications link between the conference and the new churches. Because of Baer's reports, the General Conference of Mennonites took the new step of voting funds to build a meetinghouse for the church in Stevensville, Ontario.

After Baer resigned in 1899, the Home Mission Board began reevaluating its program. Its 1902 report to the conference commented, "The traveling ministry is good, but we need more than the traveling ministry."[16] No one wanted to take over Baer's vacated position, and workers were hard to find, except during the summer. Other voices were already calling for new fields of work in home missions among Mennonites in the cities and among those North Americans who professed no Christian-

ity at all. "All around us there are those who have not professed
Christ and whose walk and conversation show plainly that they
have not yet experienced the saving grace of the gospel," Andrew B. Shelly of Milford Square, Pennsylvania, then conference president, wrote in *The Mennonite*. He advocated starting
new churches, especially in the cities. By not doing this, the
conference would lose members, he warned. "But it is not only
where our own members reside that missionary efforts should
be made. The gospel of peace must be preached to the hundreds
of thousands outside every church organization."[17]

Anthony S. Shelly, another Eastern District pastor, read a
paper on home missions at the district ministerial conference in
1890. He spoke of home missions in terms of congregational
evangelism and visits of itinerant ministers for special services.
But he also included visiting "the brethren and sisters in neighborhoods where there are but few of our people, in order to
encourage them and if possible to assist them in organizing for
aggressive work for the Master. Along this line our church has
been particularly derelict. In the past century of our church's
history in the country, we have nothing but negligence in this
line of work to point to."[18]

Farther west, David Goerz in Newton, Kansas, encouraged the 1890 General Conference to expand its definition
of home missions to include establishment of orphanages, institutions for released prisoners or alcoholics, day-care centers for
children both of whose parents were forced to work, Sunday
schools, care for the poor, immigrant missions in the cities, and
the setting up of a deaconess program. He noted that the
General Conference had not done much in this area, but individual General Conference Mennonites had contributed money to,
and had been involved in, such activities for other denominations and for the Bible and tract societies. "Also personal service in the colportage, in the city missions, etc.," he wrote, "is
already performed by brothers from our churches, who had
opportunity to be placed by other churches and would perhaps
still be working there if love for our people and loyalty toward
the church of their choice had not led them back into our circle.[19]

But the 1890 conference was not ready to act on Goerz's
ideas, and he went back to Newton to gather local support for a
deaconess program and hospital. (See Chapter 8.)

Although the concept of home missions was to expand
beyond the traveling ministry, the traveling ministry has continued in some form to the present day. J. J. Esau of Bluffton,
Ohio, was evangelist for the conference in the 1940s and 1950s,

not only holding revival meetings, but encouraging the growth of new churches. A. J. Neuenschwander credited Esau with being the first to bring together the scattered Mennonites in Toronto.[20] In 1972-73 David Whitermore traveled to 193 congregations and nine schools and colleges on behalf of the Commission on Home Ministries. In 1979 district "church planters" such as David Habegger and Mark Weidner and regional conference ministers fulfilled much of the role of the early traveling ministers. The General Conference of Mennonites found that the traveling ministry did not exhaust the definition of "home missions," but it had prepared the way for an expanded mission in North America.

Women of the Lame Deer, Montana, church, 1930

Chapter 2:
The Foreign Mission at Home: the Cheyenne and Arapaho

We as a Christian, civilized, and enlightened nation must see that they [the Indians] have their promised rights, that the laws are strictly carried out in their favor, that unchristian and unjust agents be removed and punished. In short, we must bring them, instead of the sword, the Gospel of Peace to Christianize and civilize them.[1]

To Christianize and to civilize were the goals of the first "foreign" mission of the General Conference Mennonites, the mission to the Arapaho, begun in 1880. While "mission" before 1880 had meant the traveling ministry among conference and nonconference Mennonites, "mission" now included bringing the gospel to "foreigners," that is, people who did not speak German or English. To nineteenth-century Mennonites, unschooled in anthropology and modern missiology, it seemed obvious that Christianity and white civilization—its clothing, its furniture, its ways of farming—went hand in hand. Samuel S. Haury wrote to N. B. Grubb, editor of *The Mennonite*, "Show me an Indian who has accepted Christ as his personal Savior and I will show you an Indian radically civilized."[2] With such a task in mind, Haury and his wife, Susanna Hirschler Haury, left Halstead, Kansas, on May 18, 1880, for Darlington, Indian Territory, only 200 miles south, as the first *foreign* missionaries of the young General Conference of Mennonites.

Samuel Haury and the conference had looked elsewhere for a mission field before settling on Darlington. After study at the conference's Wadsworth Academy, Wadsworth, Ohio, Haury had gone to Germany to study theology and to make contacts with the Amsterdam Mennonite Mission Society, which was sending workers to Java. But by the time Haury returned to North America in 1875, the conference had organized a foreign mission board of its own and was ready to send Haury out as its own missionary.

For five years Haury had visited congregations to build support for the new enterprise and had searched for a place to serve. Three times he had visited Indian Territory and had found a welcome from government agents and Indian leaders such as Powder Face.[3] But Haury had also found other missions already established. In 1879 he and John B. Baer, conference home missionary, had looked as far as Alaska for a place to start a mission, but other mission-minded denominations had already staked claims to most of the native people there, too.[4]

The decision to go to Indian Territory, after all, came only after the Quaker missionaries there offered to work only with the 3,500-member Cheyenne tribe and leave work with the 1,700 Arapahos to the Mennonites. (In 1884 the Quakers left the Cheyenne work as well to the Mennonite missionaries.)

From Lodge to Migration to Reservation

The Mennonites who sent the Haurys were a people who had come to North America in search of land and freedom. The missionaries went to a people who were losing their land and their freedom. Two centuries earlier the Cheyenne had lived in pole dwellings covered with grass mats in the area west of the Great Lakes near the Minnesota River. There they did simple farming and fishing. With the coming of the horse and the pressure of other tribes being pushed westward by whites, the Cheyenne and the nearby Arapaho increasingly became migrating buffalo hunters. Small bands traveled from Montana to Oklahoma to hunt the buffalo which provided food, clothing, and coverings for their tepees. From the early 1800s, the Cheyenne and Arapaho tribes were divided into northern and southern groups with separate leadership for each region.[5]

The Cheyenne were organized around a society of forty-four chiefs, who had religious and social duties. Various warrior societies organized hunts and military protection. The religious life emphasized unity with the earth and the renewal of tribal life through ritual. The most important rituals were the Sun Dance and Renewal of the Sacred Arrows. The sacred arrows and the buffalo skull are centuries-old objects which are still respected by nearly all tribal members.

After peaceful contacts with early traders, the Cheyenne and Arapaho were squeezed from their hunting lands. The Fort Laramie Treaty of 1851 gave them much of what is now Wyoming, western Nebraska and Kansas, and eastern Colorado, but that treaty was never honored by the U.S. government. From 1850 to 1880 the Cheyenne and Arapaho faced the superior military strength of the U.S. cavalry, the rapid disappearance of the buffalo, and loss of territory to white miners, farmers, and ranchers. Caught between desire for peace and need for self-preservation, the Cheyenne fought for freedom, but with little success. In 1864, troops under the leadership of Colonel J. M. Chivington, a former Methodist minister, massacred 150 Cheyenne women, children, and men camped under a white flag and an American flag at Sand Creek in Colorado. In 1868, General George Custer led a savage surprise attack on a Cheyenne village at the Washita River in Oklahoma. (The Battle of the Little Big Horn, June 25, 1876, in Montana, in which Custer and his troops were killed by a joint Cheyenne and Sioux force, was seen as revenge for the earlier Battle of the Washita.)

In 1875, an executive order of the U.S. president established a Cheyenne and Arapaho reservation, reaching from what is now El Reno, Oklahoma, west to the Texas border. (See map.) The administrative center was the town of Darlington, to which Haurys traveled five years later.

Life on the reservation was difficult, and many Cheyenne and Arapaho died. The government was unable to provide enough beef for the Indians, buffalo hunting was almost impossible, disease was rampant, and starvation was imminent for many. In 1878, 353 Northern Cheyenne, mostly women and children, escaped from the reservation and fought their way back to Montana. Ten thousand soldiers were sent to search for them. Most of the Northern Cheyenne were captured or killed, but some of the survivors and their descendents later became the nucleus of the White River Mennonite Church in Busby, Montana.[6] A military base called Cantonment was built in Oklahoma in 1879 to prevent further escapes. Cantonment soon became the center of Mennonite missions.

By 1880 when the Haurys arrived, the Cheyenne, and especially the Arapaho, were beginning to accept the realities of the reservation system. They lived in small, mobile bands, coming to Darlington weekly for the meager food rations. Early attempts at farming were thwarted by white horse thieves and

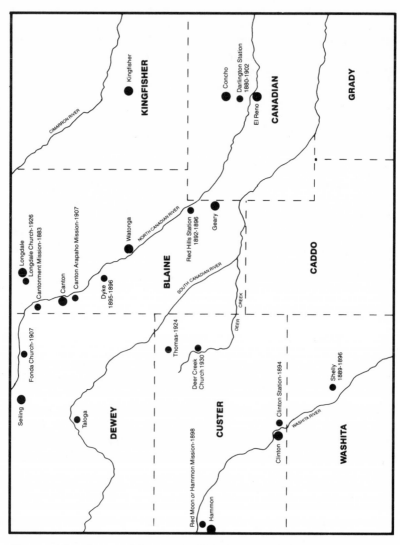

General Conference Mennonite Missions in Oklahoma

by the absence of farming tools and skills. The chiefs, under threat of further cutbacks of food, allowed Indian children to attend government schools. Already by 1880, 150 children were enrolled in the government school, and 68 older boys and girls were at an Indian school known as the *Carlisle Institute* in Pennsylvania.[7]

Education as Mission

Their nomadic life restricted by the government, the Cheyenne and Arapaho had to be taught not only the white religion, but also the white way of life in order to survive, the missionaries thought. Thus, for the first twenty years, the Mennonite mission worked primarily through schools. Supported by government food rations for the Indian children and sometimes using government buildings, three Mennonite schools were opened: Darlington in 1881; Cantonment in 1883; and, back in Kansas, Halstead in 1884. At Halstead, Indian children attended school and were trained in agriculture on Mennonite farms.

When the Haurys arrived in Darlington, the white way of life was already in evidence. Darlington was a small town not much more primitive than many Mennonite settlements on the western frontier. It was isolated because the railroad was not yet completed, but Darlington had a small newspaper and at least one church attended by soldiers from nearby Fort Reno, government employees, townspeople, and a few Indians. The Haurys were a welcome part of the community. S. S. Haury assisted the local pastor in the memorial service for the assassinated President Garfield and performed a few wedding ceremonies for whites.

While living in a rented house in Darlington, the Haurys began building the first three-story house in the area with the help of Mennonite volunteers. The building was to serve as both a residence for the missionaries and a boarding school for Arapaho children.

Some work with adult Indians went on, but it was hampered by the early missionaries' poor knowledge of the Arapaho and Cheyenne languages.[8] Sunday schools were conducted, and efforts were made to teach the Indians to settle in one location, to live in square wooden houses rather than tepees, and to raise livestock and grow crops. When the bands were dispersed away from Darlington along the Washita and Canadian rivers in 1886, 200 families were to be placed at Cantonment under the supervision of Haury and the Mennonite mission. Three hun-

dred were to be under the supervision of other agency employees.[9] The Cantonment mission was to provide the basis for a new
way of life for the Cheyenne and Arapaho.

But the colonization plan was never successful. For example, when Arapaho Chief Little Raven moved to Cantonment,
he claimed the entire property for himself, saying that God had
given it to him. Haury read him the letter from the Indian
commissioner which gave the property to the Mennonites, and
Little Raven moderated his demands. But Little Raven moved
his tents into the yard and used the brick bakery building as
shelter for his horses.[10]

Mission and Government

In both efforts—education and colonization—the missionaries' goals and those of the government Indian agents were
usually mutually supportive. Not only Mennonite missionaries, but also missionaries from many other groups, were an
essential part of the government's new "peace policy" with the
Indians. Put into effect in about 1870, the peace policy, advocated by the Quakers and other social reformers, was seen by
the churches as far superior to the earlier American policy of
eradication of the Indians or containment by war. Quakers were
placed in many administrative positions within the Indian Service. For example, John D. Miles, the Indian agent in
Darlington who had encouraged General Conference Mennonites to come to the Cheyenne and Arapaho reservation, was a
Quaker. The U.S. secretary of the interior had summarized the
peace policy as follows:

> First, to place the Indians upon reservations as rapidly as possi-
> ble, where they could be provided for in such manner as the
> dictates of humanity and Christian civilization require. ... On
> these reservations, they can be taught, as fast as possible, the
> arts of agriculture, and such pursuits as are incident to civiliza-
> tion, through the aid of the Christian organizations of the coun-
> try now engaged in this work, cooperating with the federal
> government. ... It is the further aim of the policy to establish
> schools, and through the instrumentality of the Christian or-
> ganizations ... as fast as possible, to build churches and organize
> Sabbath schools, whereby these savages may be taught a better
> way of life than they have heretofore pursued, and be made to
> understand and appreciate the comforts and benefits of a Chris-
> tian civilization, and thus be prepared ultimately to assume the
> duties and privileges of citizenship.[11]

The Darlington school, which burned to the ground only a

few months after it opened, was rebuilt with the help of federal funds. The government even offered the Mennonites the entire Cantonment military base for use as a school and mission station since the Cheyenne were sufficiently pacified and the base was no longer needed for the military. The twenty-five crude wood buildings plus two stone buildings became the property of the mission board. Joined by missionaries Heinrich R. Voth, Christian Wedel, and Jacob Moeschberger, the Mennonite group was busy rebuilding in Darlington and moving into Cantonment only a month after the last soldier left.[12] Voth wrote about Cantonment, "Here where drum and bugle called warriors together for weapons practice, in the future shall sound songs of praise to the Lord and his gospel, and an unfortunate race shall be led to the Lord."[13]

Voth, in charge of the Darlington school with nineteen pupils, and Haury at the Cantonment school, were assisted by a staff of fourteen, including cooks, seamstresses, and assistant teachers who came from Mennonite communities to help in the new undertaking. Dressed in uniforms, the Indian children learned basic English and other elementary subjects. After class the boys chopped wood and did other manual labor, while the girls helped in the kitchen, dining room, and laundry and learned to do mending, darning, and sewing. To make the mission more self-supporting and to teach agricultural skills, a cattle herd was begun, and a 6,000-acre pasture was fenced at Cantonment.[14] Following government regulations, the school required the children to speak English only, a rule which students later remembered with pain and anger.[15]

At Cantonment, Haury was superintendent of the entire mission, principal of the school, and government subagent for the main Darlington agency.[16] In this latter role, Haury intervened to try to get White Horse selected as a Cheyenne chief because he was more pliable for the agency.[17] When Agent D. L. Atkins asked Haury to evaluate reports of restlessness and potential uprising among the Cheyenne at Cantonment, Haury reported that, indeed, the Indians were unruly, and he requested that 2,500 troops be sent immediately to prevent unrest. The request was not granted.[18]

Haury saw the need not only to protect government interests, but also to protect the rights of the Indians. When a white cowboy named E. M. Horton brought 400 ponies through the reservation, he was accosted by Running Buffalo, who demanded the customary payment for crossing the reservation. Horton and his men killed Running Buffalo, and the enraged

Cheyennes cornered Horton in the nearby Indian trader's store. The trader interrupted Haury's Sunday school with news of the crisis, and Haury telegraphed Darlington for troops, meanwhile persuading the Cheyenne not to burn the building where Horton was hiding, warning them it was government property. Eventually the military arrived and took Horton into custody. Horton was tried in Wichita, and Haury testified for the prosecution, but Horton was found innocent.[19]

Haury's Resignation

In June 1887 Haury resigned as missionary. The unexpected resignation was the result of his sexual indiscretion with another missionary at Cantonment.[20] The Indian agent visited Cantonment to investigate and wrote to Washington:

> There were rumors about Cantonment involving the moral character of Mr. Haury. As he had the entire confidence of this community as well as my own, and standing so high in his church, I gave them no credence. June 4th Mr. Haury advised me by letter of his resignation as missionary among these Indians without alleging any cause. On the 22nd day of June in company with Inspector Gardner, I visited Cantonment and learned beyond question that the charges were true.[21]

Haury left the mission to become a medical doctor in Kansas. He continued a close relationship with the missionaries, but never again in an official role. He was restored to membership in the Alexanderwohl Mennonite Church, Goessel, Kansas, in 1889.[22]

The End of the School Era

H. R. Voth replaced Haury as superintendent of the mission and continued the focus on education. The schools grew and children learned to sing Christian songs and to memorize Bible verses, but no church could emerge from schoolchildren. By 1887, the Foreign Mission Board of the General Conference of Mennonites ordered that more attention be paid to adult converts. Finally in 1888 a teenage girl, Maggie Leonhard, a half-breed, was baptized by Foreign Mission Board chairman A. B. Shelly. But there was no church for her to join on the mission field. After briefly attending the Halstead school (where church attendance was difficult, since she did not speak German), she drifted away from the Mennonite community.

The Darlington school closed in 1898 because the Indian population had moved west and the school was no longer centrally located. The Cantonment and Halstead schools closed in

1901 and 1896, respectively, as the government ended subsidies to all private schools. Thus the Mennonite experiment in education among the Cheyenne and Arapaho ended with little fanfare and little controversy. Missionaries were able to do about the same amount of religious education in government schools, where students were required to attend Sunday school and church services until the 1920s.

The twenty years of operating the schools gave hundreds of Mennonites opportunity to work on the mission field as builders, cooks, seamstresses, and farmers. The nearness to the Mennonite communities in Kansas and Oklahoma had made the Indian mission an unprecedented occasion for lay involvement. This undoubtedly contributed to the later generosity of congregations toward the building of church meetinghouses and missionary residences. Three of the teachers in the Indian schools went on to head other Mennonite educational institutions: C. H. Wedel was president of Bethel College from 1893 to 1910; H. H. Ewert of Mennonite Collegiate Institute in Gretna, Manitoba, from 1891 to 1934; S. K. Mosiman of Bluffton College from 1909 to 1935.

The schools succeeded in providing some education to Cheyenne and Arapaho children. But because some of the children were attending under duress—their parents were threatened with loss of food rations if their children were not in school—the school contributed to the image of Mennonites as part of the government's occupying forces on the reservation. It is difficult to know how much former students at the mission schools contributed to the membership of the Indian Mennonite churches. The extent of their participation is perhaps indicated by the fact that missionaries in the 1930s could not recall the names of any of the thirteen students baptized at the Halstead school in 1890-91.[23]

Building Churches—the Second Phase

Until 1890, evangelism among Indian adults was usually done by the missionaries going to a camp with an interpreter, often a young graduate of Carlisle Institute, and having him laboriously interpret each sentence to whoever had assembled to listen. Since the bands were always moving around, permanent relationships with a band were difficult to maintain, and mission results were negligible.

Many of the conversions reported were deathbed experiences in which people acknowledged that they wanted to go to heaven to be with Jesus when they died. At Cheyenne funerals, missionaries found further opportunities to preach conversion-oriented sermons. Because of the staggering death rate and the availability of Mennonite cemeteries as burial sites, Mennonites had plenty of opportunity to preach funeral sermons. H. R. Voth wondered if the entire Arapaho tribe was not nearing extinction. S. S. Haury wrote shortly before his departure of the frustration of preaching:

> The people come, hear the word, give their assent to it; with this it seems to stop. There appears to be no hunger for the Word of God, no desire after salvation. By funeral occasions, of which there were more this year then heretofore, there [sic] attention was repeatedly called to the fact that, "sin was a reproach (ruination) to the people." We can admonish them, but there seems to be no manifestations [sic] of a desire on their part to forsake sin. ... The truth, that mission work among the Red Men is one of the most difficult and least promising works, is again yerified.[24]

Regular Sunday services for adult Indians had always been held at the Cantonment and Darlington schools. In 1889, J. J. Kliewer began preaching at an Arapaho camp near Shelly.

The Dawes Act. The entire program was soon changed by government intervention. In 1887 the U.S. Congress passed the Dawes Act, which called for the end of the reservation system in which land was jointly owned by the entire tribe. Each tribal member was now to select 160 acres of land and the balance was to be made available to white homesteaders. Well-meaning social reformers, missionaries, and land-hungry whites allied to lobby for the Dawes Act. Proponents of the bill argued that Indians were not using the land and that group ownership was limiting their individualism and consequently slowing their progress in farming and homebuilding. As a result of the act, most of Indian Territory was settled by whites and the entire area prepared for statehood.

The consent of the Cheyenne and Arapaho tribes was required for the allotment. Government agents applied intense pressure as well as fraud to obtain the necessary signatures for allotment. No Mennonites raised a voice except in approval of the allotment act, although missionaries did urge Mennonites to come to Oklahoma to homestead near the mission field and thus act as a buffer against the influx of less benevolent white settlers.

On April 19, 1892, at noon, a gun was fired, and the Cheyenne and Arapaho reservation was opened for white settlement. By the end of the day, the native Americans were a minority on their own land. Missionaries staked claims in

Shelly, Red Hills, and Dyke, which were to serve both as their own farms and as mission stations. Mennonite settlers homesteaded in these three areas, and for a time it was hoped that joint white and Indian Mennonite congregations would emerge. For about two years the Red Hills meetinghouse offered services for both Indians and whites, and the congregation was organized in 1897 with twenty-two white and three Indian members. But the Indians soon moved away onto their allotments, and no integrated churches emerged.[25] The Red Hills congregation became the First Mennonite Church of Geary, Oklahoma[26], and the Shelly site became the Bergthal Mennonite Church, Corn, Oklahoma (now dissolved). Dyke never materialized as a Mennonite settlement. There was severe criticism of the missionaries' staking claims, not because of what it meant to the Cheyenne and Arapaho, but because it seemed the missionaries were profiting personally from their position. Since few Indians were attending anyway, the "claim missions" were severed from the mission program in 1896.

New churches. The opening of the reservation forced the Cheyenne and Arapaho to stay on or near their allotments and required the mission to scatter new churches among them. The Hammon station, also known as *Red Moon*, was established in 1898 with H. J. Kliewer in charge.[27] The Hammon station, as well as the station at Clinton also known as *Haoenaom* (Haoena'omė) [28] established in 1894 by Michael M. Horsch, were started with only minimal consultation with tribal chiefs; they simply began where the population was. The church at Fonda was unique in that a group of Cheyenne asked for a church to be started.

At Fonda were five encampments under the leadership of Chiefs Whitehorse, Mower, and Yelloweyes. They were the most traditional of all the Cheyenne bands, so it was a surprise when they invited missionary Rodolphe Petter and native helper Harvey Whiteshield to meet with them. Petter later wrote:

> When we arrived there the large chief lodge of Voxpoham (Whitehorse) was already full of Indians waiting for us. (In these earlier meetings with the Indians only men attended, as the Cheyenne custom was.) The place was in the woods, close to the river, near the spot where several years afterwards the Fonda chapel was erected. How those Indians listened to the first gospel message they had heard from a white man! At the close of the meeting the Indians smoked the pipe as it was passed around. Then Voxpoham said, "This was a beginning and it was good. Our people want to hear more; appoint the time whenever you can come to

us. Oexova (Mower) shall call our men together. Then followed a
meal of Indian bread, cooked dried berries and meat with coffee.
In those days any important gathering was closed in this manner, as symbol that the object of the meeting had been assimilated. This was the reason why for a number of years there was
bread and coffee served at the close of our Sunday services.[29]

After the lodge tent became too small, a brush arbor was
erected and finally a simple wooden-roofed building with can-
vas sides and a dirt floor. "The Indians liked this first chapel
because it was more like their ways," reported Petter.[30] But in
1907, a small wooden building was built at Fonda from lumber
salvaged from the Cantonment complex.

Mower replaced Whitehorse as chief and was a strong
friend of the church. On Fridays he sent out messengers remind-
ing distant groups that they should gather for Sunday services.
"On Sundays he and his headman were faithfully present in the
Church, sitting on the front seat together, each holding the
Cheyenne hymnbook wrong side up, for none of them could
read. But they sang nevertheless from sheer hearing of the
words," said Petter.[31] Mower was not baptized until much later
in life, but the Fonda church was known as Mower's church
until it merged with the Seiling church in 1963. The building
was moved to Canton for use as a fellowship hall. Mower had
donated the land from his allotment and was a strong guiding
light for many years. Yet in 1921, Mower was named keeper of
the sacred arrows and left the church that was founded on his
land.[32]

Growth and Decline

Aided by the missionaries' knowledge of the Cheyenne
language, the Oklahoma churches began a slow but steady
growth beginning about 1900. But the results were too limited
to justify expending all of the energy, talent, and resources of
the Foreign Mission Board there. New fields were opened in
Arizona in 1893 and in Montana in 1904. The first overseas
mission of General Conference Mennonites was begun in India
in 1900.

Nearly 500 people were baptized in Oklahoma between
1888 and 1928. Six congregations were established, some with
nearly completely native leadership. Yet in 1928, the missionaries sent a recommendation for a cutback in personnel, which
was accepted by the board. The recommendation listed as reasons for the reduction that "the limited number of Indians, their
lack of interest and appreciation, and the proportionately

nominal results obtained do not in view of other and apparently more deserving fields, justify the present expenditures of means, time and energy in this field."[33] Missionaries said that because of cars, they could serve more than one church each. Finally, they wanted to "try to encourage greater activity on the part of these Indians by a necessity of placing greater responsibilities on them.[34] From 1928 on, Oklahoma missionaries served multiple churches as well as providing religious education (along with Baptist missionaries) at the government's Concho Boarding School, near the original Darlington school.

Whatever the justification for the cutback, church growth was not the result. Until World War II, membership in the Oklahoma Indian churches slowly declined. Church buildings were shuffled about, particularly because of the dispersion of the Cheyenne from the Cantonment area. For a time churches existed at Fonda, Longdale, and Thomas (Deer Creek), with missionaries serving these as outstations, or native helpers providing supervised leadership. In spite of the expressed desire to turn over control to Indian leaders, the remaining missionaries were clearly in charge. While membership in 1941 in the Oklahoma Indian churches total 416, average attendance in the six churches was only 167.

The Petters

For the first fifteen years of mission work among the Cheyenne and Arapaho, since missionaries had not learned the languages well enough to preach, they were consequently at the mercy of interpreters. That Mennonite missionaries did eventually learn the Cheyenne language was the result of the lifetime work of Rodolphe Petter.

Petter was born in 1865 to a French-speaking Reformed Church family in Switzerland, who claimed Huguenot ancestry. Petter's father died when Rodolphe was a child, and the family was poor. Rodolphe's brother had dreamed that he saw Rodolphe preaching to a group of Indians, and as a pious teenager, Rodolphe indeed felt the call to be a missionary.

Petter attended the Basel Mission Institute for six years, expecting to go to Africa or India. Already his proficiency for languages was evident. He had enrolled in the German-speaking school knowing only French, but he graduated with a working knowledge of German, Latin, Hebrew, and Greek and a mission theology which emphasized preaching the gospel in native languages.[35]

While doing military service in the Swiss army, Rodolphe

visited a Mennonite friend from the Jura Mountains. There he met and later married Marie Gerber and joined her Mennonite church. When General Conference Mennonite S. F. Sprunger from Berne, Indiana, visited his ancestral community in Switzerland, he persuaded the Petters to come to the United States as the first Swiss Mennonite missionaries. After touring Mennonite congregations in North America and spending a year at Oberlin College in English language study, the Petters arrived in Indian Territory in 1891 as missionaries to the Cheyenne. They were the first couple to be assigned exclusively to reaching adults and to learning the language.

The Petters lived at Cantonment, but spent full time visiting the nearby Indian camps. Rodolphe focused his attention on the oldest Cheyenne as linguistic sources, for he felt they spoke the purest form of the language. Through this method, Petter learned not only word forms, but many of the ancient myths and historical events of the tribe. These were also noted in his developing word list.

As soon as he was able, Petter began translating simple Bible verses into Cheyenne. Astounded, the Cheyenne saw marks on paper that spoke Cheyenne. Baffled by this white man who could learn their language, they decided that he must be a descendant of some long-lost part of the tribe. He was named *Zessensze* (Tsesėnetse), or "Cheyenne talker." Petter was unceasing in his determination to be near the Cheyenne. When the Cantonment school burned in 1893, he and his wife moved into a tent among the nearby Cheyenne for eight months. In 1895 he was able to publish a book of simple readings and some Cheyenne translations of European-American hymns. In 1902 he published the first edition of the Gospels of Luke and John; in 1904, *Pilgrim's Progress*; and in 1907, a Cheyenne grammar. A complete New Testament, translated from the Greek, was finished in 1935.

After his first wife, Marie, died of tuberculosis in 1910, Rodolphe married the following year fellow missionary Bertha Kinsinger, who was his linguistic collaborator and secretary. Bertha Kinsinger Petter was as remarkable as her husband. Born near Trenton, Ohio, in 1872, she earned a bachelor of arts degree from Wittenberg College, Springfield, Ohio, in 1896 and a master of arts in 1910. Possibly the first Mennonite woman to earn a college degree, she was a scholar in her own right. In college she had studied Latin, Greek, and German, as well as philosophy, calculus, and logic. Bertha came to Indian Territory as a teacher in the Cantonment school in 1896. The first single woman to make a career as a Mennonite missionary, she and her friend Agnes Williams, whom she had recruited for the mission field from Moody Bible Institute in Chicago, were in charge of the Clinton mission field for two years (1907-9) when no men were available for the work. Kinsinger and Williams conducted funerals, preached sermons, and led worship services. Kinsinger had begun to visit Cheyenne camps on horseback and later with a small buggy and team.

Independent and outspoken (the mission board by the 1930s had a policy of ignoring her "caustic letters"), Bertha was an essential part of the language team with Rodolphe. Most of her life was spent protecting him from intrusions on his time so that he could continue his language work. She promoted him to the Mennonite constituency and to the scholarly world while she also continued her own academic career.

Two years after their marriage, Rodolphe and his two children went to Kettle Falls, Washington, where he had purchased a small apple orchard, and spent two years writing and printing the 1,226-page *Cheyenne-English Dictionary*. His eighteen-year-old son Valdo handset the type and ran the multigraph machine. Bertha remained in Oklahoma to do mission work at Cantonment. When the Petters moved to Montana in 1916, Bertha drove the entire trip in a Model T, accompanied by Carrie Warren, a young Arapaho-black orphan. Bertha did the mechanical work, and Carrie was strong enough to turn the crank. The language work which had been begun in Oklahoma was continued in Montana.

Throughout his long and distinguished career, Rodolphe Petter epitomized the missionaries' ambiguity toward Indian culture and individual Indians. He appreciated the old Indian customs and wrote in 1936:

> The younger Cheyenne generation in learning English seems to have lost the ingenuity of the older Indians in their unique way of expressing themselves. Not long ago a young man dressed with headfeathers, buckskin garments, all beautifully adorned, but he was blissfully ignorant of what he wore meant.[36]

Petter also developed a reverence for the complexity and subtlety of the Cheyenne language. But he never changed in his estimation of Indians as primitive children. The 1911 General Conference of Mennonites asked Petter to present a paper discussing the possibility of Indian churches becoming full members of the conference. Petter explained that it was part of God's order that the gospel be first presented to people with a certain state of culture, the Jews, then the Greeks and the Romans. But he went on:

> And now we come to the Indians, who surely do not belong to the cultured races of the world. These were children of nature in the truest sense of the word, utterly without culture, without history. ... The fact is plain that our Indian churches in their present condition cannot be left to support and govern themselves. They have not reached the age of maturity, hence, cannot be considered sister churches by our General Conference. For this reason our Indian Churches should be considered foster children, daughters of our conference, for they will remain such for many years.[37]

The Petters developed close relationships with many Cheyenne people, and Bertha wrote a tribute to two of them: Vxzeta (Vóhtseta) (Anna Blackwolf Wolfname) and Vohokass (Vo'hokase)(Eugene Standing Elk), who assisted in the printing work. Their stories were included as appendices to Petter's own memoirs, and Bertha reported that she wept as she wrote their life stories. Yet Rodolphe was never quite willing to turn over control of the mission churches to Cheyenne leaders.

By 1924, Petter felt the Lame Deer church was almost ready for Cheyenne leadership. For the next twenty years, he gave increasing responsibility for leadership to men in the congregation, and several of these men almost entirely alone maintained the smaller mission church at Birney, twenty miles away. But Petter always found new reasons why these leaders should not take full responsibility—they did not have the proper education or enough spiritual insight or they had too many financial debts. No Cheyenne leaders were given full ordination as elders while Petter was alive.

By the end of his career, Petter began to have doubts about his language work. Few Cheyennes fully mastered reading, using his complex spelling of the language, which was dependent on the use of many archaic Cheyenne terms. He saw the decline of the Cheyenne language in Oklahoma as the more acculturated Indians there became fluent in English. Few of the new missionaries seemed to have the willingness to learn Cheyenne well.

When Harvey Whiteshield from Oklahoma, who had been Petter's collaborator on the initial language work, visited the Montana churches in 1942 and introduced Cheyenne songs with traditional Cheyenne tunes rather than the western tunes which Petter used, Petter fairly exploded with criticism of the new syncretism:

Our Cheyenne songs he [Whiteshield] simply *discarded* and tried...to introduce only his pet new Chey. songs, which are not the spiritual food or expression which *growing* Christians should have. They catch the Indians simply because their tune is like that of the heathen and peyote people. Tell our Cheyenne that the Sundance is a kind of spiritual, sacrifical replica of Christ's Passion, tell them that the Whites killed Jesus, tell them all the Scripture passages which are a pillow for them; sing their tunes, etc., etc., do never mention things that *hurt* them, then, of course they will like it. Is that Christ's Gospel? Has such a message made the Okla. Indians morally better?[38]

Petter probably developed the deepest understanding of Cheyenne culture and history of any white person up to his time. He and his wives devoted their lifetimes to the Cheyenne. He personally baptized hundreds of Cheyenne in Oklahoma and Montana. At one time nearly one fourth of the Northern Cheyenne had some tie in the Mennonite church. But Petter was never able to integrate Indian leadership and forms into the church.

When Petter began to think of retiring, the Foreign Mission Board pointed out that retirement meant going home and leaving the field. But the Petters no longer regarded Switzerland as home, and they had never established a base in any traditional Mennonite community. Their Helvetia Ranch near Kettle Falls, Washington, was now covered by the waters of the new Grand Coulee Dam. Rodolphe died in Lame Deer, Montana, in 1947. But Bertha stayed on, despite mission board protests, until 1963, when she moved to a retirement home in Billings, Montana. She died there in 1967.

Expansion to Montana

Rodolphe Petter's fluency in Cheyenne was the key to the opening of a new mission to the Northern Cheyenne in southeastern Montana in 1904. In 1889, Petter had been invited to visit the churches of the Northern District Conference. Oklahoma Cheyenne had begged him to visit their relatives in South Dakota and Montana. Lonewolf, an old man, had given Petter a thin blue scarf, in which he had tied peculiar knots, to give to Lonewolf's brother in Montana. When Petter had arrived at the Tongue River Reservation, where the 1,400 Northern Cheyenne lived, he had delivered the cloth to Chief Twomoons. Immediately, Chief Twomoons had stood up and said, "This is for me from my brother Lonewolf in the South; he tells me that you are his friend."[39]

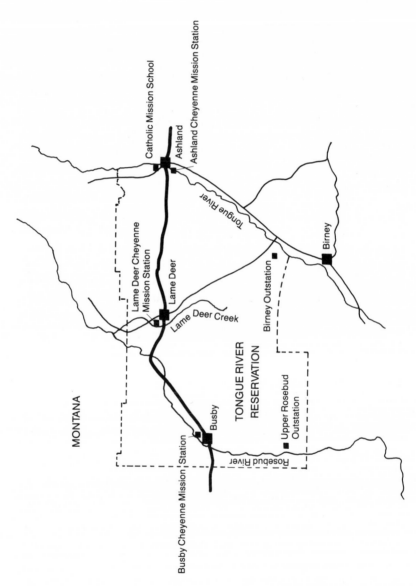

General Conference Mennonite Missions in Montana

After two later visits by Petter in 1901 and 1903, the Foreign Mission Board had decided to open work among the Northern Cheyenne. The field had been selected because the Mennonite missionaries already knew the language and because it was feared that other denominations might claim the field if the Mennonites did not.[40]

Some prior mission work had actually been done among the Northern Cheyenne. The first Christian missionaries there were the Iowa Synod Lutherans, who between 1861 and 1863 tried to learn the language. One missionary was killed, and the rest left with three young Cheyenne men whom they planned to train as missionaries. The young men died, and the work was never resumed.[41] In 1885 a Catholic mission had begun at Ashland, on the eastern edge of the reservation. It had been established at the request of a young soldier who asked his bishop to provide material aid to the near-starving Cheyenne. Mennonites felt they were not interfering with the Catholic mission, since it was confining its efforts to the eastern area of the reservation.[42] In addition to the Lutherans and Catholics, some traveling ministers from other denominations had passed through and baptized some Northern Cheyenne.

So in 1904 Gustav A. and Anna Hirschler Linscheid, who had served for three years in Oklahoma, went to Busby, Montana, to establish the Mennonite mission. The strategy was to begin at the western end of the reservation, near the government boarding school and farthest from the Catholic mission at Ashland. The Linscheids lived in a tent while carpenters built a house and barn for them. Six months later a small chapel was built, and the Linscheids were overwhelmed to find it filled with Cheyenne for the dedication service. Four years later, missionaries P. A. and Katherine Braun Kliewer began visitation work in Lame Deer, in the center of the reservation, and a station was established there. In 1910 a church and missionary house were built in the village of Birney, south of the reservation, and in 1917 a chapel was built in Ashland near the Catholic mission.

The work in Montana developed much more smoothly than in Oklahoma. There was no struggle to learn a new language. There were no attempts at opening schools or agricultural colonies. The Montana work began immediately with church development. Results in Busby and Lame Deer were slow but steady. Ashland and Birney never developed into large congregations. In spite of the emphasis on church building, the social needs of the Indians were not forgotten. Missionaries

dispensed medicine (a pharmacy was at least forty miles away),
wrote letters to the Northern Cheyenne's relatives in Oklahoma, and built coffins when requested.[43]

In 1916 Rodolphe and Bertha Petter moved from Oklahoma to Lame Deer, where they would spend almost the rest of
their lives. In 1918 Alfred and Barbara Hirschy Habegger of
Berne, Indiana, came to Busby. They served in Busby, Birney,
and Lame Deer for almost forty years. These two couples were
unique in the length of time they spent in the Northern Cheyenne mission. Unique among missionaries, they are also buried
on the reservation.

Alfred Habegger, native of Berne Indiana, and educated at
the General Conference's seminary at Bluffton, Ohio, was one
of the few missionaries able to preach in Cheyenne. The Habeggers, more than the Petters, tried to place more responsibility
for the church into the hands of its Cheyenne members. For
example, from the early years of the mission, missionaries had
solicited clothing from the home churches to be given to the
Indians as gifts at Christmas. The amount of clothing and
blankets given was based on the recipients' attendance during
the previous year. The practice was used in Oklahoma and
Arizona as well. In Busby, Montana, the practice of giving
clothing from the home churches was dropped, through the
efforts of the Habeggers. At their encouragement, the congregation itself began to buy Christmas gifts for the children.

The spirit of the early Mennonite converts on the Northern
Cheyenne Reservation is exemplified in the following letter
written for Stands in Timber to White Arm, a Baptist on the
nearby Crow Reservation:

> Dear brother. I writing short letter to you so you know my little
> baby girl died after Christmas. Your friend Bird Bear came home
> from Crow reservation after my baby died. Bird Bear told me
> your daughter died some time ago too. I sorry to hear that but at
> same time we can thank God she gone to better land where no
> sin, no heavy heart, where tears are wiped from her face.
>
> I very glad to hear you helping missionary at Lodge Grass. Be
> true to Jesus, White Arm, and show with daily life that you are
> new man and that way everything will come out to your best. It
> will not always be like you think but if you walk straight all will
> be good. You might have to wait but everything turn out all right.
>
> Remember me to Crows and be good to yourself. I now enclose my
> letter with prayer and best regards. That's all. Good-bye.[44]

After thirty years, the Montana churches began to rival
those in Oklahoma in size. There were 281 living members in

Montana and 321 in Oklahoma—although in both areas the number of active members was much smaller.[45]

Hotevilla, Arizona, 1936

Chapter 3:
A People of Peace: the Hopis

"When the Mennonites came to Oraibi to establish a mission, they were welcome, for they did not believe in shedding human blood, and they believed in living in peace." J. B. Frey[1]

The General Conference, with its doctrine of nonresistance, began its second foreign mission in 1893 among another traditionally peaceful people, the Hopi of northern Arizona. Both groups were early aware of their common peace tradition, as is evidenced by the following story, which was told often on the reservation in spite of its being unsubstantiated.[2]

When the old Hopi chief Lololma was in Washington, D.C., making arrangements for the establishment of schools in Hopi country to teach the Hopi children English and prepare them for civilized life, he became conscious of the fact that they should have a church also where the Word of God should be taught. ...

As there were a number of church organizations, the Hopi chief went to investigate and contact the different organizations to establish what their method of dealing with certain difficulties was—especially in case of war.

1. He went to the Presbyterians and asked what they would do in case of war. The Presbyterians answered that they would take the gun and fight.

2. He contacted the Christian Reformed Church group and received the same answer.

3. He went to the Methodists and again received the same answer.

4. The Baptists also answered the same.

5. He asked the Mennonites what they would do in the event of war. They answered that their belief was that they must not kill, so they would not take the gun and kill and shed man's blood.

So chief Lololma said that was the church he wanted, for the Hopis believe that if they shed blood, they can not go to heaven, for the one that lives in heaven is holy and nothing that is not holy can go there. Those who are "unholy" all have to go below.

When the Mennonites came to Oraibi to establish a mission, they were welcome, for they did not believe in shedding human blood, and they believed in living in peace.[3]

In reality, the request that General Conference Mennonites establish a mission among the Hopi had little to do with the peace position. The invitation to the Mennonites came in 1891 from Peter Staufer. Staufer, a Mennonite employed by the government Indian agency in Keam's Canyon, Arizona, had previously worked as an Indian farmer for the Mennonite mission to the Cheyenne and Arapaho in Oklahoma. Staufer described the Hopi (then called *Moqui* by the government) as follows:

The Moqui Pueblos are a very interesting, self-supporting tribe. ... These people being partly civilized, this field would afford a grand opening for mission work. It is an established fact that Christianity alone, without some civilization, will not make a lasting impression on the Indian.

These Moquis have not been so much mistreated by the Americans as by the Mexicans, therefore they do not have that prejudice against the white man, that many other tribes have. They are easily approached by the white man, and willing to learn of him whatever is to their advantage. The fact that they are not greatly prejudiced, are self supporting and are living in established villages, are favorable advantages for mission work. ...

So far I have not noticed any of the immoralities that an Indian so easily learns from degraded persons, such as card-playing, etc. ... These [school] children sing a number of hymns without any prompting. They know all the Golden Texts for this quarter, besides all of the ten commandments, can count 100 [sic] and do well in reading.[4]

As a result of Staufer's letter, mission board chairman Christian Krehbiel and Oklahoma missionary Heinrich R. Voth, visited the Hopi reservation in 1892, and the board agreed to start a new mission field, with Voth and his wife as the first missionaries.

Krehbiel and Voth saw a unique sight on their visit. The seven Hopi villages were located on the edges of three high mesas, known as *First*, *Second*, and *Third* mesas. The Hopi were desert farmers, who had been eking out a living for centuries by planting carefully in the washes and gullies. In contrast to the Cheyenne and Arapaho, the Hopi had never been forced to move by white settlement. Living in a remote area on marginally productive land, the Hopi had been virtually undisturbed by advancing whites. Hopi had been in that area for perhaps 1,300 years. The village of Oraibi, on Third Mesa, was settled about A.D. 1150. Hopi religious ceremonies and culture were also much more intact when the first missionaries came than those among the Cheyenne and Arapaho.

The Hopi's first contact with whites had come in 1540, with the arrival of the Spanish. By 1629 the Spanish had sent Franciscan priests to the Hopi villages. At first, the Spanish were greeted as the *Bahana*, the legendary lost white brother of the Hopi, who was to return as savior, bringing in an age of peace and wisdom. But disillusioned by the forced labor the Spanish required to build the mission buildings and dissatisfied by the suppression of traditional religion, the Hopi joined the Indians of New Mexico in killing the priests and driving out the Spanish in the Pueblo Rebellion of 1680.

There was little further contact with whites until the 1870s, when Thomas Keam established a trading post east of First Mesa. The Baptists established the Sunlight Mission at the village of Mishongnovi about the same time.[5] In 1887 the first permanent Indian agency was opened and a government school set up in Keam's Canyon.

Efforts of the Bureau of Indian Affairs to acculturate the Hopi to the American way of life were resisted at every step by sizable segments of the Hopi. In 1889 those who did not want their children to go to government schools were hiding them under the cliffs whenever policemen or army troops came to take them forcibly to school. Government efforts to "civilize" the Hopi went so far as to require men to have short haircuts. In 1902-3 a number of Hopi men had their hair cut forcibly with sheep shears, a humiliation not forgotten.[6]

Missionaries H. R. Voth and J. B. Epp at the time tried to disassociate themselves as much as possible with the haircut order and the order against ceremonial painting of the body. Voth wrote to *The Mennonite* that the haircut order hindered his

work in learning the Hopi language. Now the Hopi were embit-
tered against all Americans, and it was hard to convince the
Hopi conservatives that the missionaries had no hand in the
matter.[7] *The Mennonite* editorialized:

> Short hair and unpainted faces may be tokens of civilization to
> the minds of some people, but after all, the Lord looketh upon the
> heart. The idea of some people about civilizing the Indian is as
> foolish as if a man should try to break a wild horse by cutting his
> tail off an inch at a time. If red women have no right to paint
> themselves white, neither have white women any right to paint
> themselves red.[8]

The Voth Era, 1893-1902

With the approval of the General Conference of Mennonites and the raising of the money, Heinrich Richert Voth and
Martha Moser Voth went as missionaries to Oraibi in 1893. H.
R. Voth had been born in 1855 in South Russia, and his family
had immigrated to Kansas in 1874 as part of the Alexanderwohl community. Voth had attended the Wadsworth school
and, as the second ordained missionary in Oklahoma, had
served from 1882 to 1891. His first wife, Barbara Baehr, and
daughter Bertha had died in Oklahoma. He married Martha
Moser, a former missionary in Oklahoma, in 1892.

The Hopi villages in 1893 were isolated—seventy miles
from the nearest railroad station. Oraibi, which the Voths chose
as the location of their mission, was the extreme western and
the most isolated of the Hopi settlements. With difficulty, since
arable land was scarce, the Voths got permission to use twenty
acres near a wash below the Oraibi mesa. After a year of
building a house and barn and digging a well, assisted by
Staufer and Hopi employees, the Voths moved into their new
quarters.

H. R. Voth began to learn the Hopi language immediately
upon arrival, with the help of a phrase book Staufer had prepared, but his missionary work was limited at first to a small
Sunday school for children at the government day school. Since
he also had some medical training, Voth acted occasionally as
physician and dentist. But it was obviously the language and
the culture which fascinated him. The complex annual cycle of
dances and rituals was unique. Gaining the confidence of the
Hopi, Voth spent more and more time in the underground kivas
watching the ceremonies, which sometimes lasted for a week.
Sketching and photographing the rituals and collecting arti-

facts, he said, were a way of learning the culture and preparing for mission.

Increasingly, ethnologists and archaeologists from around the world were becoming aware of the rich lode of treasures on the Hopi reservation. Voth and Staufer spent much time leading archaeological teams to digs. This further increased Voth's collection.

G. A. Dorsey of the Field Museum in Chicago knew Voth from his visits to Oklahoma. So when Dorsey visited Arizona in 1897, he visited Voth. Dorsey wrote,

> From several sources, previous to my visit, I had heard of a collection which the missionary Mr. H. R. Voth had been forming during a number of years [to] assist him in his studies. ... I was at once impressed not only with its great beauty and richness, but with the detailed knowledge which Mr. Voth possessed concerning every object in his collection.[9]

After a second visit to see Voth later that year, Dorsey persuaded Voth to sell the collection to the Field Museum and to come to Chicago to "arrange the collection and construct certain altars, etc., illustrative of the religious life of the Hopi."[10] Voth left Arizona in 1898 for "health reasons." After briefly visiting relatives in Ohio, he spent twenty months working at the Field Museum, organizing his collection.[11]

When mission board chairman A. B. Shelly read in the *Fort Madison Weekly Democrat* that Voth had sold a collection of Hopi artifacts for $5,000 (about five years of a missionary's salary in those days), Shelly confronted Voth by letter with his concerns that Voth was not devoting proper attention to winning souls.[12] Thomas Keam, the trader at Keam's Canyon, had written to Christian Schowalter, another member of the mission board, in January 1899 complaining that Voth had sold fifty-two boxes to the Field Museum. Said Keam, "His sole mission appeared to be that of trading; as he accumulated more in his capacity as a missionary in that time, than I as a licensed trader."[13]

Nevertheless, the mission board allowed Voth to return to the Hopi mission field in 1900 to train new missionary Jacob B. Epp in the language. In 1901 Martha Voth died in childbirth, and H. R. felt that, for the sake of his children, he should leave Arizona in 1902.[14]

Voth's work in publishing the secrets of Hopi religion and his methods of collecting artifacts were still sensitive issues among the Hopi seventy-five years later. While the Hopi had been willing to let Voth observe secret ceremonies, they were

distressed by their publication and by what the Hopi felt was
Voth's betrayal of their religious secrets. Don Talayesva, a Hopi
traditionalist who became a Christian later in life, remembered
in 1942 how, as a child, "I traded the good bow that my ceremonial father had given me to the Rev. Mr. Voth for a piece of
calico, a few sticks of candy, and some crackers. I hated to part
with that bow..., however, my father was very poor."[15] Talayesva's autobiography had few good words for Voth, whom Talayesva accused of forcing his way into the kivas.

Part of the Hopi antagonism toward Voth was also the
natural result of Voth's advocacy of another religious system
which threatened to replace Hopi religion, which was all-
pervasive in Hopi society. Voth was also representative of the
larger threat from white civilization and the attempts to en-
force adaptation to white ways. Some claimed, without basis in
fact, that Voth was "hired to come out" by the government.[16]

The introduction of white culture among the Hopi caused
serious splits among the Hopi themselves, and by the turn of the
century, Oraibi, the most traditional of the Hopi villages, was
divided into the conservatives, or "hostiles," and the liberals, or
"friendlies," those sympathetic to some cooperation with white
ways. The dramatic split came in 1906, after the death of Chief
Lololma. In a push-fight without weapons, the friendlies, led by
Tewaquaptiwa, pushed the hostiles, led by Youkioma, over a
line drawn in the rock at the top of the mesa. The hostiles were
forced to leave Oraibi to found the villages of Hotevilla and
Bacavi. Oraibi was further split by the exodus of Christians and
others more favorable to white ways, who moved to the foot of
the mesa to New Oraibi (Kykotsmovi), the site of the government school and the Mennonite mission.

The "Voth church" on the top of the mesa—actually
finished in 1903, a year after Voth left—was controversial from
the start. Voth reportedly had got permission to build the
church building at Old Oraibi by telling Chief Lololma that the
building was to be a "healing house," which Lololma took to
mean "hospital" or "clinic."[17] The Hopi felt betrayed when the
building was used only for church services and other religious
work. Missionaries evidently intended to use the side room as a
"sick room," but this was never done.[18]

The "Voth church" was abandoned for worship services in
1917, in favor of a new building in New Oraibi closer to the
homes of most of the Christians. The older building was later
cleaned out and used again for a few years, but it burned on
April 25, 1941. Officially, the building was struck by lightning,

but one oral source insists the fire was caused by arson.[19] At a street meeting in Old Oraibi immediately after the fire, Christians shouted out a message which included a review of the legal and traditional rights of the Mennonites to occupy the church building and a message about the traditional Hopi fear of lightning.[20] Hopi traditionalists believe that natural disasters are a sign of the gods' disfavor. Some saw the fire on the mesa as a judgment on the Mennonites and the building of the church in or near the traditional path of the kachina ceremonial dancers.[21]

Voth returned to Kansas in 1902, where he did further anthropological writing and worked as an itinerant minister for the Home Mission Board. From 1914 to 1927 he served Mennonite churches in Goltry and Gotebo, Oklahoma. He died in 1931.

Voth's work as an ethnologist was seen as valuable even seventy-five years later. His many publications and his collections of artifacts were on display at the Field Museum in Chicago and at the Fred Harvey Hopi House at the Grand Canyon. In recent years, when Hopi traditionalists had forgotten details of some of the ceremonies, they consulted Voth's exhibits in Chicago.

The First Hopi Christians

The first Hopi convert in Oraibi, Kunwanwikvaya, (or Vickvaya) was baptized in 1909, sixteen years after the arrival of the first missionaries. Slowly new mission work developed in Oraibi and the nearby villages of Bacavi and Hotevilla. The Women's National Indian Association turned over their mission work in Moencopi, a colony of Oraibi about forty miles away, to the Mennonites in 1905. Missionaries Jacob B. Epp, John R. Duerksen, and Jacob B. Frey worked on learning the Hopi language and in translating portions of the Bible as well as writing a catechism and a Bible history. Gospel songs were translated into Hopi and printed in a small hymnbook without notes. By 1926, the baptismal record for the Third Mesa villages contained about fifty-two names, but no church had yet been formally organized (although missionaries said that Hopi Christians were given some decision-making power over matters such as how their offerings were spent).

Missionary Mary Schirmer found an avenue of service by raising Hopi foster children. She had discovered that when a Hopi mother died soon after childbirth, the baby was assumed to be an evil spirit who had caused its mother's death. Therefore the baby was usually buried alive with its mother. Schirmer told some of the Hopis that if such an occurrence happened again, to let her know, "for we white people love babies and Jesus loves them, too." She would be willing to take such a baby and try to raise it.

One Monday morning 1908, after she had gone to Oraibi the previous day to help Jacob B. and Nettie Harms Epp in their Sunday school, Quwanyamtiva from Hotevilla came over hurriedly to tell Mary Schirmer that his wife had died on Sunday and had left a baby boy.

> He said, "I told all of my sisters asking them to take care of the baby but none of them go near him. They are afraid of him. He is a nice pretty boy; I do not feel like killing him. He is lying on the floor. Nobody has taken care of him since he arrived." (born Sunday a.m.) So Miss Schirmer went home to Hotevilla on horseback (7 miles and 2 mesas to climb), went to the house and walked in. Two Hopi women were then already busy in the house preparing the baby boy for burial. The heathen naming ceremonial which is usually carried out the twentieth day of a child was carried out that morning.... They named him *Siwinainiwa...* [which] means "young cedar sprout." Miss Schirmer waited until they were through with their ceremony and then went and took the baby, wrapped him in a blanket she had brought with her.[22]

The act earned Schirmer the approval of the baby's uncle, Chief Youkioma, and the men of Hotevilla built her a small Hopi-style house in the village. The baby was renamed Daniel Schirmer. Later, with his wife, Amy Talesnemptewa, Schirmer served as a mission worker among the Hopi and among the northern Cheyenne in Montana.

Mary Schirmer adopted two other Hopi children and C. J. and Anna Balzer Frey adopted a Hopi orphan girl. Another single missionary, Elizabeth Schmidt, took into her home five Hopi foster children, some of whom had been orphaned during an epidemic of influenza. One of Schmidt's foster sons was Karl (Johnson) Nasewytewa, who became pastor of the Oraibi Church.[23]

Schism Among the Missionaries

The Mennonite witness to a divided Hopi tribe was itself to become divided. The fundamentalist-liberal debate that went on in many North American churches in the 1920s found its expression also on the mission field. The issue in Arizona was universalism: that is, the doctrine that all people, whether in

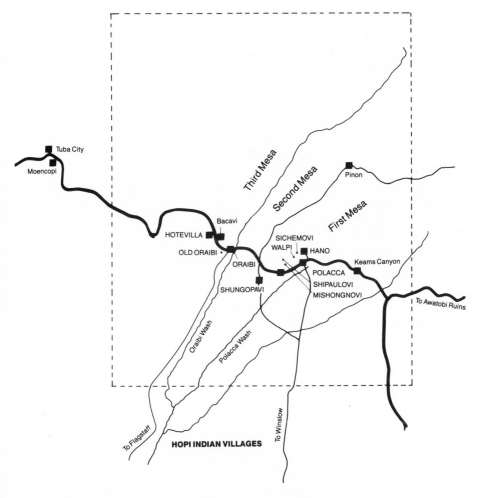

General Conference Mennonite Missions in Arizona

heaven or in hell, will eventually be saved. The theological storm centered around missionary Jacob B. Frey. Born in Marion County, Kansas, in 1875, Frey was adept with languages. He was fluent in Hopi, and knowledgeable, although mostly self-taught, in Greek, Latin, and Hebrew. Frey could hardly have been classed as a liberal except on the issue of universalism. But other Arizona missionaries, especially John R. Duerksen, insisted that Frey believed that even the devil would be saved, an idea Frey consistently denied to the mission board until his death. While Frey may have denied this extreme version of universalism, it is clear that he supported the use of a Bible translation known as the *Concordant Version of the Sacred Scriptures*, written and published in Los Angeles in 1926 by A. E. Knoch, a printer self-taught in Greek. Knoch had developed his own Greek grammar, lexicon, and expository notes and even his own Greek text of the New Testament, which differed sharply at many points from the text used by most New Testament Greek scholars. Knoch's "concordant" theory required that each Greek word be consistently translated by the same English word, a linguistically dubious notion. His doctrine of universalism came in through his insistence of the translation of the Greek words *aion* and *aionios* as "eon," meaning "a period of time," rather than as "eternity" or "forever." (For an illustration of the difference this might make, see Revelation 14:11 and 20:10.)[24]

J. B. Frey was loved by many of the Hopis, perhaps more than any other Mennonite missionary. He was, first of all, fluent in their language. Some Hopis later remembered that his children spoke Hopi as well as the Hopi children. He and his wife, Aganetha Balzer Frey, were careful to speak Hopi to each other in front of Hopi people.[25]

The effect of Frey's command of the language is illustrated in the story Frey told of his speaking at the Baptist mission at Keam's Canyon, where the missionaries did not speak Hopi.

> When the time came for my talk, I walked behind the pulpit with my black loose-leaf holder: I read the translation of the prodigal son, who left his father's house and went into a foreign country.
>
> The Hopis looked for my interpreter, but no one came. After the reading of the story, I prayed in Hopi. When I began to speak, there were many smiles, especially by the high school students. But when I described the young man's suffering—his money gone, his clothes ragged and herding hogs to have something to eat, ... and of how he decided to go home and confess his sins—many Hopis were weeping and many handkerchiefs were in

evidence. After finishing my talk, I again prayed in Hopi and sat down.

Then the Baptist missionary, who was in charge of the meeting, said, "You Indians do not come to us missionaries with your troubles, because we do not understand Hopi. And if we use an interpreter you are afraid the interpreter will tell on you. Now here is a white man who speaks your language; you can go to him and tell him everything. He will keep your secrets and be able to advise you. And now you can go to the front and shake hands with him.

Every one of that large audience came forward; many were weeping...

It took quite a while to pass that large company of people. But the last man in line was a middle-aged man who seemed to be smiling all over. When he got to me, he too gave me a hearty grip and said, "My father told us children again and again, 'A white man will come with a black book and read Hopi out of that black book and speak Hopi without an interpreter. Listen to him, he has the Word from heaven.'" Then he added, "You are that man!"[26]

While Frey may have been loved by many Hopis, he was under fire from other missionaries. Part of the reason was his alleged belief in universalism, referred to above. Part of the reason was his insistence on making the Hopi translation of the New Testament from the Greek rather than from the English King James Version, as J. R. Duerksen was doing.[27] In the stormy debate that followed, Duerksen, Frey's main accuser, was asked to resign in 1926, and Frey was asked to resign in 1928. Frey first moved near Flagstaff, Arizona, to run a sawmill and work with the Southwest Indian Bible Conference, an annual gathering of independent Indian Christians and missionaries. From 1934 to 1940 Frey taught at Oklahoma Bible Academy, in Meno, Oklahoma, where his views again got him into trouble. Frey moved back to Arizona in 1941 and helped establish independent Indian churches in Parker, San Carlos, Cottonwood, and Prescott, but he remained in contact with sympathetic Hopi Christians near Oraibi.

The furor among the missionaries spilled over into the Hopi church. One of Frey's champions among the Hopi was Oraibi pastor Fred Johnson, who had been ordained in 1926 after training at the Indian Bible Institute in Los Angeles. At the time Frey was asked to resign, Johnson took up Frey's case with the Foreign Mission Board. The board sent him an eight-point statement on why Frey had to leave. Johnson replied, "I don't understand."[28]

After Frey's return to Arizona, Johnson continued to keep up good relationships with Frey, occasionally inviting him to teach Bible classes at the Oraibi church. The Foreign Mission Board objected and sent the Oraibi church a letter explaining why the board felt Frey's doctrine was false. In 1945 the board resolved "that we advise our missionaries and Christians among the Hopis that they do not invite Frey into the Mission until he has given assurance that he does not believe and teach the doctrine of universal salvation."[29]

Both Frey and Johnson kept saying that Frey did not believe in universalism, and Johnson kept writing to the board asking for a formal hearing for Frey. Finally, at Johnson's initiation, the Oraibi church voted to request the board that Frey be given a hearing.[30] The issue now became one of who controlled the Hopi churches—the Hopi or the mission board and the missionaries. Johnson wrote, "We Indians will have Frey come. He understand [sic] our language more than any Board member or present missionary. [Are] you afraid we natives cannot judge scripture and preaching? You cannot keep him out of our homes. Your authority extends only to whom you employ."[31] Johnson continued a month later, "I want you and the Board to know and understand on the question that we Indians have rights to say who shall not be here in regards to a white missionary...and unless this rights of the Indians shall be recognized by the Board and our rights of free assembly to discuss church affairs, they may get into trouble with our people."[32]

Unable to achieve resolution of the matter with the Foreign Mission Board, Johnson and about a third of the Oraibi church left in 1946 to start the Hopi Independent Church, which later built a meetinghouse two blocks from the Oraibi Mennonite Church. Johnson continued as its pastor without support from the board.

Finally in 1949 the Foreign Mission Board met with Frey and Johnson. The board asked Frey, now seventy-four years old, "Do you believe in eternal separation from God?" "Yes," Frey answered simply. It was a time of tears and forgiveness, and the board pronounced the matter closed.

The matter was not closed, however. In 1953 Frey was invited to speak at a funeral in Oraibi. The parents of the dead girl, who had recently been attending the Mennonite church, thought they had arranged for use of the church building. But

the missionaries in Oraibi, literally following the board's resolution of 1945, refused to let the funeral be held in the Mennonite church, since Frey would be speaking. One missionary
couple attended the funeral, which was held in the home of the
girl's aunt, but just as Frey got up to speak, the couple stood up
and walked out, much to the dismay of the family. There followed a storm of letters between the girl's aunt, Elizabeth
White (Qoyawayma), Fred Johnson, Frey, and the board—
reorganized in 1950 as the Board of Missions and with no
members who had been involved in the original dispute. The
result was an apology from the board, but the request that the
pastor of the church conduct all funeral services in the local
church.[33] Frey died in Cottonwood, Arizona, in 1957.

The forty-year turmoil over a doctrinal point regarded as
minor by most Hopi Christians had a disastrous effect on the
tiny Mennonite community. Elizabeth White wrote to the Board
of Missions in 1953:

> You who are promoting mission work on the Hopi land had better
> come to unity with Christ-like love and live it before continue to
> preach about Him. ... My people are being required to make
> tremendous speed in transition almost from stone age in one
> generation into white man's pattern of life. Which causes much
> mental disturbance. Now the spiritual confusion among the mis-
> sionaries, the Hopi people question. "What is the fight about?
> Where and what is the love of Christ?"... The Hopi, whom we
> consider spiritually lost, is more quietly spiritually secured to-
> day than our missionaries in their confusion of gossip over creed
> and doctorinal [sic] split differences. It is time we all hang our
> heads in shame and humbleness before our God as Christians.[34]

A New Strategy

It was true that few Hopi converts had been won before
1950. The missionaries' list of baptized Third-Mesa Hopi (which
included those baptized at Riverside, California, or other Indian boarding schools) came only to ninety-seven people in fifty-
seven years, less than 4 percent of the target population.
Attendance at worship was often sparse, and consisted of
mostly women and children. Few people came every Sunday;
weekday sewing classes for women were better attended. The
sewing classes were not seen as "church," and attendance at
these drew less ridicule and persecution from non-Christian
Hopi.[35]

The new strategy for mission in Arizona was the Hopi
Mission School in New Oraibi. [36] One missionary wrote in *The*

Mennonite, "To the workers on the field and to others who made a study of the situation, it seemed that the only way to build up a strong Christian group and native leadership for this group would be through a mission school."[37]

The school, started in 1951, grew to include kindergarten through grade eight. Over the years it used mostly missionaries and voluntary service workers as teachers. In 1973 Ida Nowabbi (Murdock) was hired as the first Hopi teacher. The school was successful in providing quality education and attracted many non-Christian as well as Christian students, particularly during periods when the government school was relatively poor.

In an attempt to evaluate the school and the mission to the Hopi, the Board of Missions in 1960 commissioned William Rayburn, an anthropologist and Presbyterian missionary among Indians in North Carolina and South America, to visit the reservation and present a list of recommendations. Rayburn's main recommendation was to merge the Mennonite, independent, and American Baptist churches on the reservation to provide a unified Christian witness in the midst of fragmentation, both among the Hopis and among the churches—which by then included Jehovah's Witnesses, Mormons, Pentecostals, and even a Bahai missionary.

Rayburn wrote,

> There will be little interest in the Christian way as long as it remains (1) largely dominated by women and children, (2) under white missionary leadership, and (3) presenting a multiplicity of ways to the Hopi people. ... Even those for whom Hopi religion is not important, the plurality of churches and confessions creates little more than confusion.[38]

He particularly urged reconciliation between Johnson's independent church and the Mennonite church in Oraibi.

Rayburn noted the wide separation between Christianity and the Hopi world which the Mennonite missionaries had helped to create, and the sharp break with Hopi culture required of individual converts:

> So exaggerated has been the break with Hopi life that only the children who are not yet responsible Hopi people and a few old men and women who no longer function in the community life are in the Mennonite churches. There is in no sense a cross section of the life of the community in the churches.[39]

At the time of the report, none of the white Mennonite missionaries in Arizona spoke Hopi; no one had learned Hopi since the Frey-Duerksen controversy over translation. Translation of the Bible into Hopi had also stopped with the resignations of Frey and Duerksen. Rayburn recommended that missionaries not involved in the school learn Hopi and that translation be resumed under the auspices of the church. Rayburn also questioned the effect of a school such as Hopi Mission School in counteracting traditional values of the children's parents.

Although the Rayburn report seemed overly critical to some missionaries, the Board of Missions and, after 1968, its successor, the Commission on Home Ministries, attempted to carry out some of the report's recommendations. Through the efforts of Malcolm Wenger, then secretary for Indian ministries, some informal reconciliation with the Hopi Independent Church was achieved. The Hopi Mission School was turned over to a Hopi-run board with members from other churches as well as Mennonite. The commission continued to supply teachers through Mennonite Voluntary Service.

Cross-cultural gathering at Clinton, Oklahoma, 1979

Jack M

52

Chapter 4:
A Small Harvest

We prolonged our control, thus depriving the young church of the struggles and joys and the possibility of failure that leads to maturity.

We have yielded to the temptation of cultural pride. Why, one wonders, did we in our meeting places exchange the symbolic brotherhood of the Cheyenne way of meeting in a circle with all on one level for the straight rows of benches facing in one direction and dominated by a raised platform?

Yet in spite of failures and fumbles God used our lives to speak to Indian people and to draw them into fellowship with Him and with us. They in turn have been used in drawing others. . . .

Our work is then finished when we have established living fellowships for the proclamation of the Gospel, responsible churches that will continue to carry the torch. —Malcolm Wenger in "The Indian American in a Changing World," Missions Today, April 1966

By 1980, one hundred years after the first Mennonite missionaries began work among American Indians, the Mennonite churches among the Cheyenne, Arapaho, and Hopi had shown growth, but little since 1940. Of twelve Indian General Conference-related congregations in the United States in 1977, four had no official membership statistics, and two of these were not meeting regularly. The remaining eight had a total membership of about 325 adults. Average attendance was about half that number.[1] The 1974 Indian ministries report to the Commission on Home Ministries noted with concern:

> In spite of real gains in local control and responsibility and some

significant service programs, the bringing of people into fellowship with Christ and the church is at a low ebb. ... There have
been few baptisms in Indian churches. Few people, especially
young married people, have been drawn into a life of the congregations. Some congregations have declined. It has been difficult
to find Indian or non-Indian leadership to fill vacancies.[2]

One Indian church leader put it bluntly to the commission's
executive committee, "Our churches are dying."[3] In Oklahoma
and Montana, relatively large numbers of Cheyenne and Arapaho had been baptized, but church attendance was usually
low. In Hopi land, winning new church members had always
been difficult; the 1957 statistics, for example, showed only 150
baptisms in sixty years of mission activity, with twenty-five
active members.

Missionaries in Montana, Oklahoma, and Arizona had
often chafed against the comparisons with General Conference
Mennonite missions overseas. By 1941, for instance, India and
China missions had 4,389 members compared with a total membership of 748 in the American Indian fields.[4] Already in 1921,
Rodolphe and Bertha Petter felt upstaged by overseas missions,
particularly by P. A. Penner, missionary to India. Bertha Petter
felt her field was more difficult. Penner acknowledged this
when he visited the Oklahoma mission in the 1920s and reported he could never work there.[5]

The Foreign Mission Board certainly felt frustration and
bewilderment over the American Indian missions, but was willing to let the nearly autonomous superintendents of each field
continue to make policy and set strategies. When personnel and
money were available, the board shared it with Indian missions
and overseas fields.

Why was the harvest so small in these "foreign" missions
in the United States? It was some consolation to missionaries
and mission board members to know that few other denominations were attracting large numbers of Indians to their
churches. Missiologist Harold W. Turner noted that:

> The North American Indian peoples were as fine a race and made
> as good an initial response to the Christian faith as any other
> tribal peoples; that their subsequent treatment by whites was as
> bad as anywhere else, but their survival qualities have been
> unexcelled in the tribal world; that they have been the object of
> Christian missions for a period as long as that of any other people
> in modern times, and yet the overall Christian results are among
> the least impressive of all mission labours.[6]

He continued:

> Has a total indigenous population that ranged between 400,000
> and 1,000,000 ever had more mission societies and agencies,
> more men, and more resources devoted to its conversion? In
> 1923, to take a sample at one point, there were some 650 mission-
> aries, Catholic and Protestant, dealing with about 300,000 In-
> dians in the U.S.A.—one for each 460.... At the beginning of the
> 1970s one denomination, the Southern Baptists, showed 149
> missionaries on the map of their work among Indians. Only the
> Bureau of Indian Affairs could outdo these efforts, for in the late
> 1960s it was stated to have one employee for every 38 Indians.[7]

The Tenacity of Traditional Religion

Part of the reason for the missionaries' discouragement
lay in the remarkable staying power of Indian religions and
various combinations of Indian religion with Christianity. Especially in the early days of the Mennonite missions, Indians
who became Christians endured persecution from family and
friends because of conversion. One such woman in Montana,
who was the only Christian in her immediate family, ended her
own life because of the ridicule she received.[8]

In Montana, the Cheyenne medicine men viewed the Mennonite mission as a threat, and rightly so, since the missionaries expected their converts to make a total break with
traditional religion. Attendance at tribal ceremonies was
grounds for admonition; participation in the dances was
grounds for excommunication. At the same time, missionaries
consistently reported greatly diminished church attendance
during tribal gatherings for the Sun Dance and the renewal of
the sacred arrows. At times the church buildings were empty
with the note "Sun Dance" written on the attendance charts.
Although Oklahoma missionary Daniel B. Hirschler had seen
parallels to the Old Testament in Indian culture, missionaries
generally saw contemporary Indian religions as "heathen,"
and no elements of them could be permitted to enter Christian
worship. This attitude was carried to the extreme among the
Hopi, but was present to some degree in the Cheyenne and
Arapaho work.

Christians were caught between their tribal identity and
their loyalty to the church. Native helpers in Oklahoma such as
Homer Hart and Alfrich Heap of Birds (and later his son, John
Heap of Birds) attempted to play a mediating role and were
cautious in their denunciations of traditionalism. Some mis-

sionaries were frustrated that native helpers would not take a stronger stand.

In Montana, the Mennonite mission's presence was validated for missionaries and Cheyenne Christians by an incident in 1914. A tornado struck the church at Busby that year. The walls of the building collapsed, but the stove, the pulpit, and the reed organ were left intact. The tornado was seen as the result of a curse placed on the church by Black Whiteman, a traditional medicine man. But the fact that the three items important to church worship were not taken by the wind was regarded as evidence of the permanence and power of the Christian faith.[9]

The conflict in Montana became more sharply defined with regard to sexual practices in connection with the Sun Dance. In 1919 Rodolphe Petter preached sixteen Cheyenne sermons on sin to the congregation in Lame Deer. As a result, four women and several men confessed their past involvement with ritual sexual intercourse as part of the Sun Dance ceremony. While Petter had known of the practice through his linguistic research, he had earlier chosen not to make an issue of it. Now Petter took action. He translated the confessions, made copies of them, and gave them to the Indian agent at Lame Deer, a close friend. The agent made further investigations and sent the matter to Washington, D.C. The agent called a meeting of all medicine men and traditional priests on the reservation. For six hours the traditionalists denied that sexual intercourse was a part of the rituals. Finally they demanded that the woman who had made the accusations testify before the group. With Petter's encouragement, she told her story, and the traditionalists admitted defeat.[10]

"The fight is on," wrote Bertha Petter. "Christian men emboldened by the truth as proclaimed at the church have dared to bare ceremonial doings of the Cheyennes that are disgusting in the extreme. It has stirred up a hornet's nest, and Indians on the whole reservation are taking a stand."[11]

The Lame Deer congregation itself was not united in the fight with the traditionalists. Petter wrote to his wife after a congregational meeting:

> John S. T. [Stands in Timber, Cheyenne historian and author] avoided to commit himself to offend no one! Amotane spoke but advising avoidance of provoking the "older" religion! Say, a camp meeting would be pleasant with such fearful witnesses, rowing both ways?[12]

Other members of the Lame Deer congregation continued to

send their requests for government action against traditional religion. One such letter read:

> I am Yellowfox, a Cheyenne Indian, 44 years old, a man who desires the truth and anxious to keep law and order. I am glad to learn that you are going to take away all that still hinders the progress of my people.
>
> I have come to see that the religious doings of my people are conducive to wrong and immorality. ...
>
> I am an Indian police [sic] and see what is going on. I see, as it were, the law and order, as it is represented by the church and by our Superintendent, I want this state of proper living upheld among my people. When religious dancing, the giving of women to lustful Indian priests, and all the evil connected with it shall be broken, the progress will be possible and I shall believe in it. Then will my people learn to obey God's and the Government's laws. ...
>
> When all that hinders our progres[s], when all the secret doings shall be cut off, then and only then shall we be able to progress as people.[13]

The Commissioner of Indian Affairs ordered the superintendent of the reservation to take appropriate action against the medicine men. Although it was the government which took action, the medicine men never doubted that the Mennonite missionaries were responsible.[14] Petter had successfully challenged the traditionalists on the reservation. His victory was based on his close relationship to the power of the Indian agent and on his own credibility as an authority on the Cheyenne. The Mennonite churches had power also, since nearly all of the Indian police force and the Indian judge were members of the Lame Deer church.[15]

The traditionalists tried to fight back. A group of them naively petitioned Foreign Mission Board chairman J. W. Kliewer to replace the missionaries. In 1932, nearly 200 Cheyenne petitioned the Commissioner of Indian Affairs to remove the entire Mennonite presence on the reservation. That petition was motivated by the earlier incident and by the arrest of a peyote leader, urged by Alfred Habegger.[16] The traditionalists contended:

> The principal reason why we object to the presence of the Mennonite Mission is that the missionaries in question inspire their converts to become prejudiced and even malicious to all these Indians who have not embraced their specific faith. Furthermore, in consequence of this sad influence the converts are urged

to be talebearers and to be constantly on the alert to find fault and to disrupt harmony among their neighbors.[17]

Neither petition was granted.

The Ghost Dance. Early Mennonite missionaries in Oklahoma had more dialogue with participants in the Ghost Dance than with participants in the older Indian religion. The Ghost Dance was a blend of traditional Indian religion and Christianity, promoted by Wovoka, a Paiute Indian from Nevada. Some Indians reported that he was the Messiah. According to the proponents of the Ghost Dance, whites were soon to be removed, although nonviolently, the buffalo would come back, and all Indians, living and dead, would be reunited upon a regenerated earth.[18]

The Ghost Dance reached the Southern Cheyenne and Arapaho in late summer 1890.[19] Missionary Heinrich R. Voth, then serving in Indian Territory, saw the interest in the Ghost Dance as an opportunity for Christian witness. "The Indians take the thing very earnest and it appears to me there are more and better opportunities for spiritual work amongst them now than ever before," he wrote to *The Mennonite.*[20] When Sitting Bull, the Arapaho prophet of the Ghost Dance, came to instruct the Southern Arapaho concerning the new religion, Voth went to talk to him.

> The next day he [Sitting Bull] and his wife came to our Sunday school, where upon my request, he gave an address to the children. He spoke very well, encouraged the children to remain on the road which they were pursuing, to be diligent in study, and not to run away from school, etc.[21]

Sitting Bull told Voth that the Bible way was the best way, but since he and the other older Indians could not read the Bible, they were worshiping the same God and Father as well as they knew how. Later, during the Ghost Dance meeting, Sitting Bull told the Arapahos to attend Voth's church.

This opening for Christian witness was not followed up, however. Voth left Oklahoma the following year, and Bible translations were not yet ready. The Ghost Dance itself soon disappeared, partly in the aftermath of the Battle of Wounded Knee, which had been caused by white misunderstanding of the Ghost Dance. Rodolphe Petter later commented:

> Had the Indians at that time had the Gospel in their own language, I believe they would have eagerly accepted it and turned their back to their heathenism, for they were weary of it and

groped for something better. Alas, missionaries were not ready with the knowledge of the Indian language, nor had they yet the needed Bible translations.[22]

Peyote. Of far greater competition to Mennonite mission efforts was the peyote religion, in 1918 organized and incorporated in Oklahoma as the *Native American Church.* Like the Ghost Dance, the peyote religion combined elements of traditionalism and Christianity. It centered around the sacrament of peyote, a desert plant imported from the Southwest which contains a mildly hallucinogenic drug. Peyote's first appeal was to younger, educated Indians, many of whom had experience in Christian churches.

Peyote probably came to the Cheyenne and Arapaho through Comanche Quanah Parker in about 1884, but certainly by 1891.[23] Peyote was seen by many Indians as the Indian version of Christianity. Peyote ceremonies used many Christian symbols: the cross, the dove, the Trinity, and the Bible. The Native American Church preached avoidance of alcohol and tobacco, brotherly love, care of one's family, and self-reliance. But to the missionaries, the peyote adaptations were a false religion, "this curse among our Indians."[24] Throughout the existence of the interdenominational Conference of Indian Missionary Workers in Western Oklahoma from 1915 to 1943, peyote was a subject of discussion and of appeals to Congress to ban its use.[25]

Participation in peyote ceremonies was grounds for dismissal from Mennonite mission churches, yet the inroads into Mennonite churches often dismayed missionaries. When H. J. Kliewer at the Red Moon (Hammon) church called a meeting of Indian Christians to discuss peyote, he was distressed to find they did not all agree with him on the evils of peyote.[26] The missionaries' response was not to condone the use of peyote, but usually to avoid open antagonism between the two groups.

After World War II, Oklahoma churches continued to feel that peyote was a major factor in the decline of the churches. When one missionary preached a sermon denouncing peyote, the church members walked out. Few missionaries had first-hand information about the Native American Church, and no dialogue was initiated. Yet missionaries recognized that the peyote people were able to raise money for their church and provide leadership even with strong white opposition.[27]

The peyote religion made its inroads also among the Cheyenne in Montana, after its introduction there by Southern

Cheyenne Leonard Tyler. By the 1930s, a majority of the Northern Cheyenne were involved in the peyote religion.[28] Missionaries in Montana, as in Oklahoma, took a stand against peyote and considered members of the Mennonite churches who participated in peyote worship no longer in good standing. [29] Yet, members of the Native American Church seldom made such a great distinction between the Christianity of the Mennonites and the peyote religion.[30] One missionary in Montana reported he had been told of occasions when sermons by Rodolphe Petter in Cheyenne had been used in the peyote ceremonies.[31] A number of the leading members of the Lame Deer church in 1919 were former "peyote men." Bertha Petter wrote:

> Our strongest peyote leader here at Lame Deer comes frequently to our services, and told Mr. Petter after the sermon last Sunday morning, "Many lies are told about me. I am an educated man. I know the Bible. I know the commandments. I do not worship the peyote. How could I, knowing there is but one God and one Mediator, Jesus Christ. I know I am a sinner, but I am trying to overcome. I know that only the blood of Jesus can save me."[32]

Some Indian church leaders acknowledged the competition from peyote. One leader in Oklahoma, quoting another Indian, said, "The peyote people are really sincere. They really stick together. Christians don't have that yet."[33]

Modern anthropologists have compared Indian independent movements, such as the Native American Church, to the African Independent Churches, which developed independently of missionaries and mission funds. According to Harold Turner such movements "represent an intermediate stage where it is possible to respond to the Western-Christian influence with certain radical departures from the old ways but without total cultural assimilation and the loss of spiritual independence."[34] What might the results have been had Mennonite missionaries shown more willingness to dialogue with advocates of the peyote religion in the manner in which mission organizations, including the General Conference Commission on Overseas Mission, have worked with African Independent Churches in recent years?

Respect for Indian culture. In spite of the missionaries' opposition to traditional Indian dances, religious ceremonies, and even art, in some cases, Mennonite Indian churches preserved some parts of Indian culture. By the 1930s, Harvey Whiteshield and John Heap of Birds had developed hymns with Cheyenne music as well as Cheyenne words. This was the first major effort to incorporate Cheyenne culture into the Christian community. In the 1970s, some of these songs were recorded and given notation by David Graber. A Cheyenne hymnal was published in 1982.[35]

Two other forms of Cheyenne culture also had taken root in the church by the 1930s: the feast and the prayer meeting. Church members in Oklahoma gave feasts in the church on Sundays to celebrate or to give thanks for personal or family blessings. In Montana there were prayer meetings in homes. Church members came, were served a feast, and then joined in prayer for healing or gave thanks for a blessing within the host family. Both of these practices have parallels in the Native American Church and in the older Cheyenne religion.

Separation from the Hopi. In Arizona there was no such adaptation of traditional ways. That most Mennonites there from early on saw no positive values in Hopi religion is illustrated by the story of K. T. Johnson (Tuwaletstewa), one of the early converts in Oraibi. He had been head of the Bow Clan, which controlled the One-Horn and Two-Horn societies, groups which played an important role in the cycle of Hopi religion. When Johnson became a Christian, he rejected attendance at the Hopi ceremonial dances as well as tobacco, white man's dances, and picture shows. In August 1922, Johnson decided, after consultation with other Hopi Christians, to burn the Bow Clan altar and other paraphernalia connected with it, which were used in one of the most secret ceremonies of the Hopi religion.

On the next Sunday afternoon, when many white tourists as well as Hopis were gathered to watch the Snake Dance, the Hopi Christians gathered in the center of New Oraibi for prayer and singing. Johnson set up the secret altar in the public square, spoke to the crowd about the evils of idol worship, poured gasoline over the altar, and set fire to it while the Christian group sang, "When the Roll Is Called Up Yonder," in Hopi. "Thus passed away the most important Hopi religious ceremony," commented Otto Lomavitu, another Hopi Christian.[36]

In the late 1970s this sense of separation from traditionalist culture remained strong, although it began to relax in small ways. The Moencopi church, for example, decided that it was all right to go to traditional weddings. Some of the women in the church reportedly cried because they had always wanted to go but had never been able.

On the traditionalists' side, hostility toward Christians was also strong. When Hopi pastor Daniel Quimayousie began

Sunday worship in the Schirmer house in the conservative village of Hotevilla in 1970, traditionalists responded with threats to tear down the house and with letters to friends in the war protest movement in Berkeley, California. This resulted in a series of national press releases and letters attacking Mennonite mission work and claiming, without basis in fact, "Mennonites plan to build church on sacred Hopi ground" and "Aged Hopi chief brutally assaulted by Mennonite religious bigots."[37] Later, Hopi Christians and traditionalists met to discuss the issue. The Christians were told they had no legal papers for the building. The Christians agreed, but asked why Hopis needed papers when they had had the word of the chief when the building was built earlier in the century. The controversy quieted after that.[38]

Competition from Other Missions

Another factor in the growth of the Mennonite Indian churches was the competition from other missions. The Mennonite missions were seldom alone. In Oklahoma, the Quakers had briefly started a mission among the Cheyenne. In the 1870s, J. B. Wicks of Paris Hill, New York, an Episcopalian clergyman, had taken Cheyenne, Comanche, and Kiowa young men from Indian Territory to his home from the Carlisle Indian School in Pennsylvania and trained them as missionaries. By 1881, the first of these, David Pendleton, was already conducting services entirely in Cheyenne.[39]

Some sort of mission work had also been done among the Arapaho before the Haurys arrived. Powder Face, an Arapaho chief, proudly identified himself as a Christian, wore white-style clothing, and was registering his cattle herd with a brand in 1880. There is no record that he ever identified with the Mennonite mission.[40]

Dutch Reformed missionaries were well established in Seger's Colony (now Colony, Oklahoma), but withdrew in the 1920s. Relationships with the Dutch Reformed mission near Clinton were unusually tense. In 1906 Foreign Mission Board chairman A. B. Shelly virtually ordered the Dutch Reformed missionary out of the field and wrote him to stop "sheep stealing" from Clinton.[41] Veteran Clinton missionary J. B. Ediger prided himself on the fact that, while in forty years he had never mastered the Cheyenne language, he had at least outlasted the Dutch Reformed mission.[42]

Baptist, Nazarene, Pentecostal, and Mormon missionaries had made some inroads by 1928. There were so many mission

groups working among the Cheyenne and Arapaho in Oklahoma and nearby tribes that an annual conference for missionaries of Protestant groups was established in 1914.

In Arizona, Mennonites, working in the western Hopi villages, enjoyed generally good relationships with the American
Baptists who were working in the eastern Hopi villages. By the
1970s, Baptists were appointing some members to the Hopi
Mission School board. There were less cooperative relationships with some of the new mission groups: Jehovah's Witnesses, Mormons, Pentecostals, and Bahais.

In Montana, conflict with the Catholics was more open.
Mennonite missions had been aware of the potential for conflict
with Catholic missions when they first investigated the Tongue
River Reservation. Many Cheyenne had been baptized as in-
fants, and many had attended the Catholic school at Ashland.
An uneasy truce between Mennonites and Catholics existed
until 1917, when the Ashland Mennonite mission was opened
within sight of the St. Labre Mission School. Conflict was inevitable when Valdo Petter, son of Rodolphe and Marie Petter, was
appointed missionary in Ashland in 1925. Valdo was a staunch
fundamentalist (unlike his father), who had served as a noncombatant in World War I, attended Moody Bible Institute, and then
moved to Ashland.

In 1927 new priests at the St. Labre mission began to
proselyte more actively and reopened a chapel at Lame Deer.
Charges and countercharges involving missionaries, Cheyenne, and government employees began to swirl. A Catholic
publication wrote, "The Mennonites are like unto ravening
wolves seeking to ruin the souls of the Catholic Cheyennes.
Most of the faithful Indians would rather starve to death before
they would sell their souls for bribes and go over to the Mennonite Camp."[43] Rodolphe Petter wrote to the mission board about
Catholics:

> ...[T]he priest condones drinking, dancing and gambling. Accord-
> ing to the Indians he told them that since God (?) gave them their
> religious ceremonies (heathenish) they were not wrong! ...[T]he
> priests (Catholics) claim as their "sheep" any Indian baptized by
> them as infants years ago. Now they overrun the reservation to
> snatch children and baptize them, forbidding them to attend any
> of our church services.[44]

Whereas the battle with traditionalism was fought on
legal grounds, the battle with the Catholics was fought on a
moral basis. Competition between the two missions grew so
keen that eventually the Commissioner of Indian Affairs in

Washington, Charles J. Rhoads asked a third party, the Service Committee on Indians of the Federal Council of Churches, to intervene, since he suspected that both the Mennonites and the Catholics were "overzealous."[45]

Tensions gradually eased between the Mennonites and Catholics in the late 1930s as Mennonites put most of their efforts into the western part of the reservation. Valdo Petter, a key protagonist, died in 1935. His widow, Laura Rohrman Petter, continued to live in Ashland until her death in 1976. The Mennonite church in Ashland was never large—fewer than a dozen people were ever members. By the 1970s, it met jointly with a Pentecostal group.

A number of other factors probably limited Indian church growth. One was factionalism within the Indian churches, sometimes based on blood relationships. Another factor was the inability or unwillingness of Indian converts to meet all the standards of Christian ethics set by the missionaries, who carried over from their own sometimes fundamentalist backgrounds a list of forbidden activities such as smoking, drinking, card playing, movies, fairs, and so forth. In 1908 missionary J. A. Funk in Oklahoma reported that the biggest temptation to the Arapaho Christians was not the "heathen dances," but drinking and card playing. In his church in Canton, sixty-three of seventy members once had to be excluded from the Lord's Supper because of drinking and card playing. Missionaries Bertha Kinsinger (Petter) and Agnes Williams reported a similar situation in Clinton.[46] Standards and doctrines often differed from those in other Mennonite churches in North America. One Hopi Mennonite compared the legalism of the Hopi churches to what she had found elsewhere in the General Conference:

> The more I met with the Commission on Home Ministries executive committee, worked and talked with Mennonites from the Pacific District, and stayed in the homes of Mennonites in Newton, Kansas, the real Anabaptist-Mennonite became apparent. It was just completely opposite from the concept one can form by meeting and hearing about Mennonites only on the reservation. I was fully able to forgive the past history of missionaries on our Hopi Reservation and grow to share a deeper fellowship with the Mennonites of General Conference.[47]

Mennonite Missionaries and American Culture

One of the most important factors in the difficulties of the Mennonite missions may have been the unasked-for identification of the missionaries with the dominant American society.

This society had defeated the Indians politically, had left them poor, and threatened to take away their culture as well through assimilation into the larger American culture. Mennonites cooperated with the government policy of "Christianize and civilize" in the 1880s. But in so doing, Mennonites were no more cooperative than other Christian mission groups of the same era. Missionary-historian R. Pierce Beaver noted that Indian mission

> ...was undertaken by Europeans who never questioned the identification of the Gospel with European culture and with their denominational forms of Christianity. Whether Spanish, English, Russian, or German, whether Protestant, Orthodox, or Roman Catholic, the missionaries sought simultaneously to evangelize and "civilize" the Indian, conforming him to the white man's cultural and ecclesiastical pattern.[48]

Missiologist Harold Turner also noted the assumption of both church and state that the Indian would finally be assimilated into the American mainstream.

> There is nothing reprehensible in this policy—it seemed to be the best that those who held to it could offer, and it has been followed in other parts of the world where there was no justification derived from the presence of an overwhelming white majority. Indian response, however, seems to have moved from earlier cooperation, through a long period of indifference and passivity, to the more recent vocal opposition and political activism that reassert Indian identity and the renewal of Indian culture within a plural society.[49]

Thus what is notable about Mennonite missions is not that they participated in the larger attempt to assimilate the Indian, but that they differed from this assimilation policy at specific points.

——— *Anti-German feeling.* During World War I it became impossible for Mennonite missionaries as pacifists to identify totally with the aims of the U.S. government. Missionaries J. B. and Aganetha Frey in Arizona wrote of the harmful effect on mission work of those who used the Mennonites' antiwar stance and German background as an excuse to turn the Hopi against the missionaries.

> If already before the war mission work was hindered by propaganda against the same, much more was this the case during the war when poisons under the pretense of patriotism had opportunity to make such propaganda. The missionaries were apostles of peace. Thus propagandists pictured to the Indians war as the way to glory and riches, and the missionary was being de-

nounced as an enemy to the government. Finally the Indians became confused and aroused to such a degree that the worst among them took occasion to arouse their people against the missionary, telling them that, if they supported the missionary, they would be considered enemies of the government in Washington. By such threats and others they succeeded in making the Indians temporarily suspicious, especially since the godless white people helped them in this. In addition to all this, accusations were made against the missionaries to the government and investigations followed, in which the innocence of the missionaries was proven. This quieted the Indians considerably.[50]

The war also had its effects in Oklahoma, over the issue of Christmas bundles. As we have already noted, from about 1890 on, the missionaries solicited clothing from the home churches to be given to the Indians as gifts at Christmas. During World War I the practice was briefly dropped, since the clothing was directed to Mennonite refugees from Europe. The giving of clothing was never resumed with as much enthusiasm in Oklahoma thereafter. This, combined with malicious stories that Mennonites were the same German people the Cheyenne were fighting in Europe, resulted in considerable hostility toward the Mennonite Indian churches.

Collier's Indian reform. The Mennonites' and other missions' separation from government policy became more pronounced as the winds of reform began to move in the Bureau of Indian Affairs under President Herbert Hoover. Those winds became a gale when President Franklin Roosevelt appointed John C. Collier commissioner of Indian Affairs in 1932.

Collier was a romantic collectivist who saw traditional Indian culture, with its values of sharing and unity with nature, as something to be preserved rather than destroyed by acculturation.[51] Collier's policy was to encourage traditional Indian religion—including peyote and the Native American Church—and to give tribes new forms of self-government as well as material assistance through the Works Progress Administration, formed during the depression.

The reversal of policy in the Bureau of Indian Affairs was a blow to Mennonite missions, particularly in Montana. When word of the Mennonite-Catholic-traditionalist conflicts reached Collier, he asked Secretary of the Interior Harold Ickes to intervene. Ickes wrote to Waldo Petter:

Neither Commissioner Collier nor I will willingly tolerate the abuse of power in Indian Reservations by any missionary; still less will we knowingly tolerate any action by government employees designed to force Indians into any creed. We are particularly desirous of securing any information, factually supported, of the existence of abuses of these types. I should add that aggressive, provocative actions by missionaries of any group directed against missionaries of others groups, or against the native religions are entirely unfortunate.[52]

Rodolphe Petter and his son were shattered by the New Deal's reversal of Indian policy which encouraged tribal government and the peyote religion. He referred to such policies as "neo-paganism" and the "eighth beast of the Revelation."[53] He summarized its impact on the mission program in a discouraged letter to board chairman P. H. Richert:

> Because of the government's "counter influences," our Indians have, as a people, sunk deeper than they were fifty years ago. ... They are drunk with the new power and self-government granted to them from Washington, D.C., and act accordingly until chaos is fully reached. The majority of our Montana Cheyenne stand now indifferent to the Gospel of Christ.[54]

No longer was the government a trusted ally of the mission. Northern Cheyenne minister Milton Whiteman wrote:

> There was a period of time when the Sun Dance and other heathen worship was prohibited by the Indian Department in control at Washington, D.C. The Mennonite church had a large attendance at that time, and the experience was very encouraging to the Christians and Missionaries alike. But, alas, a severe change came about in the year 1933 when the Commissioner of Indian Affairs, John C. Collier; came into office. It seems the bottom just fell out of everything and the devil took over. The churches suffered a great setback. A very sad state of affairs and conditions began. Liquor and immorality went on a rampage, and heathen worship of all kinds were resumed and have full swing.
>
> There are only a few families of the Government employees here at Lame Deer who attend a service of worship. Some of the white population that the Indians live with are a poor example to the Indians.[55]

Bible translations. The major contribution of Mennonite nissionaries toward Indian cultural preservation was in terms of language. In their attempts to translate the Bible into the Indian languages, Mennonites were ahead of missionaries of most other denominations in the United States. Turner reported that by 1972, the whole New Testament was available only in seven Indian vernacular versions. Although John Eliot had translated the whole Bible into Mohican in the 1660s, no one now living can read it. Otherwise, there exists only one complete Bible in an Indian language, Dakota, after over 300 years of mission work among American Indians. "This neglect of translation has been directly due to the assimilation assumptions.... Without translation the Christian faith is never really apprehended, and men continue to live in two worlds with a language for each," said Turner.[56]

Perhaps the Mennonites' use of German in a predominantly English culture made them more sensitive to people's need for the Scriptures in their own language. Whatever the reason, Mennonite missionary translators were certainly pioneers in their field. When H. R. Voth was writing down and systematizing the Hopi language, and later missionaries J. B. Epp, J. B. Frey, and J. R. Duerksen were beginning translation, nearby Baptist missionaries among the Hopi were not learning the language at all. The results of the Mennonite mission to the Hopi might have been much different if Duerksen and Frey could have worked through their doctrinal difficulties and continued translation of the New Testament. Only a few Gospel portions, Romans 1-8, and a Bible history were completed.[57] No white missionaries to the Hopi, from the 1940s on, could speak Hopi.

Rodolphe Petter's translation of the New Testament and parts of the Old Testament into the Cheyenne language remains a monumental work, although a new, more easily pronounced spelling has since been developed. His *Cheyenne-English Dictionary* found its way into libraries around the world.

Mennonite missionaries never mastered the Arapaho language to the same degree as Cheyenne and Hopi. Missionary J. A. Funk, who served in Oklahoma from 1896 to 1920, was the only missionary to learn Arapaho well enough to translate Bible portions.[58]

Making Indian Churches Mennonite

While early missionaries may have tried to take Christian Indians out of the Indian cultures and into white culture, they were not as eager to admit Indian churches fully into the Mennonite community. No Indian church was admitted permanently into the General Conference Mennonite Church until 1956, when the Northern Cheyenne churches were approved for membership.[59]

Few Indian leaders were sent for further training at Mennonite schools, partly because few had finished high school, although two young men from Oklahoma and a young Hopi woman attended Bethel College in Kansas. The Arizona field usually relied on conservative interdenominational schools such as the Bible Institute of Los Angeles, and a few leaders from Montana went to Cook Christian Training School, Tempe, Arizona, and Mokahum Indian Bible School, Cass Lake, Minnesota. Training in such schools may have been helpful, but it did not build the ties necessary for making Indian church leaders feel a part of the wider Mennonite community. While the Board of Missions after World War II followed German-Swiss Mennonites into the cities with new churches, the board discussed much but never implemented urban churches for the growing number of Cheyenne, Arapaho, and Hopi Mennonites who had moved away from the reservation areas.

One example of the separation felt between the mission churches and other Mennonite churches was the issue of nonresistance. Individual Mennonite missionaries, such as H. R. Voth, G. A. Linscheid, and Rodolphe Petter, had strong pacifist convictions. Petter was denied U.S. citizenship in 1922 because he would not promise to bear arms to protect the U.S. constitution. The "Constitution of Our Indian Mennonite Churches in Oklahoma and Montana" enjoined a "scriptural nonresistance" on individual members. When harassed by hostile Hopis and even after an attempt on his life, J. B. Frey's attitude was: "Leave them to God. Let God judge them in His own good time." Frey pled for the release of the man who had attacked him and thus prevented his going to prison.[60]

But peace was seldom made an essential part of the gospel in the missionaries' message, even among the Hopi, where the tradition of pacifism might have provided a natural opening for the gospel. Neither did missionaries among the Cheyenne build on the peace tradition of the Cheyenne chiefs' society.[61] There is no record of any conscientious objectors to military service among Indian Mennonites in World War I. In World War II, one member of the Busby, Montana, church—Laverne Killsontop—asked for noncombatant service.[62] Six Hopis were sentenced to hard labor as conscientious objectors, but they based their case on traditional Hopi pacifism, not on Christianity.[63] In Lame Deer, Montana, numerous members of the church were armed policemen; however, Milton Whiteman, a church leader and policeman, was known for not carrying weapons. Once when he needed to arrest a man charged with murder, Whiteman succeeded in bringing him in from his hideout without a gun.[64]

Cheyenne church leader, Lawrence Hart, as a student at

Bethel College in 1961, researched "Why the Doctrine of Non-
Resistance Has Failed to Appeal to the Cheyenne Indian." He
cited a general ignorance among Cheyenne Mennonites on nonresistance and alternate programs to military service. On inter-
viewing the executive secretary of the Board of Missions, Hart
discovered that the conference had been sending out pamphlets
on nonresistance only to member churches, not to mission
churches.[65] Hart later was influenced to leave his career as a
Navy jet pilot by his former roommate at Bethel, Larry Kaufman, who accidentally drowned while in an alternate service
assignment in the Congo (now Zaire).

The General Conference Mennonites had helped bring
these Indian churches into being, but were these *Mennonite*
churches? Sometimes the conference, the missionaries, and the
Indian church leaders themselves were hesitant to say yes.

Making Mennonite Churches Indian

The first missionaries to the Cheyenne, Arapaho, and
Hopi came into an environment in which there was no nucleus
of Mennonites with which to start a church, in which leadership, of necessity, was in the hands of the missionaries alone.
However, these missionaries early saw as a goal the eventual
self-government and self-support of the Indian churches.[66]

The role of the native helper. From the beginning, missionaries in Oklahoma were dependent on bilingual Cheyenne and
Arapaho for interpretation. At first, returning students from
Carlisle Institute were used and occasionally employees from
the Indian agency. The difficulty was that young interpreters
were under intense pressure to return to traditional religion
and camp life and not be seen as white hirelings. The use of non-
Christian interpreters proved even less satisfactory. Indian and
mixed-blood persons served as teachers and staff at both
Darlington and Cantonment schools. Lucretia Arrow, for example, taught at Cantonment from about 1890 until her death
from typhoid in 1892.[67] Harvey Whiteshield taught an early
Cheyenne reading class along with Rodolphe Petter in 1894.[68]

When the development of congregations became more important, the role of "interpreter" evolved into that of "native
helper." Don All Runner's work as a native helper at the Fonda
church was described as "teaching Sunday school and interpreting when necessary. ...Since some time in August he
takes full charge of the work every second Sunday."[69] Other
native helpers included Robert Hamilton, Frank Hamilton,
Willie Meeks, Homer Hart, Don Tall Son, Redbird Black, Don

Tucker, Henry Lincoln, Frank Harrington, Arthur Sutton, Charlotte Whiteman, Bertha Adams, John Heap of Birds, Guy Heap of Birds, and Walter Fire. In Oklahoma, relationships between missionaries and interpreters or native helpers were often unstable. Pages of missionary reports to the board are filled with the stories of resignations, firings, rehirings, and frustrations with local leaders. It is hard to know how key a role such native helpers played in the development of churches. Clearly the native helpers served not only as interpreters but also as the bridges between two alien cultures.

The role of native helper declined faster in Oklahoma than in the other Mennonite Indian mission fields. Because the Cheyenne and Arapaho in Oklahoma were a minority group without a reservation after 1890, the English language was commonly understood much sooner than in Montana and Arizona. So it was easier, especially from 1940 on, for missionaries to preach in English. The role of native helper might have evolved into stronger local leadership. Instead, with some notable exceptions, it declined first in Oklahoma.

In Arizona, early native helpers and interpreters included Frank Jenkins, Nellie Johnson, Rhoda Pentewa, K. T. Johnson, and Elizabeth Qoyawayma (White). In Arizona, Christian Indians became ministers in charge of the mission churches at a much earlier date than among the Cheyenne and Arapaho missions. Fred Johnson was placed in charge at Oraibi in 1926, after the departure of J. R. Duerksen. Daniel Schirmer went as missionary to Bacavi and Hotevilla in 1934. Along with his wife, Amy Talasnemptewa Schirmer, he later served in Birney and Busby, Montana, and Moencopi and Bacavi, Arizona. Daniel was not ordained, however, until 1951.

In general, missionaries did not appoint women as native helpers, although some of them served as interpreters. Some women, however, did do more than interpret. Emma King (Hasseoveo) in Montana "gave able messages from the pulpit" in Lame Deer "when emergency called." Bertha Petter reported that one Indian had asked her, "Why not ordain Hasseoveo for the ministry? ...Although a woman she is capable as the men. Her life is consistent. She knows the Word and speaks well. We all love her."[70]

The use of native helpers was often seen as a step toward eventual all-Indian leadership of the churches. By the 1930s, missionaries in Oklahoma began talking about placing more responsibility on the Indian churches. "They would then either rise to the occasion in spite of grievous failings and show forth

the life that is within them, or they would disintegrate. I feel
that some such steps should have been taken some years ago,"
said missionary G. A. Linscheid in his 1933 report.[71] But in
practice, missionaries were hesitant to place too much responsibility on native helpers. Those who did take positions of leadership sometimes modeled the one-man-show type of leadership
they had seen for so many years among the missionaries.

In Montana it was 1950 before Milton Whiteman in the
Lame Deer church was ordained as the first Cheyenne elder,[72]
but that step was not the final step in self-government among
the Mennonite churches of the Northern Cheyenne reservation.
The Busby church, for example, still had no Cheyenne Sunday
school teacher.[73] In Oklahoma there was still no ordained native
pastor in 1961 "or even an effective church organization," two
missionaries complained.[74] In Arizona, in spite of the influence
of Hopi Mission School in educating the young, missionaries
were in charge; the Hopis were onlookers in the church, said one
former worker.[75]

The person who pushed hardest to make the vision of self-
supporting Indian churches a reality was Malcolm Wenger, a
Mennonite with a conservative, largely non-Mennonite education who had wanted to be an overseas missionary. Instead, he
and his wife, Esther Boehr Wenger, became missionaries in
Busby, Montana, in 1944. Preparing for careers as missionaries,
they became fluent in Cheyenne. They were the last missionaries to do so.

The Wengers soon became discouraged. White missionaries controlled the whole structure. When Malcolm visited one
Indian church, he saw the white missionary make the an-
nouncements as he unthinkingly poured the contents of the
offering plate into his coat pocket. Native workers had a separate salary schedule from white missionaries. The Board of
Missions even discouraged other missionaries in Montana from
including Daniel and Amy Schirmer, Hopi missionaries among
the Montana Cheyenne, in missionary staff meetings.

Influenced by the writings of Roland Allen,[76] by a year of
study at Mennonite Biblical Seminary in Chicago, and by the
General Conference's Study Conference on the Believers'
Church in 1955, Wengers began encouraging changes in the
Busby church. They got church members to take up and count
the offering. They formed a simple church council. "At first
people wouldn't talk. One older woman exclaimed, 'That
Wenger! Why does he want us to make decisions? That's what
we've got him for!'" Wenger recalled. Once, when the congrega-

tion turned to Malcolm to make the decision, he walked out of the room. By the time he returned, the congregation had decided.[77]

As the General Conference added new staff for its boards, Wenger became Board of Missions' representative to Indian churches in 1961. From 1966 to 1977, he was the administrator in Newton, Kansas, for Indian ministries. Where mission strategy had formerly been done on the field, now it was happening in Newton as well. Wenger, as well as the executive secretary, Andrew Shelly, visited the mission fields regularly on behalf of the Board of Missions. The strategy which the board, through Wenger, developed was to create independent Indian Mennonite churches. "The Indian," said Wenger, "must no longer be a guest in the white man's church but a full participant in an Indian church."[78] Local decision making by the congregation was stressed, rather than decision making by the assembly of missionaries in each field. Congregations were given a say in calling a new pastor. White missionaries left to allow local leadership to grow. Indian songs and other cultural forms were encouraged in the church. Some congregations talked about the possibility of a plural, self-supported ministry. Perhaps the idea of one full-time salaried pastor per congregation did not fit the Indian way of doing things.

The transition to new forms was not easy for missionaries nor for Indian congregations that had grown used to a white style of pastoral leadership. One woman, whose congregation was left pastorless when the white missionaries quit, told Wenger, "You took our church away."[79] Charles Yellowrobe of Busby said, "We will be orphans if the missionaries are gone." [80]

On a wider level, new responsibilities were also urged. In 1969, a Mennonite Indian Leaders Council was formed. Made up of representatives of each Indian church in Arizona, Montana, and Oklahoma, the council met at least once a year to share reports and to decide how the funds from the Commission on Home Ministries were to be divided. These funds amounted to $170,000 in 1981. Indian churches were encouraged to join district conferences and the General Conference, a step taken by 1980 by the Oklahoma and Montana churches. No Hopi churches joined the conference until 1982, when a reinvigorated Moencopi congregation joined the Pacific District Conference. Hopi Mission School became directed by a Hopi school board. Lawrence Hart, a Cheyenne from Oklahoma was elected to the Commission on Home Ministries in 1971, the same year the United Church of Christ became the first major American denomination to elect an Indian to its governing body.

In 1980 the Indian churches continued to struggle with their smallness and with the transition to new forms of church life. Most conscious attempts were being made to build ties between white and Indian Mennonite congregations through weekend or week-long cross-cultural camps in Oklahoma and Montana. Attempts were made to acquaint both Cheyennes and others with the Cheyenne peace heritage through the efforts of Cheyenne Mennonites in Oklahoma and the conference's Commission on Education. Hundreds of white Mennonites have worked in 1-W and voluntary service assignments in Indian communities.

One hundred years after the Haurys began their work, the creation of indigenous Indian churches among the Arapaho, Cheyenne, and Hopi was still in process, and the ties between the Indian churches and the rest of the General Conference Mennonite Church were still being knit.

The General Conference mission on 63rd Street, Chicago

Chapter 5:
The City as a Mission Field

"Dear Lord, let our Christmas program be good. Let us try to save someone. Please bring in drunkards. Don't let the people come just for candy and nuts and cookies, as some people do, but let them come to hear about Thee."—Girl's prayer at River Station Mission, Los Angeles, December 1913.[1]

By 1900, 40 percent of Americans lived in cities, double the percentage thirty years earlier. A much smaller percentage of General Conference Mennonites was urban, but that percentage was also growing, especially in the Eastern and Middle districts. In those districts were located most of the earlier Mennonite immigrants to North America, who were becoming more accustomed to the North American environment and to the English language.

As their members migrated to the towns and cities, the Eastern and Middle districts began starting churches there. Between 1893 and 1905, the Eastern District Conference, then located entirely in southeastern Pennsylvania, started churches in Souderton, Pottstown, Leidytown, Perkasie, Allentown, and Quakertown. A second church in Philadelphia was started for First Church members moving to the suburbs. In addition, the conference had, in 1884, taken on the responsibility for the old Germantown church, located in a section of Philadelphia. All of these churches had as their primary focus the gathering in of those of Mennonite heritage. However, some of the churches, such as Philadelphia and Allentown, also gathered in a number of people of other backgrounds. Pastor William S. Gottschall reported to the 1908 General Conference that in his congregation in Allentown only thirty-two of seventy members had come from Mennonite circles.[2]

The Middle District had been equally diligent, but with less success. Churches were begun in Canton, Ohio (1893); St. Louis (1893); Cleveland (1894); the Eisley Park sector of Chicago (1895); and Fort Wayne, Indiana (1903). But none of these churches still functioned in 1920. Many Middle District pastors had trouble giving city churches much support. Samuel F. Sprunger, pastor in Berne, Indiana, discouraged starting a new church in nearby Fort Wayne, saying that, "since these people were mostly from the Berne, Indiana, church and since there was work enough and there were homes enough in Berne, Indiana, they should not have left."[3]

Between 1900 and 1920 came a different sort of push toward the cities. Among the new residents of the cities were immigrants—most from eastern and southern Europe, mostly Catholic, mostly poor. By about 1900, foreigners by birth or parentage comprised two-thirds of the population of American cities and 47 percent of the entire country. Between 1900 and 1915 about a million immigrants a year were landing in the United States.

Protestantism, which had previously focused on the rural areas and the urban middle class, began in about 1880 to set up programs for the urban poor: settlement houses, boys' and girls' clubs, distribution of food and clothing, as well as evangelism aimed at making the new immigrants Protestant and American. It was a foreign mission at home.

This mood was evident in the remarks of H. H. Van Meter, superintendent of evangelistic work of the Chicago Christian Endeavor Union, quoted with favor in the Central Conference's periodical, *The Christian Evangel*:

> The Bible is not only under the ban in our public schools, be it remembered, but is under the same dire influence in thousands of homes of our foreign-born population. To them we are as much bound to take the message of salvation as we are to bear or to send it across the sea to the heathen world beyond, where I myself was born,...but God has brought a great foreign mission to our doors.[4]

This mood was also reflected in a 1907 editorial in *The Mennonite*, the conference's English periodical, on the "foreign element," labeling the foreign-born potentially "criminally vicious" or else an "army of paupers." "What is to be done with them? Americanize them, at least do not neglect to make their children thoroughly American in life and thought." The magazine of a conference, many of whose members spoke only German fluently, continued, "The problem of what to do with the parents who speak a strange tongue and will always do so still confronts us. There is but one thing to do if our cities are to be safe and that is to Christianize them. ...The foreign element is the burden of the whole church in America, we should be doing our part."[5]

Following the example of American Protestants, other Mennonite groups were also beginning city missions for the "foreign element." The Evangelical (formerly Defenceless) Mennonite Church had begun its mission in 1892 by supporting John A. Sprunger's work in Chicago, and the church officially opened its own city mission in 1906 in Chicago's stockyards district. The Mennonite Brethren were creating a committee on city missions in 1907 and soon took over work in Hurley and Gile, Wisconsin, and began work in Minneapolis in 1908. The (Old) Mennonites began city mission work in Chicago in 1893, followed by Philadelphia in 1899. Between 1900 and 1920 they started missions in Fort Wayne, Indiana; Canton, Ohio; Kansas City; Toronto; Altoona, Pennsylvania; and Lima, Ohio. Most of these missions included not only preaching, but clothing distribution, day nurseries, mothers' meetings, and sewing classes, and one had a medical dispensary. General Conference Mennonites looked at these examples and asked, "Why are we not at work along the same lines?"

The General Conference Home Mission Board came to the 1908 General Conference in Beatrice, Nebraska, with a recommendation to begin city mission work. Already at the 1902 General Conference in Berne, Indiana, the matter of looking after fellow Mennonites in the cities had come up, as well as the matter of providing funds for church buildings to poorer and smaller congregations. But no action was taken. By 1906 the members of the conference's Home Mission Board were raising the issue of city missions seriously. Board member J. C. Mehl of Upland, California, kept bringing up the issue in board correspondence: "I wish more effort could be made by our people to do mission work in the cities." He suggested the slums of Philadelphia as a possible location.[6]

The 1908 conference—the General Conference of Mennonites' fiftieth anniversary meeting—responded to the urging of the Home Mission Board by giving the board some new tasks.

The board was given authority to (1) establish a church building fund, (2) permanently station evangelists in newly organized rural settlements with no minister, (3) establish city missions, and (4) support and encourage young men in preparing for home mission work, as well as send experienced ministers out to travel and conduct Bible conferences and promote conference work.

The conference's action was significant in several respects. First, it marked the beginning of professional and centralized home missions. Seldom before had the *conference* stationed workers in one location for longer than a few months. The pastors for new churches had usually been furnished by stronger churches nearby or by local groups of churches or by occasional visits from a traveling minister.

The action to help educate workers for home missions was also a new departure. Prevously many Mennonite ministers had had little formal education for the ministry. The school at Wadsworth, Ohio, to train Mennonite ministers and missionaries, had been short-lived. Now those preparing for Christian ministry were attending the conference-related colleges at Bluffton, Ohio, and Newton, Kansas, and the independent schools: Moody Bible Institute in Chicago and Torrey's Bible Institute (now Biola College) in Los Angeles—or seminaries of other denominations. These more educated workers to be sent out by the conference were to be paid for full-time work. The practice was becoming common in Protestant circles in North America, but many rural Mennonite churches still expected their ministers and elders to earn a living by farming or teaching school.[7]

The conference's action in 1908 was significant, in addition, because it recognized the city as a place for Mennonites. Although Mennonites had been living in Chicago, for example, as early as 1844, little had been done to encourage urban congregations. Now voices were calling to establish churches for Mennonites moving to the city "there to engage in business or seek other employment."[8]

N. B. Grubb, of Philadelphia, for example, pled with the conference for strong inter-Mennonite urban churches:

> A strong organization representing the whole body of Mennonite believers alone will insure the keeping of those in the fold who come from a long line of Mennonite ancestors. It is about time for us to realize seriously that our children, who, on account of being separated from home churches, unite with other denominations and throw themselves into a form of Christianity which we do

not approve of and which our fathers would rather have died than accept. Let us cherish the memory of the fathers of the faith who came to America to perpetuate a church that believes in baptism on confession of faith, and that stands for peace and takes Christ at his Word, and teaches any kind of oath to be wrong.[9]

Other voices, including some of the younger leaders, were calling for the preaching of the gospel directed at the poor and the unconverted of the city.

The 1908 conference's action was not specific on which kind of mission was to be established in the cities. In implementing the action, the Home Mission Board tried to satisfy both groups who favored city missions: (1) those who wanted to prevent urban-migrating Mennonites from being absorbed into other denominations and (2) those who wanted to convert the non-Protestant urban poor, particularly the new immigrants. But the instructions the board gave to its first city missionaries were as vague as the action of the conference. Missionary E. F. Grubb wrote to the Home Mission Board March 31, 1916, "Seven years ago the Board turned me loose in Los Angeles and said, 'Go to work.' There were no definite instructions as to what or how or where; like Abraham we 'went out not knowing whither.'"[10]

Los Angeles

The mission which thirty-seven-year-old Elmer F. Grubb and his wife, Esther Johnston Grubb, started in a poor section of Los Angeles followed the pattern of most Protestant city missions of the time. The mission's aim, as conceived by Grubb, was to convince the poor and the new immigrants of the area, mostly Catholic, of the benefits of being Protestant Americans. Although the constitution of the mission church, when it was organized in 1915, included clauses on nonparticipation in warfare and swearing of oaths, there was little that was distinctly Mennonite in the message which Grubb preached in the former pool hall which he had rented and in his street meetings in the neighborhood. "To all we preach Jesus Christ, and him crucified," Grubb wrote to the board.[11] In practical terms, that meant preaching temperance (the first church building, the River Station Mission, was sandwiched between two saloons), thrift, self-reliance, avoidance of dancing and movies, and staying away from the parks on Sunday afternoon.

The Grubbs, formerly in pastorates in Stevensville, Ontario, and Wadsworth, Ohio, had arrived in Los Angeles on July

12, 1909, and Elmer had spent the first few months visiting other Protestant missions in the city, teaching a Sunday school class of black men sponsored by Torrey's Bible Institute, and riding his bicycle through the streets looking for a needy and "churchless" area in which to locate his mission. He intended to choose a predominantly English-speaking area "among people with whom we can have fellowship" without learning to speak a new language. The objects of the mission were to be "English-speaking families of working men and of the poorer class."[12]

Fifty hymnbooks were donated by the Bible Institute, and the mission held its first service on May 8, 1910, with twelve people present, including five barefoot, ragged boys just off the street.[13]

In a short time Grubb discovered that the area was not strictly English speaking. A large number of Mexican-Americans were moving into the area. By 1914 the district was 60 percent Mexican, 20 percent "other foreigners," and considerably more than 80 percent Catholic. To Grubb, a predominantly Catholic district might have seemed the area most needy of a Protestant mission, but the Home Mission Board looked at the poor results (forty conversions in five years but no church members) and recommended moving out of the Catholic district.[14]

The new station, five blocks away, on South Avenue 19 and Albion Street, was named the *Whosoever Will Mission*. Ferdinand J. Isaac of the West Zion Church, Moundridge, Kansas, who came as a Home Mission Board worker in 1914-16, surveyed sixty families on Avenue 19 and found thirty-five "American" families (that is, German, Swedish, Danish, Jewish, and black) and twenty-five of the "foreign element" (which meant Italian, Greek, and Mexican; that is, Roman Catholic or Orthodox). [15]

A major difficulty for the mission was the frail health of many of the missionaries. Elizabeth Braun and Susan M. Franz left or were asked to leave because of sickness. Grubb himself had been attracted to the southern California climate because of his hay fever and asthma. By 1915 he seemed to be on the verge of a nervous breakdown. Meanwhile, the board was raising questions about Grubb's competence as superintendent of the mission. He had trouble delegating tasks to other mission workers. Busy with buying paint and nails, Grubb was accomplishing little "mission work." "Little done. Little doing. Great ideas," board member W. S. Gottschall wrote at the bottom of Grubb's first quarter report for 1916-17. The board decided to

fire Grubb and to aim the mission at those of Mennonite background in Los Angeles as well as the poor of the mission neighborhood.[16]

The decision to direct the mission more at Mennonites had
been brewing within the board even before the mission's first
service. Already in April 1910, a month before the mission's
door opened, board member William S. Gottschall was funnel-
ing to the board the complaints of "several of our active and
influential ministers" about a so-called rescue mission: "Is this
the kind of city mission our conference had in mind? Was it not
to be more a mission among our Mennonite people in the cities,
gathering them as a nucleus for the purpose of raising congregations in cities instead of dumping our people off there for
other churches to gather in?" Board member John C. Mehl,
supported by Noah C. Hirschy, quickly countered, "Hope we
may never get so narrow as to confine our *mission efforts* to
Mennonites."[17]

In spite of such feelings, the new emphasis at the Los
Angeles mission in 1917 was toward those of Mennonite heritage, a number of whom had been attending a German Methodist church. German services now followed the English services
at the mission on Sunday morning. Pastor M. M. Horsch came
from nearby Upland,California, to take over as mission superintendent and to "more fully organize" the mission May 12,
1918, as the *Mennonite Mission Church of Los Angeles*. This
time the thirty-four charter members included thirty-one of
Mennonite background and three names of others at the bottom
of the list. This time the constitution was published in German
instead of English. For the next six years, with a series of
interim mission superintendents, the mission tried to serve
both English-speaking and German-speaking, the neighborhood and the Mennonites who drove in to the slums from as far
as twenty miles away.[18]

By the time H. Albert and Catharine Claassen came to
supervise in 1922, the mission was having to deal with rocks
thrown through windows. English-speaking people, "the
Americans," were fast moving out of the district and were being
replaced by Italians who were not attending the mission's English or German activities.[19]

The solution was another move, this time to a new middle-
class subdivision, Goodyear Park, and a concentration on the
ethnic Mennonites. "It is evident that the two lines of effort in
Los Angeles do not combine well into one work," said board
member A. P. Krehbiel, who suggested a district where Menno-

nites felt comfortable settling close to the church building.[20] So the General Conference Mennonites left their slum district in the hands of the Presbyterians, who had recently established a mission two blocks away with an Italian-speaking missionary. They built a large, attractive church building in the southern part of the city in an area of new homes occupied by Lutheran and Catholic factory workers, an area allotted to the Mennonites by the Council of Superintendents for the churches in Los Angeles.

A few adults in the new district came to the Los Angeles mission, now called *Immanuel Mennonite Church*, as did many children; by 1926, the Sunday school included 140 children from non-Mennonite parents, but an average of only five non-Mennonite adults were attending.[21] Many people of Mennonite heritage were joining the church. Under Claassen's pastorship, membership increased from 50 in 1923, to 116 in 1926, to 156 in 1932. In March 1931, the church became independent, although the Home Mission Board continued to pay assistant missionary Lavina Burkhalter's salary until the end of 1935.

However, because of the congregation's relatively high percentage of members of non-Mennonite ancestry compared to the rest of the conference and its identification with the fundamentalist theological positions of the Bible Institute of Los Angeles and Talbot Theological Seminary in La Mirada, California, the Home Mission Board was reluctant to grant the congregation the last measure of independence: the title to the church property. The first request for the title came from the congregation by 1942, but the deed was not transferred until 1948. C. E. Krehbiel, conference field secretary, visited the congregation and reported back to the Home Mission Board that he feared the church would "slip away from our Mennonite denomination and leave those who are real Mennonites stuck." "Could we insert a clause into the contract, that in case the congregation should cease to be a General Conference Mennonite church within the next twenty years, the property would fall back to the conference?" asked Home Mission Board chairman J. M. Regier. Some such clause was inserted when the deed to the property was transferred.[22]

The following years saw another move out of Goodyear Park in 1951 when blacks moved into the neighborhood, the establishment of a church in the suburb of Downey, a church split in 1956 (with thirty-seven members withdrawing to form the Bethel Community Church in Santa Fe Springs), and pastors in the late 1970s with no Mennonite church background.

The Immanuel Mennonite Church withdrew from the General Conference Mennonite Church in 1978.

A Second City Mission: Chicago

By 1913 the Home Mission Board was looking for a site for its second city mission, this time in the midwest United States. The board considered St. Louis and Kansas City, but the field quickly narrowed to Wichita and Chicago. J. J. Langenwalter, then secretary of the Western District Conference, urged W. S. Gottschall, chairman of the Home Mission Board, to choose Wichita, "which would then afford an opportunity to the students of Bethel College [in North Newton, Kansas] to help in the work."[23] The Western District ministerial conference also pledged its support. Michael Horsch and David Toews, board members, voted to start missions immediately in both Wichita and Chicago, but the decision finally was for the conference to begin a mission only in Chicago, already the location for seven other Mennonite missions, and to encourage the Western District to begin a mission in Wichita. (The Western District decided on Hutchinson instead.)

Board members Gotschall and J. J. Balzer, both opposed to Bethel College, won the day. They preferred that the mission be in Chicago where it could be assisted by the more fundamentalist Moody Bible Institute students. "I spoke to the three [students] I have in Moody Institute now, and they would be just delighted to help," wrote Gottschall.[24]

Moody students did help in the new mission, which opened on March 5, 1914. About twenty-two General Conference Mennonite young people were attending Moody Bible Institute, and many of them helped the fledgling mission in teaching Sunday school and "in singing, giving testimony, in prayer, and in preaching." Other Mennonites living in the Chicago area also helped during the early years, and a number became members in Chicago. Clint A. Lehman, manager of the Chicago branch of Lohrenz Publishing Co., directed the mission's choir for years and served as Sunday school superintendent. Other volunteers included P. K. Regier, Henry A. Fast, Daniel J. Unruh, Elizabeth Unruh, and deaconesses Lena Mae Smith and Elizabeth Goertz.[25]

William S. Gottschall, Home Mission Board member who helped survey the territory, and W. W. Miller, the mission's first superintendent, conceived of the mission as a combination rescue mission-congregation. So the mission, located at 727 West 63rd Street, began with nightly meetings. It cooperated closely with the Mennonite Home Chapel (62nd Street Mission) of the Central Illinois Mennonite Conference, only a few blocks away, which, since 1909, had been attempting a rescue mission. The cooperation was short-lived, however. Part of the reason was the hesitancy to let the General Conference Mennonite constituency know about the cooperation and its extent.[26] (Workers from both missions were participating in services at the Mennonite Home Chapel on Sunday mornings and at the new General Conference mission on Sunday afternoons.) The General Conference Mennonite workers had also surveyed the district and felt that there was not enough response from people there to support two missions in the area. So a little over a year later, the conference moved its mission to Englewood, a new subdivision of lower-middle-class workers, only one-fourth of them foreign born. The relocated mission opened its doors at 7130 South Ashland on May 15, 1915. Although other Mennonite missions in Chicago had started earlier, the Englewood mission in 1921 was one of the first to organize as a church.

In the first fourteen years the most influential missionaries at the Englewood Gospel Chapel, later named First Mennonite Church, were W. W. Miller and Catherine Niswander. Miller, who had served the Mennonite church in Pulaski, Iowa, in 1897-1914 before coming to Chicago, was fifty-five years old, an experienced pastor in the Middle District Conference, and a respected leader. During the period 1900 to 1916 he had served concurrently on the Middle District evangelistic committee, the district conference program committee, and the Bluffton College board of trustees. During one of those years he had also been chairman of the Middle District Conference. He was called to the mission because of his interest in city work and because he could preach in English.

From the beginning, Miller had a vision for building a church, not just converting individuals. Within the church, he was a tolerant listener and a peacemaker. His theology was a blend of traditional Mennonite beliefs and premillennialism, with a verbal emphasis on the latter.[27] Although Miller personally believed in nonresistance, during World War I there were no sermons on peace. But when he wanted to organize the church in 1921, he asked that the president of the Home Mission Board come to Chicago for a week of meetings "to indoctrinate the people here in Mennonitism. Little has been said thus far with reference to doctrine, [I] did not think it necessary, but before organizing and taking in members this must be done, so that all may know who come to us just where and how we stand."[28] The lack of integration of the peace teaching with the rest of the gospel was typical of many rural Mennonite churches during the period before World War II. Although committed to city missions, Miller's rural background showed in his initial reference to Chicago as "this intensely wicked city."[29] His wife, Mary Nusbaum Miller, certainly did not love the city, and because of her attitude and her poor health, he left Chicago twice. The Millers served there in 1914-19 and 1920-23.

Catherine Niswander, Miller's assistant almost from the beginning of the mission, served in Chicago from 1914 to 1928, longer than any other missionary there. Although she had, at first, wanted to be a foreign missionary, she was a home missionary for over fifty years. Niswander, who later served in Portland and Philadelphia, built up the mission by house-to-house visiting, making as many as 581 calls in one year. Influenced by her education at Fort Wayne (Indiana) Bible Institute and by the Christian Endeavor movement, she directed most of her efforts toward neighborhood children and getting them into the Sunday school. By 1921 the average attendance of Sunday school was 140, mostly children. Children by far outnumbered adults; the membership that year was 22.[30]

Niswander worked well with Miller—and without him—when the mission was without a superintendent; when Miller was away from Chicago visiting dozens of churches in the Middle and Western districts to raise money for a church building in Chicago; and when Miller went to work in a department store to support them because the General Conference, turning its funds to the Russian refugees, had failed to send its North American workers their full wages. "When Rev. Miller was gone, I saw to it that we had preachers for morning and evening. I took care of the funds; that's when we bought the mission house," said Niswander. The mission house was a duplex with apartments for the pastor's family and for her. When the board asked Niswander to go to Portland in 1928, she did so reluctantly. "I loved those people in Chicago," she recalled later. "The majority of them had come in at my invitation."[31]

By 1929 Sunday school attendance had reached 307, a new building had been constructed, and offerings were considered generous for a mission church. In 1927 a constitution was written, and lay people were elected to church offices—people such as W. H. Brown, P. P. Sprunger, Arthur McRedy, Claude Tague, Mr. and Mrs. Steuckemann, Bernard Jenks, and Pearl Harvey. The congregation was a potpourri of ethnic groups. Lay people were also involved in personal visitation and witnessing in homes in the neighborhood.

But the growth of the church was shattered by a church split in 1934 during the ministry of William Clyde Rhea. Rhea, who had married Mennonite Clara Gering at the Bible Institute of Los Angeles, had joined the Mennonite mission in Los Angeles after having been rejected for ordination by the Methodists because of his too ardent views on the second coming.[32]

Rhea came to First Mennonite Church in Chicago in 1927, shortly before Niswander left for Portland. At first, Rhea, although still recovering from a nervous breakdown, was popular in the congregation, except with those of Mennonite background, some of whom he asked to leave. Declaring that he would "rule with an iron hand," Rhea dissolved many of the organizations of the church, such as Christian Endeavor, and assumed responsibility for every activity of the church.[33]

In 1934, feeling restricted by working under a denominational mission board, Rhea decided to leave First Mennonite to form a new nondenominational mission church a block away. Only three people in the congregation then had ties with Mennonites anywhere else, and Rhea's supporters claimed that 80 percent of the congregation left with Rhea. The Home Mission Board tried to pick up the pieces of the congregation by sending in as minister A. J. Neuenschwander, an experienced pastor in the conference and a seminary graduate. But Rhea would not vacate the parsonage, and before the board could evict Rhea, Neuenschwander had had to find another pastorate. Within the next few months, Rhea's new congregation disintegrated, and Rhea left town.[34]

The Home Mission Board, discouraged, tried to turn its Chicago mission over to the Middle District Conference, but the Middle District refused to accept the responsibility. The Home Mission Board wanted to sell the property and close the mission, but the General Conference board of trustees refused permission.

So the board turned to Amos Hershey Leaman of Chicago, an (Old) Mennonite who had been director of practical work at Moody Bible Institute and had worked at some time for almost every Mennonite mission in Chicago. In fact, at the time Leaman became pastor of First Mennonite, he was still involved in a number of other Mennonite congregations. He began gathering the sheep who had scattered during Rhea's pastorate and by 1935 had built the membership back up to seventy-six. But the Home Mission Board was upset because

Leaman was not spending enough time with the congregation and refused to become a member of First Mennonite. After a stormy meeting in 1940 between members of the Home Mission Board and the congregation, the board fired Leaman against the wishes of the congregation. He later returned as minister from 1946 to 1949, when he left to start the short-lived Ravenswood Mennonite Church in Chicago.[35]

Little autonomy had been given to the congregation by the Home Mission Board. For example, when the new church building was built in 1916-17, the board forced the congregation to make changes in such matters as the shape of the windows and the location of the rear exit. But in 1940 the church council wrung from the board a decision that in the selection of a new pastor, "the church is to have a definite part."[36]

By 1940 the battles of the last decade were beginning to tell on the congregation. The church is "always a little on the sick side," reported John Warkentin, in 1939 to the Home Mission Board. Warkentin had begun attending First Church during the latter part of Rhea's ministry. In a report to the Home Mission Board he noted the poor maintenance of the building, the less-than-enthusiastic welcome to strangers, the lack of proper pastoral teaching, the lack of cooperation with other Mennonites in the Chicago area, the congregation's ignorance of the work of the General Conference.[37]

The next pastor, Erwin A. Albrecht, had a commitment to the General Conference and to its peace teaching, even during World War II. Together with John T. Neufeld, fellow Mennonite pastor at the Mennonite Bible Mission (Grace Mennonite Church), he tried to attract new people by starting monthly meetings with Mennonite students and others in the Loop area. But by 1950 the congregation had not regained its health. It was no nearer self-support than it had been twenty years earlier, and it entered the fifties with a membership of fifty-seven and a series of student pastors from the new Mennonite Biblical Seminary in Chicago.

The Snyder Churches

The Mennonite mission at Altoona, Pennsylvania, which came under the General Conference Home Mission Board in 1917, was another mission with a small Mennonite core. It had been started in December 1911 by Jacob Snyder. Snyder was an (Old) Mennonite bishop in the Roaring Spring congregation, which his father, Abram, had founded in 1898. Before leaving the (Old) Mennonite Church in 1912, the Roaring Spring congregation had been active in missions in its immediate area—starting churches in rural locations in the Allegheny Mountains like Smith Corner (organized in 1908) and in the city of Altoona, eighteen miles away. Wanting to move ahead with innovations like the Sunday school and missions among people not of Mennonite background, Snyder, together with four of the churches his extended family had started, joined the General Conference of Mennonites in 1914.

The Altoona mission became a project of the Eastern District Conference in 1914, although still under Snyder's supervision. But the project was beyond the ability of the district to support, and it appealed to the General Conference to take over the mission. This was done in 1917, still leaving the local supervision to Snyder.

Until the conference's first worker in Altoona—Elizabeth Foth of Gotebo, Oklahoma—came in 1918, none of the workers in Altoona had been salaried. Jacob Snyder, who served as overseer of the churches he had helped start, earned his living in Altoona as workmen's compensation referee for the Pennsylvania Department of Labor and Industry, a political appointment. The job gave him a compassion for working men, and he sometimes spoke on the subject of industrial accidents in Eastern District Mennonite churches. As many Americans had been killed at home in industrial accidents during World War I, he said, as had died in the trenches.[38] Snyder's son, Arthur A. Snyder, a machinist for the Pennsylvania Railroad, preached regularly at the Altoona mission in the early years.

The Home Mission Board soon sent more workers to Altoona. Martha Franz came in 1919. Gerhard M. and Ruth Foth Baergen came in 1922, with Gerhard as superintendent. With three full-time workers, the mission bustled with Sunday school, Christian Endeavor, Junior League, Bible studies, cottage prayer meetings, midweek prayer meetings, and distribution of clothing. Revival meetings were held, with catechism classes later for the new converts, many of whom were children, ages ten to twelve.[39]

New work was started in outlying rural areas among the mountain people. Daniel and Anna Braun Gerig (Anna a former missionary in India) were sent in 1921 to Smith Corner (near East Freedom) and Upper Poplar Run (near Claysburg), where the Snyders and others from Roaring Spring had been preaching. The Gerigs were later joined by Anna's sisters, Marie Braun, a missionary who supported herself by teaching, and

Elizabeth Braun, supported by the Home Mission Board first at Altoona, then in Smith Corner.

Herman Snyder, brother to Jacob, had begun holding services at Napier (Bedford) in 1913, and Mann's Choice in 1914. Both of those missions were under Eastern District sponsorship.

In 1921 Foth and Franz, while living in Altoona, began to teach Sunday school and arrange for Sunday afternoon services in Coupon, a mountain town nine miles outside Altoona. Their new project proved controversial, for Jacob Snyder began accusing them of claiming their ordinations as missionaries as proof of their right to administer the ordinances of the church. He complained to the Home Mission Board, of which he was then a member, "I am writing this letter in reference to the lady workers on the field, that they may not be able to conduct religious services outside of Altoona and select their own speakers and go around for meetings."[40]

With both Snyder and Baergen upset over Foth's actions, the board asked Foth in 1922 to move from Altoona to Coupon and work only there, while Franz was to stay in Altoona. In response, the board got a petition signed by 169 members and friends of the Altoona church asking Foth to stay. Eight days later, the board received letters of resignation from both women.

Foth, bitter at being asked to leave Altoona because of her assertive work, went to Brooklyn, New York, and started a women's Bible class. She began an independent mission, the Hoyt St. Gospel Hall, in 1929 in a red-light district, boldly walking dangerous streets and talking to the prostitutes, pimps, and underworld figures about their "undying souls."[41] Franz, later married to J. L. Westrich, also went to New York City, working at the Mariner's Temple, a mission in Chinatown, and among the "drunkards of the Bowery," and then serving with the New York City Mission Society.[42]

The personnel problems did not end with the leaving of Foth and Franz. Elizabeth Unruh, sister to Daniel Unruh in Smith Corner, left in 1924 after only a year's service. Elizabeth Braun left in 1925 after clashing with Snyder over such matters as the acceptance of members as young as eight. Baergens left in 1925. Snyder, accustomed to the control he had exerted as bishop, was in tension with most of the Altoona workers. He also clashed with Anthony S. Shelly, then secretary of the Home Mission Board, over whether Snyder should clear all Altoona missionaries' reports before they were sent to the board. Board member Gottschall wrote, "No other mission is managed like Altoona, and in no other mission is there so much trouble all the time."[43] In the end, the board, feeling it had no other choice, decided to cooperate with Snyder.

Problems in the mission did not cease with the appointment of local evangelist L. H. Glass as superintendent. Glass had been a deacon in the Altoona mission and was a retired railroad engineer. Glass was a "crying preacher," expounding an emotional, fundamentalist religion. Like Snyder and Gerig, he was more interested in immediate conversions than in bringing people into nurture within the church. Glass reported numerous conversions and new members, but a successor had less success in finding the converts and cut the membership list back from ninety to thirty-six.[44]

The neighborhood near the church building was poor and a mixture of Jews, Catholics, and black and white Protestants. The mission was aimed at the latter group, termed *Americans*. It was the only Protestant mission in the neighborhood, and it remained white as well as Protestant. Although missionary Elizabeth Foth, a former volunteer in the Los Angeles mission, had begun her work in Altoona by visiting black as well as white families, she had never invited blacks to the Mennonite mission. Instead, she urged them to join a black church. "I know they [blacks] have an undying soul," she wrote, but it didn't "always work to have them [blacks and whites] mixed."[45]

In that setting, then, where white Protestants felt threatened, the Ku Klux Klan (a secret organization advocating white, native-born, Protestant supremacy), began to show its influence. By 1926-27, near the height of the revival of the Klan, at least some members of the Mennonite Memorial Church in Altoona were Klan members. L. H. Glass, then superintendent of the Altoona mission, said he sympathized with the goals of the Klan, but objected to the organization itself because it was a secret society. Glass received support from the Home Mission Board on the latter point. Twenty-seven people threatened to leave the church, and a number of them did, when Glass refused to let the Klan use the church building for meetings.[46]

More controversy entered the church about the same time when Glass, Jacob Snyder, and A. E. Wolf, pastor at Napier, came under the influence of the Bosworth brothers, Pentecostal evangelists who emphasized physical healing as the second part of the atonement. When A. S. Shelly, Home Mission Board secretary, visited the Altoona mission in 1927, he was disturbed to find Sunday evening healing services, speaking in tongues, and reports of women and girls rolling on the floor for up to an hour. "Some of them holler and carry on like maniacs and show themselves," he was told. "People on the street call it the 'Mennonite burlesque show.'"[47]

In 1943 Jacob Snyder had died, L. H. Glass had left, and Emerson F. Slotterback, a Moody Bible Institute-trained preacher recommended by Gottschall, had just been asked to leave by the Home Mission Board without consultation with the congregation. No young people were attending. Adults who attended took little responsibility in the work of the church. The introduction of Delbert Welty, a man with more loyalty to the General Conference than some previous missionaries, as pastor in 1943 was not enough to bring the congregation out of its doldrums or into closer relationship with the conference. When Delbert and Tannis Welty left in 1945, the Home Mission Board decided to close the mission. Few of the Mennonite core which had been present when the church started were left. William T. Snyder, nephew of Jacob, who had assisted at the mission, had been drafted into Civilian Public Service in 1943. More and more blacks were moving into the neighborhood. The board sold to the Salvation Army the building, with its memorial windows honoring Mennonites in the West who had donated money. A Pentecostal group used the building in 1979.[48]

At the time the Altoona church was closed, Smith Corner, the "mountain mission," continued with a preacher out of the Roaring Spring church, and a membership of 59 (in 1947). Upper Poplar Run had been turned over in 1933 to the Dunkards, with whom Mennonites had worked jointly there. Coupon was closed about 1926; no church was ever organized. Napier continued with a membership of forty-two (in 1947). Zion Church in Mann's Choice had closed in 1935 with a membership of about sixteen.

The Calvary church in Mechanics Grove, Lancaster County, Pennsylvania, another church encouraged by Jacob Snyder, also continued. It had been started in 1914 by Joseph S. Lehman with converts from a revival he had conducted plus a number of people who had left an (Old) Mennonite congregation. The congregation came under partial support by the General Conference's Home Mission Board in 1923 and enjoyed its most rapid growth under the leadership of missionaries Daniel J. and Hazel Kuglin Unruh in 1926-29. Unruh's partents and an older brother and his family also participated in the congregation during that time. Most of the new members in the church were of Methodist and Baptist background. One

missionary-pastor conducted a Sunday school for blacks. The
Calvary congregation continued into the 1950s, subsidized by
the Eastern District home missions committee. When that com-
mittee could not find a pastor for the church, the church called a
Baptist minister, who, in 1957, led the church out of the General
Conference. Almost all of the members of Mennonite back-
ground had, by that time, joined the new Bethel Mennonite
Church in nearby Lancaster.[49]

The Altoona mission and the rural missions close by, both
suffered and benefited from Jacob Snyder's strong and sometimes rigid leadership. Without his vision for evangelism, the
churches would not have been begun and numerous people
would not have been attracted to Christianity. But Snyder was
not able to let others take leadership, particularly in Altoona,
and his interference there thwarted the effectiveness of workers
the Home Mission Board sent.

The cluster of missions also suffered from isolation from
the rest of the conference. Snyder himself, although at one time
a member of the conference's Home Mission Board, never felt
quite at home in the General Conference of Mennonites. He
retained the "Old" Mennonite style in his role as bishop. He
once installed a "baptismal pool" in the Altoona church over
the objections of other General Conference Home Mission Board
members, who couldn't support baptism by immersion.[50] The
board also contributed to the churches' isolation from the conference by sending missionaries who had few ties to the conference and who had been educated at non-Mennonite schools.
Many of these were recruited by board member W. S. Gottschall, who fervently opposed the conference's colleges, Bluffton and Bethel. The churches of this cluster that did survive
into the 1970s still had few ties to the conference.

Hutchinson

Soon after the General Conference of Mennonites started
its second city mission in Chicago, the Western District Conference decided to start a city mission in Hutchinson, Kansas, then
a city of 18,000. Mission work began in 1913 at the initiative of
H. P. Krehbiel of Newton, Kansas, with several families of
Mennonite background meeting in homes or in a rented hall.
Students from nearby Bethel College also took leadership roles.
Krehbiel considered Hutchinson "a strategic point of no small
importance for the future development and perpetuity of our
churches of that section."[51] The Western District provided

ministers, most of whom commuted to Hutchinson on week-
ends.

At the request of the Western District Conference, the
General Conference Home Mission Board, of which Krehbiel
was now a member, took over the Hutchinson mission in 1917.
Now the church had a full-time worker, H. T. Unruh, a recent
Bethel graduate. Unruh concentrated on bringing boys and
girls from the poor neighborhood surrounding the church building into the Sunday school. But few of their parents came. By
1920 the Home Mission Board had noted that the work was
changing rapidly into "church extension work" as more Mennonites moved to Hutchinson, some of them attracted to the city by
the presence of a Mennonite church there. The congregation
was organized in 1922, with thirty-eight members and experienced rapid growth, especially under the leadership of John J.
and Magdalena Neuenschwander Plenert in 1921-25 and 1927-
36. The congregation was granted its independence from the
Home Mission Board in 1936, the second General Conference
mission to get independent status. Like the Los Angeles mission, it became self-supporting by attracting large numbers of
members of Mennonite background. By 1979, about 78 percent
of the active membership of 314 had at least one Mennonite
parent.[52]

Jewish Missions

At various periods during their history, General Conference Mennonites attempted missions to another ethnic group as
closely bound together as their own—Jews in North America.
The first attempt to win Jews under official General Conference
Mennonite sponsorship was in Chicago in 1918 to 1923.

The stage was set by a Jewish-Christian evangelist named
W. M. Dickmann, who was associated with a mission to the Jews
in Brooklyn, New York. Dickmann, with the support of C. H. A.
van der Smissen in *Christlicher Bundesbote*, the General Conference's German-language publication, went on a speaking
tour of conference churches in 1917. When the General Conference leaders saw the large amounts of money Dickmann was
raising from Mennonites, they decided to try to channel that
money into a General Conference mission to the Jews.[53] In
March 1918, the Home Mission Board found its opening into
Jewish missions through Dorothy Goodman, a woman of Jewish background who had joined the Defenceless Mennonite
Church (now Evangelical Mennonite Church). Goodman had
been raised among the Amish in Pennsylvania and had been

working for the Chicago Hebrew Mission, an interdenominational organization started in 1887 to work with poor Jews, in a
program located in the basement of one of the Central Illinois
Mennonite Conference churches.[54] So in 1918, the General Conference Home Mission Board decided to open a Jewish mission
in Chicago as a joint project with the Defenceless Mennonite
Mission Board and the Central Illinois Mennonite Conference.

The board sent Dorothy Goodman on a several-months-
long tour of Mennonite churches to raise funds for the new
project. In 1920 the inter-Mennonite mission work began with
three workers: Goodman; Israel Saxe, another Jewish Christian who had worked for Chicago Hebrew Mission; and Elizabeth Hirschler, a German nurse and deaconess, who was to be in
charge of a dispensary.

Problems plagued the new mission. In the highly concentrated Jewish neighborhood selected for the mission, residents
would not allow the mission to lease a building. Saxe could not
get along with the other workers to the extent that Hirschler,
who had gone back to Germany, refused to come back to work
with Saxe. Dorothy Goodman Brundage likewise refused to
work under Saxe and continued her work under Defenceless
Mennonite Conference sponsorship only. Discarding the options
of firing Saxe or continuing with Saxe alone, the General Conference Home Mission Board voted in 1921 to accept the offer of
the Chicago Hebrew Mission to have Saxe work under its supervision but with General Conference financial support. That
arrangement foundered after two years because of difficulties
in sharing control of the mission work. The General Conference
Home Mission Board wanted to take up independent Jewish
mission work again at the beginning of 1923, but it would not
meet Saxe's salary demands. Its other missionary candidate, M.
M. Lehman, was not assigned to the Jewish mission because of
inadequate funds. Thus the conference's official Jewish mission
work ended within a span of five years.

General Conference Mennonites continued to have an interest in Jewish mission work, however. The Bergthaler Mennonite Church in Manitoba supported the Winnipeg Mission to
the Jews, in which Henry Cornelius Hiebert worked from 1947
to 1957.[55] From 1951 to 1961, the General Conference Board of
Missions served as a channel for funds to the House of Friendship, a mission to the Jews in Kitchener, Ontario, with work
also in Toronto and Tampa, Florida. The mission had been
started independently and supported by several Mennonite
groups and individual congregations in the United States and

Canada. The organization became involved in personal visitation, tract distribution, and camp evangelism in Ontario, as well as sending food, clothing, and money to the State of Israel. The House of Friendship later came under Mennonite Church sponsorship, with the General Conference Mennonite Church cooperating as a channel for funds and reports.[56]

Grace Church, Chicago

Chicago was a favorite place for starting new missions. By 1950 there were ten Mennonite missions in Chicago, sponsored by six groups. And at least three others had been started and had been closed.[57]

One of the ten, which was started independently and later joined the General Conference Mennonite Church (GCMC), was the Mennonite Bible Mission, now known as Grace Community Church. Although the mission in its early days had approval to solicit funds from the Defenceless Mennonite Brethren of Christ (now Evangelical Mennonite Brethren Church), it received little support from that church, financial or otherwise. Credit for the survival of the mission goes to the extended family of Abraham F. and Katherine Kroeker Wiens.

The Wienses started the mission after they had been asked to leave as missionaries at the Defenceless Mennonite Brethren mission in Chicago. But feeling that God had not quit calling them to city missions, in 1916 they bought a store building at 4221 South Rockwell to serve as church meetinghouse and residence for themselves and their seven daughters. In the early years financial support came primarily from the daughters' wages and from relatives in Nebraska. Later, son-in-law John T. Neufeld, a former volunteer at the mission, earned money by working as an architect, and during the Depression, by selling eggs door to door. Neufeld's home church, Bethel Mennonite Church in Inman, Kansas, also provided substantial support.

The church was a family operation: Abraham Wiens was pastor for twenty years, then his daughter Catherine's husband, John T. Neufeld, for twenty-two years, then their daughter Esther's husband, Jack Kressly, until 1963. Catherine Neufeld taught Sunday school until she had a stroke in 1976.

Brighton Park, the neighborhood in which the Mennonite Bible Mission located, was and still is primarily settled by people of Roman Catholic, mostly of Lithuanian background. The mission, as the only Protestant church in the immediate area, attracted people who were ethnically or psychologically on the fringe of the neighborhood. Many of the members were people whose needs were not being met in their own ethnic community and came as single individuals out of a family unit.[58]

As a Protestant mission in a Catholic neighborhood, the Mennonite Bible Mission was, in its early days, not always regarded highly by people in the neighborhood. One neighbor circulated a petition to get the mission closed and tried to discredit the mission by her reports of the services she heard through the open windows. Loud pounding on the doors sometimes disturbed the evening services.[59]

While the General Conference Home Mission Board was asking its workers to assent to a series of doctrines on the atonement, the deity of Christ, and the inspiration of the Bible (the emphases of the nondenominational Bible institutes), Wiens and Neufeld chose a different list of doctrines to emphasize: "Jesus Christ as Lord and Savior, the life and conduct of the believer, overcoming evil with good, the believer's trustworthiness, and the simple life." Neufeld in particular was a staunch pacifist. He had spent time in the disciplinary barracks at Fort Leavenworth during World War I for refusing to wear the army uniform. During World War II, as pastor of the mission, he attended the conscientious objectors' conference and the monthly meetings of pacifist ministers in Chicago (possibly he was the only Mennonite minister to do so).[60]

In spite of Neufeld's convictions about nonparticipation in warfare, the peace stand was not made a test of fellowship in the congregation. Of seven members of the church in military camps in 1942, none took a stand as conscientious objectors. "However, they almost all tried to get into some branch of the service where they would not be in active combat," Neufeld told the Home Mission Board.[61]

The mission was also somewhat unique among Mennonite city missions in that its workers liked living in the city and working in home missions rather than foreign missions. While some missionaries saw home mission work as a temporary internship until they were sent overseas, Katherine Wiens was initially disappointed when her daughter Elizabeth and her husband, John Thiessen, chose to go to India. "Had not she and Papa Wiens been doing mission work in Chicago?"[62] While some missionaries complained about having to raise their children in the city, John and Catherine Neufeld felt living in the city "was good for our children as they grew up in the environment of the mission work. Oftentimes, too, we were told that city work was not for the Mennonites because they were a rural people. It

seemed strange to us that so many Mennonite people succeed
very well in business and should not succeed in city mission
work," Neufeld wrote.[63]

By the late 1930s the Mennonite Bible Mission was developing closer ties to the General Conference. Three families from
the church had gone into foreign mission work under the
General Conference. Financial support was coming from the
General Conference church in Inman, Kansas. So in 1939 the
congregation came under the General Conference's Home Mission Board, with the Inman church's contributions counting
toward the board's budget for the mission. The church joined
the General Conference in 1942 and changed its name to *Grace
Mennonite Church* in 1950. In 1978 it became *Grace Community Church*. The congregation, now springing back from a fire
which destroyed its meetinghouse in 1977, has had a peak
membership of eighty. It receives mission support through the
Central District Conference.

The Central Conference Missions

The Central Illinois Conference of Mennonites (which became part of the General Conference Mennonite Church in
1946) also developed an interest in city missions in the early
1900s. It began its first mission in Chicago in 1909, later located
at 6201 Carpenter Street. It was known first as the *Mennonite
Home Chapel*, then as *First Mennonite Church*, then as the
Mennonite Gospel Mission. Encouraged by what seemed to be a
quick attainment of self-support by "First Mennonite," the
Central Conference started its second mission, in Peoria, Illinois, in 1914. Its third city mission was added in 1923, when the
26th Street Mission left the Mennonite Church and asked to
join the Central Conference.

The 26th Street Mission, established September 23, 1906,
was an outgrowth of the Mennonite Home Mission, begun by
the Mennonites' (MC) Local Mission Board of Illinois (which
later came under the Mennonite Board of Missions and Charities). Its first superintendent was Amos M. Eash. Born in
Middlebury, Indiana, Eash had come to Chicago in 1903 as a
stenographer for *Mining World*, had done volunteer work at the
Mennonite Home Mission, and had married one of its converts,
Anna Annacker, a German immigrant.

Within three years after the mission was opened, its Sunday school had an enrollment of 325. The Eashes and other,
shorter-term workers quickly built up a program of boys' and
girls' clubs, teachers' training classes, a day nursery for chil-

dren whose mothers were employed, and industrial training for
young men. The mission dispensed food, clothing, fuel, and
money to those in need and offered free services from volunteer
physicians. Mothers' meetings included Bible study, as well as
instruction on sewing, housekeeping, and birth control. A fresh-
air program sending children to Mennonite farms, offered the
children "a choice between a city alley and real life."[64]

But in spite of the large enrollments at these activities, the
mission had few members. To become a member of the 26th
Street Mission meant to shed much of one's culture as a new
immigrant in Chicago and to take on the cultural practices of
another ethnic group: Swiss Mennonites. This meant adopting
a different mode of dress, among other things.

When Eash returned in 1921 from two years in Palestine
as director of the Syrian Orphanage in Jerusalem, he found the
work "had gone down considerably." The Mennonite mission
board (MC) had decided to sell the building and close the mission, so Eash applied to the Central Conference of Mennonites
to take over the work, which they did in 1923.[65]

Eash became an active part of the Central Conference,
serving as field secretary for Congo Inland Mission (an inter-
Mennonite mission of which the Central Conference was a
member) in 1928-36. But he soon found that the Central Conference, while less restrictive in some areas, would not help him
fulfill all his dreams for the 26th Street Mission. Eash wanted a
"rounded out" ministry, meeting the religious, social, and physical needs of the people. The Mennonite constituency, he complained, felt that, "the entire expression of the city mission
shall be primarily evangelistic."[66]

In spite of difficulties, the mission grew slowly to a membership of seventy-two in 1935. But the mission began to decline
after Eash offered his resignation in the face of an impending
separation from his wife.[67] Anna Eash went back to the Mennonite Home Mission, and Amos Eash took the pastorate of a
Congregational church in Chicago. He came back to the Central
Conference just before his retirement when he pastored the
rural mission church in Comins, Michigan, in 1947-48.

After the Eashes left, the mission seldom prospered. The
neighborhood was becoming poorer, with stronger representa-
tions of Italian and Mexican ethnic groups. The mission building was in need of renovation. Carl J. and Martha Graber
Landes of Bluffton, Ohio, became workers there in 1939 and
tried to initiate some social service programs, working under a
theology similar to Eash's. Under Landes's leadership and un-

der the auspices of the Mennonite Peace Society, a group of Mennonite young people from seven states participated in a voluntary service project at the 26th Street Mission in the summer of 1939. A group of young Mennonites—students and professionals—organized a fellowship which met quarterly at the 26th Street Mission.[68]

But the 26th Street Mission did not recover, and the Central Conference dismissed its workers there and sold the building to a Baptist group in 1942. Some people in the neighborhood continued to have some Mennonite loyalties, however; the Central Conference minutes of 1944 and 1945 show contributions given by "Twenty-Sixth Street."

The 62nd Street Mission, the Central Conference's other mission in Chicago, also had a life span of about forty years. It opened June 20, 1909, at 843 West 63rd as the Mennonite Home Chapel in a Dutch Reformed neighborhood. The mission's first superintendent was Albert B. Rutt, who, as a Mennonite (MC), had been doing mission work in Chicago for several years. Interested in publications and in doing "more progressive" mission work in the city, he offered his services to the Central Conference. He became the first editor of the Central Conference's periodical, *The Christian Evangel.*

The mission's program included rescue mission work, club work, a fresh-air program, monthly women's meetings, street meetings, and tract distribution in the red-light district. By 1914 the Central Conference mission committee had given the mission its independence and it took on the name *First Mennonite Church of Chicago.* But its independence was short-lived. In 1917, Rutt resigned, and the mission came back under the mission committee as the *Mennonite Gospel Mission.*

After a series of interim superintendents during the next year and attendance falling from 130 to 35 in six years, E. T. Rowe was appointed superintendent in 1918. Rowe, a former Methodist minister in Chicago, had been born in Scotland and enlisted in the British army at an early age. Upon his conversion in 1904 he had left the army to do traveling evangelistic work in England. He came to Chicago in 1913, joined the 62nd Street Mennonite mission in December 1917, and he and his wife, Violet Edmunds Rowe, were appointed as missionaries six months later. Rowe gave the mission an evangelistic atmosphere, buying a "gospel car" for street meetings and installing on the front of the church building a large electric sign that flashed, "Jesus Saves."

After the Rowes' departure in 1929 the Mennonite Gospel

Mission had a series of superintendents with tenuous ties to the
Central Conference. The mission committee asked one superintendent to resign because of his uncooperative attitude toward
the conference and his espousal of postmillennialism. Another
superintendent openly rejected the peace position, telling the
congregation on Sunday morning, "All of this working for peace
is useless. Peace will not come until the Prince of Peace
comes."[69]

By the early 1940s attendance was decreasing. Of forty
parents represented by children in Sunday school, only four
attended church. The former residents were moving to' the
suburbs, and the new residents were black, Jewish, or Catholic.
The Central Conference mission board saw little response from
the new residents and closed the mission in 1948. Most of the
property was sold, and the flags and hymnbooks were given to a
nearby mission.[70]

The Mennonite Gospel Mission in Peoria, Illinois, the Central Conference's second attempt at city mission, is the only one
of that conference's city missions with results still in evidence,
having merged in 1971 with a Mennonite Church mission in
Peoria. The joint venture is known as Peoria United Mennonite
Church. The Mennonite Gospel Mission was begun in 1914 with
Jacob and Sarah Augspurger Sommer as the first workers in
"this wicked whisky-soaked city of Peoria," as Sarah Sommer
reported.[71] Sommers gave leadership to the church for almost
twenty-five years, offering a program of worship, Sunday
school, women's meetings, Christian Endeavor, summer Bible
school, children's weekday meetings, and choirs to a membership largely of non-Mennonite background. Its peak of membership was 158 in 1957, with Samuel Ummel as superintendent
and pastor. The Peoria church's struggles in a racially changing
neighborhood in the 1960s are told in Chapter 10.

Evaluating the City Missions

The Mennonite city missions of the early twentieth century were a response to the new urban situation: large numbers
of new immigrants to the city, living in neighborhoods with few
churches, and a growing number of employed and unemployed
poor. Like other Protestant denominations in North America,
Mennonites (of all groups except the most traditional) began
mission churches in the city, a foreign environment to most
rural Mennonites.

Most of the missions not only provided preaching, but also
sought to deal with the needs of the whole person on an individ-

ual basis. In Los Angeles, one result of the extensive house-to-house visiting of the missionaries was the identification of many people who lacked basic necessities such as food and clothing. The mission spent a good part of its budget buying groceries and sewing supplies, and it solicited contributions of money and clothing from Mennonite congregations across the continent, particularly women's sewing circles and children's Sunday school classes. Homeless men were furnished with beds and meals. Sewing classes were organized for girls taught by Mennonite volunteers, many of them students at Torrey's Bible Institute. Indeed, relief work occupied so much of the mission workers' time that one little girl at the mission quoted Matthew 11:28 thus: "Come unto me, all you who are tired and heavy laden, and I will give you a dress."[72]

The 26th Street Mission in Chicago probably had the largest social service program of any of the Mennonite missions and was classified by Fretz as the most "progressive" of the Mennonite missions in Chicago.[73] Amos Eash, superintendent at the 26th Street Mission, departed from the usual Mennonite practices of the day in developing a Sunday school teachers' training class for new members, keeping careful records of Sunday school membership and attendance, and cooperating with Chicago social agencies.

Blended with the social service approach in these relatively poor city neighborhoods was a fundamentalist doctrine in some of the missions. City missions, like other churches in the conference were torn by the fundamentalist-modernist controversy in the 1920s and following. Although there were exceptions, most of the city missionaries were influenced to some degree by fundamentalism. The conference's Home Mission Board recruited students at Bluffton and Bethel colleges (the conference's schools) as well as at Moody Bible Institute in Chicago and Torrey's Bible Institute in Los Angeles, but most of the board's workers came from the Bible institutes. When board members recommended a place for preparation for city work to new mission candidates, it was almost always Moody or Torrey's.[74]

There was more than one reason why few new home missionaries had had Mennonite schooling. First, although many connected with the Mennonite colleges served in foreign missions, few graduates from the colleges were interested in home missions.[75] In 1920 the board lamented that during the past year, not one such person was available from these institutions.[76] But of those Mennonite college graduates who did apply, few were chosen. As a matter of routine, college graduates were asked for statements of faith by the Home Missions Board; Bible institute grads were seldom questioned formally. When board member William S. Gottschall asked one candidate, a college graduate, for a statement of faith, the candidate declined, saying, "There were men in the Board to whom he would not submit in a test; they were prejudiced against Bethel or Bluffton College and the seminary."[77] Indeed, Gottschall, a powerful figure on the board during his tenure from 1893 to 1938, was prejudiced against the Mennonite colleges and practically all seminaries, which he suspected of modernism. When the board was looking for a replacement for W. W. Miller in Chicago, he wrote,

> There would be available men here at the Seminary [in Bluffton], but they are all taught to be prejudiced against Moody Institute, from whence we get our efficient voluntary workers and who make up a considerable part of the audience and help in SS-YPS and in the contributions. Beside their instructors here and at Garrett Institute, where many of our theological students, as well as some of the seminary instructors, have been, also prejudices them rather radically against the Premillennial Return of the Lord, which all the workers and members as well as the voluntary workers in Chicago believe. There is no seminary student belonging to our conference that we could use in Chicago.[78]

When the Home Mission Board, in its 1923 report to the General Conference, endeavored to "correct the false impression that the Home Mission Board is not favorably disposed to our schools," the board's statement sounded more like an admonition to the conference schools to "be spared from the spiritually blighting influence of the materialistic and faith-undermining teaching which is creeping into so many institutions of learning in these days of widespread apostasy from the faith 'once delivered to the saints.'"[79]

Some board members took a more moderate stance. John M. Regier, for example, once objected to Gottschall's blanket condemnation of University of Chicago graduates. But the fundamentalists were successful enough in weeding out those candidates they felt were not doctrinally sound that Gottschall could boast to the 1935 General Conference, "So far as we know we have no disturbance in our field on account of liberalism in theology, although it has several times endeavored to enter our ranks when a change in workers became necessary."[80]

The result of this selective screening of home mission

candidates was that the home mission churches had few theological ties to the traditions of the General Conference Mennonites. J. Winfield Fretz's 1940 study of Chicago Mennonite
churches said only three of thirty leaders in the Chicago Mennonite missions had "the proper combination of personal qualifications, experience, and social outlook to adequately carry on
the task of religious work in an urban community." The ministers, he observed, lack a Mennonite consciousness. Their source
of guidance and inspiration came from the Moody Bible Institute, and not from the churches which supported them.[81]

Although almost every congregation in the conference was
affected by the fundamentalist-modernist dispute, those congregations with a core of people with Mennonite background
usually remained loyal to the General Conference of Mennonites in part because of the social and familial ties with Mennonites in other congregations. City congregations like First
Mennonite in Chicago had almost none of these cultural ties,
except through the missionary—and sometimes not even then.

Some city congregations felt "that the larger Mennonite
church was against us. They didn't care to be with us. They
didn't care to find out what's going on here."[82] Sometimes the
lack of interest was on the part of the city congregations. An
observer of one such congregation reported in 1939,

> The congregation seems quite ignorant regarding the work of
> the General Conference; in fact, there was even indication of lack
> of sympathy with the Home Mission Board, or perhaps even
> active antagonism.... The young people attend religious rallies of
> other denominations, but show no interest in Mennonite re-
> treats. [The pastor] is said to be in favor of making this church
> interdenominational. It seems that for some time the congrega-
> tion was entirely ignorant that its pastor was receiving any
> financial support from the Home Mission Board.[83]

What cultural forms the new city missions should adopt
had been a difficult dilemma, for Mennonites themselves—
particularly the sons and daughters of immigrants—were themselves taking on American cultural forms in their own church
life. Before the sobering experience of World War I, North
American Mennonites had been tempted to believe that their
nonresistant stand would soon become the norm of North
American Protestantism. Some General Conference Mennonites embraced ecumenical contacts enthusiastically, and the
conference was a charter member of the Federal Council of

Churches, the forerunner of the National Council of Churches of Christ in the United States.

Thus the early efforts of the Los Angeles mission, for example, were to assimilate the new urban immigrants into the American mainstream, just as many Mennonites themselves were trying to be assimilated. Missionaries such as Elmer Grubb saw it as their duty to make city dwellers both Protestant and American. He described one Sunday school picnic thus:

> We had German, Russian, Italian, English, Mexican, and native-born—but all *Americans*. We are reminded of our duty as a nation to assimilate these various peoples and make them good citizens and of the duty of the church to bring Christ to them that they may have eternal life.[84]

Even though much of the neighborhood around the early Los Angeles mission was not English-speaking, missionaries never considered learning Spanish or Italian.

P. W. Penner, missionary in Los Angeles in 1918-21 and a second-generation American, had a German accent so thick that fellow worker, Ina Feighner, felt it was a detriment to the work. Yet he had a great concern for the Americanization as well as conversion of the neighborhood children who attended the mission and who were "without the slightest discipline." "America has within her border indeed a vast 'foreign' field to work on. What about the American citizenship of these upgrowing [sic] children? Oh, the heart nearly fails when one thinks about it," he wrote.[85]

Other city missions, however, were less concerned about Americanizing and did make more attempts to conduct meetings in the languages of the neighborhood. The 26th Street Mission in Chicago had, at various times, services or classes in German, Bohemian, and Italian. In the mission's later years a Spanish-speaking worker was hired. Mennonite Bible Mission in Chicago also had meetings in Lithuanian and Polish. Talk about Americanizing disappeared after World War I.[86]

Most of the General Conference Mennonite missions placed relatively more emphasis on creating a church membership, than did standard fundamentalism with its emphasis on producing conversions. The two emphases, of course, were not mutually exclusive, but one could get in the way of the other. One of the difficulties the Home Mission Board had with the early Los Angeles "rescue mission" was its greater emphasis on conversion. From October 1914 to April 1916 Grubb reported forty-five converts, but there were only nine church members.[87]

Grubb had witnessed decisions for Christ and baptized numerous people before being pushed by the board to organize a church with the help of board member Michael M. Horsch. But even after organization of the church on February 21, 1915, little emphasis was placed on church membership or on discipleship, one of the fundamentals of Anabaptism. Board member H. P. Krehbiel complained, "Sister Feighner speaks of three conversions, which are supposed to have occurred recently. Neither Bro. Grubb nor Bro. Isaac makes mention of these. It would seem that they should. Who was instrumental in bringing about these conversions? Where are these people now? Are they receiving Christian nurture?"[88] Although individual missionaries showed reluctance to organize churches and develop a membership roll, the General Conference Home Mission Board's position was always clear: church extension was of primary importance.

Another characteristic of most of the city missions was an emphasis on children's programs and the conversion of children as young as ten or even eight. That emphasis owed less to traditional Mennonite beliefs in adult baptism than to the views of salvation promoted by the nondenominational Bible institutes. In most of the missions, many more children than adults attended, for children from non-Mennonite homes were more likely to come than their parents. While children in attendance might number in the hundreds, adults often numbered in the dozens at missions like 26th Street in Chicago and the Immanuel Church in Los Angeles.

The Mennonite Bible Mission in Chicago, for example, had an extensive children's program of Sunday school, vacation church school, and Bible memory work. But Abraham Wiens felt that preaching from the pulpit was of first importance, so the preaching came before the Sunday school, and all children were expected to come for the preaching service. The preaching was geared to the children, who made up the majority of the audience, and the blackboard was often used to illustrate sermons.

The large numbers of children attending without their parents usually produced some discipline problems, and missionaries found a variety of ways to deal with the offenders. Elmer Grubb in Los Angeles commented on the boys coming in off the street and disturbing the meetings, "but we [are] winning them by the use of moral and well-nigh muscular suasion," he said. The Grubbs sympathized with the boys and took a number of them as foster children into their home, but some of the volunteer Sunday school teachers were less sanguine about the discipline problems. "Some say, 'I never saw such children,' and I presume they never want to see such again, for some never come back," Grubb wrote.[89]

In the early 1920s, U.S. legislation was drying up the stream of immigrants from southeastern Europe. At the same time, General Conference Mennonite Church efforts at starting city missions among the poor stopped. Home missions had never held the appeal of foreign missions, neither could they now compete with relief needs of the Russian Mennonites. Many of the relatives of General Conference Mennonites were in Russia suffering in the famine of 1920-22. Then came the immigration of 20,000 Russian Mennonites to North America, most of them to Canada, beginning in 1923. Relatively large Home Mission Board sums were devoted to helping ministers among the immigrants to organize churches. Of all the boards of the conference, the Home Mission Board suffered most by the diversion of funds for Russian relief. During the triennium ending in 1923, funds contributed to emergency relief increased from $186,924 to $281,298, while home missions contributions decreased from $88,029 to $59,745. The income of most other boards remained fairly steady.[90] City mission work never recovered its momentum in home missions.

Even in the decade before the Depression, the Home Mission Board was deeply in debt. While foreign mission and education boards climbed out of indebtedness in the mid-20s, the Home Mission Board could not. In 1921 the board cut home missionaries' salaries because funds were not available to pay them. Some board members blamed the state of home mission finances on the diversion of contributions to nonconference causes. With the coming of the Depression, funds ran low again. Sometimes board members themselves borrowed the money to pay Home Mission Board bills. One bank in which Home Mission Board money had been deposited closed. By 1932 the board had reduced all its workers' salaries. At the 1933 General Conference, it was noted that some workers' salaries had been reduced by as much as 50 percent. At times the board could not even send all of the reduced salaries it had promised. During 1932 it sent workers only 46 percent of the *reduced* salaries.[91]

Only by 1939 could the Home Mission Board again think of expansion among people not of Mennonite background. But the only city work it took on was the already established work of the Mennonite Bible Mission (Grace Mennonite Church) in Chicago.

The efforts to convert the poor of the cities had been cur-
tailed. But the earlier emphasis on the cities had had its effects.
Not only had the conference affected the cities by preaching the
gospel to hundreds of persons, but the missions in the cities had
also affected General Conference Mennonites. Scores of long-
and short-term workers, raised in rural settings, had been introduced to the cities and to the squalor and the beauty there.
Many home missionaries served under the conference who
would have sought other opportunities to serve in the cities.
Women, in particular, were given places of service seldom available in their own congregations. Workers like Catherine
Niswander, Elizabeth Foth, Lavina Burkhalter, Elizabeth Unruh, Pearl Ramseyer, and Martha Franz took on the responsibility of home visitation, teaching of Bible classes, taking care of
mission finances, and mission administration. But by the 1940s
few of these single women were still serving, and most missions
were staffed only by married couples. In 1942 the Home Mission
Board responded with little encouragement to one young
woman who had applied for home mission service, "We have
only one such worker, Miss Niswander."[92]

By the 1940s, the Home Mission Board was evaluating its
city mission work—and those who saw the essence of Mennonitism as rural were evaluating it, too, in a negative light.
Sociologist J. Winfield Fretz, an advocate of Mennonite rural
life, in a 1940 study pointed out the failings of all eight
Mennonite-related missions in Chicago.[93] Others in both the
General Conference and the Central Conference had been saying all along that Mennonites did not belong in city missions,
that they should stick to rural missions where they could be
more successful in building up Mennonite churches.[94]

In some respects, the situation in the city churches the
conferences had established thirty years ago did not look good.
The Altoona mission closed in 1947, the Jewish mission had
never really gotten started, and First Church, Chicago, was
still recovering from the split of 1934. But the city missions that
had aimed at attracting those of Mennonite background—Los
Angeles and Hutchinson, in particular—were thriving. The
Central Conference closed both its Chicago missions, 26th
Street Mission in 1942 and Mennonite Gospel Mission (62nd
Street Mission) in 1948, leaving that conference with Peoria as
its only city mission. The city missions which attracted the poor
or the lower-middle class of other backgrounds had not been
attractive to the upwardly mobile Mennonites who moved to the
cities as business people or as professionals. Fretz's study of

Chicago churches in 1940 found that 92 percent of the members of the eight Mennonite churches (of all branches) came from non-Mennonite stock.[95]

But while the city missions attracted these persons of other backgrounds into the Mennonite church, the missions could not hold them after they became more affluent and moved from the neighborhood of the church to the suburbs. Attendance at the missions was based primarily on geography, not on a distinctive Mennonite theology or way of life. Most missions did mention the Mennonite peace position, but few members of the missions ascribed to it in practice during World Wars I and II.[96] The doctrine preached by most of the missions, except for the antiwar stance, could have been heard in almost any evangelical Protestant mission, so there was little incentive for these church members at the missions to search out a Mennonite church after they moved. The Mennonite Community Church, in Markham, Illinois, although intended to attract such people, had only small success in doing so.[97] So when the inner-city neighborhoods around the missions changed, most of the missions experienced a loss in members.

The integration of members of city mission churches into a conference bound by family and cultural ties was difficult. Even Home Mission Board members W. S. Gottschall and H. P. Krehbiel had a hard time thinking of new members of the mission churches as Mennonites. In Los Angeles in 1916, when Grubb wanted to hire Ina M. Feighner, the mission's first convert, as a replacement for missionary Susan Franz, Krehbiel objected, saying, "So long as we have persons of our own denomination who are offering themselves for this work, as we now have, we should not ignore them and give these positions to outsiders." Board member M. M. Horsch, a former Indian missionary in Oklahoma, quickly retorted that Feighner *was* a Mennonite, "not by birth but by adoption.... I for one will not be a party to such *an injustice* [as hiring someone other than Feighner]."[98]

With such difficulties to overcome, the city missions established before World War II—at least those aimed at their neighborhoods rather than at migrating Mennonites— were only slowly integrated into the total life of the conference. The General Conference Mennonite Church had begun or acquired six city missions (and the Central Conference, three) and had become involved in half a dozen small rural missions, mostly in Pennsylvania. Churches had been born, but were these *Mennonite* churches? Neither the constituency nor the mission churches themselves were sure.

Members of the Board of Colonization

CMC Arc

Chapter 6:
The Scattering Mennonites

"It has become clear to the Board that our first duty is toward them of our own household; that by doing this form of home mission work we are really getting at the primal purpose for which our Home Mission department was created by the Conference."[1] H. P. Krehbiel, 1915

While the city missions among the non-Mennonite poor were creating a broader vision for many General Conference Mennonites, others within the conference were more concerned about a different kind of home missions—missions among their own people, ethnically and religiously. Some, like Martha Woelke of Beatrice, Nebraska, wrote to the Home Mission Board asserting that such work among members of the General Conference was not really home missions.[2] But the Home Mission Board and most conference leaders were giving priority to establishing churches among the Mennonites who were moving away from the rural centers of Mennonitism. Board member W. S. Gottschall voiced the feeling of those others when he wrote in 1915,

> I fear our people will begin to wonder why we spent so much money and have so many workers in a place that after six years shows no better returns [Los Angeles]. We must impress our people with the fact that city missions is a side issue in Home Mission work and Saskatchewan is the place where we ought to concentrate our forces. Our work there pays much better and we are indebted to our people there.[3]

By 1908 a second generation of Russian Mennonite immigrants, looking for land and opportunity, was moving away
from the West Reserve in Manitoba; from Goessel, Kansas; from
Freeman, South Dakota; and from Mountain Lake, Minnesota,
to places like Great Deer and Waldheim, Saskatchewan; Deer
Creek, Oklahoma; Lake Charles, Louisiana; Arena, North Dakota; Ashley, Michigan; and Joamosa, California—places where
no Mennonite church had been before. Many of the migrating
Mennonites were giving more thought to economic need than to
spiritual need, and even if several Mennonite families were in
the same location, they sometimes would not or could not start a
Mennonite congregation. Perhaps some wanted to escape a
Mennonite environment and its disciplines and "peculiar" beliefs. Some joined Nazarene, Adventist, Mormon, or "union"
churches in the communities to which they moved; others simply did not attend church. General Conference leaders soon
realized that if the conference were to survive, either churches
must be started in these places to which its members were
moving or the migration must be halted.

At first, it was hard for many General Conference Mennonites, particularly in western U.S. and Canada, to envision a
Mennonite life outside of a solid Mennonite community. Reporting on his trip to Pennsylvania in 1930, P. P. Wedel, minister of
the First Mennonite Church of Christian, near Moundridge,
Kansas, and president of the General Conference, marveled at
the differences between life in Kansas "where we still have a
large number of churches that enjoy the privilege of a solid
Mennonite settlement, or almost so," and life in Pennsylvania,
where "in most communities our people therefore live among
other people, that is, among folks of other denominations."[4] The
Canadian Conference home mission report of 1912 observed
with concern,

> We are also surrounded more by worldly people and by Chris-
> tians of various denominations. Especially in the city and in the
> new settlements we are influenced in the ways of these people....
> We recommend that our fellow church members be reminded
> that, if they emigrate, they might consider not only outward
> advantages, but also spiritual care.[5]

The Pacific District Conference minutes of 1901 warned:

> ...when members of our denomination from the east move to the
> west, they should ask themselves the question, "Will we be
> spiritually fed there?" If there is no prospect of this, then we
> should remember the biblical accounts of Abraham's trip to
> Egypt, Isaac's moving into the Philistine countries, or Elime-

lech's moving into Moab country and the consequences that followed.[6]

Concerned about the out-migration, the Western District Conference from 1910 to 1918 had a colonization committee which was "to prevent the dispersion of the members leaving the settlements by either inducing them to establish themselves in settlements which already exist or to gather in new settlements." The committee was to inform itself of land settlement opportunities and direct the people who wanted to leave to areas where good cheap land was available and where other Mennonites could settle. The Bordeaux Tract in southeastern Wyoming was promoted this way in 1915. But the committee was never given any budget monies, and the conference made the committee stop taking the free trips offered by the land companies. Finally in 1918 the conference dissolved the committee because its activities seemed to promote emigration from the Mennonite settlements.[7]

Other conference leaders also tried to stop the flow of Mennonites out of the communities in which immigrants had first settled. C. E. Krehbiel, field secretary for the General Conference in 1923, cautioned the conference, "Concerning the small scattered groups, the advice can hardly be given too often: Don't do it! Don't break away thoughtlessly from the mother church. Consider that doubly first. You owe that to yourself and your family. The branch that is torn off the vine dies!" But perhaps realizing that words alone would not stop the migration, he added some advice for situations where "isolation" had already taken place: elect a leader and send his name to the conference statistician, elect a correspondent to both church papers, read our church papers so members will give through conference channels, take regular offerings, and send delegates to the conference.[8]

The question was whether these Mennonites, moving to the fringes of Mennonite settlement and beyond, could be a Mennonite church even if all their neighbors were not Mennonite. Could Mennonite values be preserved outside the Mennonite settlements?

Both the General Conference Home Mission Board and the home missions committees of the regional conferences felt responsibility for the spiritual care of these people. The traveling ministers of the General Conference, Eastern District Conference, and Middle District Conference continued to visit scattered Mennonites in towns and in the country. The Western District Conference was shepherding the dozens of rural settlements of Mennonites in Oklahoma Territory, first opened to white homesteading in 1889. The Pacific District Conference organized its first evangelization committee in 1908, and the four-year-old Conference of Mennonites in (Middle) Canada appointed its first traveling ministers in 1906.

Wherever a traveling minister found a few General Conference Mennonite families settled on farms or in farm-based towns, he visited and encouraged these families to start or to continue a Mennonite church. In general, the regional conferences took responsibility for settlements close enough to send in nearby ministers for a few days, while the General Conference sent workers to settlements farther away from the Mennonite centers of population.

Northwest Canada

After the 1908 General Conference, which authorized both city missions and the stationing of permanent (that is, not traveling over a wide region) workers in rural settlements, the General Conference Home Mission Board set to work. At the same time the board was arranging for a city mission in Los Angeles, the board was also beginning to send workers to the Canadian Northwest, especially Saskatchewan. There a large number of Mennonites had settled, beginning about 1891, most of them moving from Kansas, Oklahoma, Nebraska, Minnesota, the Dakotas, and Manitoba, although some came directly from Russia and Prussia. The largest settlements were just north of Saskatoon, between Langham and Rosthern; southeast of Saskatoon, near Drake; and in the Swift Current-Herbert area in southwestern Saskatchewan.

The General Conference Board of Home Missions sent its first stationed workers to Saskatchewan in 1909: Nicholai F. and Anna Dick Toews, who had earlier been in southern Manitoba on behalf of the General Conference. Toews went to the Langham-Waldheim area, where he organized the Zoar Mennonite Church in 1913.[9] John M. and Regina Franz—like Toews, from Mountain Lake, Minnesota—labored at nearby Great Deer, Saskatchewan, from February 1915 to July 1916.

That Saskatchewan was as needy a mission field as Los Angeles was clear to Franz. He reported back to the Home Mission Board,

> Now the field is beginning to look altogether different: there is now a hunger for God's word and a desire to pray. Of these conversions [thirty-four], twenty-three were members of some church, but had never personally excepted [sic] Christ, and had

never had the assurance of sins forgiven. This is one of the biggest difficulties of this field, there is a remarkable change but room for much more. Lots of church members, but so very few Christians.[10]

Most of the workers sent to Northwest Canada were not simply assigned to one local congregation, but had responsibility for visiting a number of local meeting places. For example, N. W. Bahnmann at Hague, Saskatchewan, also served at Aberdeen, Warman, and Patience Lake beginning about 1915. N. F. Toews also visited Didsbury and Sunny Slope, Alberta, and Renata and Nelson, British Columbia. Other Saskatchewan locations served by General Conference home mission workers between 1909 and 1926 included Osler, Wymark, Swift Current, Herbert, Drake, Morse, Enz, Copeland, and Friesens. Between 1914 and 1926 Gerhard Buhler and P. P. Tschetter visited numerous settlements in Manitoba.

The Canadian Conference had its own traveling ministers working in these same areas, beginning in 1907. Because of its concern for fellow Mennonites scattered widely with few preachers, the conference had set up a home mission committee in 1906, consisting of Peter Regier, Johann Gerbrandt, and Benjamin Ewert. Regier had been ordained as elder of the Rosenort Church in Prussia and had immigrated to Manitoba in 1893 and to Tiefengrund, Saskatchewan, in 1894. Gerbrandt had immigrated from Prussia to Kansas in 1875, then to Drake, Saskatchewan, in 1906. Ewert's migrations had taken him from West Prussia to Hillsboro, Kansas, to Edenburg, Manitoba, where he taught school and was ordained as a preacher in the Bergthaler Church in 1895. He later served as the Canadian Conference's first full-time traveling minister in 1917-38.[11]

Within the next few years, ministers designated by the Canadian Conference were visiting Mennonites in thirty-two locations in Saskatchewan, as well as in Winnipeg, Morden, Haskett, Dominion City, and Stuartburn, Manitoba; Renata, British Columbia; and Didsbury and Sunny Slope, Alberta. In some cases, local ministers and elders were asked to take responsibility for nearby areas. The North Star Mennonite Church at Drake, Saskatchewan, for example, was responsible for work among the Hutterites near Guernsey. About fifteen General Conference-related congregations were established in Saskatchewan and Alberta between 1891 and 1914.

With both the Canadian Conference and the General Conference sending workers to many of the same areas, misunderstandings arose. The problems were particularly serious in 1913 in Alberta, where workers from the two conferences were not working together harmoniously, and the General Conference workers had not even attended the 1913 sessions of the Canadian Conference. To help solve the problem, the General Conference Home Mission Board and the Canadian home mission committee divided the field, leaving Alberta to the General Conference and giving Manitoba and part of Saskatchewan to the Canadian Conference. In addition, the General Conference Home Mission Board appointed David Toews of Rosthern, Saskatchewan, who had been elected to the board in 1911, as superintendent of the "Canadian field" "with full power to look into matters and get our workers and the ministers of the Canadian Conference upon a brotherly and cooperative basis."[12]

As superintendent, Toews had the authority to dispense funds to workers, almost at his own discretion, with minimal reporting back to the board. For over thirty years, Toews operated in this manner, at times serving as the only link between the General Conference Home Mission Board and the Canadian Conference. Toews, born in Russia in 1870, had immigrated from Russia through Turkestan to Kansas, and after finishing his schooling, came to Manitoba with H. H. Ewert to teach. He came to Rosthern, Saskatchewan, to teach in the *Deutsch-Englische Fortbildungsschule* (German-English Continuing Education School) in 1904 and remained there until his death in 1947, serving as an elder in the Rosenort Church, member of the General Conference Home Mission Board, officer of the Canadian Conference, liaison with government for Mennonite conscientious objectors, and head of the Mennonite Board of Colonization, which brought over 20,000 Mennonites from Russia in 1923-30.

The appointment of Toews as superintendent for the Canadian home missions of the General Conference did not eliminate all frictions. In August 1914 the Canadian home mission committee wrote to the General Conference board suggesting that the General Conference Home Mission Board turn over its work in Canada to their committee.[13] Toews himself, frustrated by "a very general indifference to our Canadian work," suggested the same action in 1922. But the rest of the General Conference Home Mission Board members protested, and that action was never taken.

Part of the problems revolved around the attitudes of the General Conference workers. Some of the General Conference's workers in Canada before 1926 had been educated at Bethel College, like John J. Voth in Herbert, Saskatchewan, whose work caused little friction. Others, like Daniel J. Unruh, had been trained by Moody Bible Institute in the new evangelistic methods. Unruh ran into problems in Didsbury, Alberta, when he tried to make changes too fast for the church, many of whose members were of Old Colony, Bergthal, or Sommerfeld Mennonite background. The German versus the English language was the primary issue. Unruh's wife, Hazel Kuglin Unruh, did not speak German, and Unruh took the position that the church should use whatever language would glorify God. At nearby Sunny Slope he was conducting a Sunday school in English for children from Mennonite, Swedenborgian, and Presbyterian homes and those with no church connections. The congregation refused to go along with the transition to English, and Unruh resigned in 1923. "No move in which I was the initiator has been accepted without some suspicion, and the general opinion is to watch me lest I bring in something they haven't had before," he complained.[14]

The Pacific Fringe

Beginning about 1876, General Conference Mennonites began moving to the West Coast. In 1888 Elder Jacob R. Schrag of Freeman, South Dakota, and his followers moved to Polk County, Oregon. The group in 1891 moved to Lane County, Oregon, and in 1900 to near Ritzville, Washington, where it became the Menno Mennonite Church. The Waldo Hills (later Emmanuel) Mennonite Church at Pratum (near Salem), Oregon, (mostly immigrants from Ohio) was organized in 1890 with the help of conference traveling minister J. B. Baer. Mennonites came to other western states as well. Congregations organized in the years that followed included Onecho (First) Church, Colfax, Washington, in 1893; Paso Robles, California, in 1897; First Church, Upland, California, in 1903; First Church, Reedley, California, in 1906; and First Church, Aberdeen, Idaho, in 1907.

The early work of the General Conference Home Mission Board was in California. Except for the city missions, the first stationed Home Mission Board workers in the United States were Ferdinand J. and Anna Penner Isaac, former missionaries in Los Angeles, who went to Woodlake, California, in 1916. Isaac was to be paid $300 a year by the First Mennonite Church of Woodlake, organized in 1915, to serve as its pastor; the General Conference Home Mission Board contributed $400 a

year toward his support and was entitled to half his time of
itinerary work around towns like Porterville, Bakersfield,
Woodville, Dinuba, Fairmead, Winton, Denair, Tulare, Delano,
and Lerdo. Isaac's task was to look up people of Mennonite
persuasion in these areas, arrange for meetings, and organize
the groups into churches. At Porterville, for example, he found
about six Mennonite families who had not known of each other's
presence; regular monthly meetings were started. The
Woodlake church was short-lived, however. The Isaacs left
Woodlake in 1918 and three years later began service in
Champa, India. The congregation held its last service in 1929,
with many of the members attending the Reedley church thereafter.[15]

Following Mennonites who moved, often on the basis of
economic opportunity, made it difficult to start and maintain
churches. A church was organized in Dos Palos, California,
northwest of Fresno, in about 1930 with workers supported
jointly by the General Conference and the Pacific District Conference. Members consisted of Mennonites who had moved
there from other parts of the state. But the church dissolved
only three years later when many of the members moved because the water promised for irrigation was not provided.[16]

In Escondido, California (San Diego County), a church was
organized in 1912 with the help of Michael M. Horsch of Upland. But shortly afterwards, a number of families moved away,
and attendance declined. That church dissolved in 1934.[17] Eden
Valley, Wyoming, was visited by the Pacific District Conference
evangelization committee, but soon all the Mennonites had left
the settlement.[18] A more successful effort of the Pacific District
Home Mission Committee and the General Conference Home
Mission Board was helping the Zion Church at Polk Station,
Oregon, move from its rural location into the town of Dallas,
Oregon, and become the Grace Mennonite Church in 1928.

Other rural locations of scattered Mennonites which received Pacific District Conference or General Conference help
before 1950 included DuBois, Idaho (1916-20); Minidoka, Idaho
(about 1925); Deer Park, Washington (1936-44); Winton, California (1937-41); Caldwell, Idaho (1945-62); and Lynden, Washington (1945-   ).

Colonization on the Plains

Mennonites also moved out of concentrated settlements to
new locations on the Great Plains of the United States. In the
Western District Conference, large numbers of Mennonites

from Kansas moved to Oklahoma Territory. Between 1892 and 1920, about twenty General Conference Mennonite churches were organized in Oklahoma. Some were near the Cheyenne-Arapaho mission stations of the conference. As noted earlier, Indian missionaries, such as J. S. Krehbiel at Darlington, Oklahoma, made the run for land in 1892 and became pastors of white Mennonite churches. The First Mennonite Church of Geary, Oklahoma, was organized in 1897 with twenty-two white and three Indian members. But the government soon moved the Indians to another location, and Indian participation in the church ceased.[19] At Shelly, Oklahoma, the building of the Indian mission was sold to a white Mennonite church.

Other Mennonites moved farther away from the central Kansas settlements. Churches were started in Vona, Colorado, in 1907; Perryton (also known as Waka) in 1922, Texline in about 1930, and Dalhart in about 1933, all in the Texas Panhandle; Ransom in 1886, Hanston in 1892, Kismet in 1917, Greensburg in 1919, Montezuma in 1920, Colby in 1921, and Syracuse in about 1931, all in western Kansas; and Neodesha in 1941, Fredonia in about 1939, and Independence in about 1946, all in southeastern Kansas.

Because of its larger financial and personnel resources, compared to the Pacific and Canadian conferences, the Western District Conference took responsibility for most of this home mission work. At first, little of the work was done in cooperation with the General Conference. Indeed, communication between the two conferences was sometimes strained. In 1921 the General Conference sent Gustav Frey to a new Mennonite settlement near Colby in Thomas County, Kansas. The Western District home mission committee had recommended to the General Conference board that it not help Gustav Frey settle in Thomas County to minister to the Mennonites who had moved there from the Goessel area. The primary reason, according to P. P. Wedel of the district committee, was that the district had "at least eleven such settlements, some larger, some smaller that are without a minister. ...We shall be pleased if the Home Mission Board continue its arrangement there, and are willing to cooperate as much as possible, although we think that it perhaps would have been better if this had been considered as our territory from the very start," Wedel told Anthony S. Shelly, General Conference Home Mission Board secretary.[20] The General Conference Home Mission Board was involved later in helping churches in Fredonia, Neodesha, and Independence, Kansas, Texline, Texas; and Wheatland, Wyoming (1914-26).

Of the many home mission churches in the Western District, the churches most isolated from other General Conference Mennonites had the most difficulty continuing. All of the churches started in Texas and in southeastern Kansas before World War II are no longer in existence, while many of the Oklahoma churches, which are closer to each other, have remained vital.

In the Northern District Conference, smaller in membership but larger in area than the Western District Conference, the General Conference Home Mission Board was more active. Beginning in 1918, P. P. Tschetter, as a worker under the General Conference board, settled in Yale, South Dakota, and visited Hutterites and scattered Mennonites in the Dakotas and in Manitoba. After leaving Saskatchewan in about 1915, Nicholai F. Toews settled in Alsen, North Dakota, and ministered to the churches there and in Langdon. Edward Duerksen served in that area from 1926 to 1941, a period of membership growth for the North Dakota churches.

The Northern District Conference home mission committee was active in starting churches, sending workers from about 1917 on to Lustre and Wolf Point, Montana, and to Huron, South Dakota, in 1945. But the standard church-planting pattern in the Northern District before World War II was for established churches to start daughter churches nearby. Thus the Bethesda Church in Henderson, Nebraska, helped start the church in Madrid, Nebraska (also supported by the General Conference Home Mission Board); First Church in Butterfield, Minnesota, was started by First Church in Mountain Lake, Minnesota; the Bethlehem Church in Bloomfield, Montana, was organized by H. A. Bachman of Freeman, South Dakota, from whence most of the members had immigrated.

Southern Settlements

The General Conference Home Mission Board also helped organize churches in two southern U.S. settlements. The Palm Lake Mennonite Church of Lake Charles, Louisiana, was made up of immigrants from the Grace Hill Mennonite Church, Whitewater, Kansas. The church never had a resident minister, but the General Conference Home Mission Board sent Albert Claassen, former missionary to the Indians in Oklahoma, there for about four weeks. The settlement dissolved about 1925 when many of the members moved to California and Kansas. Those who stayed joined a Nazarene church.[21]

Around 1923 the General Conference Home Mission

Board also helped a group of Mennonites from Herbert, Saskatchewan, who had settled near Yellow Pine, Alabama, hoping to make a profit by distilling oils from pine stumps. The board briefly supported Walter Kephart of Gadsden, Alabama, formerly a deacon in the Roaring Spring Mennonite Church in Pennsylvania, in serving this short-lived settlement.[22]

The New Immigrants

In the 1920s the shape of the General Conference Home Mission Board's work was altered radically by the immigration of over 20,000 Mennonites from Russia to North America, the bulk of them to Canada, between 1923 and 1930. About 85 percent of this number were *kirchliche* Mennonites. Most previous *kirchliche* Mennonite immigrants had affiliated with the General Conference Mennonite Church, and the conference considered them "our people." Having just come away from famine and revolution, the new immigrants had little money for the support of their pastors. The General Conference and Canadian Conference therefore revised their budgets to allow for monthly payments partially to support up to twenty immigrant ministers and to free some of their time for organizing new churches. The General Conference Home Mission Board at first designated $100 a month, then $210 a month for this activity, and later increased this sum to as much as $560 a month.[23] In 1935-38, these funds to immigrant ministers represented about half of the salaries which the Home Mission Board paid.

The entire sum to be used in Canada was given to board member David Toews of Rosthern to distribute as he saw fit, except for what went to Jacob H. Janzen, elder of the United Mennonite Church in Ontario, and to the girls' homes in Winnipeg and Saskatoon. By 1932, three-fifths of General Conference home mission funds were being spent in Canada, with a good part of that going to immigrant preachers and elders. In 1938, twenty-eight preachers were being supported in Canada. Part of the money going to Canada was being used for the girls' homes in the cities, but it was clear that city missions was a sideline for the Home Mission Board; taking spiritual care of Mennonites took priority. Home Mission Board secretary J. M. Regier wrote in 1932 to the General Conference churches,

> The 20,000 souls that have been rescued out of dark Russia will need assistance until the worldwide depression will let up. To keep them for Jesus Christ is as necessary as to win heathen converts in India and China. And we trust and believe that these

very immigrants and their children will in the next generation be the main supporters of our missionary endeavors in India and China.[24]

Among the immigrant ministers assisted by the General and Canadian conferences in the 1920s and 1930s were Jacob H. Janzen, who founded the United Mennonite Church in Ontario in 1925; Franz F. Enns, who founded the Whitewater Mennonite Church in Manitoba in 1927; Johann P. Klassen, who founded the Schoenwieser Mennonite Church in Winnipeg in 1928; Johann J. Klassen, who began the Nordheimer Mennonite Church in Saskatchewan in 1925; and Cornelius D. Harder, who started the Westheimer Mennonite Church in Alberta in 1930 and organized the Conference of Mennonites in Alberta. All these men had been ordained as preachers or elders in Russia.[25]

To establish churches for Mennonites who had fled the drought of the prairies or who sought other opportunites, workers were also sent to British Columbia, beginning with Jacob H. Janzen in 1935 in Vancouver. Permanent workers were stationed at Yarrow and Sardis in 1939. The United Mennonite Church at Yarrow and the First Mennonite Church at Sardis (Greendale) were the first General Conference churches to be organized in British Columbia. Both were organized by Nicolai W. Bahnmann, an ordained minister who had most recently been serving in Pretty Prairie, Kansas.

Efforts in home missions in Canada were again strengthened after World War II, when 8,000 more Mennonites from Russia swelled the membership of existing churches and founded a few new ones. In 1968, about 60 percent of the members of the Sargent Avenue Mennonite Church in Winnipeg had immigrated to Canada since World War II.[26]

Although most of the Russian Mennonite immigrants of the 1920s went to Canada, others went to the United States, Mexico, Paraguay, and Brazil. In the United States, the Spring Valley Church, Newport, Washington, and the Emmanuel Church, Reinholds, Pennsylvania, were organized in 1928 and 1939, respectively, with recent Russian Mennonite immigrants.

In 1930-32 about 2,000 people from Russia migrated to Paraguay and set up the Fernheim Colony, close to the Menno Colony, to which more conservative Mennonites in Canada had migrated seeking to escape the secularization of the schools. About 1,200 went to Brazil in 1930. After World War II, more immigrants went to these two countries, as well as to Uruguay. Although these settlements were thousands of miles from the

United States and Canada, because of the common ethnic background, help for these churches in organizing and in providing traveling evangelists also fell to the General Conference's Home Mission Board. The board sent its first workers to Paraguay in January 1941.

Two other small groups of Russian immigrants settled in Mexico in the 1920s. From about 1926 to 1928 some support was sent to Elder P. P. Janzen of the San Juan Mennonite Church at Irapuato (El Trebol) in central Mexico. But the settlement dissolved in 1928 and its members moved to the United States.[27]

Contact was also made with a group which settled near Cuauhtémoc, Chihuahua, in northern Mexico, near the Old Colony and Sommerfelder Mennonites who had recently immigrated there from Canada. As early as 1927, the Hoffnungsau church was requesting the Western District Conference to send an elder to conduct baptisms. Contact with the group increased in the 1940s. In 1941 the congregation was accepted into the General Conference and J. M. Regier, then chairman of the Home Mission Board, visited Cuauhtémoc and ordained the Hoffnungsau minister, Jakob Janzen, as an elder.

When Elder Janzen retired in 1945, the General Conference Home Mission Board, on request of the congregation, began sending workers to serve as elders. By that time, the Hoffnungsau church was attracting a number of people who had left or been expelled from the more traditional Old Colony. But the church leadership, particularly one extended family who comprised almost the entire church membership of twenty-six in 1949, was not ready to include people of Old Colony and Sommerfelder background into the church, at least partly to avoid hard feelings with Old Colony leadership. One pastor sent by the Home Mission Board complained, "I am supposed to confine my services to the twenty-six members and their children only" with no outside mission work, not even with other Mennonites in Cuauhtémoc. "According to the Scriptures I cannot adjust myself to their way of dealing with lost, seeking souls."[28] Meanwhile, in 1947, Mennonite Central Committee had sent workers who were involved in a health project, and later in relief and agricultural work among the Old Colony people as well as Mexican nationals around Cuauhtémoc. These workers later came under the General Conference's Board of Christian Service.

The matter of evangelism in the Hoffnungsau church came to a head in 1963, when the church leadership asked all

former Old Colony people in the church and those who associated with them (meaning, the General Conference workers
under the boards of Missions and Christian Service) to leave the
church. The workers and the other ousted members then set up
the Mennonite Church of Mexico, now divided into three congregations at Cuauhtémoc, Steinreich, and Burwalde, all
served by workers under what is now the General Conference's
Commission on Overseas Mission. These churches are made up
of those who became excommunicated after sending their children to the General Conference Mennonite schools or who had
been excommunicated from the Old Colony Church for adopting
a more modern lifestyle. The Hoffnungsau church continues as
a small, independent group. Thus, the General Conference in
Mexico now serves a different Mennonite group in Mexico from
the group which originally requested help. Throughout the
history of the General Conference's work near Cuauhtémoc,
relationships with Old Colony leadership have been poor. Some
Old Colony members have felt the threat to their way of life
from the General Conference churches and elementary and
secondary schools and have responded with opposition and, in
the early 1970s, at times with threatened violence to mission
workers.[29]

Dispersion in the Central Conference

Like the General Conference, the Central Conference of
Mennonites, before its merger with the General Conference,
also experienced the scattering of its members as farmland in
central Illinois became more scarce. Several of its new churches
established in 1900-20 were the result of movements of members into towns; Tiskilwa, Illinois (1911); Carlock, Illinois
(1914); Eighth Street Church, Goshen, Indiana (1913); and Con-
gerville, Illinois (1896).

All the new rural churches of the Central Conference
during those years were started outside of Illinois. The South
Nampa Church, Nampa, Idaho, existed from 1908 to 1927. The
Belleview Church in Columbus, Kansas, joined the Central
Conference in 1920. Located in a poor farming area, it had only
twelve members in 1955. It disbanded in 1972. The congregation in Kouts, Indiana, began in 1916 and closed in 1947.
Pleasant View Church, Aurora, Nebraska (a charter member of
the conference), another rural church far from the hub of Central Conference activity, closed in 1965.

New Churches from Schisms

From 1925 to 1950 the only new churches in the Central Conference and in the Eastern and Middle districts of the General Conference were city churches and churches which left the Mennonite Church in protest of stricter church discipline, particularly in matters of dress, and more conservative leaders. Joining the Central Conference in the 1920s, from the Mennonite Church were the Warren Street (now Pleasant Oaks) Church, Middlebury, Indiana; Maple Grove Church, Topeka, Indiana; Barker Street Church, Mottville, Michigan; and the Comins, Michigan, church, which became known as the conference's "rural mission." First Church, Sugarcreek, Ohio, left the Mennonite Church to join the Middle District Conference in 1929. The Fairfield, Pennsylvania, church split from the Lancaster Conference congregation at Mummasburg in 1926 and later joined the Eastern District Conference.

The Pacific District also received two congregations which had split from Mennonite Church congregations: the Calvary Church in Aurora, Oregon, in 1944 and Filer, Idaho, in 1955. Other such congregations include the Stirling Avenue Church, Kitchener, Ontario, which separated from the First Mennonite Church of Kitchener in 1924 and joined the Eastern District Conference in 1946. Since 1970 it has been a member of both the Conference of the United Mennonite Churches of Ontario (affiliated with the General Conference Mennonite Church) and the Ontario Conference (Mennonite Church).

The City as a Home for Mennonites

Although many of the churches in the new settlements of Mennonites did not survive into the 1970s, more than 100 of them did, now making up about one-third of the churches belonging to the General Conference. Additional town and country churches organized during the period 1890-1945 relate to the General Conference through one of its regional conferences. The statistics showed that it was indeed possible to be the Mennonite church in rural and town locations far from Gretna, Manitoba, and Moundridge, Kansas.

By contrast, fewer than thirty churches now in the General Conference are the result of home mission work among Mennonites who moved to the cities in 1890-1945. Before World War II, most of General Conference Mennonites were still farm-based, although the urban population came into the majority in Canada as a whole between 1921 and 1931 and in the United States between 1910 and 1920.

Beginning in 1862 in Philadelphia, General Conference Mennonites had had a concern for their fellow church members who moved to the cities. In 1893 the Eastern District voted to concentrate its work in the cities of eastern Pennsylvania, and the churches at Allentown, Quakertown, Norristown, and Pottstown were soon begun. In the Middle District, efforts to encourage city churches among migrating Mennonites by sending traveling ministers to visit them were unsuccessful. In St. Louis, for example, the Middle District tried to nurture a small group of Mennonites by asking C. H. A. van der Smissen, pastor in Summerfield, Illinois, to visit St. Louis as frequently as possible, beginning in 1894. The proposal to station a minister there came to the conference often, but that action never materialized. The Western District in 1887, 1891-92, and 1911 had contacted Mennonites living in Wichita.[30]

By 1923, the only city churches in the General Conference outside of Pennsylvania were those under the General Conference Home Mission Board. Chicago and Altoona had been "won from the unchurched and unconverted non-Mennonite population around the Mission," and Los Angeles and Hutchinson were "composed largely of Mennonites and persons out of Mennonite families," the 1923 General Conference was told.[31]

If General Conference Mennonites were unsure that the Chicago and Altoona missions were *Mennonite* churches, they were equally unsure that Mennonites moving to the city could produce Mennonite *churches*. Leaders who did see the need for Mennonite churches in the cities were often criticized. Peter Schantz, pastor of the East White Oak congregation in Illinois and organizer of eight congregations in the Central Conference, had considerable opposition from others in the conference when he began a Sunday school at Normal, Illinois, in 1910 and then decided to live in town himself.[32] Benjamin Ewert, a pioneer home mission worker in Winnipeg, commented in 1956, "It should be noted here that from the side of the old congregations in the settlements it was not considered good, for single persons or families out of their own people, to settle in cities or even in Winnipeg. When Benjamin Ewert with his family moved to Winnipeg thirty-five years ago, that was also condemned."[33] Others were skeptical of the ability of Mennonites in large cities to form organized congregations that could become self-supporting.[34] P. A. Penner, veteran General Conference missionary in India, wrote Ewert upon his retirement, "We want to tell you that we believe your work was vastly harder than ours, though we are in a foreign field.... When have we met with such

extreme poverty as you have met? When have we been sub-
jected to criticism, such as you have been exposed to?"[35]

Many Mennonites who moved to the cities were unsure of
their identity. Ambitious Mennonites often felt uncomfortable
about being identified with a group commonly regarded as
"peculiar" and as conscientious objectors to war. Would such
identification lessen their standing among their peers at the
work place? When large Protestant denominations made no
issue of faith about participation in military training and war,
how could a very small denomination declare that war is sin?[36]

The issue of city churches for those of Mennonite background was debated at the 1926 General Conference, meeting
in Berne, Indiana. The side against city missions was presented
first by J. M. Regier, then pastor in Pandora, Ohio, and a
member of the General Conference Home Mission Board. Regier argued that the conference did not need to make a special
effort to establish churches for Mennonites who moved to the
cities because (1) most of them are attending some church anyway; (2) only one-fifth of the absentee members of rural
churches join other denominations; (3) it would cost too much to
build a church building nice enough to attract city people; (4)
mission funds are needed more for India, China, the "Christless
Indians" in North America, and the multitudes in the cities
without any church; and (5) other Protestant denominations
already in the cities subscribe to Mennonite beliefs including
the objection to war. "Are we sure that as a Mennonite church
we have something to offer that other Protestant churches do
not have, that would make it necessary to supply these members with Mennonite services?" he asked. It was all right to
start an urban Mennonite church if there were enough in Wichita or Lansdale who wanted to work under the name *Mennonite*
or if there were a needy community with no church at all, he
conceded. But he felt urban Mennonites were just as well off
working as a leaven for peace in various denominations.[37]

The case for city missions among Mennonites was made by
Albert Claassen, General Conference missionary in Los
Angeles, where the congregation was just making the transition from nonethnic to ethnic Mennonite focus. Claassen was
not encouraging Mennonites ("a rural people") to move to the
cities. "The city is truly no place to raise your family," he
warned. But Mennonites do move to the cities, and the conference should do church extension work there. "It is just human to
dismiss them [Mennonites in the city] with a shrug of the
shoulder because they will not listen and are drifting, hoping

that some other denomination might care for them or, as some
hold, that Mennonites cannot and will not lose their faith,"
Claassen said.

> But, my brethren, is that the attitude of Jesus, our Good
> Shepherd? Does he not leave the ninety-nine in safety and go
> after the lost and straying one? and dare we do less?—Is not the
> very fact that many of our brethren go to the cities the very
> starting point of our city mission tasks! In Los Angeles the
> faithful brethren of our denomination formed the nucleus of our
> congregation there. It would be very difficult for us as Mennonite
> workers to do city mission work without their presence and
> help.[38]

The 1926 conference did enlarge its city home mission
work to include the establishment of girls' homes in Winnipeg
and Saskatoon, but by the 1929 conference in Hutchinson,
Kansas (held for the first time in a city auditorium), the nature
of its home missions was still ill-defined. Henry A. Fast, then a
new member of the Home Mission Board, told the conference,
"Our conference has never formulated a statement of policy in
its home mission work or in any definite way given expression
as to what it conceives its home mission task to be. [39]

Without a particular strategy, the Home Mission Board
proceeded. By the time of the 1929 General Conference, the
Home Mission Board or district home mission committees were
involved in new mission work in five cities: Lansdale, Pennsylvania; Portland, Oregon; Saskatoon, Saskatchewan; Wichita, Kansas; and Winnipeg, Manitoba. Regier himself must
have had second thoughts about city missions, for he wrote in
1932, "Our success in foreign missionary work depends upon
the home base. Many of our Mennonite people are moving to the
cities. We must establish strong centers in these places."[40]

Indeed, Mennonites were moving to the cities in the 1920s.
Not only were cities near Mennonite settlements, such as Wichita and Saskatoon, swelling with new Mennonite immigrants
from the rural areas, but many of the new immigrants from
Russia were settling in cities. The United Mennonite Church in
Kitchener-Waterloo, Ontario (Kitchener had a population of
35,657 in 1941), was organized by Jacob H. Janzen in 1925.
Soon that congregation had organized branches in surrounding
towns: Leamington (1929), Vineland (1936), Niagara-on-the-
Lake (1938). Janzen also made some attempts to start a Mennonite congregation in Windsor, Ontario, beginning in 1926.[41]
That group worshiped with German Lutherans, but had its own
catechism classes, Bible studies, and choir practice. Because of

anti-German sentiment, services were discontinued during World War II. After the war, an attempt was made to reintroduce a Mennonite church service in a Lutheran church, but by now interest had slackened and the venture had to be abandoned.

The immigrants of the 1920s also settled in large numbers in Winnipeg, forming the Schoenwieser Mennonite Church (First Mennonite Church) in 1926 and the North Kildonan Mennonite Church (in a Winnipeg suburb with a dense population of Mennonites) in 1935.[42]

To those who cared to observe these urban immigrant churches, the growing congregations in Hutchinson and Los Angeles, and many of the Eastern District churches, it was becoming clear that some Mennonites could move to the cities and establish viable Mennonite churches.

The Girls' Homes and City Churches in Canada

Among the Mennonites moving to the cities in the 1920s were young single women working as domestics in the wealthier homes and in other jobs. Many of them were recent immigrants, trying to help their parents pay back the debts incurred in transporting them from Russia to their new homes in Canada. Many came to the city with little money and little knowledge of English. Hundreds of such young women were in Winnipeg alone. To help these women find work and to give them a place to live and to gather for worship and social occasions, the 1926 General Conference authorized the establishment of "girls' homes" in Winnipeg and Saskatoon. (The Home Mission Board's resolution had come at the initiative of Canadian board member, David Toews.)[43]

The Eben-ezer Girls' Home was begun in Winnipeg that same year under the leadership of Gerhard A. Peters and his wife, Helene Froese Thiessen Peters. Gerhard Peters had immigrated to Canada from Russia in 1923, but was already fluent in English, having spent a year in the United States as a young man. The Peterses managed a large house where some of the young women lived, and as many as 150 came to worship services and social evenings there. From 1926 to 1964, the home served about 1,500 girls.[44]

The Mennonite Girls' Home in Saskatoon was slower getting started because of the difficulty in finding a house to rent. But finally the home was opened in 1931 with Jacob J. and Katherine Kornelsen Thiessen as workers. Mennonites—domestic workers, university students, and others living in

Sastaktoon—had been meeting since 1923, served by ministers
from Dundurn or some other rural settlement. By 1930 the
group had grown and asked for a minister. J. J. Thiessen was
hired part-time in July 1930 by the General Conference Home
Mission Board, and when the work grew to full-time, he moved
his family to the city in January 1931. His task was a double
one: to run the girls' home and to organize a congregation.
Through the years about 500 women, both Canadian-born and
recent immigrants ranging in age from sixteen to forty-four,
were served by the home.[45] Thiessen later described the situation of the young women thus:

> Some were getting $6 a month, others $8, perhaps $10 or $12.
> After a number of years of service they might get $20 or $25 a
> month, and this was considered an exceptionally good wage.
> These girls, perhaps your mothers have been among them, have
> established a very good reputation for the Mennonites in Saska-
> toon. The ladies would phone us again and again asking for
> Mennonite girls. And why? The ladies would praise them that
> they were not smoking, not stealing, they were of good beha-
> viour, industrious, trustworthy, attended the church and worked
> hard. There were instances where the girls were exploited and
> did not receive their day off. According to law, every domestic
> had a Thursday afternoon and evening off. Our churches, know-
> ing the spiritual needs of our girls, established a Mennonite
> Girls' Home. This was a private house, in which Mrs. Thiessen
> and I and our children lived, and the girls who would come to the
> city for work were received and assisted in finding a job, if they
> were out of work, they would come back and again we would help
> them get established again. Whenever they had their sorrow and
> griefs to tell somebody, they would come to our house and I
> always had time to listen to them, and to counsel them.[46]

The girls' home evidently met a need for these domestics, for in
1935 the Thiessens reported that, of 110 Mennonite girls in
Saskatoon, about 90 visited the home.[47] The congregation, too,
was meeting a need, growing from twenty-five members in 1932
(all with Russian Mennonite surnames) to 115 in 1939 and to
500 in 1978, even after helping start five other congregations in
the city. The General Conference Home Mission Board later
started girls' homes in Vancouver, British Columbia, and in
Calgary, Alberta.

Traveling ministers had visited Mennonites in Vancouver
in the early 1920s, but most of the Mennonites were attending
other German-speaking churches and did not want to return to
a Mennonite fellowship. By the early 1930s, however, the situation had changed; new Russian immigrants were coming to

Vancouver, and "working girls" were finding jobs as domestics and in factories.[48] So in 1935, the General Conference Board, through David Toews, its representative in Canada, sent Jacob H. Janzen, elder in Waterloo-Kitchener, and his wife, Tina, to Vancouver to gather Mennonites into a congregation and to organize a girls' home, the Mary-Martha Home for Girls. After two years, the Janzens returned to Ontario and turned the work over to their son-in-law and daughter, Jacob B. and Erna Janzen Wiens. The church struggled for several years with low attendance: in morning services fifteen to twenty-five people; on Sunday evening when the working girls could attend, seventy to eighty.[49] After World War II, however, the congregation grew quickly, attracting recent immigrants from the Soviet Union, and several daughter churches were later started.

As in Winnipeg and Saskatoon, the aim of both the church and the girls' home was to draw in those of Mennonite background. Later writers commented, "These girls had no place for fellowship or worship and might soon have lost their Mennonite heritage had not the Canadian Conference taken steps to prevent this."[50] Both a church and a girls' home were also started in Calgary, Alberta. Through the visit and encouragement of J. J. Esau of Mountain Lake, Minnesota, then a traveling evangelist for the General Conference, a group of Mennonites in Calgary decided to come together in 1944 and asked Abe Koop of Pincher Creek to preach for them. The Alberta Missions Committee was at first responsible, but feeling unable financially to handle the new work, it asked the General Conference Home Mission Board to take over the Calgary mission.[51]

An English Church in Canada

Winnipeg was one of the first Canadian cities in which Mennonites lived. Mennonites of the Bergthaler Church were living there as early as 1907, and Henry H. Ewert visited them there as early as 1909.[52] The Mennonite Brethren established a city mission there in 1913. But it was not until 1938 that another church for Canadian-born Mennonites was established in Winnipeg.

The church's founding was largely the result of the work of Henry Ewert's brother, Benjamin Ewert. Born in Prussia in 1870, Ewert came to Kansas with his family in 1874. In 1892 he moved to Manitoba, where he taught in Edenburg, was elected a minister in the Bergthaler Church, and assisted his brother Henry at Gretna in developing Sunday school conventions. Although Benjamin Ewert's assignment for over thirty years as

Canadian Conference traveling minister took him to rural and small-town Mennonite settlements across Canada, he had a special concern for cities. His sermon at the 1917 mission festival in connection with the Canadian Conference annual sessions is unusual for its place and time in its inclusion of cities as a place for mission: "Just as the Savior preached the gospel in cities and villages, so it is our task to follow his example and proclaim salvation in city and country and to let ring out in all the land the invitation to the supper of the Lamb," Ewert said.[53]

In 1920 Ewert began surveying Mennonites in Winnipeg and found fourteen, although he was sure there were three times that many. He set up a Winnipeg committee and started worship services there four times a year. In 1921 the Ewert family moved to Winnipeg. That year, while also traveling for the Canadian Conference, he started monthly services in Winnipeg. By 1925, there were thirty services a year, and by 1926, forty-eight services as well as twenty baptisms.

The new Russian immigrants started the Schoenwieser Church about this time, but the need was felt for a church appealing to Canadian-born Mennonites, mostly of Bergthaler background. So in 1938 Ewert left his assignment as traveling minister and began the Bethel Mennonite Mission Church. The mission, however, was not supported by the Bergthaler Church (although the entire Bergthaler *Lehrdienst* was invited, only two Bergthalers attended the founding service for the church)[54], but by the General Conference and the Canadian Conference.

Ewert's ministry began with Mennonite young people in Winnipeg who had not been reached by other churches in the city. I. I. Friesen, the church's second minister, also drew in young people and gave them responsibilities alongside older adults as choir director or even as deacon. By 1940, the Bethel Church had introduced English services in the evenings. Attendance there was more than double attendance at the German services on Sunday morning.[55] Sunday school, choir, and ladies' aid were also in English by 1943. The congregation, as the first all-English-speaking church in the Canadian Conference, was not always well accepted by other churches in the conference. Even by 1951, Bethel was still the only English-speaking church in the Canadian Conference. Pastor David Schroeder then wrote to G. G. Epp, "Being the only English church in the Conference, we sometimes feel we are not appreciated, and so I thank you again for coming to us."[56]

About 1942-43 Benjamin Ewert tried to start an inter-Mennonite English-language congregation in Winnipeg. The

Bruderthaler (Evangelical Mennonite Brethren) had been holding meetings one Sunday evening a month in the Bethel building, with about one-third of the attenders being Bethel people.[57] Ewert envisioned a "First English Interdenominational Mennonite Church," and an inter-Mennonite committee of six was appointed to study the matter. The committee held several meetings, but after making several inquiries of Conference representatives in Canada and the United States, did not see its way clear for the promotion of such an interdenominational Mennonite Church.

U.S. Churches for Urban Mennonites

At about the same time the girls' homes were starting in Canada, district conferences in the U.S., sometimes in cooperation with the General Conference Home Mission Board, were beginning city churches aimed not at the "foreign element" or the unconverted, as twenty years earlier, but at fellow Mennonites. Some were just then moving to the cities as part of a general American trend toward urbanization; others had lived there for forty years already. The year 1928 saw the beginnings of three new city churches, all near rural settlements of Mennonites: Wichita, Kansas; Portland, Oregon; and Lansdale, Pennsylvania. In addition, as Mennonites looked for work in cities during the Depression, congregations were started in Lima, Ohio, in 1932 and in Enid, Oklahoma, in 1935.

Wichita. Before 1928, the Western District Conference had found it difficult to believe that there might by Mennonites in the larger cities within its boundaries who might want to be part of an urban Mennonite church. In about 1920 when the home missions committee compiled a list of thirty-three Mennonite settlements in twenty counties in Oklahoma where there was no organized Mennonite church, there was no mention of Oklahoma City, Tulsa, Enid, Lawton, or Ardmore, the state's largest cities.

As early as 1886 the Kansas Conference (a predecessor of the Western District Conference) had asked Dietrich Gaeddert to visit Mennonites in Wichita, which he apparently did once— on March 25, 1887. Further brief attempts to survey the need for a Mennonite church in Wichita were made in 1891-92 and 1911. The district home mission committee brought up the subject of Wichita again only in 1926, and soon after, Christian E. Krehbiel—field secretary for the General Conference and president of the Western District Conference organized the first meeting on June 8, 1928, in a Wichita park. The Western District committee sent Arnold and Edna Funk of Hillsboro, Kansas, there as full-time workers from November 1929 to February 1931. However, much of the credit for gathering the congregation goes to Krehbiel, who, after Funk resigned, traveled to Wichita from Newton each Sunday to preach and to nurture the small congregation composed primarily of Mennonite families and "working girls." Although Funk had had a vision of a church which would serve the immediate community as well as the Mennonites in town, the charter membership of the Lorraine Ave. Mennonite Church in 1932 was ethnically homogeneous. The September 1939 report to the home mission committee listed 93 Mennonite attenders and 12 non-Mennonites; in 1940 it was 135 Mennonites and 15 non-Mennonites; but by 1941 the report listed 160 Mennonites and no non-Mennonites. In 1970, 49 of 481 members were of non-Mennonite parentage.[58]

The Wichita work remained entirely under district supervision, although the General Conference Home Mission Board did contribute to the church's building fund in the 1940s, albeit reluctantly. When Ben C. Frey, chairman of the Lorraine Avenue Church expansion committee, requested help from the General Conference Home Mission Board, Chairman J. M. Regier responded that most of the Mennonites coming to Wichita were defense plant workers. Would they be committed to pacifism and would they contribute to CPS work? "It may be up-hill to solicit in these rural churches, in spite of the fact that they [Lorraine Avenue Church members] are their own sons and daughters who have gone to the city. But, are not sons and daughters seeking independence when they leave home?"[59]

Portland. Another district-initiated city mission in which the General Conference Home Mission Board became involved was in Portland, Oregon. The mission opened on December 16, 1928, with Catherine Niswander, former mission board worker at First Mennonite Church in Chicago, as the only staff person. The mission had been intended, by its planners, to attract the Mennonite families moving to Portland, but attending German Baptist, German Lutheran, and German Methodist churches. But the mission did not locate in the German-speaking district of Portland and its services were never in German. Most of the adults who came to what became known as the *Alberta Community Church* were of Mennonite background. But Niswander was as diligent as she had been in Chicago in visiting families in the neighborhood and inviting children to Sunday school.[60] Some of the children who attended the church, not only did not influence their parents to come with them, but their parents refused them permission to be baptized. W. S. Gottschall, board member, reported in 1933:

> They had a series of evangelistic meetings and nearly all the older boys and girls of the Sunday school came forward and expressed a desire to be Christians and be baptized. Most of the parents who are not Christian objected, so that only three were baptized, and one man previously baptized received by the right hand of fellowship.[61]

Until the first male worker came in 1933, Niswander did all the pastoral work except the preaching. Preaching was done at times by S. S. Baumgartner, minister of the Mennonite church in Dallas, Oregon, and later by Mahlon H. Day, a Baptist minister, and students and faculty from the Baptist seminary and Portland Bible Institute.

The congregation, now called *Peace Mennonite Church*, relocated in a Portland suburb, in 1974. It has experienced a high turnover of members, with membership since 1938 fluctuating between thirty and ninety-two. Its members come from both Mennonite Church and General Conference as well as other backgrounds, and it is still receiving support from the Pacific District home missions committee.

Lansdale. The third city mission to begin in 1928—now called *Grace Mennonite Church*, Lansdale, Pennsylvania—was also aimed at people of Mennonite background, although it later included members of other background and organized a Spanish-speaking congregation-within-the-congregation in 1958. With the encouragement of the General Conference Home Mission Board, the church was begun by the Eastern District home missions committee, particularly Nathaniel B. Grubb, pastor of First Church, Philadelphia, and Allen M. Fretz, pastor of Deep Run, Perkasie, and Springfield churches. The first meeting of seventeen interested families was held February 2, 1928, and by February 27, 1930, a constitution had been adopted for Grace Mennonite Church, with a charter membership of sixty-five. Membership grew to 353 in 1978, and, in addition, the congregation has helped start congregations in Norristown, Kempton, and Harleysville, Pennsylvania. In 1970, about one-third of its members were of non-Mennonite parentage.[62]

Lima. The Mennonite Gospel Mission (now First Mennonite Church) of Lima, Ohio, begun in 1933, was only a few miles from the Mennonite settlements around Bluffton and Pandora. It was begun by P. A. Kliewer, pastor of the Ebenezer Church near Bluffton, to gather the Mennonites living in Lima into a church that would preserve their heritage—and to provide a place for Christian service.[63]

In 1933 the Middle District Conference took over the Lima mission as an "experiment" and called J. J. Esau, "the blind evangelist," as its first full-time pastor. The congregation remained under the Middle District home mission committee until 1957, although that committee never supported it wholeheartedly. Handicapped by the Depression, the congregation built a basement first and met in it for fifteen years while waiting for funds from the district to build the rest of its building. One pastor wrote to the Middle District home mission committee in 1943 complaining of per-member assessment for the Lima mission: "Other members feel that when the individual churches have their hands full trying to maintain themselves in the old Mennonite areas, the matter of supporting an additional church in a city already full of churches is not of first importance."[64]

As in Portland, most of the adults who came were of Mennonite background while the Sunday school was made up of children from the neighborhood surrounding the church. Groups of young people from Bluffton and Pandora Mennonite churches did volunteer work in Lima, supervising children's meetings on Wednesday afternoons, canvassing the neighborhood, and teaching Sunday school. During the Depression the Lima congregation's Women's Missionary Society sewed clothing to distribute to needy families. The service projects were an attraction to the church for some neighborhood people, such as the woman with a large family who was invited to come to church early in the fall and immediately asked whether the church gave out food baskets at Christmas. Growth for the congregation was slow, but in 1970, forty-one of eighty-one members were of non-Mennonite parentage.

Enid. When the Western District home mission committee started its mission in Enid, Oklahoma, in 1935, Henry N. Harder of Rosthern, Saskatchewan, its first pastor, set out to make the "Mennonite Gospel Hall" (now Grace Mennonite Church) a church for Mennonites in the city as well as for others in the community. But immediately a group of about thirty Mennonites, led by Heinrich T. Neufeld, broke away to form a second church. They wanted a "church for our brothers and sisters of the faith (*Glaubensgeschwister*), not a city mission," they told the home mission committee. Particularly they wanted to use the German language. But in spite of opposition both within and without the congregation, Harder continued in his task, visiting non-German-speaking homes and inviting people to church. Usually only the children from these homes came. Harder reported in 1940, "We have had fine contact with non-Mennonite families. These send us their children, some very regularly, others not so much. When sickness comes to their members they call on me." Tracking down Mennonites who moved into the city was difficult also, he reported, "since a number of people [who] will not come to the church probably never did much attend. In some cases our Mennonite ministers will not take the trouble to encourage the people to come or tell them there is a Mennonite church in Enid." In 1940, twelve non-Mennonite and twenty-six Mennonite families were attending.[65] How many of those were members is not known, but in 1970, only 15 of 192 members were of non-Mennonite parentage.

Contact with Non-Mennonites

A major result of the creation of Mennonite churches in new places across the continent was increased contact with people of other church backgrounds and people of no church background. In Mennonite towns like Henderson, Nebraska, or Steinbach, Manitoba, contacts with non-Mennonites were few; even public schools were solidly Mennonite. But in Lansdale or Saskatoon or Woodlake, most of one's neighbors or schoolmates or business associates were not Mennonite, and one often saw one's fellow Mennonites only within the church walls.

Outside the original Mennonite settlements in North America, one had more opportunities to untangle faith and culture. To be sure, some Mennonites in the dispersion gave up on that task. Some simply threw away both Mennonite faith and Mennonite culture and quit considering themselves Mennonite; that had been the fear of the conference leaders who cautioned against moving out of the Mennonite settlements. Others could not untangle the strands and wanted to set up an ethnic fortress within the church of the dispersion. Albert Claassen, pastor in the Toronto mission, commented in 1948, "We have folks there that are interested and desirous of having a Mennonite church here, but it shall be for Mennonites. Sometimes we are more exclusive than we realize."[66]

Sometimes the scattered Mennonites were not quite sure what to do with members of other backgrounds once they had them. C. Ramseier, organizing a Mennonite church in Swift, Alabama, in 1908, wrote to the General Conference Home Mis-

sion Board about his dilemma. In Swift there were three Mennonite families—eight members—who had been meeting weekly
for over two years. Now some others from the community
wanted to be baptized. "Do we baptize them as members in the
Christian church or as members in the Mennonite brotherhood?" Ramseier wanted to know.[67]

The first generation of scattered Mennonites tried to hold
on to as much of their culture as they could, particularly the
German language. At the 1980 Pacific District Conference it
was reported that German private schools were being conducted by the churches at Aberdeen, Idaho; Upland, California;
and San Marcos, California. Three other congregations were
interested in starting such schools. The attitude of the delegates
is evidenced by the following discussion:

> It was agreed that if we want to continue our services in the
> German language we must have German schools. We must not
> rush into the English until we have our children well grounded
> in our beliefs since the English schools teach no religion. Uphold
> the German as long as possible, but give it up when young people
> begin to leave. We will eventually pass over to the English
> language. We should also keep in mind how we can serve God
> best in our communities.[68]

In Canada, where later waves of immigration from Russia
prolonged the use of German in the churches, city churches
even in the 1940s could be oases of German in the city. In
Calgary "it was told of a case where an old man met some
brothers [upon coming to the new church] and among tears told
that it had been ten years since he had spoken our language."[69]
But even if English were the only language used, churches
could still become ethnic strongholds in which outsiders felt
uncomfortable. Even most city churches remained predominantly of Mennonite background into the 1970s.

While the Home Mission Board was clear that its first duty
was to gather in scattered Mennonites, it also told its workers,
"That does not preclude giving the same attention to others not
of our Mennonite extraction who reside in a community where
we take up work."[70] Many of the Mennonite churches of the
dispersion did reach out in service, if not in evangelism, to non-
Mennonites around them. Lima, Ohio; Portland, Oregon; Lansdale, Pennsylvania; Wichita, Kansas; Drake, Saskatchewan;
Bethel in Winnipeg; Warden, Washington; and Ransom, Kansas, all tried to set up ministries to the communities around
them and drew in some people of other backgrounds. Often, as
in the "foreign" city missions, these ministries were aimed at

neighborhood children, and few of their parents became members, or even attended. The Eben-ezer Girls' Home in Winnipeg served some non-Mennonite as well as Mennonite young women.[71] Almost all of the churches of the dispersion were somewhat less homogenous ethnically than the churches their members had left behind, although many of the new nonethnic members came through marriage. In Upland, California, for example, during the congregation's first sixty years, 100 of 907 new members were of non-Mennonite parentage, and half of these were married to a member of Mennonite background.[72]

During the Depression, the spirit of mutual aid which was valued in the rural Mennonite communities was translated, especially in the cities, into social service to all the poor of the community. The Lima church distributed clothing and food. The First Church, Philadelphia, set aside a portion of its building for a reading room to "give the unemployed of the district an opportunity to spend the time in reading good books and magazines instead of walking the streets in discontent." It also set up a relief system in the congregation with a designated person to contact "if you are out of work; if you want work done; if you need food, coal, or clothing; if you have donations to make."[73]

In Wichita, under the leadership of Pastor Edward D. and Ella Schmidt, some members of Lorraine Avenue Church and people from at least five other churches in Wichita began a ministry to the poor in the southwest part of the city in the late 1930s and received financial help from the Western District home mission committee in about 1940-43. The program included Sunday school, worship services, rug-weaving classes, sewing bees, building houses,health classes, and prayer meetings. The ministry also provided an opportunity for students from Bethel College to volunteer their help. But the Western District home mission committee was never enthusiastic about the social service aspects of the program. When Schmidt, who later became a naturopathic physician, wanted to set up a free medical clinic there and to expand the services into a Wichita "Hull House," the home missions committee replied that it did "not see its way clear to make the work at the southwest side a social enterprise. Social work would be outside of the sphere of the Home Mission Committee's responsibilities." The entire program was terminated during World War II, when the economic conditions of the people improved as defense industries in Wichita stepped up their production and more jobs became available.[74]

Regional Conference Involvement

In general, the regional conferences before World War II did not give priority to ministries to people not of Mennonite background, or sometimes even to setting up churches for Mennonites in the cities. Around 1916 the understanding was that the General Conference Home Mission Board would be responsible for "city mission and church extension mission work" and that district conferences would be responsible for rural church extension.[75] That division of responsibilities continued until 1933, when, feeling the financial pinch of the Depression, the General Conference board asked the district conferences to take over home mission stations in their districts. However, that request was successful only in the case of Smith Corner, Pennsylvania, where the Eastern District took on the missionary's salary for one year "as an experiment." The division was not always adhered to, for the General Conference and the regional committees kept stepping on each other's toes, particularly in the Canadian Conference and the Western District Conference, where the General Conference did get involved in some rural church extension work. It was not until August 3, 1938, that a joint meeting of the General Conference Home Mission Board and the evangelistic committees of the district conferences was scheduled to revise the division of labor and discuss such matters as a standard pay scale for workers, summer internships for seminary students, and the need for more consultation with local groups.[76] Even after that, some of the regional conferences were reluctant to be involved in city churches. In 1944, the Canadian home missions board wanted the General Conference board to take over all city missions in Canada so the Canadian board could concentrate on rural fields.[77]

The General Conference Home Mission Board often supported district projects by providing loans or gifts for church buildings in places such as Wichita, McPherson, and Burns, Kansas; Vineland, Ontario; Swift Current, Hanley, and Wymark, Saskatchewan; McCreary and Morris, Manitoba; Vancouver and Sardis, British Columbia; Shafter, California; Allentown, Pennsylvania; and Arena, North Dakota;

Like many other district home missions committees, the Western District committee, even though willing to take on city churches among scattered Mennonites, had little interest before World War II in churches directed at those of other backgrounds. In 1927 George Kaufman, who said he was the only Mennonite in Lookeba, Oklahoma, wrote to the Western District home mission committee asking for an evangelist to hold meetings there. Kaufman was superintendent of a Sunday school organized five years earlier by the Christian and Missionary Alliance. H. D. Wiebe, a teacher at the Mennonite Brethren school in Corn, Oklahoma, had been preaching in Lookeba two Sunday evenings a month. But otherwise, there had not been any worship services in the town for years. Kaufman said that in his young people's Sunday school class, only four out of forty-three were Christians. P. P. Wedel, then chairman of the home missions committee, replied that the home missions committee could not take up the work but that Wedel personally might try to fit the visit into his busy schedule. His correspondence does not indicate that he ever did.[78]

In spite of missed opportunities, such as at Lookeba, the definition of *Mennonite* was changing in the General Conference during the period before World War II. A survey of the delegates to the conference sessions would show not only Mennonites from the solidly ethnic rural settlements, but Mennonites from the city missions and Mennonites from the scattered rural settlements. Mennonites were no longer only farmers or teachers, but accountants and factory workers. Instead of only fearing the changes that the scattering was bringing, Mennonites, particularly in the cities, were looking at the issues and asking new questions. One person looked at the ambiguities of being both Mennonite and urban thus:

> The question of the role of a Mennonite church in the city has never been clearly defined and means different things to different members. To some it is a gathering place of the "church family" which includes many real family ties. To others, the Lorraine Ave. Mennonite Church serves as a bridge for rural Mennonites on their way to eventual urbanization. Some see it as a mission station in the "foreign" land of the city, with responsibilities for outreach to its neighbors far beyond those expected of rural churches in their comfortable closed communities.[79]

The first generation in the city was often still rural-oriented, but attitudes and self-images were changing. Said another urban Mennonite, "This is both threatening and exciting for all of us."[80]

Civilian Public Service, 1945

Chapter 7:
The General Conference, a 1945 Perspective

"We further acknowledge our common guilt of not having taught and lived more fully our Christian life as a way of peace and love and good will toward all, and so recommend that when the men are demobilized we engage in a service of humble penitence and prayer for the forgiveness of our common sins and rededicate ourselves to a more honest effort to follow the Prince of Peace and to spread His Gospel of peace and love among all men." Resolution passed by the 1945 General Conference

---

The 1945 sessions of the General Conference, held May 31 to June 5 in North Newton, Kansas, were shaped by World War II. War conditions had forced the postponement of the usually triennial sessions for an additional year. Among those attending the conference were a number of men on leave from Civilian Public Service, the alternative service option for conscientious objectors to military service in the U.S. The conference delegates praised the CPS men, yet conscientious objectors were in the minority among drafted men in the General Conference in both the U.S. and Canada. In the United States only 26.6 percent, or 828, of General Conference Mennonite men who were drafted chose alternative service rather than some form of military service. Over 15 percent served as military noncombatants, and over half (57.7 percent) chose full military service.[1]

The U.S. government's Selective Service System was in charge of the CPS camps, to which the conscientious objectors were assigned, but the historic peace churches—Mennonites,

Friends, and Brethren—actually administered the camps and supported them financially. The Selective Service had army officers in charge of the section dealing with conscientious objectors, and the churches felt unhappy about the lack of civilian direction. In addition, some of the CPS men were dissatisfied with the soil conservation and other projects which they regarded as make-work activities. However, some of the CPS men received other duties, such as public health or work in state mental hospitals.

While the CPS camps had some aspects of a concentration camp (restricted movement and work without pay), they also provided an opportunity for the men to struggle with what it meant to be a Mennonite and a conscientious objector. Mennonite pastors visited the camps. Mennonite camps, under the direction of the Mennonite Central Committee (MCC), developed a series of studies on Mennonite-Anabaptist beliefs. Out of the CPS camps came a generation of Mennonite leaders who were acquainted with Anabaptist thought and who were trying to put it into practice. And because Mennonites of different groups were in constant contact with each other in the CPS camps, out of the camps came a new interest in cooperative Mennonite work and exposure to the world beyond the Mennonite communities.[2]

In Canada, Mennonite conscientious objectors were generally given the opportunity for Alternative Service Work (ASW), although some were sent to prison for refusal of military service.[3] Exact numbers of General Conference Mennonite men serving in Canadian Alternative Service are not available, but John A. Toews estimated that about 72 percent of the 10,870 conscientious objectors in World War II in Canada were Mennonites.[4] In 1941-43 most of the conscientious objectors worked for maintenance, travel, and fifty cents a day in camps operated by the Department of Mines and Resources; but after 1943 some conscientious objectors were assigned to work of "national importance" in agriculture or industry. As in the U.S., in Canada, also, many of the men who returned from ASW camps brought with them an enthusiasm for work in the church. But Canadian Mennonites, like those in the United States, were chagrined at the large numbers of young men from their churches who entered the military. In the Rosenort churches of Saskatchewan, for example, about half of the men eligible for service took up arms, and the other half served as conscientious objectors.[5]

The 1945 General Conference responded to the World War II experience of having so many men from a "peace" church enter the military by reaffirming its 1941 statement on peace and military service (which rejected both combatant and noncombatant military service) and by confessing that the church had not sufficiently taught the way of peace.

The General Conference had entered the twentieth century full of optimism that its peace position would soon be adopted by Protestantism in general. It joined the Federal Council of Churches in 1908 and generally felt that its theology was little different from most other Protestants in North America except for the emphasis on world peace and nonparticipation in the military. Most other social issues on which the General Conference took a stand before World War II (secret societies and temperance, for example) were issues which also concerned many other Protestant groups. While some General Conference Mennonites leaned in the direction of the social gospel, others leaned toward fundamentalism. But few had a vision of a Mennonite theology which treated peace as an integral part of the gospel and not merely as an adornment. W. S. Gottschall, a member of the Home Mission Board, insisted in 1915 that a missionary candidate "express himself on his belief about the Inspiration of the Bible, the Deity of Christ, and the Atonement through the blood of Christ, before considering his application." Only later did Gottschall think of adding to the examination proposed for candidates two other topics: Conversion and Regeneration, and Distinctive Tenets of the Mennonite Church.[6] While the peace position was important, the early Home Mission Board had not related peace to the rest of the gospel.

During World War I, many of the Mennonites' former allies in the peace position began supporting the war, and Mennonites were jolted into the realization that their nonresistant belief would probably always be a minority position within North American Christendom. The General Conference withdrew from the Federal Council of Churches in 1917, at least partly because of the peace issue, and began to turn toward more contacts with other Mennonite groups and with the Quakers and the Church of the Brethren. A series of nine All-Mennonite Conventions were held from 1913 to 1936. The historic peace churches held conferences beginning in 1922. The General Conference itself set up a peace committee in 1926 and gave it a budget in 1933. An independent Mennonite Peace Society was formed in 1932 and was a predecessor to the present-day Mennonite Central Committee Peace Section.[7]

World War II gave Mennonites a second jolt. Conference

leaders came to realize that many of their own members were not conscientious objectors to war. Mission churches where many of the members were not of Mennonite parentage particularly felt the struggle with the peace position. In Portland, Oregon, Arnold J. Regier, pastor of the Alberta Community Church, wrote to Home Mission Board chairman, A. J. Neuenschwander for advice in 1942:

> How shall we regard our nonresistance stand in this war time. Our people have been very open-minded and gracious toward our peace views so far. But I feel that under the increasing pressure some are finding it hard to continue to appreciate some of the peace literature that is coming out in our church papers.... How much emphasis do you think should we place upon this particular teaching at the present time? I realize that our Sunday school work is largely dependent upon the attitude we shall take. Should we continue to subscribe to *The Mennonite* or shall we refer this matter to the conference officials or publication board?[8]

Neuenschwander suggested substituting the publication of the Union Gospel Press, Cleveland, Ohio, for *The Mennonite* as the Sunday school paper.[9]

Other churches had to deal with members or attenders who worked as civilians on military bases or in defense industries. Clyde H. Dirks, minister of the First Mennonite Church in Hutchinson, Kansas, wrote to the Home Mission Board, "Our city has an airplane factory, a naval base and will have an army unit soon. All of these tell heavily on city church life. Only the faithful to Christ will be able to take it."[10]

Acculturation

Could the peace witness and other Mennonite beliefs survive acculturation? General Conference Mennonites who came to the 1945 conference, particularly those who were at least one generation away from immigration, were adopting a culture more and more like that of the society around them. Like their non-Mennonite neighbors, they lived on separate farmsteads rather than in compact villages. They drove automobiles and used gasoline-powered tractors. They listened to the radio and bought mass-produced consumer goods, but fewer Mennonites joined labor unions or got divorces. Some left farming and found new professions in the towns and cities, although they usually chose the fields of education or medicine. Some Mennonite congregations put flags in their meeting places, yet Mennonite young men were less likely than their schoolmates to join the military.

The accommodation to society may have happened more quickly in the cities, but it affected the country as well, as Chicago missionaries John and Catherine Neufeld found out:

> We discovered very often that worldliness had crept in among our rural areas almost as much as it had in the cities. I remember once when our children came home from a Mennonite retreat, they said, "All those young people talk about is clothes and movies." In our conservatism we had advised our children about the evils of the movies, but we found to our amazement that many bars had been let down among our Mennonite people in general.[11]

One measure of acculturation was the dropping of the German language, for the use of English often brought with it the religious influences of American Protestantism: revivalism, fundamentalism, or the social gospel. For a time, it almost seemed as if Mennonites had to keep the German language to remain Mennonite. C. E. Krehbiel, conference field secretary, had reported to the 1926 General Conference that, of forty-eight churches speaking German only and forty-five churches using both German and English, all but three had *Gesangbuch mit Noten*, the German hymnal published by the General Conference. Krehbiel continued,

> No such loyalty to our *Mennonite Hymnal* exists. Of the thirty-four churches that use English exclusively, only eight report having our hymnal, and of forty-five that use both languages, only three report having our hymnal, and some of them have but do not use the book. Without exception they have other hymn books of which some are of the commercialized revival type.[12]

On the other hand, some Mennonites urged more extensive use of English in order to break down one of the barriers which hindered English-speaking people from attending Mennonite churches. Silas M. Grubb asked in *The Mennonite* in 1900:

> How can we propagate scriptural truths among English-speaking people if we insist upon them becoming German? English is used in our Mission Work. Would we consistently permit the Heathen to become an English Mennonite and insist upon the civilized communicant remaining a German one?
>
> Some hold a preservation of German in our family and church to be a duty we owe to our fathers in the faith. But our duty to our fathers is to teach their doctrine, not their language; a religious duty, not a secular one. All the effort our church can command is needed today to rebuke the military spirit of the English-speaking people, by a clear setting forth of the Christ doctrine of

Peace....Why not then make the one who speaks English a
brother instead of an intruder?[13]

The language transition was apparent at the 1945 General
Conference sessions. Most of the discussion was in English, but
the delegates sang in both English and German. The printed
copy of the *Official Minutes and Reports* was primarily in English, with only the foreword and the texts of the resolutions
printed also in German. The English minutes, however, noted
that the Saturday morning Scripture and prayer were "in the
universal Mennonite language, German."[14] In 1945, the Wom-
en's Missionary Association voted to quit publishing a German
section in *Missionary News and Notes.*

The switch from German to English in the General Conference began first about 1874 in the Eastern District Conference
(eastern Pennsylvania), where the earliest Mennonite immigrants had settled. In most other districts in the United States,
the language transition happened between 1920 and 1930. In
Canada, where later waves of immigration prolonged the use of
German, Canadian Conference minutes were not printed in
English until 1956. The Canadian Conference executive secretary reported in 1968, "In terms of language transition we are
over the halfway mark. Culturally we are becoming thoroughly Canadianized."[15]

The chroniclers of the Sargent Avenue Mennonite Church
in Winnipeg, established in 1949 to meet the needs of post-
World War II immigrants from Russia and Paraguay and others
who wanted German services, described the language shift in
that congregation in an extensive history covering both culture
and religion. By 1963, some members were pressing for an
English Sunday school for their children who could not speak
German well. By 1964 the congregation had elected a preacher
who could speak both languages and had noted that more and
more members were forming "marriages with people of other
religions—most leave; only a few remain true to us." By 1965
most church members were better off financially, working as
managers or foremen or owning their own companies. By 1967
the historian noted that most of the young people's first names
were different from those of their ancestors. In later life the
young people won't know who they are or where they have come
from because of their names, she commented. "May they so live
that they do not thereby be lost in the general population."[16]

Another indicator of the General Conference's being influenced by its environment was the effort to reorganize and
consolidate the conference's boards and committees. This cul-

minated in the acquisition of a headquarters building in 1943 and in the consolidation of boards and committees in 1950: the efficient equipment of the modern corporation. Before 1940, the General Conference had no central office. The secretary of each board or committee kept his own files at home, and some of them were later lost. Each board had its own treasurer and its own bank accounts until the 1945 conference established one central treasury. There were few administrative staff people; board officers did their own administration on a voluntary basis or left most of the decisions up to the field workers. The 1938 General Conference minutes listed only four appointed staff people: a field secretary, a conference statistician, a conference treasurer, and a treasurer for the Board of Foreign Missions. Three of these four were living in Newton or North Newton, Kansas, but the fourth lived in Idaho. Boards and committees had grown in number. Another board or committee had been created every time a new need arose. By 1947 there were to be eight boards plus seven committees that were not related to any of these boards.

"Unity, efficiency, and economy demand an effective and simple integration of our service operation," reported H. A. Fast, chairman of the committee appointed to rectify the situation, to the 1947 conference.[17] Fast's committee, "the coordinating committee," had been created at the 1941 General Conference after Fast had presented a talk on "The Duplication and Overlapping of the Duties of the Various Boards and Committees of the General Conference" at the request of the Board of Education. The conference was ready to organize, standardize, and professionalize. The coordinating committee's solution was to be a new constitution, which was adopted at the 1950 General Conference sessions. The new constitution consolidated the many boards and committees into four boards: Missions (both home and foreign), Education and Publication (Christian education, young people's work, higher education, the seminary, and publishing), Christian Service (relief, peace, mutual aid, and voluntary service), and Trustees and Finance. Board members could no longer be employees as well. An annual "council of boards" was to provide for coordination and cooperation among the boards.

In 1945, the General Conference officially accepted the gift of an office building at 722 Main Street, in Newton, Kansas, through the initiative of H. P. Krehbiel and his daughter, Elva Krehbiel Leisy. She donated or partially donated four adjoining buildings to the conference between 1943 and 1975. The central

treasury was in Newton. Staff began to be added: first, retired
foreign missionary P. A. Penner as office manager in 1943, then
staff of the boards of Missions and Publication. The Board of
Missions had an executive secretary with an office in Newton
by 1951.

New Interest in Foreign Mission

By 1945 the Conference of Mennonites in Canada, after
meeting the needs of the new immigrants, was expressing a
new interest in missions, particularly foreign missions. Before
World War II, the Canadian Conference churches had contributed to the foreign mission program of the General Conference,
but not until 1946 did the first Canadian-born missionary go
out under the GC Foreign Mission Board. In 1947 (the same
year in which Canadian Mennonite Bible College was founded)
the Canadian Conference appointed a committee on foreign
mission which not only encouraged giving to overseas mission,
but began looking for its "foreign" mission, investigating work
among the Indians in Manitoba and Saskatchewan. The Bergthaler Church, at the time affiliated with the Canadian Conference but not the General Conference, organized Mennonite
Pioneer Mission in 1945, which at first attempted a mission to
Indians in Mexico, then turned to northern Manitoba. (The two
Canadian mission boards amalgamated in 1957-60.) A second
generation following the immigration of the 1920s was ready to
venture into missions away from the East and West Reserves
and away from the scattered Mennonite communities across
Canada. But the objects of mission for Canadian Mennonites, as
for American Mennonites a generation earlier, were to be people who were unlikely to want to join ethnic Mennonite congregations because they did not live in Mennonite communities.
Mennonites could carry out the missionary mandate without
disturbing their ethnic solidarity.

Overseas missions got new priority. At the 1945 General
Conference, the Board of Foreign Missions gave a fanfare for
new work in Colombia, South America. Less prominent was the
Indian mission work in the United States, by then sixty-five
years old, where progress was unsteady at best. The Oklahoma
report to the conference noted, "It is up-hill work, especially in
times like these. But there is progress in spite of all hindrances." Bertha Petter, missionary in Montana, stated, "The
reaction among the heathen Indians against the 'White man's
religion' has grown in so far that the old heathen ceremonies
paired with mongrel peyote religion have lifted their heads,

insisting that their way of worshiping God is best for the Indians." But some progress was noted; since the last General Conference sessions, the first native helper among the Cheyenne had been ordained to the ministry.[18]

Urbanization

Most of the 160 congregations that sent delegates to the 1945 General Conference were town and country churches, as were all ten of the new churches accepted as members of the conference that year. Yet, increasing numbers of Mennonites were living in cities, and even many members of rural churches no longer earned their living by farming.

Urbanization was happening among Canadian Mennonites even faster than in the United States. To keep pace with it, the Canadian and General Conference home mission boards started eight new city churches in Canada during the 1940s, compared with two or three in the United States. In Ontario, the United Mennonite Conference, at the encouragement of Jacob H. Janzen, established a home mission committee in response to the needs of Mennonites moving to Toronto and St. Catharines. The new city missions began with visiting ministers under the sponsorship of the Ontario missions committee in 1942, but within a year both missions were transferred to General Conference sponsorship. Janzen had wanted to make the missions a provincial conference project, but he felt the Ontario churches did not yet have strong enough ties among themselves to manage two city missions, so Janzen asked the General Conference Home Mission Board to supervise the missions and in return, the Ontario churches were to send regular offerings to the GC Home Mission Board.[19]

Although the Toronto congregation was directed primarily at those of Mennonite background, there were attempts to draw in others as well. The first General Conference worker was Arnold A. Fast, a graduate of Moody Bible Institute, and he and the other three ministers who served between 1943 and 1950 tried to establish a mission to the neighborhood, particularly to children. In 1953, the Sunday school had "Japanese, Estonian, Canadian, and Mennonite" children.[20] But the Toronto church was not successful in bringing in adults of non-Mennonite background. In spite of its boys' and girls' clubs, the congregation had little identification with the neighborhood around the church building. Most of the members were scattered across the city, and only the pastor lived in the neighborhood. A conservative Protestant approach did not appeal to a Roman Catholic neighborhood.[21] The congregation remained predominantly of Mennonite background—about 92 percent in 1959.[22]

The group which became the St. Catharines United Mennonite Church also began worshiping in 1942 and organized in 1944 under the leadership of Wilhelm Schellenberg, minister until 1950. Some of the nearby Mennonite ministers were reluctant to see the church begin. One minister wrote to A. J. Neuenschwander, chairman of the GC Home Mission Board, "The people from there could really come to Vineland and Niagara. It is only ten miles here or back. Many do come." [23]

In spite of this attitude, the congregation experienced rapid growth as a result of the migration of Mennonites from Russia and Poland after World War II and from Mennonites moving into the city from the surrounding area. A small number of people of non-Mennonite background have come into the church through marriage. Membership in 1977 stood at 700.[24]

Farther west, new churches were being started in Prince Albert, Saskatchewan; a second congregation, Mayfair, in Saskatoon; First Church, in Calgary, Alberta, and Sargent Avenue Church in Winnipeg. In Regina, Saskatchewan, David Toews and Gerhard Penner had been meeting monthly with about ten Mennonite families during 1940-44, but beginning in 1944 they decided to meet with the Mennonite Brethren church in Regina. A General Conference-related church was not started there until 1955. In other locations as well, earlier barriers between Mennonite groups were breaking down as contact with each other grew more frequent. The General Conference congregation in Prince Albert wanted to give new members the option of sprinkling or immersion as the form of baptism, an effort to make the church more attractive to those of Mennonite Brethren background, who had a tradition of baptism by immersion. But G. G. Epp, member of the Canadian Conference home mission committee, discouraged the action, "To change our mode of baptism and to make it optional likely would cause confusion in the minds of some."[25]

In the United States only two new city churches were organized during the 1940s: McPherson, Kansas, in 1945, and Bethel in Lancaster, Pennsylvania, in 1947. The McPherson church, sponsored by the Western District Conference, was made up almost entirely of Mennonites from the Swiss Volhynian community around Moundridge, Kansas, who had moved to town. The core of the Lancaster church was General Conference volunteers and former Civilian Public Service workers from the Akron, Pennsylvania, headquarters of Mennonite

Central Committee. The group had begun meeting on their own, but the Eastern District Conference assumed sponsorship.

The General Conference Home Mission Board got involved in encouraging city Mennonite fellowships which had started on their own. Many of these fellowships were composed of Mennonite students. In 1943 a Mennonite group in New York began meeting, and General Conference Mennonite students at the Biblical Seminary of New York gave leadership. About a year later the General Conference Home Mission Board asked Paul F. Barkman, secretary-treasurer of the group, to become contact person for Mennonites in the city. Another student group was active in the Chicago Loop area about 1944, led by General Conference mission pastors John T. Neufeld and Erwin A. Albrecht. Neither of these groups grew into organized churches, but another university-related group in Edmonton, Alberta, begun in 1949, was the nucleus of First Mennonite Church in Edmonton. The group began meeting at the initiative of John Unrau, a Mennonite professor at the University of Alberta. The home mission boards of the Alberta, Canadian, and General conferences helped support the Edmonton church.[26]

Not all such spontaneous Mennonite fellowships were encouraged, however. In 1945 J. A. Duerksen, a resident of Washington, D.C., wrote to the General Conference Home Mission Board asking for help for a fellowship there, in which General Conference members were in the majority. J. M. Regier, chairman of the Home Mission Board, offered little support, "They are a capable group and well able to take care of themselves." The group wanted social, not religious, gatherings and were well entrenched in the non-Mennonite churches they attended, Regier added.[27] The Washington fellowship never organized as a church.

Back to the Country

In the midst of the rapid urbanizing of American and Canadian societies, however, the mood of many in the General Conference in 1945 was to preserve a religious heritage that was rural in attitude and geography. In 1942 the Mennonites, Brethren, and Quakers had formed the Rural Life Association, organized in response to a challenge from Luigi Ligutti, executive director of the National Catholic Rural Life Conference. Based at the churches' colleges, it promoted rural church extension and agricultural missions. Howard Raid, a General Conference member and a teacher at Bluffton College, served as an officer of the organization.

In home missions, too, hopes were placed in rural missions. Earlier, board member A. J. Neuenschwander had noted that although the rural population in America was declining, General Conference church membership had increased almost 20 percent in the last seven years. He neglected to mention that those seven years had seen the immigration of thousands of Mennonites from Russia to Canada. If the Home Mission Board enlarged the rural phase of its work, in a few years the confer- ence would be able to show even more substantial growth, he said.[28] Evaluators of urban missions were pessimistic about the city. J. Winfield Fretz's 1940 study of Chicago Mennonite mis- sions concluded, "Mennonites should use their rural talents where they know what they are doing and where the money could be more effective in furthering the kingdom." [29]

The Central Conference mission board voted in 1940 to get out of its two Chicago missions and investigate fields of rural work.[30] The Middle District Conference, already thinking of merger with the Central Conference, also concluded, "Similar views have been expressed by some of the ministers of the Middle District Conference, since our city mission work seems to drag along and does not seem to make much headway.... If our home mission board plans to cooperate more closely with the mission board of the Central Conference, then we, too, would have to consider rural fields more than we have done up to this time."[31] The Canadian mission board in 1944 asked the General Conference board to take over all city work in Canada, feeling that the General Conference board was the more appropriate place to lodge city concerns.[32]

Meanwhile, thousands of young men were soon to be leav- ing Civilian Public Service (CPS) camps in the United States and alternative service assignments in Canada. The plan of the General Conference Home Mission Board was to mobilize the resources of the conference to help these young men to return to the rural areas, to farming, and to the General Conference Mennonite churches. Many of the earlier colonization efforts by conferences had not been too successful. The Mennonite Set- tlers' Aid Society, a nonprofit corporation set up in 1927 by five Mennonite ministers, had contracted for a 50,000-acre tract in northeastern Washington and northwestern Idaho, to be re- served for Mennonites only for ten years. But the project did not attract enough people to form a successful colony.[33] The 1938 General Conference had looked favorably on the report of the Emergency Relief Board calling for "a committee whose duties it would be to help young people and older ones, too, to find a home in such a closed settlement. This would be real home mission work," said board secretary John C. Mueller. "Many of our people are lost by our churches because of present circumstances. A soul kept is a soul saved." A motion to include the problems of scattered young people in the cities, as well as in rural areas, was tabled.[34] The project, however, was given not to the Emergency Relief Board, but to the Home Mission Board. That board's solutions in 1941 were first to ask David Toews to appoint a Canadian committee and second to focus the U.S. work on the Western District. Eight members from the Western District were appointed, but no one wanted to chair the committee. The committee's accomplishments were not noteworthy.

As World War II drew to a close, the colonization issue grew more urgent. The Home Mission Board decided to enlist the help of the entire conference in the service of Mennonite colonization. The board sent William H. Stauffer of Sugarcreek, Ohio, in 1943-44 on a year-long tour of the conference, visiting churches and CPS camps promoting the idea of colonization and presenting to the CPS men "the Mennonite way of life." The problem, as Stauffer saw it, was that Mennonites were not staying on the farm, but were moving to the cities, with their "paganism, corruption, and artificiality." He argued, "As Mennonite people we have a much better heritage, we are much better equipped to bring the unsearchable riches of Christ to the country than to the city. There are others who can more effectively bring Christ to the cities."[35] At the same time Mennonite Central Committee was also promoting colonization among the CPS men with the booklet "Mennonite Colonization" written by General Conference member J. Winfield Fretz.

MCC organized a new section on Mennonite Aid in 1944. The 1943 General Conference created its own Board of Mutual Aid. The new board was to provide vocational counseling to young people, provide information on colonization and settlement opportunities, and to assist young people—particularly ex-CPS workers—with low-interest loans which would help them get an education, buy a modest home, or get a start in farming, business, or a profession. In its first two years of existence, the Board of Mutual Aid collected $45,000 in loans and gifts and made forty-six loans, mostly to CPS men and mostly in the Western District Conference. Twenty-two of the forty-six loans, averaging about $1,000, were used to buy livestock.[36] The board's program was focused on the U.S. situation; until 1955, no loans were made in Canada.

After 1950, the Board of Mutual Aid became a committee

under the Board of Christian Service and was later incorporated separately as *Mutual Aid Services, Inc.* The program
always remained small, from 1950 to 1955 making an average
of ten to eleven loans per year of $1,000 to $2,000 per loan. A
special fund within the Mutual Aid Committee was set up to
enable church college faculty and other church workers to buy
homes. Mutual Aid Services made its last loan in 1967 and
began phasing out after that. Part of its function continued
through General Conference participation in the health plan of
the inter-Mennonite organization, Mennonite Mutual Aid Association.

Because of the Board of Mutual Aid's mandate to deal with
colonization, it got numerous inquiries from small rural Mennonite congregations, asking the board to promote their communities as places for Mennonite young people to settle.
Colonization efforts in the 1940s led to the birth or growth of
churches in locations like Lynden, Washington; Caldwell,
Idaho; Burns, Kansas; Huron, South Dakota; Codette, Saskatchewan; Lymburn, Alberta; Carman, Manitoba; and Ke-
lowna, British Columbia. In contrast to the less than a dozen
city churches started during the decade, about thirty rural or
small-town churches had their beginnings during this period.
But to Mennonites, now moving more frequently as individuals
or families rather than in church-related groups, the new Mennonite colonies were not as attractive as the colonies' promoters
had hoped. In spite of conference encouragement for colonization near Caldwell, Idaho, for example, the First Mennonite
Church there never reached a membership over thirty-nine
from 1947, when it was organized, to 1963, when it dissolved.

The itinerant ministry of the General Conference was
revived in the 1940s with the appointment of J. J. Esau, of
Bluffton, Ohio, an evangelist, to visit conference churches. In
1942 he was asked to visit Canadian churches "to develop a
deeper spiritual life and also to link the churches in Canada
more closely to the churches in the United States."[37] Esau
visited not only established churches but groups of unorganized
scattered Mennonites. He is given credit for being the first
person to bring together scattered Mennonites in Toronto.[38]

The rural emphasis of the 1940s was also evident in the
General Conference's missions to people outside the Mennonite
fold. Both the Central Conference (now Central District Conference) and the Pacific District Conference began "rural" missions during the 1940s. The Central Conference, eager to find a
mission field which promised more success than its two Chicago

missions, chose to emphasize Comins, Michigan, as its "rural mission" and to expand its ministry in 1948-49 to McKinley, a new logging community eleven miles away. The Central Conference Yearbook of 1948 praised the Comins church as "the fastest growing and in many respects the most encouraging and challenging field in our conference."[39] The Comins church owed much of its success to the fact that it had started with a core of Mennonites who had separated from the Mennonite Church congregation near Fairview, Michigan, over conference rules on dress and discipline. At their request, Emmanuel Troyer, then field secretary of the Central Conference, came to Comins in 1925 to organize the group of twelve members into a Central Conference church. By 1935 the church had grown to 82 members and by 1947 to 151, many of them blue-collar workers not of Mennonite background. In 1970 about 30 percent were of non-Mennonite parentage.[40] Especially under the leadership of Frank Mitchell in 1931-41, the congregation emphasized peace theology and had a representative in the Mennonite Peace Society and the Fellowship of Reconciliation.[41]

The new mission at McKinley, Michigan, although considered a daughter church of Comins, did not have the advantage of a core group of Mennonites in its beginning. The church organized there, without the word *Mennonite* in its name, suffered leadership problems, and never gained a foothold in the community. It was closed in 1966.

The Pacific District voted in 1948 to start its first congregation aimed specifically at people not of Mennonite background. It also chose a rural logging area: Sweet Home, Oregon. Begun at the suggestion of P. A. Kliewer of Albany, Oregon, former missionary among the Cheyenne in Montana, the mission had as its first pastor Alfred Schwartz of Monroe, Washington. He began with children's classes and home visitation. The congregation's membership never grew above 100 until about 1971, when the congregation experienced a renewal under the leadership of Larry Sloan, a logging truck driver, and began attracting many young people. Membership in 1978 was 186.[42]

The General Conference itself had had some experience before 1940 in rural missions aimed at non-Mennonites. The western Pennsylvania churches started under the influence of Jacob Snyder had been mostly rural. By 1940, Napier, Smith Corner, and Mechanic's Grove were still functioning. Coupon, Upper Poplar Run, and Mann's Choice had closed or been turned over to another group.

The General Conference board had also tried to establish a

mission at Eldon Camp, five miles east of Flagstaff, Arizona, in 1926. But that effort was concluded only three years later. The mission was started on the property of J. B. and Aganetha Balzer Frey, General Conference missionaries to the Hopi Indians in Arizona in 1903-29. Marie Schirmer, another missionary to the Hopis, was Eldon Camp's first mission worker among the white, middle-income farmers. Freys were the only Mennonites living there. The work was abandoned without a congregation ever being organized, partly in the face of depleted finances of the Home Mission Board.[43]

The General Conference Home Mission Board turned again to rural missions in the 1940s. These ventures into non-Mennonite rural areas were not the result of a well-planned rural strategy, but rather the result of the initiative of several local Mennonite groups whose work the General Conference was persuaded to take over.

The Home Mission Board got involved at Paint Rock, North Carolina, (located between Asheville, North Carolina, and Knoxville, Kentucky) in 1940 by accepting the request to add four dollars a month to the support of Elsa Grantland, a member of First Mennonite Church in Chicago. She had begun conducting an interdenominational Sunday school among white mountain people in about 1936. The project had been the idea of A. H. Leaman, pastor of the Chicago church at the time, and that congregation partially supported Grantland in her work. Grantland's mission work met with opposition from the people in the area, but in 1947, the General Conference voted to enlarge its "southern mountain mission work" and put more funds into the project. One board member wrote of Grantland: "Great opposition—great field—great saint of God working. This is real home missions."[44]

The Home Mission Board categorized the Paint Rock work as a "foreign" mission, implied in such descriptions of the mountain folk as people "with underdeveloped religious, economic, and cultural standards."[45] Andrew Holliman, a native of Oklahoma, became the first pastor in 1947 of a new congregation, Grace Chapel in Paint Rock (organized in 1948). A second congregation, Belva Bible Church, was organized near Marshall, North Carolina. Some additional work was done in Houston Valley, Tennessee. The General Conference Home Mission Board in the 1950s turned over both missions to the Eastern District Conference, whose home missions committee terminated its involvement after 1965, when it could not find staff for the mission. The Belva church was probably the more thriving of the two congregations, and it was turned over to the Methodists. The Grace Chapel dissolved.

In the 1940s the General Conference also became involved in two other mountain missions—like the Paint Rock work—through little initiative on the part of the Home Mission Board. Here, the General Conference took on support of workers administered by other mission agencies.

In 1945 the General Conference took on the support of Margaret Slotter and Elsa Pfister, members of the Grace Mennonite Church, Lansdale, Pennsylvania, who had been working for about eight years with the Scripture Memory Mountain Mission in Hoskinston and Hyden, Kentucky—later in Cumberland and Incline, Kentucky. In 1949 the General Conference Home Mission Board took over responsibility for three other women working with mountain children: Marie Liechty, Lillian Lehman, and Lorraine Burkhalter, of Berne, Indiana, who were working near Greenville, Tennessee, with the Children's Bible Mission, a nondenominational group which required its workers to find their own financial support. First Mennonite Church in Berne agreed to continue contributing the amount of the women's salaries, but the Home Mission Board became the channel through which that was done. The Berne church also used the Middle District home mission committee to funnel money to a worker at a Jewish mission in Los Angeles and to five workers in the Go Ye Mission, Chouteau, Oklahoma.[46] In 1949 the Home Mission Board gave partial support to Carl Wahlstedt and his wife of Barbourville, Kentucky, supervisors of a nondenominational children's camp known as *Emmanuel Bible Camp*.[47]

Most of the work of these mountain missions consisted in teaching school children Bible verses during released-time classes. Children who learned at least 200 Bible verses went to camp in the summer, where the missionaries sought to lead those children to accept Christ. But as GC Board of Missions executive secretary John Thiessen noted in 1954, there was no program of follow-up work and no gathering of believers into congregations or strengthening of existing congregations. "We are not clear as to what to recommend to the Board for these areas, because at present our workers there work under an organization over which we have no influence," Thiessen told the board.[48]

After 1959 the General Conference sent to these workers only funds received and earmarked for them. Such channeling of funds continued until 1970, when the last of the General

Conference workers terminated her service with the Children's Bible Mission.[49]

Another home mission work begun in the 1940s among North Americans of another culture was a mission among migrant farm workers. By 1941, the California Mennonite Sunday School and Christian Endeavor Conference sponsored full-time Mennonite migrant workers at Shafter, California.[50] A second migrant work began in 1941 under an inter-Mennonite women's group known as the *Mennonite Women's United Service Committee*, formed at the initiative of Mary Burkhart of Goshen, Indiana. The committee included representatives of the General Conference, the Central Conference, and the Evangelical Mennonite Church. From 1944 to 1952 it supported both men and women as summer workers among migrants in the central United States, working under the direction of the Home Missions Council of North America (later know as the *Division of Home Missions of the National Council of Churches in the United States*). After the Service Committee disbanded in 1953, the General Conference Women's Missionary Association directly supported migrant work under the General Conference Board of Missions and under Mennonite Central Committee.

The General Conference Board of Missions' own migrant work was begun in 1951 in a desert hamlet known as *Friendly Corner*, near Eloy, Arizona, among black, Anglo, and Spanish-speaking migrant workers in the surrounding cotton fields. The work had actually been begun a number of years earlier by a Tucson, Arizona, man known as "Brother Smith," who had been preaching in the migrant camps and helping people with food and clothing whenever he could. Smith tried unsuccessfully to convince his own denomination, the Christian and Missionary Alliance, to start a church near the migrant camps. But Mr. and Mrs. John P. Janzen, General Conference Mennonites attending the same Christian and Missionary Alliance church in Tucson, carried the concern to the General Conference Board of Missions, which agreed to begin the work in 1951.

Rebecca Nickel, Glen and Ruth Habegger, Elsie Heppner, and a number of shorter-term workers began a Sunday school for children of migrant farm workers, first in a public school building, then in an old store building. In 1954, a church building was built by eleven men from the Newton and Whitewater, Kansas, area churches, including Walter H. Dyck, a member of the Board of Missions. Sunday worship services, midweek services, and a young people's group were begun soon after the building was finished.

Bible classes for children in the migrant camps were carried on during the week. Glen Habegger described the early efforts:

The children were usually seated on cardboard spread on the ground. Bible choruses were sung by the children, the teacher told a Bible story, the children memorized Bible verses, and the children usually did coloring of pictures, or had other handcraft. The children could earn small prizes such as a pencil or a little puzzle for memorizing Scripture portions and could receive a Bible for memorizing a certain number of Scripture portions.[51]

Through the 1960s the mission's emphasis continued to be on children, with the program including daily vacation Bible school as well. During the early years, most of the people who attended services were children. Young people were transported to and from the chapel in the mission workers' cars.

By the mid-1960s, however, farmers in the area were replacing people with machines in the cotton harvest, and the population declined as most of the farm labor camps were vacated or torn down. In 1977 Pastor Glen Habegger asked the congregation whether it wanted to continue meeting, since Sunday school attendance during the previous months was often as low as four. But the group decided to continue. A little over half of those attending the Friendly Corner Chapel were of ethnic Mennonite background. The group finally disbanded in 1980.

An Anabaptist Evaluation

Of the work which the General Conference or Central Conference began among other ethnic groups in North America before 1950, neither the advocates of rural missions nor the advocates of city missions could claim advantage. Both rural and city missions had had successes and failures. (See Table 1.) Of nine city missions started in the first half of the century, four were still in existence and members of the General Conference in 1978. Of about thirteen rural missions, four were part of the General Conference in 1978. The problem with Mennonite city missions was not so much that Mennonites were better suited to carry on rural missions; it was that General Conference Mennonites were still a close-knit ethnic group—or rather, a collection of related ethnic groups. Missions before 1950 had assumed that following the evangelistic formulas of conservative Protestantism would bring church members in the same way it had for other North American Protestants. Mennonite mission workers had assumed that one simply had to add a few Mennonite "distinctives" (like peace and not swearing oaths) to the formula, in the way one would garnish a casserole with parsley, and one could create a Mennonite church.

But that method of doing missions had two flaws. First, parts of the evangelistic formula did not work for anybody: stable churches were not created through children's programs alone. Reaching the parents through their children was seldom successful. Second, General Conference Mennonites were not typical North American Protestants. Without the strong ethnic ties to other parts of the General Conference, mission churches felt isolated from the conference and felt just as comfortable going in the direction of other denominations or of no denomination at all. That was a rural problem as well as an urban one. The missionaries at Comins, Michigan, asked the Central Conference in 1937 for closer relationships, saying, "We feel that the Conference is our foreign field." The people knew little about the conference institutions and its interests. Couldn't other ministers in the conference visit Comins on their vacations? the mission workers pleaded.[52] What was needed was a Mennonite theology, distinctive in its entirety, not just one or two optional points—a theology that could tie the conference together when ethnic identity could not.

The 1940s saw the beginnings of the development of a theology that sought to meet that need by going back to the theology of Mennonites' sixteenth-century spiritual forebears, the Anabaptists, who had formed churches based on common conviction, not family relationships. The emphasis on Anabaptist theology followed about sixty years of renewed interest in Anabaptist history, first in Europe and then in North America. The historical interest which began in 1884 with Anna Brons's Anabaptist history published in northern Germany, continued into the 1940s in North America with the beginnings of work on the *Mennonite Encyclopedia*.[53] The landmark article on Anabaptist theology, which appeared in 1944, was "The Anabaptist Vision," written by the Mennonite historian Harold S. Bender.[54] Through the next decades there followed a string of articles, research, and rethinking on Anabaptist theology of the sixteenth century and its meanings for the twentieth century.

As Mennonites became more urban, they looked to the urban Anabaptists for clues on how to do evangelism in ways that were not necessarily tied to a rural culture of closed ethnic communities. Conference leader Erland Waltner commented:

> As a traditionally rural and conservative people confronts the
> liberalizing and secularizing influence of this urbanization, can

it find effective ways of not only maintaining its faith but also of communicating it in an increasingly urban culture in which it must now exist and grow?

To suggest that the survival of an Anabaptist-Mennonite heritage is in some way dependent on the preservation of a rural culture is probably to misunderstand and to misinterpret this heritage. Significantly it has been observed that both early Christianity (Jerusalem, Antioch, Ephesus) and early Anabaptist (Zurich, Strassburg, Amsterdam, Emden) were cradled in urban rather than in rural cultures. It may even be, as Paul Peachey has proposed, that urban culture may be more congenial to true Anabaptism than is the rural.[55]

The mission emphasis of eighteenth- and nineteenth-century Protestantism, which had inspired Mennonites to do evangelism outside their own boundaries, was now being tested by a new discovery of the theology of their spiritual forebears and a reinterpretation of what it meant to be Mennonite in a changing culture.

The problems and possibilities which World War II presented to Mennonites provided the setting for the Anabaptist reawakening. The generation of Mennonites who had had to make a clear choice about military service was committed to the peace position and was ready to hear how their Anabaptist forebears had articulated the gospel of peace and had found no contradiction between a stand for peace and evangelistic zeal. Those who had served in alternative service camps had found it was possible to be Mennonite away from the home communities. They had found new possibilities for service and for mission in North America.

Table 1

Membership of churches started before 1950 as missions to those of non-Mennonite background (date work started)

GENERAL CONFERENCE	1950	1981
Urban		
Los Angeles (1909)	295	withdrew 1978
First, Chicago (1914)	57	92
Altoona, Pennsylvania (1911)	closed in 1947	
Hutchinson (1913)	195	473
Grace, Chicago (1917)	76	89
Jewish mission, Chicago (1920)	closed in 1923	

Rural

Napier, Bedford, Pennsylvania (1913)	53	128
Smith Corner, East Freedom, Pennsylvania (1908)	38	31
Coupon, Pennsylvania (1921)	closed in 1926	
Upper Poplar Run, Claysburg, Pennsylvania (1920)	transferred 1933	
Mann's Choice, Pennsylvania (1914)	closed in 1935	
Mechanics Grove, Pennsylvania (1914)	47	withdrew 1957
Eldon Camp, Flagstaff, Arizona (1926)	closed in 1929	
Paint Rock, North Carolina (c. 1940)	?	dissolved
Belva, North Carolina (c. 1940)	organized 1962	withdrew 1967
Scripture Mountain Memory Mission (1945)	no organized church	
Sweet Home, Oregon (1948)	organized 1951	186
Friendly Corner, Eloy, Arizona (1951)		closed in 1980

CENTRAL CONFERENCE	*1950*	*1981*

Urban

26th Street, Chicago (1909)	closed 1942	
Mennonite Gospel Mission, Chicago (1909)	closed 1948	
Peoria, Illinois (1914)	142	79(merged)

Rural

Comins, Michigan (1925)	164	102
McKinley, Michigan (1948)	organized 1951	closed 1966

Mennonite Voluntary Service, Hammon, Oklahoma

Eugene Stc

Chapter 8:
Relief and Service as Witnesses for Peace

"It is often frustrating for a suburban congregation to face the dire needs of the inner city. Yet in our time, we must learn to live with such creative tensions. It is our growing experience that suburban congregations can learn from the insights of poverty communities, and the poverty community can benefit from the resources and skills of those who are willing and able to help." —Richard D. Krause, voluntary service worker in Fort Wayne, Indiana, 1969.

General Conference Mennonites' programs in relief and service were later in coming than programs in missions. Home missions in the form of the traveling ministry had begun as soon as the General Conference was formed, and missions to American Indians began in 1880. But in one sense, relief and service programs were already in operation before the conference created separate boards and committees to administer relief.

The first "foreign" mission, to the Cheyenne and Arapaho in Oklahoma Territory, was an effort not only to build churches, but also to provide for the Indians' needs in food, shelter, health, and education. White Mennonite churches sent food and clothing to meet emergency relief needs in Oklahoma. Scores of short-term workers came as farmers, gardeners, seamstresses, cooks, matrons, and teachers.[1]

Institutions such as hospitals and homes for the aged were also thought of as mission projects. In a speech to the 1890

General Conference sessions David Goerz of Newton, Kansas, included such benevolent institutions in his definition of home missions. "The basis for home mission is the belief in Jesus Christ and the Samaritan love born out of this belief, which places itself selflessly in the service of the kingdom of God," Goerz said. This love included not only preaching services, but schools for poor children, orphanages, and institutions for epileptics, the insane, deaf and dumb, blind, released prisoners, "fallen girls," and alcoholics. Other manifestations of this love included day-care centers for children, kindergartens, and Sunday schools, as well as immigrant missions and tract distribution.[2]

Only gradually did General Conference Mennonites separate missions from service and begin setting up separate institutions for charity. The first relief project in which the entire General Conference participated—as well as the then-unorganized Mennonite Church (MC), spurred on by John F. Funk's *Herald of Truth*—was the helping of 18,000 Russian Mennonites to immigrate to the plains of Canada and the United States in 1874 and the years following. The project was an expansion of the idea of mutual aid from the congregational level to the international level. From 1873 to 1881 North American Mennonites gave about $40,000 through the Mennonite Board of Guardians to help the new immigrants settle.[3] But with the end of the immigration, the conferencewide and inter-Mennonite relief machinery was dismantled.

In 1896 the General Conference suggested the organization of a permanent relief commission "to aid needy members of our faith, following the example of the district conferences," each of which had an *Armenkasse,* or treasury to aid the poor within the church. When the 1899 General Conference created the Emergency Relief Board, its task was expanded to include relief of "all catastrophal suffering in our own group or anywhere in our land, and in the world."[4]

The famine in India in the late 1890s provided the first opportunity for the Emergency Relief Board to go into action and also provided the springboard for General Conference mission work in India. The General Conference had at first cooperated in the India relief program with the Home and Foreign Relief Commission of the Mennonites (MC), organized in 1897. But the inter-Mennonite cooperation which had been envisioned did not succeed, and the General Conference Mennonite Church organized its own relief board.

In the early years, almost all of the funds of the Emergency

Relief Board went overseas through General Conference missions in India or China or through other benevolent agencies such as the Red Cross or the Christmas Ship or the American Friends Service Committee, although some help was given in North America intermittently. The board gave its first relief contributions in North America to victims of the San Francisco earthquake in 1906.

City missions in the United States, the first begun in 1909, also provided a channel for sending food and clothing to the poor. Sunday school classes, women's groups, and others within General Conference Mennonite churches sent boxes of cookies or children's clothing for home missionaries to distribute in the neighborhoods around the mission buildings. Missionaries used additional funds to buy food or sewing supplies for poor families. At times, money for this work came from the Emergency Relief Board.[5] Many General Conference Mennonites thus became acquainted with North American poverty through mission literature, through their Sunday school classes and women's missions societies, through short terms of service in the mission, or through visiting their friends and relatives who were serving in the missions.

Institutions of Mercy

Just as the city mission movement among Mennonites had got its cues from European and North American Protestants, so General Conference Mennonites also borrowed from their environment in setting up church-related hospitals and homes and deaconess institutions.

The first Mennonite hospital for the acutely ill was the Mennonite Bethesda Hospital Society, begun in Goessel, Kansas, in 1900. It was soon followed by hospitals in Mountain Lake, Minnesota, in 1905; Newton, Kansas, in 1908; and Beatrice, Nebraska, in 1911. All of these hospitals, although not directly related to the conference, were started and managed by local Mennonite groups and were located in heavily Mennonite communities. The General Conference itself sponsored only one hospital, a tuberculosis sanatorium in Alta Loma, California. The sanatorium opened in 1914, at first under the sponsorship of the Pacific District Conference, and closed about 1921 for lack of patients and a shortage of Mennonite nurses in its isolated rural location. The Central Conference of Mennonites took over a hospital in Bloomington, Illinois, in 1919, which was later named *Mennonite Hospital.* After the immigration in the 1920s of Russian Mennonites (who had had hospitals in Russia as early as 1880), Canadian Mennonites started hospitals, beginning with Concordia in Winnipeg in 1928.[6]

Homes for the aged also had their beginnings around the turn of the century, as Mennonites became town-dwellers and it became less common to house older people in the home of a son or daughter. The first such institution among Mennonites was the Mennonite Home for the Aged in Frederick, Pennsylvania, established in 1896 through the efforts of Nathaniel B. Grubb, pastor of First Mennonite Church in Philadelphia, and starter of mission churches. He first bought the property himself in 1895 and turned it over to the Eastern District Conference a year later.

The Bergthaler Mennonite Church in Manitoba had a home for the aged in Gretna in 1918-38, and the Central Conference of Mennonites established a home for the aged near Meadows, Illinois, in 1923. The Bethel Home for the Aged was begun in Newton, Kansas, in 1926. But most of the Mennonite-related homes for the aged were started in the 1940s, 1950s, and 1960s as urbanization hit the bulk of Mennonites.[7]

Orphan work also occupied General Conference Mennonites. The Salem Orphanage near Flanagan, Illinois, founded in 1896, got the support of the Central Conference. The Eastern District Conference had orphan work, initiated in 1905 by the Ladies' Aid Society of First Church, Philadelphia. Earlier, orphan work had been attempted in Kansas by the Leisy Orphan Aid Society, organized in 1884 at Halstead, and the Mennonite Orphan and Children's Aid Society, organized in 1893 at the same place. The two groups later united and, until 1905, homeless children were housed at Christian Krehbiel's farm near Halstead until they could be adopted by other families. After 1919 the General Conference Home Mission Board administered the orphan fund, and about thirteen children were placed in new homes. In 1941, the Home Missions Board recommended liquidation of the Orphan Fund because there had been no call for help in the last six years, but the General Conference voted to retain it.[8] After World War II some help was given to Mennonite orphans in South America. In 1979 the General Conference still distributed annually a small amount of interest money from the orphan fund through Mennonite Central Committee and the General Conference Commission on Overseas Mission, but none through the Commission on Home Ministries.[9]

General Conference Mennonite involvement in mental hospitals began after World War II although Mennonites in

Russia had established an institutioin for the mentally ill, epileptics, and the mentally retarded as early as 1910.[10] During World War II, 1,500 Mennonite conscientious objectors did alternative service in state mental hospitals and training schools, and some young women volunteered for such work under Mennonite Central Committee. Their experiences awakened Mennonites to the need for improved, compassionate care for the mentally ill. With the encouragement of the 1945 General Conference as well as other Mennonite bodies, MCC approved a mental health program in January 1947. Brook Lane Farm (now Brook Lane Psychiatric Center), Hagerstown, Maryland, was opened in 1949. Five other Mennonite mental health institutions opened between 1951 and 1967.

All of these mental health centers relate to each other through Mennonite Mental Health Services, Inc., a psychiatric service of Mennonite Central Committee, although MCC no longer directly administers the centers. MCC has retained only the power to appoint the board members and approve the budget of Mennonite Mental Health Services. Community ties within the centers' boards are being strengthened through inclusion of representatives-at-large on the boards in addition to the church representatives. The secular relationships are also felt through the increasing funds available from federal, state, and provincial governments.

The Mennonite mental health centers perhaps have received more praise from non-Mennonite sources than any other venture which Mennonites have begun. Mennonites have been recognized as leaders in progressive mental health care. Prairie View received the Gold Award of the American Psychiatric Association in 1968 and Kings View the same award in 1971.[11]

While Mennonites concentrated on running their own mental health institutions as a model for others, Quakers emphasized lobbying for national mental health legislation. The three historic peace churches were partners in 1946 in forming the National Mental Health Foundation, which emphasized national education efforts on mental health.

Deaconesses in Service

Like the city missions and the hospitals of the early twentieth century, the deaconess movement among North American Mennonites was influenced by the widespread deaconess movement of Pietism. Mennonites in Europe had had congregational deaconesses since Reformation times. These were usually individual women, married or single, elected by the local congregation, who carried on pastoral work among women much as male deacons did among the men of the church.

In the nineteenth century a new model for deaconesses was developed in Germany and was successfully institutionalized in 1836 by a Lutheran pastor in Kaiserswerth named Theodor Fliedner. Fliedner was acquainted with the Mennonite deaconess work in Amsterdam, but he used as his primary organizational model the Catholic religious orders— particularly the Sisters of Mercy. The resulting structure was a sisterhood of single women who served society in the care of the poor and sick, taught both normal and retarded children, supervised orphanages and houses of correction for women prisoners, set up institutions for training women working as domestics, and served as assistant pastors in congregations. The deaconesses belonged to a "motherhouse," presided over by a deaconess mother and usually a male pastor. There most of them lived and there all could return in old age. Deaconesses did not receive salaries; the motherhouse provided them with room, board, and a small monthly allowance for personal expenses. By 1911 there were over 19,000 deaconesses in eighty motherhouses in Europe.[12]

The deaconess movement came to the United States in 1849 and grew rapidly after 1880. Nearly 150 deaconess institutions were established in the United States between 1885 and 1900, especially by the German-American religious bodies. In North America the deaconess movement was an urban movement, with deaconesses working primarily in the large cities among the urban poor—in house-to-house visiting, work among women and children, and medical services.[13]

Perhaps the first Mennonite (or rather, ex-Mennonite) to be involved in the institutionalized deaconess movement was J. Shelly Meyer, a Presbyterian pastor and a former member of First Mennonite Church in Philadelphia, whose wife, Lucy Rider Meyer, provided the impetus for starting deaconess work in the Methodist Episcopal Church in 1888.[14]

John A. Sprunger (1842-1911), a Mennonite lumber dealer from Berne, Indiana, also pioneered in deaconess work. Inspired by the European deaconess work, he founded an interdenominational deaconess home in Berne in 1890, which was moved to Chicago in the same year. Sprunger's Light and Hope Mission Society, organized in 1893, built a deaconess home and hospital in Chicago and an orphanage in Berne. Later branch hospitals were opened in Cleveland and Detroit, while deaconesses were sent to help institutions at Evansville and

Indianapolis, Indiana, and Bloomington, Illinois. (The Mennonite deaconess hospital in Bloomington related to Sprunger's
work was taken over in 1896 by Brokaw Hospital, a Methodist
institution, and has no connection with the present-day Mennonite Hospital in Bloomington.) Sprunger's work was plagued by
difficulties, however. The Cleveland hospital was destroyed by
fire in 1895; the Berne buildings burned in 1899. In 1897,
eighteen deaconesses left Sprunger's organization on doctrinal
grounds and established their own deaconess home. About 1900
the Sprunger deaconess homes were closed, and the remaining
deaconesses managed an orphanage at Berne and served as
foreign missionaries. At no time was Sprunger's work affiliated
with the General Conference Mennonite Church, although it
did receive some support from the Defenceless Mennonites
(Evangelical Mennonite Church).[15]

The deaconess work most closely connected with the
General Conference Mennonite Church was that established in
Newton, Kansas, at the initiative of David Goerz, a Russian-
born Mennonite who between 1873 and his death in 1914 served
as editor of *Zur Heimath,* secretary of the Mennonite Board of
Guardians, organizer of the Mennonite Teacher's Conference (a
predecessor of the Western District Conference), organizer of
the Mennonite Mutual Fire Insurance Company, relief worker
in India, a founder and the business manager of Bethel College,
and minister of the Halstead and Bethel College Mennonite
churches in Kansas. Goerz first suggested deaconess work to
the General Conference Mennonite Church at the 1890 conference, and the Board of Home Missions made some inquiries
about places for training deaconesses. In 1899 the issue was
brought up again at the conference session in which the wom-
en's organization took leadership. There Sara Sprunger of
Berne, Indiana, read the paper, "Deaconesses and Their Work."
When the issue came up again during the Home Mission
Board's report, Goerz asked if the conference would object if a
local area began the deaconess work on its own. No resolution
was passed, but Goerz took the delegates' comments as assent
and proceeded to start deaconess work in central Kansas.[16]

In 1900, just before Goerz left for India with a shipment of
grain to relieve the famine, he was contacted by the first deaconess candidate, seventeen-year-old Frieda Kaufman of Halstead, Kansas, who, as a child, had had contact with Lutheran
deaconesses and Catholic nuns in Germany. Goerz then "vowed
to the Lord, that if a safe return from India would be granted
him, he would give his sincere and untiring effort to the Deacon-

ess cause after his return."[17] Goerz came back from India via Russia and brought with him the first donation for American deaconess work: about $150 donated by Mennonites in Russia, who had had some deaconesses beginning in 1894.[18] Some additional funds were forthcoming, and three young women prepared for the deaconess work—first at Bethel College, then at the interdenominational deaconess hospital in Cincinnati or the Evangelical Deaconess Home and Hospital in St. Louis.

But Goerz had a hard time finding an organization to sponsor the work. From 1903 to 1911 there was much controversy about who should carry on the deaconess work: the conference, an independent organization, or individual congregations. At first the deaconess work was to come under the Bethel College Board of Directors, which organized a subsidiary Bethel Deaconess Home and Hospital Society in 1903. But "under the pressure of opposition," the society's ties with the college were severed in 1905. The Western District Conference was also approached about sponsoring the deaconess work in 1903. From 1905 to 1950 the conference had a three-member deaconess committee which was to "receive money for this work, to arrange for the training of sisters for the service in the church and general deaconess service, and in general to promote this cause according to ability." But little or no financial support came from the conference. For the most part, support of the deaconess work was through the Bethel Deaconess Home and Hospital Society, whose members consisted of donors of $50 or more. They came not only from Kansas, but also from Minnesota, Illinois, Ohio, Nebraska, Iowa, California, and South Dakota.[19]

The first three deaconesses—Frieda Kaufman, Catherine Voth, and Ida Epp—were ordained and installed on June 11, 1908, in Newton, Kansas. The majority of the sixty-six women who joined the Bethel Deaconess Home over a span of almost fifty years worked in Bethel Deaconess Hospital in Newton—as nurses, X-ray technicians, receptionists, kitchen or laundry workers, or as instructors in the Bethel Deaconess Hospital School of Nursing, although the deaconesses had always intended that some of their members be involved in work other than hospital work. Sister Gertrude Penner in 1916 served as a visiting nurse in Newton homes, a forerunner of the present public health nursing program in Harvey County, Kansas. From 1917 to 1921 she was school nurse for the Newton public schools. Sister Elfrieda Sprunger served as parish deaconess (an assistant to the pastor) at First Mennonite Church in Berne,

Indiana, for six months in 1919 while she was waiting being sent as a missionary to China. In 1921 both she and Sister Elizabeth Goertz embarked on thirty years of mission service in China and wore the deaconess garb there until the Foreign Mission Board told them to discontinue the garb. Sister Eliese Hirschler was a candidate for Jewish work in Chicago under the Home Mission Board.[20] But the number of deaconesses in Newton never grew large enough that the motherhouse felt that more could be spared from hospital work. The largest number of deaconesses at any one time was thirty.[21]

Some deaconesses were sent from the Newton motherhouse to other hospitals related to General Conference Mennonites. In 1911 a sister was stationed in Mountain Lake, Minnesota, at the request of a few friends, and in the following year the Mountain Lake hospital became a branch of the Newton organization, with two sisters stationed there. In 1930 the hospital became independent. Three sisters were lent to a hospital in American Falls, Idaho, for two years while its deaconess candidates were training in the Newton motherhouse.

In addition to Goerz, the driving force behind the early deaconess work in Newton was Sister Frieda Kaufman, deaconess mother from 1908 until her death in 1944. Full of energy, she was superintendent of the hospital until 1938; she did almost all the planning for the building of the new home for the aged; she solicited funds; she was instrumental in the plans for the student nurses' home; she helped in planning of construction and methods of operation for the Mountain Lake hospital and home; and she edited the Bethel Deaconess periodical *In the Service of the King.* A member of First Mennonite Church in Newton, she was on the building committee for that church's educational wing and organized there the first Sunday school teachers' training class in the General Conference.[22]

After her death, few women joined the Bethel deaconesses. The last two became deaconesses in 1954. In 1976 fifteen deaconesses were living either in the deaconess home or in the Bethel Home for the Aged; all were at least sixty years old.[23]

Smaller groups of deaconesses operated the Mennonite Deaconess Home and Hospital in Beatrice, Nebraska, and the Salem Deaconess Hospital in Salem, Oregon. Established in 1911, the deaconess home in Beatrice had a staff of five deaconesses in 1956.

Deaconesses always thought of themselves as missionaries, with a commitment at least equal to that of any other full-time church worker. A recruitment pamphlet of 1911 referred to the deaconess work as "this important branch of home mission."[24] "All deaconesses are missionaries," said deaconess mother Lena Mae Smith in 1976. "It was the Christian work that attracted us to the deaconesses. We didn't become nurses just to go out and earn money.

"Now," said Sister Lena Mae, "everybody in our society is so independent. A woman has to look out for herself. Women are not doing things in groups as we used to."[25]

Women in Church Vocations

The deaconess movement put women into the forefront of the mission movement, but by the end of World War II, few women were joining the deaconesses. The Western District Conference voiced its concern in 1949 by asking the General Conference executive committee to study establishing a deaconess program on the General Conference level, "to include foreign missions, home missions, relief and parish work."[26] A conference-appointed committee came to the 1950 General Conference with a recommendation that a General Conference board be designated to assume responsibility for promotion of the deaconess cause. The committee also suggested that the deaconess structure might be changed to provide for pastoral counseling, closer cooperation with the church, a broader scope of service, more opportunity for individual deaconesses to choose their own field of service, modification of the garb, clarification of the vow, shorter terms of service, a broader educational program, and a more specific enlistment program. The 1950 General Conference approved the report and assigned the deaconess concern to the new Board of Christian Service.

Other denominations were also reevaluating their deaconess programs in the early 1950s in the light of decreasing numbers of sisters. "With the exception of the Methodist deaconesses in England, the others seem to be in a similar position as ours, retaining a system which apparently does not fully meet the requirements of the present day without some changes," the General Conference deaconess committee noted in 1950.[27]

Some people blamed the shortage of deaconesses on the required dress, or the commitment to singleness, or the identification of deaconesses as nurses only, or the restrictions of a communal lifestyle. The Board of Christian Service began conversations with women particularly on ideas for a modified sisterhood of women involved in full-time church work. Deaconess mother Lena Mae Smith in Newton proposed a revised deaconess program which would work more closely with the Board of Christian Service and the Western District and would allow for "associate deaconesses" with five-year terms of service.[28] A vocations conference for young women was held in Wichita in 1955. A study commission was formed. In 1956 the General Conference sessions approved setting up an organization called "Women in Church Vocations" to "provide a form of ministry for women within the church."[29]

On May 24, 1959, the first four members of Women in Church Vocations were commissioned at Mennonite Biblical Seminary: Virginia Claassen as a teacher of missionaries' children in Japan, Martha Giesbrecht Janzen as a missionary in Japan, and Cornelia Lehn and Muriel Thiessen (Stackley) as writers and editors under the Board of Education and Publication.

At first, qualifications for Women in Church Vocations (WCV) included a college degree plus a year of seminary training. An annual conference of WCV members provided "inspiration and fellowship."[30] Gradually, in an effort to attract more women to the program, the membership boundaries were relaxed to include secretaries or virtually any woman working for the church in some way, and the college degree was no longer mandatory. In late 1961 the Board of Christian Service voted to discontinue membership recruitment and commissioning, and the program became a generalized encouragement of both young women and men to consider church-related vocations. In evaluating the problems of Women in Church Vocations, the Board of Christian Service asked, "If we really are honest, have we created an organization, but not properly created a ministry?"[31]

The General Conference had tried to make the deaconess program more appealing to women by making it more individualistic: women were no longer under the authority of the deaconess mother; no lifetime commitment to a particular job or to singleness was implied; practically any form of service within the church was acceptable for the program. But, in the end, the conference made Women in Church Vocations so individualistic that the program could not hold together. It came to demand so little of its members that it offered few benefits. The commitment to a Christian lifestyle and to Christian service which the deaconesses had embodied was now being lived out in a different manner in a different program: voluntary service.

War and Relief

Both voluntary service and relief programs of the Mennonite churches were deeply affected by World Wars I and II. During World War I, Mennonites had been reluctant to wear the army uniform, but they were willing to give money and material aid to relieve war suffering. A few young people had served with the American Friends Service Committee reconstruction units in France and with the American Committee for Relief in the Near East. The war spirit and the pressures of conscription and the war bond drives, especially in the United States, had put Mennonites—who were both German and pacifist—on the defensive. In Canada the government had recently restricted the immigration of Mennonites.[32] In the aftermath of the war, Mennonites of all branches were eager to prove themselves as responsible citizens who cared about the rest of the world and who could respond to hunger and want in time of peace as well as in time of war.[33]

The new emphasis on relief work found expression in 1920 in the organization of Mennonite Central Committee, the first long-term inter-Mennonite organization to receive the cooperation of so many Mennonite groups. The occasion for organization was the famine relief in Russia which affected Mennonites in South Russia as well as others. The first relief goods and workers were sent to the Mennonite settlements of Chortitza, Halbstadt, and Gnadenfeld. A portion of General Conference relief funds between the two World Wars was channeled through Mennonite Central Committee (between 1938 and 1950 ranging from 10 to 80 percent).

General Conference aid went to both Mennonites and others. The 1938 report of the Emergency Relief Board told of aid to Mennonite families in Canada who were new immigrants and had experienced heavy debts because of sickness; to Mennonites in Mexico and Paraguay; to mission fields in China, India, and American cities; to a child-feeding program in war-torn Spain.[34] But the giving of relief involved mostly the giving of money, not of personal time on the part of the General Conference constituency. Only a few General Conference Mennonites went overseas, for example, to distribute relief goods in the period between the World Wars. Only twenty-eight Mennonites of all groups had served under Mennonite Central Committee before 1941.[35] The goods were distributed either by General Conference missionaries already at the location or through other relief agencies.

Not until World War II were large numbers of people mobilized in the cause of relief and service. In 1941-47 eight hundred twenty-eight General Conference Mennonite men served in the United States in Civilian Public Service camps, in work in hospitals for the sick in body and mind, and in other work, most of which could be considered Christian service. In Canada, over 10,000 conscientious objectors served in forestry or farm assignments in 1941-46, about 72 percent of them Mennonites. The exact number of General Conference Mennonites in alternative service work in Canada is not known. By May 1, 1947, sixty-one General Conference Mennonite men and women were involved in relief and service work through Mennonite Central Committee, in postwar reconstruction in Europe, China, India, South America, Puerto Rico, and Gulfport, Mississippi. Dollars were being given for relief in unprecedented amounts, but more than that, people were giving of their time in service at needy places far from the concentrated Mennonite settlements.

Relief work, said Henry A. Fast, chairman of the Emergency Relief Board in 1947, "stimulated among us an interest in the people being served. Never had our people on so wide a scale identified themselves intimately with such a variety of people." With more personal involvement in serving the needs of the poor, Mennonites gained a new appreciation of the meaning and power of service "in the name of Christ."[36]

World War II improved Mennonites' vision of the world in need. That vision was expressed in the 1950s, not only with expanded overseas mission and service programs, but with expanded North American programs. Mennonite young men doing alternative service to the military had discovered new areas of need—for sanitary privies in Florida and Mississippi, for humane mental hospitals across the continent. Mennonites had discovered that lay people—not just ordained ministers or missionaries—could help meet those needs.

One result of that new vision in North America was Mennonite Disaster Service, a lay-led, almost ad hoc organization to help those suffering from natural disasters such as tornadoes and floods. The first local unit was organized in Hesston, Kansas, in 1950. MDS later got international coordination under the auspices of Mennonite Central Committee; however, it has always gained its strength from its grass-roots nature, depending on men and women to leave their homes or jobs for a few days or even months to help those who need immediate disaster aid. Although MDS has worked closely with the Red Cross and government agencies, including the U.S. National Guard, it was seen as an alternative to Mennonite participation in civil defense programs.[37]

The second major result of the new vision for service in North America was the development of voluntary service, which since World War II has mobilized thousands of Mennonites—mostly young lay people—to become acquainted with human need and to try to do something about it.

The Beginnings of the Voluntary Service Idea

Mennonites have been pioneers in the organization of voluntary service programs, setting up programs which many other agencies, both private and public, use as a model. However, Mennonites themselves were influenced to begin voluntary service by a number of factors.

The first influence on Mennonite voluntary service was the long history of volunteer workers at Mennonite city missions and Indian missions. Scores of workers served as short-term missionaries on the Home Mission Board payroll; others served without pay. The 1920 report of the Home Mission Board, for example, listed thirteen mission workers on the board payroll and thirty-three volunteer workers in city missions. In the first ten years of the Twenty-sixth Street Mission in Chicago, only four of thirty-six workers served longer than two years. Twenty-eight served one year or less.[38] But the Home Mission Board did not organize the volunteer work centrally. There was no central recruitment for voluntary workers, and not every mission had such workers. A structured program of voluntary service was formed only after the Mennonites experienced being pacifists in wartime.

Both long-term (one year or more) and short-term voluntary service as organized programs had their origins in World War I. Long-term voluntary service grew out of the experience of the American Friends Service Committee, which had established reconstruction units in France soon after the AFSC's founding in 1917. In 1920 the AFSC created the Home Service Section to provide for young people and others a way of giving a year or two of service in dealing with social problems in North America. Together with the desire to serve was coupled the desire of pacifists to prove themselves responsible and sensitive to social needs, even though they did not take responsibility for military defense of the nation. The AFSC's 1925-26 annual report noted that such service was "in direct opposition to the idea that patriotism or loyalty to one's country can be expressed only in time of war." The report continued, "The real conscientious objector is the last person in the world to shun social responsibility."[39] By 1936 the Friends had sixty-eight volunteers in twenty institutions in eleven states: in detention homes, migrant work centers, health camps, settlement houses, mining towns, and Negro schools.

Another influence on Mennonite voluntary service was the summer work camp, which also started in the aftermath of World War I. The first work camps were begun in France about 1920 by a young Swiss named Pierre Ceresole. Ceresole's organization, Service Civil International, sometimes dubbed the "pick-and-shovel brigade," set up work camps to rebuild houses which had been damaged during World War I. The work camps were intended for convinced pacifists who wanted to show that their concern to do constructive work was as strong as that of the soldier to do destructive work.[40]

The American Friends Service Committee took Ceresole's secular work camp idea and began sponsoring its own work camps in the United States. The AFSC's first work camp in 1934 attracted fifty-six campers, all paying their own way. The program expanded to include thirteen summer work camps by 1946. While building playgrounds, painting buildings, constructing a reservoir, or clearing land, work campers were taught about economic and social injustice and came to know individual poor people.

Among the Mennonites acquainted with Quaker voluntary service were Carl J. and Martha Graber Landes. Carl Landes, former pastor of the First Mennonite Church in Philadelphia, had begun work in June 1936 under the American Friends Service Committee, doing community work among resettled coal miners in Orient, Pennsylvania. In the summer of 1938, under the auspices of the Mennonite Peace Society (a forerunner of the Mennonite Central Committee Peace Section) and the Central Conference mission board, Landes led the first Mennonite-sponsored work camp, at the Twenty-sixth Street Mennonite Mission in Chicago. In this "Volunteer Community Citizenship Camp," fourteen participants, eighteen years and older, spent the month of July surveying the neighborhood, painting the church building, and building recreation equipment for children in the mornings. The afternoons and sometimes evenings were spent in field trips or study of nonviolence, alternative service possibilities, relief programs, and peace education. Work campers published a mimeographed newsletter, which included editorials on nonviolence as more than passive submission.[41]

Other Mennonites became acquainted with the work camp idea through participation in the work camps of the American Friends Service Committee and the Fellowship of Reconciliation in the late 1930s and early 1940s. Henry A. Fast had attended an AFSC volunteer orientation. Robert S. Kreider, William Stauffer, and Donovan Smucker were in AFSC work camps. Smucker was part of the first AFSC work camp in 1934 at Westmoreland Homesteads, Mount Pleasant, Pennsylvania, where the AFSC had set up cooperative gardens, canneries, and stores to support unemployed coal miners. "Westmoreland was the prototype project for CPS-VS," he said.[42] Elmer Ediger and Edna Ramseyer (Kaufman) participated in work camps of the Fellowship of Reconciliation.

The FOR work camp in which Ediger participated was billed as an "opportunity to experiment with the full application of Christian love in the slums of New York City. The people will live and learn in the context of an *ashram*, or communal village." The work camp combined a recreation program for the children of the Harlem neighborhood with education of the work campers in the ways of nonviolence. The work camp also included nonviolent direct action to end racial discrimination. The peace teaching that Ediger's Bethel College education had given him in theory, the work camp gave him in practice. When Ediger participated a few years later in the shaping of the Civilian Public Service program for conscientious objectors during World War II and, after the war, in developing the idea of Mennonite voluntary service, his work camp experience served him as a model, both in service and in group life.[43]

The Mennonite Witness for Peace

The service idea was growing slowly in the shadow of impending war. But World War II and military conscription in both the United States and Canada hurried the development of some organized service for peace, within governmental restrictions. In Canada, conscientious objectors were required to serve in national parks and fire prevention until the order in council was amended in 1943 and 1944 and agricultural and other employment was permitted as alternative service. In the U.S. alternative service was conducted primarily through Civilian Public Service (CPS) camps, with a few conscientious objectors allowed to serve outside of camps in agriculture, mental hospitals, public health, and so forth. Mennonites, Brethren, and Friends cooperated with the U.S. Selective Service System in setting up the CPS units, and Mennonites like Elmer Ediger tried to incorporate into the government-regulated camps as many of their ideals as possible. Also influencing alternative service during World War II was Mennonites' experience with forestry service in Russia as an alternative to the military.

The alternative service experiences of the war broadened the horizons of Mennonites. Conscientious objectors who had hardly left the farm before the war had found distressed and oppressed people in North America with whom rank-and-file Mennonites had had little previous contact. The war had brought General Conference Mennonites out of secluded communities and had given them contacts not only with other Mennonite groups, but with the rest of their society.

As Mennonites were looking farther beyond their ethnic and geographical boundaries, they were also looking more deeply within—examining their theological roots. They were discovering that what governments had been compelling them to do in service to humanity, their spiritual forebears—the sixteenth-century Anabaptists—had been compelled by the Holy Spirit to do. The educational programs of the Mennonite CPS camps had taught the Anabaptist theology of discipleship, just then being restated and popularized by Harold S. Bender, Donovan Smucker, and others. Mennonites were rediscovering the vision of the church as:

> the community of professing servants, whose mission was to call men to discipleship, in proclamation, in service and offered fellowship. They were the community of people who care. Just as God had once dared to risk His Son, the church could now dare to give herself fully for her neighbors.[44]

World War II had also taught General Conference Mennonites that the peace position was weaker in their congregations than they had thought. Some Mennonites saw the need for a program which would teach as well as provide an outlet for the peace witness.

Some of the younger Mennonites who had been in alternative service or who had served in the prewar work camps came to the end of the war with a vision for continuation of service for peace after the end of the war. They wanted to put into practice their vision of the church, as well as to show their fellow citizens that Mennonites were not just *against* war, but *for* peace and service, that Mennonites were willing voluntarily to contribute to the well-being of the nation in peaceful rather than military ways. "Why witness . . . only when coerced by the state—why not do it without the compulsion, save for the love of Christ?" these Mennonites asked.[45]

Organizing the Vision

The vision for a peacetime peace witness took organizational form in Mennonite voluntary service programs. The first to establish voluntary service programs were Mennonite Central Committee and Mennonite Board of Missions and Charities (Mennonite Church) in 1944 and the General Conference Mennonite Church in 1946. (The Mennonite Brethren Church established a separate Christian service program in 1960.)

The transition from wartime alternative service to voluntary service was not automatic. After World War I, Mennonite Central Committee and the conferences had neglected energetic teaching on peace and service, and some conference leaders thought that would happen again after World War II. The General Conference's Committee of Seven disbanded after World War I, and a peace committee was not formed until 1926. But this time some of the people who had been through the earlier work camps and through CPS were determined to see a peace witness continue past the end of World War II. Through persuasion and negotiation, voluntary service programs were approved by the governing boards of both the Mennonite Central Committee and the General Conference.

The General Conference executive committee then gave administration of the voluntary service program jointly to the Peace Committee and to the Young People's Union, then an organization of young adults up to age thirty. The aims of the MCC and General Conference programs, both of which Elmer Ediger helped to organize, were to benefit the people served, the people serving, and the sending church. Voluntary service was to provide projects to help alleviate human need, tension, and spiritual confusion; to provide a means of testifying more widely to the gospel and its way of love and nonresistance; to provide a channel of service for young people; and to provide an experience of internship in Christian service through which more individuals might be led to enter full-time ministry or missionary service.[46] Voluntary service was to help young people learn what it meant to be part of a believers' church, after the manner of the Anabaptist vision. An article written for the 1956 General Conference Yearbook summarized the vision for voluntary service:

> In a day when much Christianity is creedal, verbal, and without the cross, such discipleship also witnesses to the conscience of many nominal Christians . . . For Christian young people here is a way to fulfill a responsibility to help meet the welfare needs of

the larger society. This is a way of reaching out of our secluded comfortable community life to multiply the number of "missionaries" going from our midst into the world.[47]

The First Voluntary Service Units

Beginning in 1944 Mennonite Central Committee, on behalf of all cooperating Mennonite groups, organized summer voluntary service for women at Ypsilanti, Michigan, and Howard, Rhode Island, in connection with the work men were doing in mental hospitals in Civilian Public Service. In addition, MCC began looking ahead to the possible end of the war by setting up CPS camps involved in projects which could be continued during peacetime. MCC established public health units in 1943 in Mulberry, Florida, and in 1945 in Gulfport, Mississippi. Most of the work involved building sanitary privies in poor black areas. After 1947 the Gulfport unit was turned over from CPS administration to voluntary service administration within MCC.

After the war MCC set up additional summer and longterm voluntary service units. In 1947, for example, MCC had six summer units involving seventy-three women and nineteen men, all college age or older. By 1950, two years before the United States again began drafting conscientious objectors, MCC had established twenty-five service units, about half connected with hospitals, for 240 people in service in North America. Sixty-six of these people were in longer-term units. MCC began overseas voluntary service, called *Pax*, the Latin word for "peace," in 1951.

Within MCC, the new voluntary service program simply took over the administrative machinery of MCC-administered Civilian Public Service. Elmer Ediger, the last CPS director for MCC, continued as director of MCC voluntary service until 1951.

The General Conference sponsored its first voluntary service unit in the summer of 1946, with nine young adult volunteers working with the three Chicago Mennonite missions—First, Grace, and Woodlawn. They served primarily as vacation Bible school teachers and youth activity leaders at public playgrounds. The General Conference Home Mission Board provided funds for room and board. The voluntary service committee, of which Elmer Ediger was chairman, sponsored four units the next summer: the Chicago project; vacation Bible school teaching and other work at the Northern Cheyenne mission in Lame Deer, Montana; a Mennonite youth team which itinerated among the Indiana and Illinois churches; and a Canadian-U.S. youth exchange team. Every summer since then, summer service projects have been sponsored by the conference with the number of volunteers eighteen years and older reaching as high as 153 in 1960.

For the first ten years of the General Conference voluntary service program's existence, voluntary service opportunities were offered only in the summer in projects ranging in length from one to twelve weeks. Those who wanted longer terms of service in North America or abroad served through Mennonite Central Committee. In 1953, for example, about 200 General Conference people were in voluntary service, only about a quarter of them in General Conference summer service. The rest were about equally divided among MCC summer service, North American longer-term service, and foreign service.

General Conference summer service differed from MCC summer service primarily in the fact that most of the GC summer units were directly related to General Conference missions—about two-thirds of the service projects in 1956.[48] Locations varied from rural settings like Oraibi, Arizona, or Camp Friedenswald, Michigan, to urban settings like East Harlem Protestant Parish in New York City and the Bethel Mennonite Church in Winnipeg. Some summer volunteers even went overseas to Colombia.

Women dominated summer service. Every year since its beginning, General Conference summer service has had a majority of women, with the ratio of women to men sometimes running about seven to one. Until June 1957 the voluntary service directors were women: Bertha Fast (Harder) in 1947 and 1950, Erna Friesen (Graber) in 1948-49, Edith Claassen (Graber) in 1951-52, and Leola Schultz in 1952-57.

Beginning in the late 1950s the Board of Christian Service developed several new approaches to short-term service. Winter service opportunities, averaging about a month, were developed to appeal to adults who might have more time to give in the winter.[49] Weekend work camps, known as "WE-Service," brought young people from Mennonite churches and colleges to cities like Wichita for one-day work projects, beginning about 1957. Other weekend work camps tried to give exposure to the urban environment and its opportunities for service and vocations. The voluntary service office also developed "earning units" to attract college students who could not afford to spend the summer in a totally "voluntary" project. In locations like North Battleford, Saskatchewan, volunteers could earn money

in the provincial mental hospital while living in a unit house
and relating to the Mennonite church there. In 1960 this earning service was called the *Students-in-Industry* program. It was
a three-month program of study, work, and group life for seminary students, high school teachers, and upper-level college
students. Fourteen participated in 1960.

The new approach to short-term service which was pur-
sued with the most enthusiasm was the teenage work camp. In
1956 the Young People's Union, meeting in connection with the
General Conference triennial sessions in Winnipeg, encouraged the Board of Christian Service to begin voluntary
service for high-school-age youth the following summer. The
new program, later called "Servanthood Work Camps," began
with only one project a year—usually construction work at a
Mennonite campground. A General Conference report described the teenage work camps as combining "six hours of
rigorous work with the joys of simple living, cooperative housekeeping, and roughing it. Planned periods of discussions, worship, prayer, and Bible study put depth into group living."[50]

The teenage work camps became more popular than summer service for older youth and adults. By 1966 more participated in senior high work camps than in regular summer service,
and in 1967, 355 work campers and their leaders participated.
Since that time, staff has not given as much priority to work
camps, but they continue to draw 110 to 160 work campers and
leaders annually. The Mennonite Voluntary Service office and
the youth office of the Commission on Education now take joint
responsibility for administering the teenage work camps as
both a service and an educational experience for youth. As a
rule, work campers pay their own transportation and room and
board. The 1977 work camps for teenagers included experiences
in theater (Kansas City, Kansas), community living (Koinonia
Partners, Americus, Georgia), work with the mentally retarded
(Wheat Ridge, Colorado), and work in an inner-city community
center (Hamilton, Ontario).

Meanwhile, participation in college-age summer service
has dwindled since the 1960s, now involving less than twenty
people annually, excluding work camp leaders. Most summer
service workers are now placed in existing long-term units
rather than in special summer units.

Long-term Service Units

Long-term voluntary service in the General Conference
Mennonite Church developed slowly. At first, volunteers who

wanted longer terms of service were referred to Mennonite
Central Committee's program. But MCC's stated policy, encouraged by some other Mennonite groups, was not to under-
take voluntary service projects in locations where there were
Mennonite churches. The General Conference units were developed precisely to tie in longer-term volunteers with city missions and Indian missions, and also to provide a uniquely
General Conference channel for service that could be more
closely related to local and district programs.

As early as 1947 the General Conference Peace Committee
was discussing the possibility of one or two year-round volun-
tary service projects. But it was 1955 before the first two "mis-
sions Paxmen" were sent to Congo (now Zaire) to work with
Congo Inland Mission, and 1957 before the first two North
American long-term units—Gulfport, Mississippi, and
Cuauhtémoc, Chihuahua, Mexico—came under the General
Conference.

Within a year the General Conference had five long-term
voluntary service units. The Chicago unit related to a city
mission church. The Lame Deer, Montana, unit related to the
Cheyenne mission work. In Rosthern, Saskatchewan, volunteers worked on a farm which supported a home for handicapped and retarded persons, a project sponsored by
Saskatchewan Mennonite churches. Two other projects—
Gulfport and Cuauhtémoc—were transferred to the General
Conference from Mennonite Central Committee, but both had
some previous connections with the General Conference. In the
case of the Mexico unit, General Conference Board of Missions
was already involved with a small church of German-speaking
Mennonites from Russia. The Gulfport unit was led by General
Conference workers Orlo and Edna Kaufman. From 1957 to
1965 the number of long-term volunteers serving under the
General Conference stayed between sixteen and thirty-four,
with the majority of long-term workers serving under MCC
programs at home or abroad. In 1964, for example, only thirty-
two volunteers were serving in General Conference long-term
service, while fifty-eight General Conference Mennonites were
serving in MCC's North American voluntary service.[51] The
largest Mennonite voluntary service program in North
America was under the Mennonite Board of Missions and
Charities (MC), which had begun its first long-term unit in
1948.[52]

A long-term voluntary service assignment generally
meant living in one house with other volunteers, sharing all

income and household duties, and receiving as compensation room, board, transportation, medical expenses, and a small monthly allowance—at first $15, later $30 for a first-year volunteer.

Gulfport

At least 80 percent of General Conference long-term voluntary service units have been located near or worked directly with General Conference churches and missions. Others provided workers for ongoing institutions initiated by agencies other than voluntary service. The Gulfport unit neither attempted to start a General Conference church nor identified itself with a particular institution. It simply came to serve a poor and racially segregated community in southern Mississippi.

Part of the Gulfport unit's uniqueness stemmed from its origins with Mennonite Central Committee. The unit began in 1945 as one of the last Civilian Public Service camps set up during World War II. It had the task of building sanitary privies in Harrison County. Outside the city limits of Gulfport were houses of poor, all-black North Gulfport, where many houses lacked sanitary facilities, and hookworm and typhus thrived in the unsanitary conditions. As the war ended and CPS was phased out, the Gulfport unit received MCC summer service volunteers and, after a special meeting of MCC approved the new voluntary service program in late 1946, became MCC's first long-term voluntary service unit in North America.

The central forces behind the program of the Gulfport unit were Orlo and Edna Goering Kaufman, General Conference Mennonites from the Eden Mennonite Church near Moundridge, Kansas, who served in Gulfport from 1947 to 1975. Edna was a graduate of McPherson (Kansas) College, a Church of the Brethren institution. Orlo had graduated from Bethel College (Kansas) and Garrett Theological Seminary in Chicago. They began their service in Gulfport under Mennonite Central Committee and continued in Gulfport after MCC turned the project over to the General Conference boards of Christian Service and Missions.

The Gulfport unit was located just outside the city—first at Camp Bernard, then after 1947 at Camp Landon, where the volunteers were housed in old army barracks. After completion of the health and sanitation project, the Camp Landon unit focused its program on activities for children and support and development of existing black institutions; that is, the churches and the schools. Camp Landon sponsored boys' and girls' clubs, shop classes, and sewing classes. Volunteers taught in released-time Bible classes in the black public schools and organized summer Bible schools, which black churches then lacked. Volunteers built chairs and tables for the almost totally unequipped black churches and schools and built playgrounds throughout the county. Beginning in 1953 the Camp Landon unit leased a building in North Gulfport as a Christian Community Center for children. It began a library there in 1954 and a swimming pool across the street with the aid of a new organization it helped to start: the Good Deeds Association. The unit arranged for "fresh-air" visits of black children to white Mennonite farm families in Kansas, South Dakota, and Ohio. In later years, volunteers served as teachers to integrate the faculty of the all-black North Gulfport school.

Formal ministries to adults were fewer: the radio program known as the "Sunday School Class of the Air," help in organizing a Community Action Program to receive federal Office of Economic Opportunity funds, and in establishing a credit union in 1966.

Over the thirty years of the Gulfport unit's existence, 68 CPS men and 371 VS workers served there—with terms ranging from a few weeks to two years. In the absence of a General Conference church or mission to which to relate, the voluntary service unit gained continuity through long-term personnel. These people were Orlo and Edna Kaufman and Harold and Rosella Wiens Regier, who served in 1953-55 and 1961-70. Primarily through the Kaufmans and Regiers, Camp Landon related to adults of the community and tried to serve as reconcilers between blacks and whites in a time of high tension over segregation issues.

The Gulfport unit had begun its work among poor whites and poor blacks, but in 1953 came the decision that Camp Landon would minister to blacks and the Wayside Mission to whites. The Wayside Mission—later named *Crossroads Mennonite Church*—had grown out of a Sunday school started by the nearby Gulfhaven Mennonite Church (MC). Although voluntary service workers at Camp Landon did direct their efforts toward blacks, Kaufmans and Regiers strove to maintain contact with the white community. Harold Regier and Orlo Kaufman were members of both the black Interdenominational Ministerial Alliance and the white Gulfcoast Ministerial Association and promoted a few joint meetings of the organizations. Regiers sponsored private interracial dinners in their home.

Even the relatively quiet witness of the Mennonite program in Gulfport brought angry reactions from whites who favored racial segregation. When a young black woman became a voluntary service worker in summer 1959, suddenly all voluntary service workers were refused service at coffee shops, ice cream stands, and filling stations. The Mississippi State Sovereignty Commission, formed to uphold segregation, visited Camp Landon in November 1959 as a part of a statewide investigation into "communist" activities. The White Citizen's Council investigated Camp Landon in 1964, and Camp Landon received a bomb threat after hosting an integrated dinner in 1968.

However, except on one occasion, Camp Landon staff and volunteers did not join in direct action in the civil rights movement.[53] In order not to jeopardize their program, they determined that their witness was through a long-term Christian presence of white people who could be friends with black people. Amos Crouch, a resident of North Gulfport, commented, "One very real benefit that has been derived in this community from the Camp Landon staff and its activities is to make people comfortable and at ease with white people."[54]

One area in which they did take risks with a stand for racial integration was in church. Camp Landon staff, although involved during the week with blacks, attended church on Sunday with whites at the Crossroads Mennonite Church, where Camp Landon personnel held positions as Sunday school teachers and song leaders. After pressure from Camp Landon and the denominational agencies of the Mennonite Church and the General Conference Mennonite Church, the Crossroads Church voted in 1968 to open its doors to all races. Regier became pastor in 1969 and attempted "to show that the Mennonite view of the church was a viable alternative in the South." But a charter family left the church, attendance declined, Regiers left in 1970, and worship services were discontinued in summer 1971.

By the late 1960s the voluntary service program of Camp Landon was searching for new directions. Summer Bible schools had been turned over to the black churches. The community center was under the direction of the Good Deeds Association. Federal poverty programs were meeting some of the needs which Camp Landon had met earlier. Released-time Bible classes in the schools had ended in 1966 because of white opposition. The primary involvement of volunteers was through teaching in the black public school. A team of administrators from the General Conference and the Central District Conference recommended closing the unit unless work could be started in forming a new Mennonite church in Gulfport. Personnel for that task was not found, and Camp Landon closed in 1976.

David Haury's history of Camp Landon, commissioned by the Commission on Home Ministries in 1976, commented on the unit's contributions:

> Orlo Kaufman believes that Camp Landon probably brought more benefits to the Mennonites who served there than to the people of North Gulfport they served. VSers often had very meaningful experiences which produced new outlooks not only on the problems of poverty and injustice, which they first encountered while at Camp Landon, but also on their own roles as Christian servants. Moreover, the unequaled fellowship in living, working, and worshiping as a unit revitalized the meaning of faith and the church for many VSers. For most VSers this was their first acquaintance with blacks, segregation, and the South, and Camp Landon was very important simply as a learning center.[55]

Haury evaluated Camp Landon not as "a simple VS project but exhibiting many characteristics of a foreign mission." [56] Yet Camp Landon personnel chose to cooperate rather than compete with the existing black churches and no General Conference church was ever established. The benefit was greater acceptance by black leadership in North Gulfport because of service without strings attached. Yet the drawbacks of that strategy were the lack of a Mennonite church in which blacks could feel welcome and learn to know the words behind the Mennonites' deeds, and the identification of Mennonitism with whiteness. Even Camp Landon's witness against racial discrimination did not dispel the idea among many North Gulfport residents that only whites were Mennonites.

Service Sponsored by Regions

The Conference of Mennonites in Canada first had a Board of Christian Service after the reorganization of its boards in 1956. With a few exceptions, the Canadian board did not sponsor voluntary service projects itself, but supported the voluntary service programs of the General Conference and Mennonite Central Committee. In 1957 about 40 percent of the budget of the Canadian Board of Christian Service went to the General Conference Board of Christian Service. In addition to its other work in peace and mutual aid, the Canadian board also promoted voluntary service at Fort Vermilion, a northern Alberta settlement of Old Colony and Sommerfelder Mennonites.

A nursing station was built and teachers were sent for public schools which the more traditional Mennonites attended.[57]

In other areas as well, congregations or groups of congregations organized social service programs and recruited workers on a voluntary service basis. The Crossroads Center, an inner-city community center in Winnipeg, began in 1970, initiated by a group of concerned individuals from several Winnipeg congregations. The Charleswood and Home Street Mennonite churches each supported a volunteer, beginning in 1970. John Brenneman, a member of First Mennonite Church in Lima, Ohio, set up a summer service project in 1976 under his congregation's sponsorship. By 1974, twenty General Conference congregations sponsored or helped to sponsor nursery schools or day-care centers.[58]

The Board of Christian Service tried to encourage this kind of local voluntary service by the placement of a board staff person, Walter Paetkau, in the Fraser Valley of British Columbia in 1965-70. Paetkau's assignment was to help local congregations in Alberta, British Columbia, Washington, and Oregon discover ways of witness and service at home. Among the new projects started at his initiative were Twin Firs, a receiving home for socially disadvantaged youth, sponsored by Mennonite churches in British Columbia; a "candy-striper" MVS corps in the Cottage Private Hospital near Abbotsford, British Columbia; Matsqui-Sumas-Abbotsford (MSA) Community Services; and some voluntary service projects which MCC (Canada) administered.[59] After the conference reorganization in 1968, the new Commission on Home Ministries continued the theme of congregational involvement in service with an emphasis on "living, active congregations."

Beyond Alternative Service

In the United States, most Mennonites connected "voluntary" service with a compulsory program: conscription for the military or alternative service. Mennonites had set up their voluntary service programs not only to provide a channel for Christian witness, but also to provide a church-controlled alternative to the military, in the event of a renewal of the military draft. The 1950 General Conference voted to endorse voluntary service as the type of program it wanted for its young people "in case they are being drafted." [60]

As the U.S. government was considering conscription legislation in 1950 and 1951, Mennonites and other peace churches petitioned the government for a program under civilian direction in which men could be assigned overseas as well as in the United States, in which they could receive wages, where churches would be allowed to hold religious services, and in which men could serve under a variety of agencies: the church or service agency's regular program, a church-related special program for conscientious objectors, a government-sponsored program, or civilian employment in fields in the interest of the national health and welfare.[61] The lack of some of these options had been a sore point among Mennonites in the Civilian Public Service program of World War II.

The Universal Military Training and Service Act, approved by the U.S. Congress June 19, 1951, went into effect in July 1952 with most of the provisions for which the peace churches had petitioned. The classification given to conscientious objectors doing two-year alternative service was "1-W." Such men had the option of working in church-related voluntary service programs or finding their own jobs which qualified under Selective Service regulations. Under the latter option, a 1-W man could find a job as a hospital orderly, for example, draw the same wage as anyone else in a similar job, pocket the money, and live as connected or unconnected to the church as he wished.

The GC Board of Christian Service, seeking to give guidance to drafted men (generally ages nineteen to twenty-six), outlined four possible service choices for men in 1951, shortly after the draft law was passed. Overseas *Pax* and voluntary service were the two preferred ways of doing 1-W service. Getting less enthusiastic endorsement were the 1-W mission option (described as a commitment to contribute monthly one's net earnings toward an ongoing mission or service program of one's choice, or to turn over the whole paycheck to the church in return for room, board, travel, and twenty-five dollars a month allowance—almost the same financial arrangements as in voluntary service) and 1-W earning service, in which men kept their entire wages.[62]

Although the conference preferred drafted men to take options one and two, it also encouraged young men in options three and four, since those were also conscientious objector positions not connected with the military. The Board of Christian Service recognized that the peace position had been too long taken for granted in the General Conference and that GC churches had been lacking in education for peace. In both the United States and Canada, the majority of Mennonite young men drafted during World War II had entered the military.

Now, spurred on by the recovery of the Anabaptist vision and its witness against killing in war, the Board of Christian Service called a conference April 10-11, 1953, at the Eden Mennonite Church near Moundridge, Kansas, to discuss "The Church, the Gospel, and War." Out of that conference came a reaffirmation of the church's historic peace position, a rededication to strengthening the peace position in the General Conference, and a call to the total Christian church to "take its hands off the sword, abandon the theories of the just war and of the lesser evil, and, through the grace of God, summon its members to a ministry of forgiveness, suffering love, and trusting faith."[63] Some speakers at the Eden conference wondered whether nonresistance was really a part of Mennonites' Christian beliefs and practice or whether it was simply a matter of social culture. "In looking back over my own experience in Mennonite communities, including both eastern and western Canada, there is little recollection of nonresistance having been stressed or that it was a significant part of the daily attitudes in Mennonite groups," said conference speaker John C. Sawatzky. "It is known that there is a heritage of nonresistance and this distinguished Mennonites from other Protestant churches for centuries. Many of us have rested our consciences on this heritage, assume that we have sort of inherited this belief, and have not found it necessary to develop the essential underlying personal faith."[64]

A Canadian peace study conference was held in Winnipeg in 1954 as a follow-up to the Eden Conference. Like the Eden Conference, it, too, expanded Mennonites' definition of nonresistance. One young man said after the conference, "Man! I learned a lot these days. I always believed in nonresistance, but I never knew there was so much to it!" The conference stressed the biblical basis of nonresistance and its relationship to the gospel. The doctrine of peace, in many Mennonites' eyes, grew beyond being a "Mennonite distinctive" to becoming a part of the total missionary message. P. U. Giesbrecht of Homewood, Manitoba, wrote following the conference, "If, as the case is, this is a biblical doctrine, and not merely a tradition of Mennonites, it has been learned that it is our duty to teach others also. Not only ourselves or our children, but also our neighbor, our fellow Christians. This we have failed to do."[65]

Both the Canadian and General Conference boards of Christian Service gave priority in the 1950s and following to peace education within the congregations. Brochures were written and distributed. Encouragement was given to Henry A.

Fast to publish *Jesus and Human Conflict,* a statement of the
biblical basis for nonresistance, not resting "primarily on certain 'proof texts.' ... Instead it [nonresistance] is so inseparably
bound up with the character and will of God as revealed in
Christ Jesus and supremely in His way of the cross that no one
can well deny its claim without repudiating to that extent his
faith in God and His way for man." [66]

The Canadian Board of Christian Service attempted a
peace registration of all draft-age Mennonite young people. The
GC Board of Christian Service sent predraft mailings to
General Conference teenagers—first boys only, then to both
sexes. The board sponsored preservice training schools for men
about to enter 1-W service, beginning in 1960. Predraft "boot
camps" were developed, beginning in the Western District Conference, to educate seventeen-year-old boys about the church's
peace teaching and alternative service options. In 1971, just
before the U.S. draft ended, nine such peace training camps
were held in four U.S. districts and the Canadian Conference.

New General Conference statements on peace elaborated
on and expanded the 1941 Souderton statement on war and
peace, with a major new statement, "The Way of Peace," being
adopted by the 1971 General Conference in Fresno, California.

The educational efforts toward conscientious objection had
some effect in the General Conference. Although the United
States as a whole had fewer conscientious objectors in the early
1950s than during World War II, the percentage of General
Conference conscientious objectors increased from about 27
percent in 1944 to 47 percent in 1957.[67] A much larger number of
Mennonites than men from any other church group registered
as conscientious objectors. From 1952 to 1962, 70 percent of the
13,769 men who served as 1-Ws were Mennonites.[68] But far
fewer 1-W men were serving in church-related voluntary service than in 1-W earning service. When the 1-W program began,
Mennonite Central Committee had estimated that 30 percent
would serve in voluntary service and Pax, but the actual figure
in 1957 was only 15 percent, among all Mennonite groups.[69]
Among General Conference Mennonites the percentage was
higher, with about 25 percent of 1-Ws in church-related programs in 1955. That percentage increased to 43 percent by
1967. The result was a scattering of Mennonite "earning 1-Ws"
across the United States independent of any connection with
the church. In 1954, for example, 113 General Conference 1-Ws
worked in Denver; 53 in Topeka, Kansas; 14 in Ypsilanti, Michigan; 13 in Kansas City, Kansas; and 11 in Chicago. The other

214 General Conference 1-Ws were scattered: four in one state, nine in another.[70]

At first, the various Mennonite groups and MCC tried to provide pastoral care for the scattered 1-W men, just as they had to the CPS men in camps during World War II. Where Mennonite 1-Ws were concentrated in a city, MCC bought unit houses in which 1-Ws could choose to live, local pastors related to the unit, and social as well as religious programs were planned for the 1-Ws. District peace committees and the Board of Christian Service appointed ministers whose duty it was, on a part-time basis, to visit 1-W men and their families at least once every two months. But when 1-Ws chose locations for service hundreds of miles from the nearest Mennonite church, pastoral care was difficult. There were attempts to carry on the ministry to 1-Ws on an inter-Mennonite basis through MCC, but the Mennonite Church's insistence on a separate ministry made it difficult for MCC to provide extra 1-W services to the smaller groups.[71]

Within the first two years of the new draft, it became apparent that 1-W was an individual, not a corporate Mennonite, peace witness. Elmer Ediger, then executive secretary of the Board of Christian Service, told the 1953 MCC annual meeting that 1-Ws had to be won to cooperation with MCC, since they had made no commitment to MCC. He noted the decided absence of community and community controls in most 1-W situations, in contrast with the situation in many rural Mennonite communities or in CPS. The new system may produce stronger individual belief and greater individual initiative, but it will also produce more moral casualties and more who will leave the Mennonite church altogether, he predicted.[72]

About 1956, General Conference Mennonites and other Mennonite groups began raising questions about the churches' relationship to the 1-W program and to the 1-W men. Some were critical of the behavior of the scattered 1-W men who experimented with activities that would have been banned at home. Others placed much of the blame on Mennonite communities which fostered a sense of conformity more than responsibility. In spite of some of the problems of men in 1-W, the majority of Mennonite pastors reported an improvement in the spiritual condition of 1-W men by the time they were released.[73]

In Denver, where there was a high concentration of Mennonite 1-Ws, the men participated in a number of volunteer activities outside their regular hospital jobs. These activities included flood cleanup, going as peace teams to Mennonite churches, sponsoring their own Saturday-morning prayer breakfast, providing transportation for a girls' club, and contributing from their relatively small salaries to charities. One Denver 1-W summarized his feelings about 1-W service: "I feel I've been doing work here which helps other people, and at the same time I've come to know other men of my faith and come closer to my church. The whole experience has given me new direction in life.[74]

Some critics were less sure of the value of earning 1-W work. "Can 1-W be considered a witness for peace?" asked Edgar Metzler. "Can it even be considered Christian service? The two years of 1-W are not voluntary service, which would be the only kind of Christian service, but dictated by the demands of law." Metzler charged that the 1-W program had not channeled men into the areas of greatest need, since 55 percent were serving in mental and general hospitals, "where the level of medical care is . . . unbelievably high."[75]

In 1959 the Mennonite groups sponsored a major study of the church and the 1-W program. Out of this study and other reflections came the conviction that earning 1-W was the government's program, while voluntary service and Pax were the church's programs. "1-W earning service may be a legitimate legal alternative to military service, as defined by the statutes of Selective Service on authorization of Congress, but it is not the church's program of witness for peace. . . . It can be a witness for peace *only* if the participants make it such," wrote Wilfred Unruh, staff member for the Board of Christian Service.[76] He proposed a ministry to Mennonite young men in the government's civilian 1-W alternative service similar to the ministry to those in military service or anyone else in the church. After 1967, the Board of Christian Service staff spent little time in the administration of 1-W earning service. Their ministry for 1-Ws outside of VS and Pax consisted of a general list of recommended locations for 1-W service and an annual meeting with other Mennonite 1-W administrators to compare notes.[77]

Along with this new attitude separating the ideology of 1-W from the ideology of voluntary service grew an emphasis on voluntary service as an appropriate activity for all church members, not just draft-age young men. However, throughout the 1960s about half of the General Conference's voluntary service workers were earning 1-W credit through Selective Service. Were such people in voluntary service because of the Selective Service requirement or because of their desire simply to serve through the church? The motivations of most such men were probably mixed. The test of motivation did not come until 1972 when neither the United States nor Canada had conscription any longer. Immediately after the end of the U.S. draft, the number of new placements dropped, the average age of volunteers dropped, and the percentage of men in the program fell.[78] By 1977, however, as many volunteers were in service as in 1971.

Voluntary Service Directions in the 1970s

At the same time as the escalation of U.S. involvement in the war in Vietnam in the mid-1960s—and an increase in the number of men drafted—came a sharp increase in the number of workers in the General Conference voluntary service program. From 34 volunteers in service in 1965 the number jumped to 82 in 1966 and rose to a peak of 140 in 1971. Mennonite Central Committee programs experienced a similar increase in General Conference volunteers. Board of Christian Service staff strengthened their efforts in setting up new voluntary service units, especially in connection with urban mission churches and poverty communities. From 1965 to 1969 thirteen new units were added, with projects ranging from a day-care center in Oklahoma City to an Indian youth center in North Battleford, Saskatchewan.

Such a large increase in personnel and number of projects required more funds, but the churches' contributions for General Conference service programs were dropping. The solution was a requirement for each unit to be self-supporting.[79] In practice, the requirement meant that each voluntary service unit could not depend for its support on the voluntary service office in Newton, Kansas. Support had to be gathered locally—from the jobs in which volunteers worked or from local churches. Previously, some volunteers had been in jobs in which they earned wages, which were then turned over to a common fund from which all the unit members were supported. But now there was pressure for more of the unit members' assignments to be in earning jobs. In 1967 earning MVS workers brought in $119,288, or 78 percent of the total GC voluntary service investment for the year, including administration. In 1970, when the Commission on Home Ministries faced a severe budget cut in all areas of its work, the voluntary service budget also decreased, and funds for subsidy of long-term units decreased from $42,800 to $23,800.[80] For 1978, 73 percent of the program's income came from the volunteers' earnings or other local sources. The new philosophy of local self-support enabled the expansion of the program, but it also placed some volunteers in jobs which had marginal service value in order to support other volunteers in more service-related assignments.

Together with the shift toward local self-support was a shift toward more local participation in the administration of voluntary service units. The Commission on Home Ministries, created by the new General Conference constitution in 1968, was further developing a policy of decentralization. Instead of the commission's directly administering mission churches, for example, the commission was to serve as an enabler for local or regional groups to be in mission. The same policy was applied to the voluntary service program with the move toward local self-support and the attempt to relate each voluntary service unit to a local congregation. The Commission on Home Ministries' policy allowed for developing more local involvement in voluntary service, but it did not lend itself to using a voluntary service unit to start a new congregation. In practice, however, the policy was flexible, and a few units were created in areas without Mennonite churches. But even these (Washington, D.C., and Lakeview in Chicago, for example) related to other local support groups. The 1970 CHM report restated the goal of the voluntary service program: to help local Mennonite congregations be actively involved in service to people in the vicinity of their congregations.

Paradoxically, together with this effort to tie voluntary service units more closely with Mennonite churches came an increase in the number of non-Mennonite volunteers in Mennonite Voluntary Service. In 1969, only 6 of 119 volunteers going into service were not General Conference members. In the late 1960s, however, more people from outside of the historic peace churches were coming to the conviction that the Vietnam War and all wars were wrong, and a number of these were attracted not only to secular service programs like VISTA, but to MVS. "Some of our most concerned, serious volunteers have come from non-Mennonite background," said voluntary service director George Lehman in 1970.[81] Many non-Mennonite volunteers found out about Mennonite Voluntary Service through a publication called *Invest Yourself,* published by the interdenominational Commission on Voluntary Service and Action.

By 1978, 40 percent of the participants in Mennonite Voluntary Service were not Mennonites, and another 10 percent were from other Mennonite groups. Some of these had more commitment to their particular service project than to the Mennonite church to which their unit was to relate, but others became acquainted with the church and its teachings and became Mennonites themselves. Wilfred Unruh found in 1965 that about 5 percent of other Protestants in all Mennonite service programs became Mennonites.[82]

Fulfilling the Congregations' Mission

The priority locations for the thirteen voluntary service units started in the late 1960s were urban poverty neighborhoods and cities where new Mennonite churches were starting.

One location which had both qualifications was Fort Wayne, Indiana. Initiative for a new MVS unit in Fort Wayne came from Leonard Wiebe, pastor of the suburban Maplewood Mennonite Church, which had been established in 1960. The church included both affluent and lower-income members, and at least six members of the congregation were already involved in the East Wayne Street Community Center. The East Wayne Street Community Center, where many of the voluntary service workers were to serve, had been started by the Crescent Avenue Evangelical United Brethren Church in 1964 in cooperation with the East Central Neighborhood Association. The neighborhood was low-income and 50 percent black; within five years that percentage increased to 95. Bringing in Mennonite volunteers to staff the East Wayne Street Center was an experiment in encouraging a suburban Mennonite congregation to relate to an inner-city neighborhood.

The first volunteers came in February 1966, and by 1969 the unit had grown to include a maintenance man at the community center, a teacher in the center's preschool program, two workers in East Central Improvement, Inc. (a nonprofit housing reconstruction corporation), three young men earning wages at Lutheran Hospital, and two MVSers' wives also in earning jobs. One of the volunteers described life in the MVS unit thus:

> Since everyone has a different job during the day and different activities and responsibilities in the evening, each unit member plans his own day. However, all the unit members get together at 5:30 for the evening meal to share the day's activities. Every two weeks, the unit meets with Len Wiebe, pastor of the Maplewood Mennonite Church, for an evening meal and a period of discussion.
>
> A recreation fund of $2.50 per month is provided for each person. Occasionally, all the unit members go to a movie, bowling, a theatrical play and so forth. During the summer the unit has picnics and goes swimming.
>
> Everyone is encouraged to become involved in the community and to do more than work an "eight-hour shift." It is everyone's

responsibility to keep the unit house in order and to use free time constructively.

Several members find themselves involved with the Boy Scout Troop at the Center on Thursday evenings, and about once a month on Saturday hikes or campouts. Some members are involved with the recreation program four nights a week or with the tutoring program two nights a week. Other members are involved with the newly formed East Wayne Soul Club as well as make contacts with the neighborhood people to help them with their problems or just to chat and visit.[83]

MVS also meant less structured involvements.

VS is—getting a young Negro teenager out of jail and taking him into the unit for several weeks giving him a temporary home. . . .

VS is—helping move a family to another house on a Friday evening so they won't be evicted the next morning and be literally put out into the street. . . .

VS is—expressing your concern and conviction of being a conscientious objector. Very seldom does one run up against opposition when given a chance to explain the nonresistant position and tell what you are doing.[84]

In about 1972, the Fort Wayne unit turned to minor home repair as Lincoln Life Insurance Company developed a home improvement corporation and finance agency to do the same job in housing reconstruction that East Central Improvement had previously done. Another volunteer became director of a consumer action center, which dealt with complaints about substandard housing, poor workmanship, overpricing, and dirty grocery stores. Action to remedy the problems sometimes took the form of picketing if private negotiation had not been effective.[85]

In Hamilton, Ontario, a city of 300,000 in 1969, the voluntary service unit worked in an inner-city neighborhood, while the more white-collar, sponsoring congregation, the Hamilton Mennonite Church, was located five miles away. Mennonites sponsored a drop-in center called the "Welcome Inn." "The Inn [isn't] a rescue mission, yet we try to rescue people from being sucked further into poverty," commented one volunteer.[86] As in Fort Wayne, Mennonites cooperated with other church groups in a united Christian approach to helping a poor neighborhood. A number of activities were aimed at children (recreation and tutoring, for example), but others were intended for adults (sewing classes, informal family casework services).

The unit in Markham, Illinois, a suburb of Chicago, also related to a Mennonite church in the suburbs, but in this case, the unit worked in the suburbs, too. At the time the unit began in 1964, Markham was a lower-middle-income suburb of 16,000 which was just beginning to experience racial integration. The congregation, with the help of MVS staff, began the first full-time day-care center in the city.[87] Later volunteers became involved in such activities as a city recreation program for youth and a sheltered workshop for the handicapped.

In 1982 most volunteers in the United States and Canada served in day-care centers, housing rehabilitation, and other inner-city ministries. Smaller numbers were involved in peace education, alternative education, native American concerns, prison ministries, mental health, home health care, and environmental concerns. One hundred twenty volunteers participated in twenty-six units, eighteen of them in urban areas.

Intentional Communities in MVS

Another trend in the 1970s was the connection between Mennonite Voluntary Service and Mennonite intentional communities, groups which, like voluntary service, emphasized group living, income sharing, simple living, and a corporate religious life. The secular counterculture movement and its communes influenced the growth of Mennonite intentional communities. But, like voluntary service, the intentional community movement was also influenced by the recovery of the Anabaptist vision and its emphasis on the committed group of believers whose faith is manifested in their lifestyle and in their concern for those around them. Reba Place Fellowship in Evanston, Illinois, probably the first of the Mennonite intentional communities, began in 1957 out of the "Concern" movement in Goshen, Indiana. That movement itself had roots in the experiences of Mennonite volunteers in Europe after World War II and their wrestling with it meant to be a church in the Anabaptist tradition. Many of the later Mennonite intentional communities included members who had formerly served in Mennonite volunteer programs either in North America or overseas. Their question was, If the voluntary service lifestyle has value for one or two years, why can't this lifestyle be valid for a lifetime?[88]

A few of these intentional communities became voluntary service units under the General Conference program: the North Chicago unit in 1969; Fairview Mennonite House in Wichita and The Bridge in Newton, Kansas, in 1971; and La Familia Mennonite House in Albuquerque, New Mexico, in 1974. The inclusion of intentional communities into the MVS program—

particularly those units where some members were over thirty years old and were planning on terms of service of indefinite length, rather than the standard one or two years—raised new issues for the Commission on Home Ministries and the General Conference as a whole. Some felt their own lifestyles threatened by the intentional communities' commitment to simple living and the extended family. Others feared a loss of the voluntary service program's tax exemption because of the intentional communities' open resistance to payment of war taxes. In 1973 the Commission on Home Ministries decided to allow Anabaptist-oriented intentional communities to relate to the conference as voluntary service units, but emphasized that such relationships should not be considered permanent and that communities should view themselves as congregations rather than MVS units and look for other long-term relationships with each other or with conference bodies.[89] Since that time, no intentional communities have been voluntary service units for longer than three years. The successor to The Bridge, New Creation Fellowship, became a member congregation of the Western District Conference in 1973. The other three communities have dissolved.

Voluntary Service and the People Served

Mennonite Voluntary Service workers, as much as anyone else in the General Conference Mennonite Church, were working with the poor, oppressed, and minorities in North America. In places where it was difficult to create a congregation whose members transcended racial and economic barriers, Mennonite volunteers were working with these people, learning their needs, trying to meet them, and being advocates so that public and private agencies would help them. At first, many volunteer assignments served existing institutions—hospitals, mental hospitals, Mennonite campgrounds—or existing mission programs. Gradually some volunteers began to work out of institutional settings, sometimes creating their own programs to meet needs no one else had been able to meet. In Fort Wayne, Indiana, and Wichita, Kansas, volunteers were instrumental in starting housing rehabilitation programs in poor neighborhoods. Oklahoma City volunteers started Our Wonder House, a preschool education program where none had been before. In other locations, volunteers provided the staff necessary to keep going agencies which served the poor. In Gulfport, race relations were improved, and integration happened in the community without open conflict.

Voluntary Service and Volunteers

In 1965, almost two-thirds of the volunteers in all Mennonite service programs came from farm homes. The vast majority of these served in cities where the variety of cultures and the new experiences of service broadened their horizons. A man from a rural all-Mennonite community could discover a new sense of Mennonite identity while living among people of other faiths or no faith and find a new appreciation for his Anabaptist-Mennonite heritage. A woman trained only for traditional "women's jobs" could find satisfaction in directing a community action program in the inner city. One study of volunteers in Pax found that 40 percent changed their vocational plans after service.[90] For example, Paul and Pauline Holsopple who had been in service in Fort Wayne joined another couple in starting a Christian bookstore there in 1971.

Voluntary service also showed many volunteers new ways of being the church. After discovering it was possible to live joyfully on a subsistence-level income, some volunteers left service with a resolve to continue a simple lifestyle. Many of the volunteers came from churches where the articulation of their faith was done only in formal settings: Sunday morning worship, prayer meetings. In voluntary service they attempted, sometimes successfully, sometimes not, to share their faith in nonchurch language and in a nonworship setting. Voluntary service staff hoped that even a two-week experience in a work camp would make volunteers more sensitive to community needs when they returned home. One-year MVS gave opportunity for more intense grappling with the issues of the world and the issues of personal relationships. "The twenty-four hour rubbing of group living wears down good resolutions after about two months. As one young college junior in one-year VS said, 'I'm just beginning to realize what nonresistance means in my personal relations.' "[91]

Many volunteers found it easier to remain in the community where they had done their service than to return home. Unruh's 1965 study found that only 33.4 percent of all Mennonite volunteers remained permanently in their home community after service. In Mennonite Voluntary Service in North America, virtually every voluntary service location could boast some former volunteers who had stayed on as church members or employees of social service programs. Irvin and Lillian Enns and their eighteen-month-old daughter, Karan, of Inman, Kansas, stayed in Gulfport in 1965 after two years of voluntary

service to live in the black community, work at a secular job, and
stay involved in Camp Landon's Bible classes, community center, and maintenance work. Others like Martha Wenger, a Mennonite Voluntary Service worker for Clergy and Laity
Concerned in Washington, D.C., in 1979, simply remained in
the job which they had served in MVS.[92]

Voluntary Service and the General Conference Menno-
nite Church

Wilfred Unruh's 1965 study called voluntary service
"among the most influential of the renewal movements in the
Mennonite church, for voluntary service is a movement of the
nonprofessional church people."[93] The impact of voluntary service can be measured in part by the sheer numbers of General
Conference Mennonites who have served either in short-term or
long-term service under the General Conference or MCC: ap-
proximately 7,000 between 1944 and 1978. This represents
almost 12 percent of the total 1978 General Conference membership in North America. (See pp. 293-96.)

In some cases volunteers have made a noticeable impact
not only on the people whom they had come to serve, but on the
Mennonite congregation to which they related. A pastor of a
city church noted,

> When volunteers have been able to establish really warm friend-
> ships with the people here, and have by the sincerity of their
> coming to live and to serve without cost, unheralded, but simply
> serving and enjoying their opportunity to serve . . . the people
> here witness a kind of expression of living the Christian life that
> they have never seen before in this way. This has made a notice-
> able impression on our members urging them to a more dedi-
> cated Christian discipleship. Some have been profoundly moved
> by the whole idea of volunteering one's time for a period of two
> years.[94]

In other locations, tensions developed between the church
and the voluntary service unit, especially when most of the
church members lived in a neighborhood different from that in
which the volunteers worked. The Fort Wayne, Indiana, unit,
for example, experienced some typical conflicts with the Maplewood Mennonite Church to which it related. The pastor wrote,

> There are a number of people within the congregation who have
> strong concerns about the East Central Neighborhood. Unfortu-
> nately, there are others for whom this is of little concern, or at
> least it is not a priority with them. A growing conviction of mine
> is that we will need to work with a certain bloc of the congrega-

tion in continuing the concerns of low-income people. Perhaps we
have expected everyone in the congregation to make this their
priority which is somewhat unrealistic. The feeling of both
VSers and the congregation last evening was that we want to
build a stronger support group among those within the congregation for whom these concerns are a priority.[95]

Some units and churches were able to resolve tensions through
congregational participation in MVS projects, MVS participation in church activities, or "foster parent" programs for volunteers. In other locations, such tensions were not resolved, and
units were closed.

Most voluntary service workers considered themselves as
a kind of missionary. Unruh's study showed that 87.4 percent of
all Mennonite volunteers agreed with the statement "Voluntary service workers, (MVS, summer service, Paxmen, 1-Ws)
are just as much Christian witnesses as are foreign missionaries."[96] Indeed, by 1978 voluntary service workers constituted
the bulk of the "home missionaries" of the Commission on
Home Ministries. Indian ministries was scaling down its staff
to give more local control of programs. Responsibility for starting new churches was primarily in the hands of the regional
conferences. Mennonite Voluntary Service remained almost the
only department of the Commission on Home Ministries with a
centralized administration and placement service, where
workers regularly consulted with each other at retreats.

The wide use of relatively short-term personnel (with few
serving more than two years) in the church's mission brought
both problems and benefits. On the one hand, short-term,
mostly young personnel hindered the development of long-
range goals and continuity in programs. On the other hand,
voluntary service provided for flexibility in programming. "Voluntary service," said one MVS director, "can be an experimental arm of the church on mission. It can try new ideas, new
patterns. It can risk failure with less anxiety than career missions."[97]

Many questions about voluntary service remain for the
future. Should the voluntary service lifestyle be encouraged for
the entire church, or is this lifestyle reserved for a select group
of Christians, mostly young? Should terms of service longer
than two years be encouraged? How can the rest of the church be
more involved with oppressed and hurting people in North
America? Can mission and service be recombined?

Voluntary service programs are probably the Mennonite
church's most unique contribution to the Christian church as a

whole. Mennonites borrowed the structure from others, and
about forty other organizations—public and private—now have
some kind of volunteer corps in North America.[98] Yet Mennonites have developed the idea beyond the scope of most other
church groups in terms of the percentages of their members who
have served and in terms of correlating service programs with
their entire theology of the church.

Table 1 General Conference-Related Institutions for the Physi-
cally and Mentally Ill

Hospital	Location	Date Founded
*Mennonite Bethesda Hospital Society	Goessel, Kansas	1900
Bethel Hospital	Mountain Lake, Minnesota	1905
*Bethel Deaconess Hospital	Newton, Kansas	1908
*Beatrice Community Hospital and Health Center	Beatrice, Nebraska	1911
⁰*Alta Loma Sanatorium	Alta Loma, California	1914
Salem Deaconess Home and Hospital	Salem, Oregon	1917
Salem Hospital	Hillsboro, Kansas	1918
*Mennonite Hospital	Bloomington, Illinois	1919
Concordia Hospital	Winnipeg, Manitoba	1928
Bethania Hospital	Altona, Manitoba	1936
Bethesda Hospital	Steinbach, Manitoba	1937
Bethel Hospital	Winkler, Manitoba	1935
Henderson Community Hospital	Henderson, Nebraska	1951

Homes for the Aged		
*Frederick Mennonite Home	Frederick, Pennsylvania	1896
Bethesda Home for the Aged	Goessel, Kansas	1898
Hillsboro Home for the Aged (successor to Salem Home)	Hillsboro, Kansas	1912
⁰Bergthaler Home for the Aged	Gretna, Manitoba	1918
Eventide Home	Mountain Lake, Minnesota	1921
*Meadows Home for the Aged	Chenoa, Illinois	1923
*Bethel Home for the Aged	Newton, Kansas	1926
⁰Invalid Home of the Mennonite Youth Society	Rosthern, Saskatchewan	1944

Mennonite Home for the Aged	Rosthern, Saskatchewan	1944
Home for the Aged		
and Infirm, Bethania	Winnipeg, Manitoba	1946
Pleasant View Home	Inman, Kansas	1947
Herbert Nursing Home	Herbert, Saskatchewan	1954
Menno Home	Abbotsford, British Columbia	1954
Mennonite Home for the Aged	Coaldale, Alberta	1955
*Mennonite Memorial Home	Bluffton, Ohio	1955
Salem Home for the Aged	Winkler, Manitoba	1956
Salem Home for the Aged	Freeman, South Dakota	
*Memorial Home	Moundridge, Kansas	1958
*Menno Home (for the retarded)	Waldheim, Saskatchewan	1962
Swiss Village	Berne, Indiana	1965
Sierra View Home	Reedley, California	1968
Glencroft Retirement Community	Glendale, Arizona	1970
Parkview Home	Wayland, Iowa	1961
Prairie Sunset Home	Pretty Prairie, Kansas	1959
Buhler Sunshine Home	Buhler, Kansas	1945
Meadowlark Homestead (for the mentally ill)	Newton, Kansas	1951

Mental Health Centers

*Brook Lane Psychiatric Center	Hagerstown, Maryland	1949
*Kings View	Reedley, California	1951
*Prairie View	Newton, Kansas	1954
*Oaklawn Psychiatric Center	Elkhart, Indiana	1963
*Kern View	Bakersfield, California	1966
*Eden Mental Health Center	Winkler, Manitoba	1967

*Officially recognized by the General Conference Mennonite Church
°No longer in existence

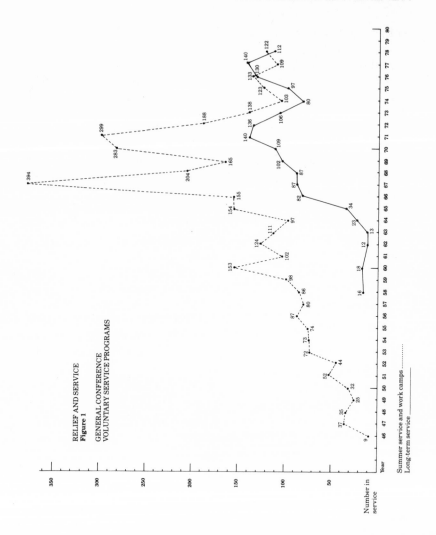

RELIEF AND SERVICE
Figure 1

GENERAL CONFERENCE
VOLUNTARY SERVICE PROGRAMS

Summer service and work camps ....
Long-term service _____

Gordon Keeper (right), lay minister of Little Grand Rapids, and a fellow Christian from Pauingassi with Henry Neufeld

Ike Froese

Chapter 9:
Mission in the North

two peoples
of Hiawathan and Simonian origin
now
are touching one another

they have met
by the circumstance of ethnohistories
and
by our ecclesiastical design

now that there is geographic coexistence
we dream about
proximity of mind and soul

Father of all peoples
give your assent
we ask
for the building of this dream
　　　—Menno Wiebe[1]

The new interest in missions after World War II not only affected the General Conference, but also the Bergthaler Mennonite Church of Manitoba (many of whose worshiping centers became members of the General Conference beginning in 1968). The Bergthaler church in the 1940s was a centrally administered organization with a number of worship centers in southern Manitoba. As one of the moderately traditional groups of Mennonite immigrants from Russia in the 1870s, the Bergthaler church had been sending financial support to General Conference Mennonite missions, but no foreign missionaries had come from within the Bergthaler church.

Mexico

By the 1930s a few Bergthalers began offering themselves as foreign missionaries. One of these was Randall Groening, a member of the Lowe Farm Bergthaler church and a graduate of Winnipeg Bible Institute, a nondenominational school. Groening, who had been working in an orphanage in Mexico, suggested in 1939 to the Bergthaler leaders that they support him in a mission to the Tarahumara Indians near Creel, in the northern state of Chihuahua, Mexico. The Bergthaler church showed its interest, gave token support to Groening as he investigated a field in Mexico, formed a missions committee in 1940, and accepted Groening as a mission candidate in 1942.

By 1944 the Bergthaler church had formed Mennonite Pioneer Mission (the name suggested by Groening), had on paper an agreement to cooperate loosely with the General Conference Mennonite Board of Foreign Missions, and had engaged Groening and his wife, Maria, a Mexican citizen, as missionaries among the Tarahumaras. In 1945, Henry and Susan Gerbrandt, also of the Lowe Farm Bergthaler congregation, joined the Groenings in Mexico.

The mission had difficulties from the start. Gerbrandts were never legally in the country as missionaries. The Mexican government prohibited the entrance of foreign ministers or missionaries, and the Gerbrandts had to reenter the country periodically under tourist visas. Opposition from the Roman Catholic church, already established among the Tarahumaras, mounted. Tensions developed between Randall Groening and the Mennonite Pioneer Mission board over the issues of nonparticipation in war and Groening's desire for the mission to be nondenominational. In 1974 Groening sent the Bergthaler committee his resignation, saying that he was not a conscientious objector and didn't feel that he should be working for a Mennonite organization. Later he said the People's Church of Toronto would take over the work in Creel; however this development did not happen.

The mission board was then faced with the problem of how to continue. The land which the board had paid for was in the name of Groening's wife, since under Mexican law only those families who had been living in Mexico since the time of the revolution in the 1920s could own land. Groenings repaid the board for the land, but Mennonite Pioneer Mission was left without a mission station.

Gerbrandts continued in Mexico until 1948, spending some of that time with the Wycliffe Bible Translators, helping the Tarahumaras with the reading of the newly translated Gospel of Mark. Faced with governmental and ecclesiastical opposition, and with no land, the Bergthaler church chose to withdraw from Mexico, and the Gerbrandts returned to Canada.[2]

The Mission Goes North

The Mennonite Pioneer Mission board, meanwhile, had become involved financially, although not administratively, in other mission ventures. Anne Penner, of the Rosenfeld Bergthaler congregation, had been ordained as a missionary for India under the General Conference in 1946.

However, the Bergthaler church wanted its own mission. This time it looked north to the Indian and Métis (half-breed) communities around Lake Winnipeg, where some Mennonite conscientious objectors had taught in government schools and served in United Church missions during World War II.[3] Already during the era of Mexican work, Bergthaler Bishop David Schulz and J. N. Hoeppner had gone as far as Matheson Island to look for a new mission field.[4]

The location of Mennonite Pioneer Mission's first mission station in northern Manitoba was the Métis community of Matheson Island, 150 miles north of Winnipeg. Matheson Island was chosen because of a letter the Mennonite Pioneer Mission board had received from Matheson residents requesting a missionary. The board responded by sending Jake and Trudy Unrau in 1948. It was not until about a year later that Unraus discovered that the request had really been meant for the Anglican church, to which many of the residents of Matheson Island already belonged.

The Unraus and the mission board had been aware that the majority of Indians and Métis in the north were members of the Anglican or Roman Catholic churches. Yet neither church held regular services in many of the northern communities or had resident priests or deacons who could carry on services in the absence of missionaries. Thus the Mennonite missions felt it was justified in starting another church among people whose religion was seen to be nominal or formal and unrelated to their daily life, or who were troubled by alcohol abuse. One chronicler of early Mennonite Pioneer Mission efforts commented:

> Most of the missions of these churches have been established for many years and seem to have succumbed to the pressures of time developing such symptoms as lethargy and indifference producing a kind of religious formalism lacking power of conviction and a maintenance of Christian ethics.[5]

The Matheson Island community in 1948 was poor and partially isolated. Situated in Lake Winnipeg, it was accessible in summer only by boat or plane. In winter one could drive a car from the "end of the road" across the frozen lake to the island. Most buildings were of logs, and many people lived in tents during the winter trapping season. Income was generally low. Even the best type of employment such as trapping, fishing, or lumbering was inadequate to maintain a reasonable standard of living.[6]

The form which the mission first took was little different from that of most foreign missions or the North American city missions. A house was built for the missionaries, along with a church building, a dispensary, and a 32-volt power plant. A Sunday school for children and adults was started on Sunday morning, and worship, in which Christians took turns leading the singing, reading Scripture, and praying, was held Sunday evenings. Bible studies, prayer meetings, and choir practices were organized. Woodwork and sewing classes were held. Later there were boys' and girls' clubs and women's meetings.[7]

The theology of the early efforts of Mennonite Pioneer Mission also resembled that of many General Conference-related missions at mid-twentieth century. Sunday school materials were predominantly those published by Scripture Press, a conservative nondenominational publishing house, although some Mennonite material was also used.[8] The fundamentalist approach changed somewhat after missionaries received more training in Mennonite institutions. Missionary Jake Unrau later commented that a year of furlough as a student at Canadian Mennonite Bible College in Winnipeg had changed his preaching:

> We wanted to present the gospel as our own, not third hand. The peace witness had to be part of it. It was only then I found out that the native people had a mission to me. The way they settle quarrels—they are so peaceful, so patient, giving people time. So I didn't push them on it [the peace stand].[9]

Social services also formed a part of the early mission at Matheson Island and elsewhere, as nurses were sent under the mission board, and Mennonite teachers were encouraged to apply for jobs in the government schools.

A second mission station was opened at Pine Dock, another Métis community near Matheson Island, in 1949. But because of local opposition to the mission, it was moved to Anama Bay in 1952. This work, too, was discontinued in 1954 because of the strong Pentecostal mission here.

While missionaries reported no baptisms in the early years at Matheson Island, attendance at Sunday services was reaching as high as sixty, and the mission program of the Bergthaler church drew the admiration of the Canadian Foreign Missions Committee, which had been organized at the 1949 sessions of the Conference of Mennonites in Canada. Because the Canadian Conference had no foreign mission program of its own, support for the Bergthaler mission began to come from the Whitewater Mennonite Church and elsewhere in the Canadian Conference. Mennonite Pioneer Mission reports were read at the annual sessions of the Canadian Conference. Eventually, the Canadian Conference Mission Committee and the Bergthaler board agreed to amalgamate over a three-year period. By 1960 Mennonite Pioneer Mission belonged not only to the Bergthaler Mennonite Church, but the whole Conference of Mennonites in Canada.

Influenced in part by a larger source of funds and workers, Mennonite Pioneer Mission expanded to more northern communities: to the Métis communities of Loon Straits (population 79) in 1955 and Manigotogan (population 173) in 1957, to the Saulteaux (pronounced "So-toe") village of Pauingassi (population 125) in 1955 and the Bloodvein River reserve (population 176) in 1960, and to the predominantly Cree community of Cross Lake (population 1,050) north of Lake Winnipeg in 1956.[10] Mennonite Pioneer Mission also made a short attempt at involvement in a mission on a Blood Reserve near Cardston, Alberta, in 1966. That effort had been started independently by a Mennonite living nearby.

Pauingassi

One of the strongest churches which evolved as a result of the Mennonite mission in the north was in Pauingassi, an isolated village east of Lake Winnipeg. The residents were Saulteaux but had never been given separate reserve status by the government. Thus there was no school in the village, and few of the residents had been to any school. Only one person spoke English. The standard of living was quite low. Alcohol abuse was a problem. Thirty-five percent of the children died before the age of four. [11] Because they lived off the reserve, Pauingassi residents got no government benefits and were totally dependent on their own efforts to earn a living from hunting, fishing, and wild rice harvesting. Many of the houses had no windows, but only a large hole in a low roof. Inside the dirt floor was covered with spruce boughs. [12]

In contrast to many other native communities around Lake Winnipeg, there had been relatively little Christian mission activity in Pauingassi by 1955. Methodist missionaries had come to the area in the late nineteenth century, and the denomination, as part of the merged United Church, had had a resident missionary for many years in Little Grand Rapids, twelve miles away, but not in Pauingassi, where traditional Indian religion still had a strong influence.

To Pauingassi, Mennonite Pioneer Mission sent Henry and Elna Neufeld, former students at Canadian Mennonite Bible College, to start a school as well as a church. The school, begun at the request of the Indians, continued under mission supervision until 1971, when it was taken over by the government.

Like most other missionaries in the north, the Neufelds were not only teachers and preacher, but dispensers of medicine, legal advice, transportation, repair work on motors and other machinery, advice on home economics, and communication with the outside world. But unlike most other Mennonite missionaries in the north, Neufelds were forced to learn an Indian language. Supported by a linguistics course at Caronport, Saskatchewan, and the interpreting of the one English-speaking Indian at Pauingassi, Neufelds set about to learn Saulteaux. At first, the hymns at the mission worship services were in Cree (later also in Saulteaux), from a book prepared by the independent Mennonite organization, Northern Light Gospel Mission, in northern Ontario. The sermon was in English, interpreted into Saulteaux when the interpreter was there. When the interpreter was absent, there was no sermon. Gradually, Neufelds began to speak more and more Saulteaux, and by late 1959, Henry was preaching in Saulteaux.

Neufelds worked in Pauingassi for eleven years before a church formed. In 1966, St. John Owen, Jacob Owen, and Lucy Owen completed an instruction class and were baptized. As the church grew, Neufelds encouraged native Christians to take more and more leadership. In 1970 Neufelds insisted on moving from Pauingassi to Winnipeg, and Vic and Norma Funk, the new workers, intentionally did not consider themselves as ministers, but as resource people, Vic speaking at the worship service or the Bible study only when invited to do so.[13]

At about this time, St. John Owen received a call to the pastoral ministry in a dream, and in 1972 he was ordained as elder. Jacob Owen, Spoat Owen, and David Owen were ordained as additional pastors for the small congregation. After 1976 there was no resident white missionary in Pauingassi. However, Henry Neufeld visited the community about six times a year for counsel and support. The church, with thirty-four members in 1981, was a stable group and the only congregation in the community. Jacob Owen spent some time traveling in surrounding Indian communities on behalf of the church, visiting in particular Poplar Hill, Ontario, where the Northern Light Gospel Mission had worked earlier, but strong local leadership had not developed. "When you left," Jacob Owen told Henry Neufeld, "you gave us the authority to continue."[14]

Cross Lake

The other showpiece of the Canadian Mennonite mission effort was Cross Lake, Manitoba, a predominantly Cree community where Otto and Margaret Hamm and Helen Willms, a nurse, went in 1956.[15] In Cross Lake the Elim Mennonite Church was established and came to be led by Cree pastor Jeremiah Ross. Like St. John Owen, Ross received his call to the ministry in a dream. According to Ross, when he was sick and unconscious he received a vision of a ladder going up to heaven and a beautiful city. "And that's why I'm working at this now, that God has chosen me to tell to the other people about this eternal life that this man told me about when I saw him when I was unconscious," Ross related. Ross was the first ordained Indian pastor in Mennonite Pioneer Mission history. He was converted in 1964, baptized in 1966, and ordained in 1968. Partly supported by the mission board and partly by his own hunting and trapping, Ross led a congregation of less than a dozen members, and in the 1970s gave daily Bible meditations in Cree over the local radio station.[16]

The Cross Lake mission bore many similarities to the one at Pauingassi. The two locations were the only ones where the earliest missionaries learned to speak a language other than English (English was the predominant language at Matheson Island, Loon Straits, Pine Dock, Manigotogan, and Selkirk) and where special efforts were made to understand and identify with the Indian culture. Missionary Ernie Sawatsky at Cross Lake in 1964, for example, went out on the trapline for three weeks and attended an Indian dance, activities which natives had never seen a missionary do before. But in spite of Sawatsky's sensitivity to Indian culture, he recognized that Cross Lake was a society thrown into turmoil by the impact of white culture. He wrote, 'There is no unambiguous language and cultural pattern here. Instead there is flux and insecurity.[17]

Mennonites and Other Missions

Also unique to Pauingassi and Cross Lake was the cooperation among denominations. At Pauingassi, the United Church tried to reinstate its mission in the 1960s with visits from a nearby minister, but finally left the work in the hands of the Mennonites.

In Cross Lake, as at Matheson Island and most other Mennonite mission locations, Mennonites were not the first missionaries. The first Protestant work on the reservation had begun in 1841, and a United Church in Cross Lake was the result of that effort. Roman Catholics had sent workers in 1911, and by 1961 they claimed 800 of the reserve's 1,050 people.

The early Mennonite Sunday worship services in Cross Lake were well attended in spite of the presence of the other churches. Otto Hamm commented,

> Having been baptized as infants, all feel a sense of belonging to their respective church, yet the essence of Christianity has gripped but a few of them. Many say they respect all religions, and the fact that they attend mass in the morning, United Church in the afternoon, and the Mennonite mission in the evening proves their point.[18]

Most Indians and Métis saw little reason to choose one church and attend only there. Some people had been baptized several times by different church groups. Denominational competition was as difficult for mid-twentieth-century Indians to understand as it had been for the nineteenth-century Cree chief who had been approached at various times by priests or ministers of three different churches who each had told him that theirs was the only true way to heaven. He suggested they ought to call a council among themselves; until they agreed, he could wait.[19]

In Cross Lake, the three mission groups cooperated, but elsewhere there was opposition.[20] At Bloodvein, the local Catholic priest opposed the entry of the Mennonite mission, declaring, "The devils are coming."[21] Indians on the reserve sent petitions and counterpetitions opposing and supporting the establishment of a Mennonite mission and school at Bloodvein. Finally the Department of Indian Affairs granted permission. A Roman Catholic school was already in operation at Bloodvein. Eventually the Mennonite and Catholic schools merged and were placed under government supervision.

More serious conflict developed between Mennonite missionaries and the Pentecostals. The Pentecostals did not station resident missionaries. Instead, itinerant evangelists would come to a town for meetings, ask for converts, and then move on, a strategy some missionaries called "hit-and-run tactics."[22] The Pentecostals attracted native people partly because of the emotional services, which contrasted with the mission's more staid order of service. The bodily movement of the Pentecostal services was sometimes compared to the Indian powwow. Part of the attraction was also the Pentecostals' "assumption that the Indian is capable of accepting and expressing Christianity in his own way." Pentecostal churches provided an avenue for Indian leadership which white churches often did not.[23]

At Loon Straits, Mennonites tried to work with an independent Indian group who called themselves Brethren. But soon the group told the missionaries they were no longer welcome, and the Mennonites established a second place of worship in the community.[24]

A Pentecostal evangelistic team came to Bloodvein in 1962, baptized thirty-five people, and formed the Bloodvein Bible Chapel. Four years later the group had about a dozen active members.[25]

At Matheson Island there was direct competition with Pentecostal evangelists from 1948 to 1954, when the Pentecostals and the Mennonites agreed not to duplicate efforts in any one area.[26] The Pentecostal influence, however, was evident even in the Mennonite chapel. The form of baptism posed a problem at Matheson Island as early as 1953 because the congregation wanted immersion as its form of baptism, while the Canadian Conference required its member and mission churches to pour the baptismal water. In 1958, the Mennonite Pioneer Mission board voted that baptism at Matheson Island and Loon Straits should be in the church building (that meant pouring), and in exceptional cases in the river by pouring "to prevent confusion of the issue at home."[27] Organization of the congregation was delayed until 1965, when delegates at the

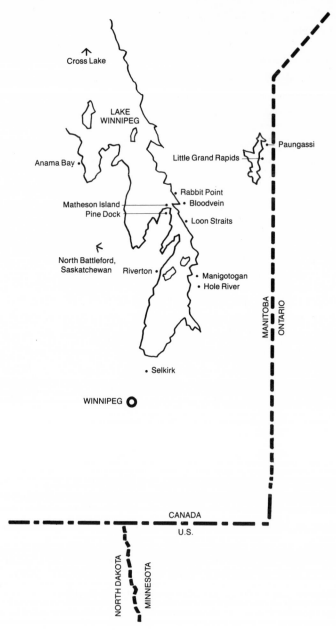

Native Ministries Conference of Mennonites in Canada Locations

Canadian Conference annual sessions agreed that the new congregation could regularly immerse members, but asked that
members should also be accepted if they had been baptized by
pouring or any other form.[28]

A self-sustaining congregation at Matheson Island did not
develop. By the 1960s, most of the active participants in the
Mennonite programs had moved away, mostly to urban areas.
By 1968, only one member was left, although a small group
continued to meet for worship. At Loon Straits, Bloodvein
River, Little Grand Rapids, and Manigotogan, worship services
were held when a missionary was present. However, few residents of these communities were ready to change their membership from Anglican or Catholic or United churches to the
Mennonite church.

At Hole River, Native Ministries chose not to develop a
Mennonite church, but to cooperate with the Anglicans and to
focus on a social service ministry. In 1980 Murray and Ruth
Martin went to Hole River under the joint sponsorship of the
Conference of Mennonites in Canada and Mennonite Central
Committee (Canada).

Community Development

By the mid-1960s, church growth statistics among the
Mennonite Pioneer Mission stations were small. The board told
the Canadian Conference in 1963, "All confessions have experienced that mission work among the Indians goes slowly. We,
too!" [29] Twenty years' experience with native people in northern
Manitoba was teaching missionaries and board members that
one could not simply announce the gospel at Sunday services
and expect a church to emerge automatically. Missionaries
were learning that they had to bridge a cultural and ethnic gap
between themselves (primarily of Low German-Russian background) and the Saulteaux, Cree, and Métis.

Their solution to this problem was an emphasis on community development which began in the 1960s. "Preaching has
very little meaning in the Indian community unless we also
help these people to a more decent existence," said Ike Froese,
Mennonite Pioneer Mission board leader and later executive
secretary for MPM-Native Ministries.[30] Adolph Ens, then a
teacher in Loon Straits, wrote, "The church has pioneered in
bringing education and medicine to the Indians; I believe it may
have to pioneer in the economic field, too."[31] Missionaries lob-
bied successfully to get a post office established at Bloodvein. A
group of Mennonite businesspeople from southern Manitoba

called *Christian Investors* established the first general store in Pauingassi.

The most ambitious community development project was at Manigotogan, a predominantly Métis community of less than 200 people. Trying to raise the standard of living of the residents while allowing them to continue traditional occupations, missionary Jake Unrau helped in organizing the Wanipigow Producers Co-op Ltd. in 1963. The community was at the brink of economic destruction with the threatened closure of the fishing industry, the negative effects of inflation on fur profits, and the restriction of pulp-cutting contracts. During the first year, eighteen fisherman got jobs through the co-op, and the co-op turned a profit. Eventually as many as forty men participated in the cooperative, which allowed its members to get better prices for their fish and pulpwood and to get credit to buy equipment.

Missionary Neill von Gunten, who followed Unrau at Manigotogan, continued working with the cooperative and for two years was mayor of the town. Taking a political position caused some struggle "within myself, within Native Ministries, and within the Mennonite constituency," von Gunten admitted, [32] but he took the office with the purpose of training a native to do the job. Native representatives got experience in writing grant proposals and going to Winnipeg to confront the government. The town was successful in getting government money for a park, a hockey rink, and renovation of community buildings. The cooperative which the Mennonite mission helped to start had the distinction in 1981 of being the only church-initiated native cooperative in western Canada—of the hundreds started in the 1960s and 1970s—that was still functioning successfully. [33]

At Matheson Island, Peter Warkentin not only preached on Sundays, but ran a mechanics shop during the week from 1968 to 1972. He and his wife, Anne Marie, decided against direct evangelism and made casual visits instead. They told the board,

> One individual shared that in the past the Bible had always been read upon visits. They had also been preached at and they greatly resented that. Our not reading the Bible has brought us closer to the people. Now some are beginning to share and ask questions on their own. [34]

Attendance at worship services, particularly for adult males, was low during that period at Matheson Island. However, the Warkentin workshop was a place for contact with men in the community. The Mennonite Pioneer Mission board sent Warkentins to Matheson Island because "to have specialized clergy, that is, theological experts who have no accompanying additional skills in a community where such specializations have never existed, would be ill-advised," the board reported to the conference.[35]

Another attempt at community development came in 1973, when a handicraft project was started with seed money from the General Conference Poverty Fund. Coordinated by John Funk, the project encouraged the production of beadwork, mukluks, and other native handicrafts in northern communities and helped find markets for them. The handicraft project closed in 1975.

In downtown Winnipeg, Mennonite Pioneer Mission-Native Ministries operated a drop-in center for native youth from 1965 to 1976. Called *Youth Opportunities Unlimited* (YOU), the center sponsored tutoring, counseling, and native sports teams. There was no direct attempt to establish a church, although a youth group called *Club 12* met regularly for worship and study. Social service to native people in Winnipeg continued after 1976 with the establishing of reception homes. These were temporary lodging for out-of-town native people who had come to the city for medical attention for themselves or their family members.

A Voice for Native People

The social service ministry extended as well to attempts to influence government on behalf of native people. Menno Wiebe, executive secretary of Mennonite Pioneer Mission from 1964 to 1974, saw the function of the church not only to preach the Word but also "to put pressure on the political structures to develop a better deal for the Indian and to suggest direction."[36] In 1969, for example, the Canadian Board of Missions asked the federal government to reevaluate its Indian policy "which threatens further social upheaval with the Indian communities." The board asked the government "to listen sensitively to the Indian people, to allow them ample time to voice their concerns and alternatives, to adequately interpret the far-reaching implications of this policy."[37] Together with other denominations, the Conference of Mennonites in Canada in 1974 attempted to make the Indian voice heard regarding plans of Manitoba Hydro to flood native lands for a hydroelectric dam.[38]

Mennonite Pioneer Mission workers began to talk more

about the good in Indian culture and had a new emphasis on anthropology, the study of which was becoming more common in Christian mission fields around the world. Mennonite missionaries in northern Manitoba began to look for ways in which native people could be Christian without leaving their social context. A 1973 consultation of mission workers, native Christians, board members, and others discussed how the gospel could fit into Indian culture rather than requiring Indians to "act white" in order to be Christians. "Are we combining two religions, or can Jesus be seen as the fulfillment of Indian history, just as he was the fulfillment of Hebrew history?" asked some consultation participants.[39]

Wiebe, who had acquired a graduate degree in anthropology, talked of a special mission Mennonites might have to their Indian neighbors. "Mennonites, because of their own history of minority oppression," he said, "might have an edge in sensitivity to the harboured resentment of the Indian peoples."[40] Workers got new encouragement to learn Indian languages, even where English was commonly used, and a series of language workshops were held in cooperation with the Northern Light Gospel Mission, beginning in 1974.

"Red power" and Indian self-determination were taken seriously by MPM workers. For example, Wiebe went to Matheson Island in December 1972 and called a public meeting on the need for MPM to continue its work there, since most of the island's residents were either Anglican or Catholic. Wiebe got encouragement to continue.[41]

The 1975 name change from *Mennonite Pioneer Mission* to *Native Ministries* came as a result of the increased emphasis on listening to the Indian. Isaac Beaulieu, executive director of the Manitoba Indian Brotherhood, invited to speak at the 1969 sessions of the Conference of Mennonites in Canada in Saskatoon, told the delegates, "After 400 years, do you still need missions? To us the word *mission* designates an inferiority even if it is not intentional. Why can't we just become regular congregations?"[42] The word *pioneer* also had negative connotations for some native people.

The new interest in anthropology had the unexpected by-product of increasing interchurch cooperation. In 1967, when Wiebe as executive secretary was planning a Mennonite Pioneer Mission anthropology institute for mission workers, he discovered that mission programs of other denominations were facing the same questions. Thus developed the first Inter-Church Seminar for Workers in Native Communities. Held in cooperation with the extension department of the University of Manitoba, the first seminar had as its subject "Cultural Change and Christian Mission." Mission anthropologists Jacob Loewen and Richard Pope were the main lecturers. Wiebe attributed to the institute the development of decision-making groups at Bloodvein River Reserve, the encouragement of Jeremiah Ross's ministry at Cross Lake and the development of a Cree language course.[43] The seminars became an almost annual oc- curence, drawing Mennonite, United, Anglican, Roman Catho- lic, Presbyterian, Lutheran, and Christian Reformed workers, but not the more evangelical groups nor the Pentecostals.

Urban Native Churches

An additional mission effort toward native people came with Mennonite Pioneer Mission-Native Ministries' efforts to start churches in urban areas. Especially in the 1960s and 1970s large numbers of native people moved to cities. In 1959, there were a total of 55,656 Indian and Métis in Manitoba; by 1963, about 6,000 were living in Winnipeg. By 1980, estimates of the Indian and Métis population of Winnipeg ranged from 20,000 to 60,000.[44]

The first effort to start an urban native church was in Selkirk, population 8,500, twenty-one miles north of Winnipeg. By 1966, several families who had been associated with the Mennonite missions in Manigotogan, Loon Straits, and Mathe- son Island were living in Selkirk. Raymond Settee and Hannes Bell asked the Canadian Conference to help them establish a church. Missionaries Jake and Trudy Unrau, formerly at Matheson Island and Manigotogan, were the first workers, coming in 1968. A worshiping group soon developed, but be- cause of the ebb and flow of members and the wide variety of backgrounds from which the white and Métis participants came, a constitution for the congregation was not adopted until 1980, when Malcolm Wenger was pastor.

Two newer efforts at developing urban native churches have been in Winnipeg. In 1980 Elijah McKay, a Saulteaux who had earlier worked with the YOU center, began meeting with a developing Native Christian Church. In 1981 Jake Unrau re- sponded to the request from some Métis in Winnipeg for a Mennonite-related congregation.

Congregations in Mission

The development of native congregations in Selkirk and Winnipeg brought the issue of white-Indian relationships clo-

ser to Mennonites in southern Manitoba. No longer was missions something far away; the Selkirk church could be visited
easily by car or bus. After a visit to Selkirk, one southern
Manitoba Mennonite commented, "For some of us the mystery
and romance of missions is gone forever, but the significance
and meaning of the mission of the church of Christ took on a new
dimension."[45]

Manitoba Mennonites had actually had long-standing contacts with natives. There were Métis squatters in 1873 on the
West Reserve, settled by Mennonites only a few years later.
Mennonites on both the East and West reserves in Manitoba
had numerous contacts with Métis in the first years after immigration from Russia.[46] Many Métis continued to be present in
southern Manitoba as migrant laborers. In 1972, an estimated
1,500 people of Indian ancestry were entering the Altona area
during the beet-hoeing season.[47] Some mission workers noted
wryly that it was "easier to support a program in the north
away from our doorsteps than to befriend and show love and
concern to the fellow next door."[48]

Some Mennonites of German background in the south
tried to become better acquainted with natives and the mission
program through visits to the mission stations. Many students
from Swift Current Bible Institute in Saskatchewan and later
also Elim Bible Institute, Altona, Manitoba, spent January
terms volunteering in the northern communities. Some summer volunteers helped with vacation Bible schools.

The 1967 Mennonite Pioneer Mission report to the Canadian Conference analyzed the problem thus:

> The test in the MPM program has already come in part, but
> largely lies ahead. It has to do with our stance to the Indian
> person as such. Apparently we are much more ready to do mis-
> sion work among the Indians in the north who are removed from
> our churches than we are among the Indians who are coming to
> live as our neighbors. It is painful to discover that the very
> churches who show considerable interest in the MPM program
> "out there" show almost no interest to the very same Indian
> people when they come to live in our communities. We accepted
> Indians as converts. Perhaps it is now time that we accept these
> converts as brothers and open our churches to them.
>
> ...If we cannot accept the Indians as brothers in the Mennonite
> constituency, then we will find little or no opportunity with
> northern Indian communities. It is a test that can be evaded
> largely in the foreign missions program because the converts
> remain in their respective countries. It is a test that can not be

evaded in the MPM program because the Indian people live in our midst and are very quick to observe the sincerity or insincerity of our mission motives.[49]

The question became whether these native Christians could really be a part of the Mennonite people. In the early years of Mennonite Pioneer Mission, it was difficult for native converts to feel a part of a Mennonite constituency not only because of the racial prejudice of some Mennonites,[50] but also because of lack of contact. When native young people were sent to Bible schools, Mennonite schools were seldom chosen because much of the instruction was still in German in the 1950s. Everett Monkman of Matheson Island did attend Elim Bible Institute in Altona, Manitoba, but transferred the next year to Winnipeg Bible Institute, a nondenominational school, because of the language problem.[51]

While Indian leadership often wanted to be identified as "Mennonite," missionaries sometimes suggested that "Mennonite" be left out of the names of the new Indian and Métis congregations. There was reluctance in the Canadian Conference to list the new native congregations in the conference's yearbook alongside the more established, non-Indian congregations. Could an Indian congregation be a Mennonite church?

As an awareness of the native people as neighbors and fellow Mennonites grew, some efforts were made to involve native Mennonites in decision making and to build the contact necessary for making the mission churches feel a part of the Mennonite constituency. In 1967, the question was raised at Canadian Conference sessions: "Why are no Indians attending conference?"[52] In the following years, native pastors and other church leaders from Cross Lake, Pauingassi, Little Grand Rapids, and Selkirk spoke to the delegates (some of them through an interpreter) and attended many of the conference sessions. In 1979 Norman Meade of Manigotogan was appointed the first native member of the Native Ministries board.[53] But in 1982 none of the native churches were members of the Canadian Conference or the General Conference.

The first Mennonite congregation in the Canadian Conference to begin direct work with neighboring Indians was the North Battleford Mennonite Church in Saskatchewan. In 1973, the congregation invited Mennonite Pioneer Mission to send a half-time worker to serve the surrounding Indian communities, mainly Cree. The worker would also serve as half-time pastor for the congregation. Through the efforts of workers David and Sue Neufeld, former Mennonite Central Committee volunteers in Vietnam, the congregation helped to start a day-care center in the church building, a legal aid services center, and a Community Closet thrift store. Because of tensions within the church over such activities, the congregation withdrew its sponsorship in 1978, and Native Ministries ended its official involvement in 1979. The work continued on a private basis.

Newer involvement in Indian ministries included the Grace Mennonite Mission Church, Meadow Lake, Saskatchewan, to which Native Ministries sent workers first in 1977. In 1978-79 former Cross Lake worker Ernie Sawatsky served as Native Ministries resource person to the Mennonite Conference of Alberta. Florence Driedger of Regina, Saskatchewan, began work in 1980 raising congregational awareness of possibilities of local native ministries and helping congregations understand the aspirations and struggles of native people.

In 1981, Native Ministries had relationships with four organized native congregations (Cross Lake, Pauingassi, Selkirk, and Winnipeg) and continued in ministry in about ten other locations. As in other conference missions in North America, the Native Ministries program still struggled with untangling Mennonite faith from Mennonite culture and trying to find a way to tie that faith together with the culture of another people: the native people of Canada.

Arvada Mennonite Church

Chapter 10:
Making Missions Anabaptist

"We must realize more fully that the Believers' Church. . .was born primarily in the large cities in Europe. It became rural only during later generations because of the severe persecution. We have not yet regained the insight, conviction, and vision that a Believers' Church has a special mission in the urban life of our day." —Cornelius Krahn. 1955[1]

In the 1950s, '60s, and '70s General Conference Mennonites tried to apply their rediscovery of the Anabaptist vision to home missions. There were parallels between post-World War II North America and sixteenth-century Europe. As Mennonites became more urban, historians discovered the urban roots of Anabaptists. They found that initially Anabaptism was an urban movement. Early Anabaptists served in a variety of occupations, and only later, under persecution, did Anabaptists withdraw to the countryside and take up farming as their principal occupation.[2] The voices that had earlier identified the Mennonite way of life with the rural community were quieter now, as some, like Paul Peachey, argued that "the freedom and diversity of the city make it a better setting for the 'believers' church' than does the closed rural community."[3]

As Anabaptists had confronted the church-state, so were there needs for modern Mennonites to make their voices heard in a militarist, materialist society. As Anabaptists had met in small, intimate groups for fellowship, worship, and discipline, so Mennonites now felt the need for a more personal church in a more impersonal world. As Anabaptists had preached with enthusiasm to their neighbors and friends, so Mennonites were beginning to feel more comfortable in reaching out to their non-Mennonite neighbors. As the cultural differences that had once distinguished Mennonites from their neighbors grew fainter, Mennonites wanted a distinctive theology that could give themselves and their neighbors a fresh vision of what it meant to be the church in the world.

The Urban Mennonites

Almost every new General Conference church started after World War II was a city church. One of the reasons for this new direction in Mennonite home missions was quite simple: General Conference Mennonites were moving to the cities at an ever faster rate. Although urbanization of Mennonites before World War II had happened more slowly than in the general population, now the rate of Mennonite urbanization was far more rapid (although Mennonites' degree of urbanization was still below national averages).[4] In 1943, 54 percent of General Conference Mennonites had been farmers; in 1964, only 30.7 percent earned their living by farming.[5] Even rural churches like the Alexanderwohl Mennonite Church near Goessel, Kansas, had fewer farm families. Among adult men in that congregation, the percentage of farmers dropped from 62 percent in 1946 to 38 percent in 1956, and member families living in towns or cities rose from 29 percent to 43 percent during the same period.[6] By 1956, General Conference Mennonite churches were found in twenty-seven cities of over 9,000 population. Seventeen percent of all General Conference members were in city churches; however, the percentages varied considerably from one region to another, ranging from 1 percent in the Northern District (north central states) to 40 percent in the Conference of Mennonites in Canada.[7] In Canada, many of the Russian immigrants of the 1920s had settled first in cities rather than on farms, and their numbers were swelled by more Mennonite refugees from Europe after World War II.

Increasing the numbers of Mennonites moving to U.S. cities were the hundreds of young men doing alternative service to the military (1-W). Of 1,042 Mennonite men in 1-W in June 1957, 708 served in cities of over 10,000. Most of these men came from rural areas, but many of them remained in urban areas after their service ended. An inter-Mennonite 1-W workshop in 1957 noted that "1-W service is accelerating an already existent trend toward the urbanization of the church and the shattering of community. 1-W men are becoming socially, psychologically and economically oriented toward urban ways, and many are permanently changing vocations and locations."[8]

Especially in the Western District Conference, home mission committees provided initiative and personnel to start new churches in cities where larger concentrations of 1-W men were working: Kansas City, Topeka, and Arvada (Denver). The 1953 study conference on "The Church, the Gospel, and War" encouraged the building of Christian communities "even in urban areas" and encouraged 1-W men to "form churches now while they have large numbers of men, to provide an outlet for a Christian witness."[9]

Underlining the renewed urban emphasis in the General Conference was the fact that the conference's new seminary, Mennonite Biblical Seminary, established in 1945, was located in Chicago. Men and women who attended the seminary preached in Chicago-area churches, visited patients in the Cook County Hospital, and, most importantly, *lived* in the city. Mennonite Biblical Seminary in 1951 hosted a conference on the city church, with major addresses by Donovan E. Smucker, professor at the seminary, and John T. Neufeld, seminary business manager and long-time pastor of the Grace Mennonite Church in Chicago. Under the leadership of seminary faculty and students, a new Mennonite church grew up in Chicago, the Woodlawn Mennonite Church. Many students at the Chicago seminary graduated feeling that the city was the place where they wanted to minister. After the seminary moved to Elkhart, Indiana, in 1958, the seminary and the Board of Missions attempted to continue the city emphasis through the interdenominational Urban Training Center in Chicago, and later through the Seminary Consortium for Urban Pastoral Education, but few Mennonites took advantage of educational experiences there.

The City Church Movement

As the General Conference Mennonite Church was moving from a majority of rural members to a majority of urban members in the early 1950s, the General Conference's Board of Missions was placing relatively little emphasis on city missions. The 1950 constitutional change had combined home and foreign missions under one board, and the result was that foreign missions, expanding rapidly after World War II into Colombia and Taiwan and Japan, received most of the board's attention. The Board of Missions urged district conferences to take over all home mission work within their boundaries, and the Canadian Conference home mission committee took more direct supervision of Canadian work. The Board of Missions still provided some subsidies to new churches and kept more direct ties to "non-ethnic" missions such as Gulfport, Mississippi, and Eloy, Arizona. But even in the latter cases, the board and its staff spent little energy on these missions and did no long-range planning for them. Regional conferences, especially those which had no staff and meager finances, were sometimes ill prepared to assume full responsibility for home mission work within their areas. Furthermore, some potential sites for new missions were far from other General Conference Mennonite churches, and it was not clear which district should be responsible.

Most of the new churches started by districts were aimed at people of Mennonite heritage who had moved to an area without a Mennonite church. The Canadian Conference supported at least fourteen city churches in 1956. Among all five U.S. districts were only ten city mission churches, compared with about twenty-five district-sponsored rural mission churches. The Western District Conference, however, was on the brink of a new emphasis on city churches. The 1956 district conference session doubled its home missions budget from $25,000 to $50,000 and authorized six new city churches. Added to the city churches just starting in Topeka and Kansas City were Oklahoma City; Newton, Kansas; Arvada, Colorado; and Liberal, Kansas—all started in 1956-57.

Such was the background of an informal meeting of seventeen city church workers and their spouses, as well as the executive secretary of the Board of Missions, on August 19, 1956, at Child's Restaurant in Winnipeg during the 1956 General Conference sessions.[10] Called by Leland Harder, then pastor of First Mennonite Church in Chicago, the meeting was intended for fellowship and for discussion of what it meant to be an Anabaptist church in the city. Out of the meeting grew a newsletter, *The Mennonite Church in the City*, published from September 1956 until 1968, and a resolution to be presented on the conference floor. A similar but more general resolution, drafted by the resolutions committee passed without dissent. It asked for increased efforts in home missions during the next triennium and consideration of the appointment of an additional staff worker to promote this work.[11]

The General Conference Board of Missions had difficulty following up on the Winnipeg resolution. A proposed annual home mission study conference happened only once. The proposal to add a staff person was "a pigeon-hole minute on the secretary's register," complained *The Mennonite Church in the City* in 1959.[12] The publication noted that the separate Home Mission Board had been dissolved after eighty-four years of existence "just at the time when home missions was due for new emphasis and the departure of thousands of our members required profound and courageous action for the sake of church preservation and extension." The Board of Missions report for the 1956-59 triennium made little mention of missions in North America except those among blacks and Indians.[13]

About two months before the 1959 General Conference, the Board of Missions drafted a resolution, which the conference upheld, setting up a committee on city churches, to include board representatives, city church workers, and others. In addition, a city church staff person was to be hired. (The first was Peter Ediger, who began full-time work with the Board of Missions as city church field worker in 1961. Stan Bohn served part-time in1965-68.)[14]

District committees sometimes called on the staff of the committee on city churches to investigate a possible site for a new church: Were there people there who were interested in starting a Mennonite church? Was the population in the area growing? Should an established city church set up a voluntary service unit? The Pacific District Conference, for example, asked Ediger to investigate possible work in Phoenix and to evaluate the already established work in Portland. The committee on city churches also sponsored an inter-Mennonite city church seminar in 1962 and a research project on the Mennonite church in the city conducted by Paul Peachey under the direction of the Institute of Mennonite Studies, Elkhart, Indiana.

Those who inspired and supported the committee on city churches asked anew what forms a Christian existence in the city would need to take to be in keeping with the Anabaptist doctrine of the church.[15] One author suggested a ministry of the laity, Bible study, a caring fellowship, positive disciplines, and servanthood as the issues of church renewal.[16] Another suggested a binding fellowship, discipleship, discipline, evangelism, nurture in the church, servanthood in the world, wide distribution of leadership responsibility, stewardship, worship, and love and nonresistance as the marks of authenticity in the church.[17] John Esau rejected the "simple believism" of the early city missions, which tended to duplicate what other churches were doing, as well as "survivalism," which was concerned primarily with self-preservation and rushed in a panic to start churches in urban areas where Mennonite people had gone. The peace position, which had been soft-pedaled for fear of driving away potential members, could actually be an attraction, said Esau.

> Perhaps the time has come to call for a radical discipleship in the sense of our Anabaptist tradition. Perhaps if we were to do this we would discover that our distinctives are really our greatest point of appeal rather than an unnecessary offense. . . . Urban congregations by the very nature of their competitive situation with numerous other churches and denominations will have to take the lead in developing a peculiar Mennonite theology.[18]

Yet while the city church committee looked to Anabaptist distinctives for the theory, it often looked outside the Mennonite groups for practical models. The committee noted with approval such churches as East Harlem Protestant Parish in New York City with its storefront ghetto missions; West Side Christian Parish in Chicago; and Church of the Saviour, a house church in Washington, D.C., requiring high commitment to the church and to mission.[19]

City churches also dealt with people of predominantly rural background who had certain expectations (nurtured in a close Mennonite community) of what constituted a church. City pastors often had to deal with the difficulty "of finding and keeping the essential elements of our faith without carrying along the rural trappings and the resulting problem of satisfying the rural constituency that it is still a Mennonite church."[20]

Some less avant-garde models were also borrowed. From mainline Protestant circles and from the methods of social science research came an emphasis on analyzing a town or neighborhood before starting the church. Whereas Elmer Grubb in 1909 had ridden his bicycle up and down Los Angeles streets looking for a needy area to start a church, John Hiebert—in investigating a new church in Kamloops, British Columbia, in 1966—wrote a twenty-three-page report to the B.C. missions committee describing the city in detail and telling of his interviews with former Mennonites and other local ministers. Mennonites in the '50s and '60s also borrowed a definition of success based on rapid church growth. Its primary ingredients were full-time leadership, a growing suburban location, and an attractive building, built early in the life of the church—or even before the church began meeting. To help new churches to finance meetinghouses more systematically, the

General Conference established Church Extension Services, Inc., in 1958, a revolving loan fund set up as an alternative to direct loans from the Board of Missions. Emphasis on a building was not always beneficial, however. Two city missionaries in Saskatchewan reported in 1957, "Basically I think the group got off on the wrong foot by insisting on having a church building and a pastor before beginning services. This meant that formal organization took the place of fellowship as the motivating factor."[21]

Another issue debated more vigorously was whether Mennonite city churches should be "community churches" (that is, trying to reach the immediate neighborhood of the church building) or whether city churches should be "regional churches," drawing in people from all over the city who shared common beliefs. On the one hand were those who charged that the community church was

> a modern version of the medieval parish church and the Reformation Protestant concept of the church. It is the idea that all citizens in a given area go to the one church in that area, the assumption being that all Protestant churches are in the last analysis very much alike. This assumption is that a community church operates on a broad-minded rather than a narrow-minded philosophy; that in reality personal convictions should be sacrificed for group harmony. . . . It is church development on the basis of the lowest possible common denominator. [22]

Others attacked the community church more obliquely.

> As a sociological fact, it is clear that the residential community, on which the parish is based, is coming to be less and less the community in which the work of the world is done and the crucial decisions are made. In our urbanized society, most men do not really *live* where they reside.[23]

On the other hand there were those city church leaders who asked for the church to identify with the neighborhood in which it was located. The neighborhood was the focus of service and of working for social change. Churches such as the Woodlawn Mennonite Church in Chicago adopted a neighborhood as their parish and sought to minister to people through a church-sponsored coffeehouse and through participation in a secular community organization. "Community organization can be sharpened as a tool for mission and a demonstration of one way in which the body of Christ penetrates the world," Ed Riddick of Chicago told an urban pastors' seminar in 1966.[24]

From 1950 to 1970 about fifty new churches were started in the General Conference Mennonite Church. Twice as many city churches were organized in 1950-60 as in any prior decade of conference history.[25] Leland Harder noted that "in no previous period in the history of the conference had there been such concentrated church-planting activity on our continent."[26] The flowering of so many new churches—most of them in cities— followed a long dormant period in which few churches were started in many areas of the conference. The Bethel Church in Lancaster, Pennsylvania, erected in 1952, was the first new church building in the Eastern District Conference in forty years.[27]

But the city church movement itself slowed about 1968. Part of the reason was that the regional conferences were heavily burdened with support of many of the churches already started, which were not becoming self-supporting as fast as the conferences had hoped. Other factors also diverted energy from the city church movement: the North American effects of the Vietnam War and the reorganization of the Board of Missions and the Board of Christian Service under the new constitution of the General Conference adopted in 1968. Then, too, mobility and anonymity were becoming rural as well as urban concerns. The new Commission on Home Ministries had no separate committee on city churches.

In spite of the city churches' too frequent dependence on attractive church buildings, middle-class suburban neighborhoods, ethnic identity, and traditional forms, the city church movement showed more clearly what earlier city churches in Wichita and Winnipeg had tried to say: Mennonites of rural background could live in the city and still be Mennonite. Whereas earlier city churches had tried to reach out to the poor non-Mennonites or to transplanted Mennonites, the city church movement tried to reach out to middle-class neighbors of transplanted Mennonites. It was an important step in untangling faith and culture.

Developing a Social Conscience

With the new emphasis on Anabaptism came an expansion in the number of societywide social issues with which the General Conference was concerned. Before World War II, social issues on which the conference took a stand were few: conscientious objection to military service, temperance, and membership in secret societies were the primary issues. Thrust more deeply by the war into the affairs of the world beyond Mennonite circles, General Conference Mennonites took an interest in more social issues after World War II. A study conference on

"The Church and Its Witness in Society" in Winnipeg on January 9-11, 1951, packed seventeen major papers into three days and drew 300 delegates from 80 percent of the Canadian Conference congregations.[28] A 1961 conference on "The Church in Society" covered such topics as labor-management relationships, underdeveloped nations, civil defense, race relations, church and state, the offender, alcohol, and urbanization and agriculture. By the 1970s, the General Conference peace and social concerns office was dealing with such topics as nuclear energy, use of the automobile, abortion, the role of women in the church, the Christian and economics, war taxes, and aging. The Washington and Ottawa offices of the Mennonite Central Committee U.S. Peace Section and MCC (Canada) kept Mennonites informed about legislative developments in these areas, working under the assumption that Mennonites wanted to influence their members of Congress and Parliament on issues of social welfare and human rights.

Among the most emotion-laden of the social issues was race. In Canada the frictions were between white and Indian or Métis. In the United States most of the frictions were between white and black. Although Mennonites themselves were a minority ethnic group in both countries, they had become upwardly mobile fairly quickly and often had trouble identifying with other minorities, particularly those of lower socioeconomic status.

The issue of black-white relations gained prominence in the General Conference in the late-1950s as the United States as a whole was dealing with the implications of the 1954 Supreme Court decision outlawing separate but equal schools for blacks. The Mennonite Central Committee Peace Section began an active interest in race issues in 1955, and the 1959 sessions of the General Conference adopted a statement on "The Christian and Race Relations." After vigorous discussion of such concerns as interracial marriage, the 1959 delegates adopted the resolution calling for each congregation to welcome persons of "whatever color or national origin" as members and leaders. The resolution also asked conference-related institutions not to discriminate in personnel and admission policies.[29]

Some General Conference Mennonites got involved in the freedom movement in the U.S. South by sending food and clothing to Tennessee black farmers who were put off their land because they had voted. Some sponsored voluntary service projects in black neighborhoods. Others hosted "fresh-air" children in Mennonite farm homes, walked in peace marches for civil rights, and rebuilt bombed black churches through Mennonite Disaster Service. The civil rights movement was perhaps the first occasion in which General Conference Mennonites got involved in nonviolent civil disobedience on behalf of people who were not Mennonites.

The 1950s marked the beginning of General Conference home mission work among American blacks. The Mennonite Church had begun a mission among blacks as early as 1891;[30] however, before World War II the General Conference Mennonite Church had no mission work among blacks and had only a handful of Indian members. The first Indian mission churches were not fully admitted as members of the General Conference until 1956.[31]

After the conference reorganization in 1950, the new Board of Missions set as a priority starting missions among Jews and blacks in North America. The strategy did not include bringing members of these groups into General Conference membership, however, and straining the sense of ethnic solidarity. Instead, with both groups, the Board of Missions chose to support interdenominational missions: in the case of the Jews, the House of Friendship in Kitchener, Ontario (see Chapter 5); in the case of blacks, East Harlem Protestant Parish, started in 1949 by a group of pacifist students at Union Theological Seminary. Among these students was Hugh Hostetler, a Mennonite, who applied for and received support from the General Conference Home Mission Board.

East Harlem Protestant Parish leaned heavily on social action approaches to human need and the use of existing facilities for worship—an apartment house, a rented storefront. The project, located in a thirty-block slum area of New York City, had five churches in 1953 with a membership of 323. In addition to partially supporting Hostetler, the General Conference funded summer voluntary service units in East Harlem in 1950-52, 1965, and 1968. The East Harlem project was controversial with the General Conference Board of Missions because of its social-service approach to ministry, and official General Conference sponsorship ended in 1956.[32]

Black Churches in the General Conference

As job opportunities drew Dutch-German-Swiss Mennonites to the cities after World War II, they also drew blacks to the cities, and the larger black urban populations began expanding out of the earlier ghettos into previously all-white residential areas. Racial tensions and fears often resulted in white residents' fleeing to the suburbs and such neighborhoods becoming virtually all black. Such was the case in several cities where the General Conference had established city missions: Philadelphia, Chicago, Peoria, and Los Angeles.

Churches chose different ways of coping with the issues of neighborhood change. In Philadelphia, First Mennonite Church chose to leave its center-city location and go to suburban Huntingdon Valley, while Second Mennonite Church chose to stay in its location and serve both blacks and Puerto Ricans. It became a mission church for a second time in 1961. The Mennonite Gospel Mission in Peoria, Illiinois, sold its church in an area of growing black population and merged with the Ann Street Mennonite Church (MC). The Immanuel Mennonite Church in Los Angeles sold its building and moved to suburban Downey, California. First Mennonite Church in Chicago stayed in its neighborhood. Although the congregation was divided in 1965 on the race question, a few long-time members stood by Pastor Harry Spaeth during the transition in the neighborhood and invited black families to join the church. First Church now has a small but active group of black members, a black lay pastor (John Burke), and one elderly white member. In Oklahoma City, attempts to establish a Mennonite church were less successful than carrying on service projects in the black community. Mennonite workers there chose to affiliate in 1970 with an interracial Presbyterian congregation, which became the Trinity United Mennonite-Presbyterian Church. That affiliation ended in 1979.

For a number of years, leaders of the city church movement pointed with pride to the Woodlawn Mennonite Church in Chicago as the first organized church in the General Conference to have an interracial membership and integrated pastoral leadership. The congregation had not started with racial integration in mind; it began meeting in 1950 as a Sunday school for children of students and staff at the new Mennonite Biblical Seminary in Chicago. The seminary rented a nearby church building, and J. N. Smucker, then editor of *The Mennonite*, served as part-time pastor, assisted by seminary students.

Almost as soon as the new church was organized in 1951, middle-class black residents began to move into the neighborhood around the seminary. The congregation actively sought black participation, but at first it attracted mostly neighborhood children. By 1957 more nonseminary people held leadership positions, and for the first time several black women from the community were serving as Sunday school teachers. "This restores in some sense the goal, even in a transitional inner-city situation, of an indigenous leadership and congregation," noted *The Mennonite Church in the City*.[33] By 1959, a year after the seminary left Chicago for Elkhart, Indiana, the congregation had twenty-nine black members and twenty-five white members plus a white pastor—Delton Franz—and a black associate pastor—Vincent Harding, the first black church leader in the General Conference. The congregation got financial support from the General Conference Board of Missions (and later the Central District Conference), beginning in 1953.

When Curtis Burrell, Jr., became the congregation's second black pastor in 1966, the neighborhood was changing again—from middle-class black to poor black. Burrell chose to emphasize a ministry to the neighborhood over a ministry to his own church members, becoming involved in the Kenwood-Oakland Community Organization (of which civil rights leader Jesse Jackson had been the first coordinator in 1965) and in ministry to local gangs of young men, particularly the Black P. Stone Nation. Coupled with this neighborhood ministry were the slogans of "black power" and black self-sufficiency. Burrell renamed the congregation the "First Church of MAN (Making a Nation)" and wrote of black peoplehood and of the necessity of black people's religion picturing "blacks as the 'people' having been predestined to triumph over all times and circumstances and ordered of the Father to lead the way in building a world for all people."[34]

Such a ministry ran into trouble after the church building was burned on July 29, 1970. The arson was blamed on members of the Black P. Stone Nation whom Burrell had hired in the community organization and later fired. Burrell, the congregation, and some conference leaders quickly organized a fund-raising campaign to rebuild the church building. But the Central District home missions committee felt it was receiving double messages on whether Burrell wanted white help in rebuilding. The committee felt Burrell was not giving adequate financial reporting of mission funds, and it was further disturbed by Burrell's statements on some Mennonite college campuses in 1971 about his personal life. Support for Burrell was also waning among most of the middle-class black members of the congregation. The Central District ended its subsidy in 1971, and the congregation dissolved.[35]

The Community Mennonite Church in Markham, Illinois, a southern suburb of Chicago, had more success in maintaining a racially integrated congregation. Part of the reason for this

was the fact that the city itself remained integrated, with significant numbers of white residents remaining as blacks moved in.
The Markham congregation was one of the first new mission
projects of the Middle District (later Central District) in 1955,
intended to attract members of First and Grace churches who
had moved to the suburbs as well as to reach the unchurched. In
the latter objective, the church was more successful; in 1964
only eight of forty-six members had come from other Chicago
Mennonite churches. The congregation took in its first black
members in 1961 after considerable controversy.[36] Pastor Larry
Voth actively visited both blacks and whites in the neighborhood, inviting them to church. By 1978, the participants in the
congregation were about equally divided between blacks and
whites. Participants came from a variety of backgrounds:
Methodist, Baptist, Lutheran, Catholic, Presbyterian, and
Mennonite. "White families have come because we are a socially active church. Blacks have come because they are interested in an alternative to their own tradition," said one
member of the Markham church.[37] In the 1960s members of the
congregation participated in civil rights demonstrations and
went to Washington, D.C., to talk to congressmen about the
Vietnam War. The congregation sponsors a day nursery and a
Mennonite Voluntary Service unit.

The Rainbow Boulevard Mennonite Church in Kansas
City, Kansas, established in 1957, also had an interracial membership within its first decade. The interracial youth program
involved the church in discussions with the Young Men's Christian Association, and a city recreation league which had turned
down the requests of the youth group to use the swimming pool
and other facilities. The church sponsored a "freedom school"
for black children boycotting the illegally segregated public
school system. Several members were involved in an integrated
neighborhood association that met in the church building, in
some civil rights demonstrations, and in some equal-
opportunity housing efforts. "I think it would be true to say that
black people's rights were a cause Mennonites responded to,"
said Stanley Bohn, pastor in Kansas City in 1957-66.[38]

The Poverty Fund

In 1968 the social atmosphere in the United States included the black power movement and James Foreman's demands for "reparations" from white churches for past injustices
to blacks. In that atmosphere came a "Resolution on Poverty in
North America" to the 1968 General Conference sessions. Initi-

ated by a Sunday school class at the Arvada (Colorado) Mennonite Church and presented by the conference's Board of
Christian Service, the resolution called for education of General
Conference members on the plight of the poor, finding ways for
the poor to help themselves out of their situation, and establishing a million-dollar fund over the next triennium to finance
poverty-related programs.[39]

Although the conference adopted the resolution without
an amendment to expand the scope of the program to overseas
projects, the Poverty Fund, as it was set up by the General
Board, divided its activities among North American and foreign projects. Under the staff leadership of Gary Franz, the
Poverty Fund launched a campaign to educate General Conference Mennonites about poverty and provided some seed money
for projects designed to alleviate the plight of the poor. From
1969 to 1972 the Poverty Fund collected $208,613.86. The Pov-
erty Fund, however, was abolished by the 1971 triennial conference because of the conference's commissions feeling of
financial competition. Beginning in 1973, each of the three
conference commissions—Home Ministries, Education, and
Overseas Mission—included some money for poverty concerns
in their budgets, and Home Ministries and Education created a
joint Poverty-Affluence Reference Council to distribute poverty
monies to North American projects related to community
ministries, Indian ministries, voluntary service, and education.
From 1973 to 1979, poverty monies averaged about $47,000 a
year.

War, Counterculture, and Taking Stock

The years 1965-75 brought new emphases to the General
Conference. The starting of new churches came almost to a halt
as conference mission committees felt they could extend themselves no further, and as the Vietnam War brought new issues to
consider. By 1970, near the height of the war, more General
Conference young men in the United States were registering as
conscientious objectors than ever before during a time of the
draft: 63 percent, compared with 52 percent in 1960 and 27
percent in 1944.[40] But now the historic peace churches no longer
constituted the bulk of conscientious objectors. The Vietnam
War was an unpopular war, and thousands of young men
refused to serve in the military. Mennonite pastors served as
draft counselors for many non-Mennonites.

Many of those who could not get conscientious-objector
status from their draft boards fled to Canada; an estimated

30,000 to 40,000 draft resisters were in Canada in 1974. Although Canada was not directly involved in the war in Vietnam, Canadian Mennonites became involved in the plight of American resisters in cities like Toronto, Vancouver, and Ottawa. For example, Mennonites were represented on the Winnipeg War Resisters Committee, and some kept draft immigrants in their homes. In the United States, Mennonites had to deal with the fact that many of the Vietnam pacifists were not Mennonites and some were political rather than religious pacifists.

General Conference Mennonites, like many other religious groups in North America, were divided in their opinions about the war, but the official conference stance was one of opposition to this war, as to all other wars. Conference resolutions asked for reduction of military acts and for increased economic aid to Vietnam.[41] Students in Mennonite colleges, delegates to the Amsterdam Mennonite World Conference, and other Mennonites in various places gave money through Mennonite Central Committee (Canada) to aid war sufferers in North Vietnam. CFAM, a Mennonite radio station in Altona, Manitoba, sponsored a drive for food in Vietnam. The Markham, Illinois, church wrote a statement on Vietnam, but the local papers refused to print it, even as an advertisement.[42] Some draft-age Mennonite young men chose not to register for the draft, even for alternative service, and served prison terms. Such draft resisters won some official support from conference bodies, including the Western District Conference in 1969 and the General Conference in 1971.[43]

Some Mennonites, like other pacifists, were also applying their scruples about participation in the armed forces to the payment of taxes used for war. As early as 1959, the General Conference encouraged the Board of Christian Service "to give attention to this problem, seeking for an acceptable solution to the same for all who have convictions against so supporting military efforts."[44] The levying of war taxes was another form of conscription, the tax resisters said. The tax issue was a new attempt to apply the Anabaptist principle of peacemaking to a situation which had not confronted the early Anabaptists: the almost universal federal income tax which funded a vast military operation more dependent on technology than on people. The issue got its most intense discussion around the request in 1974 of a General Conference employee, Cornelia Lehn, that the conference not withhold federal income taxes from her paycheck so that she could have the opportunity not to pay war taxes, to which she was conscientiously opposed. A special session of the General Conference February 9-10, 1979, still had not settled the issue of whether the conference should break federal law in order to meet the demands of conscience.[45] In 1982 the General Conference planned to take the government to court to gain the right not to withhold employee's taxes, but an unfavorable ruling on a similar case in the Supreme Court caused the conference to stop pursuing the case.[46]

The Vietnam years also involved Mennonites in other issues of North American culture: a renewed concern for protection of the environment, a questioning of materialism and efforts to simplify lifestyles, a questioning of old structures and rituals and, on the other hand, a feeling of threat at the passing of old forms.

One of the new forms which Mennonite churches were taking, beginning about 1960, was inter-Mennonite affiliation. Gone now were the days when congregations left the Mennonite Church to join the General Conference. Now they joined both conferences. Earlier distinctions were becoming blurred, and inter-Mennonite cooperation took place in consultations about overseas missions and in cooperation between Mennonite Biblical Seminary (General Conference) and Goshen Biblical Seminary (Mennonite Church), which began a joint program in Elkhart and Goshen, Indiana, in 1958.

The General Conference Mennonite Church had had the unity of all Mennonites as a goal since its founding in 1860, but in the hundred years after its founding, that goal had been realized only with individual independent congregations and with the Central Conference of Mennonites.

The urge to set up inter-Mennonite congregations often came from Mennonite students and faculty at state universities. Mennonites on many secular campuses had been meeting together for fellowship since the early 1950s. Where few Mennonites were located, differences among Mennonite groups seemed small in comparison with the differences from other churches.

One of the first such student groups to affiliate with both the General Conference Mennonite Church and the Mennonite Church was at Ohio State University at Columbus. Sunday school classes for students and their families began November 24, 1957, but the new group had no pastor. Since it was composed of almost equal numbers of General Conference and Mennonite Church students, the group decided to request Sunday morning speakers from both conferences.

Although the decision to function on an inter-Mennonite basis had been at the initiative of the Columbus group, the suggestion to affiliate officially with more than one conference came in 1962 from the denominations and their student services committees, which had been meeting jointly once a year. The congregation organized in 1962 as the Neil Avenue Mennonite Church and began the negotiations with the Central District Conference (GC) and the Ohio and Eastern Conference (MC) on joint affiliation. Lay leader Alton M. Shelly told the conference representatives in 1963,

> We as a Mennonite church continue to hope that Mennonites who come to Columbus will join our group and enter into the life of our church regardless of former conference affiliation. We have been concerned that joining one conference might gradually hamper our ministry to Mennonites from other conferences. There is a strong desire among members of our church to have a closer tie and working relationship with the total Mennonite church. We are very much interested in considering the possibilities and implications of affiliating with both Conferences.[47]

By 1964 the congregation and the conferences had worked out the details on conference relationships and toleration of some doctrinal differences, and the Neil Avenue Church was accepted into both the Central District Conference and the Ohio and Eastern Conference. The church first began receiving financial support from both conferences in 1967, when its part-time pastor began full-time service for the congregation.

Other congregations became inter-Mennonite by the merger of two churches affiliated with separate denominations. The Rainbow Boulevard Mennonite Church in Kansas City, Kansas, was the first inter-Mennonite congregation in North America. It was formed by the merger in 1964 (a few months earlier than the Columbus action) of Grace Mennonite Church, which was affiliated with the Mennonite Church, and the Rainbow Boulevard Mennonite Church, which was a member of the General Conference. The new congregation simply kept the conference affiliations of the original churches.

Since 1964, at least thirty Mennonite congregations have affiliated with both the General Conference Mennonite Church and the Mennonite Church. Some have been in university settings (Urbana, Illinois; Ames, Iowa; Boston, Massachusetts; Ann Arbor, Michigan). Others were new urban churches that wanted to attract all Mennonites into one congregation rather than into two struggling, competing congregations in the same city (Tucson, Arizona; Cincinnati, Ohio). Still others were congregations which had belonged to one conference for a number of years and later decided to join a second conference as well— usually because of a growing number of new members who had previously been part of the second conference (Minneapolis, Minnesota; and Smithville, Ohio, for example). Other inter-Mennonite churches came about through the merger of two congregations (Normal, Illinois; Kansas City, Kansas; and Peoria, Illinois). Although conference officials did not discourage dual—or in one case, triple—affiliation, initiative for inter-Mennonite churches usually came from the local level.

Some General Conference congregations have also been affiliated with non-Mennonite conferences. The Trinity congregation in Oklahoma City was both Mennonite and United Presbyterian. Ecumenikos, a lay-led house church in suburban Kansas City, Kansas, began as an experimental mission of five denominations—General Conference Mennonite Church, Christian Church, United Church of Christ, United Presbyterian Church in the U.S.A., and United Methodist Church—and is affiliated with all five.

In Ontario, the Conference of the United Mennonite Churches of Ontario (GC) cooperates closely with two Mennonite Church conferences in missions as well as education and other matters. The Pacific District Conference and the Southwest Mennonite Conference have started joint missions in Arizona and California.

A new Mennonite congregation seeking affiliation with only one conference may soon be the exception. As additional inter-Mennonite churches are formed, informal pressure builds for more cooperation at the denominational level and for merger of Mennonite programs and publications.

The inter-Mennonite churches were, almost by definition, composed of strong cores of Mennonites by heritage who valued their denominational ties and attempted to attract other scattered Mennonites to their churches. However, the inter-Mennonite churches were about as successful as single-conference city churches in reaching out to those of non-Mennonite backgrounds.

Another new form of the church which took shape particularly in the 1970s was the house church. Although churches which met in homes were prevalent in the first three centuries of the church and among the sixteenth-century Anabaptists, modern interest in the house church can be traced to Ernest Southcott, an Anglican parish priest, who published the book *The Parish Comes Alive* in 1956, and to Hans-Ruedi Weber of the World Council of Churches whose article on house churches was reprinted in the Mennonite pamphlet *Concern* No. 5.[48] Another source of inspiration was the Church of the Saviour in Washington, D.C.

In some Christian circles, the term *house church* came to include any small group meeting within a congregation for fellowship, psychological healing, and spiritual growth, but the house church was not necessarily "the church," empowered to administer the sacraments and take on all other functions of a congregation. Mennonites were perhaps unique in promoting the house church as an authentic structure for the church, not just a temporary condition until a congregation could buy a building and become a "real church."[49]

Beginning in 1957 with Reba Place Fellowship (an intentional community in Evanston, Illinois, now affiliated with the Church of the Brethren) and continuing with The Assembly in Goshen, Indiana; the Cincinnati Mennonite Fellowship; Mennonite Church of the Servant, Wichita; Covenant Mennonite Church, Hesston, Kansas; Kitchener-Waterloo House Churches; and others—house churches became a part of North American Mennonitism. Such house churches usually met in groups of ten to twenty in homes, although they sometimes met in rented facilities. The term *house* referred more to a quality of face-to-face interaction than to a place of worship.[50] When a group grew too large for such close interaction, the frequent solution was not to find a larger meeting place, but to subdivide into two or more house churches.

Mennonite house churches tended to look for precedent for their actions and structures in the house meetings of the Anabaptists. John W. Miller wrote in 1958 of the "household church" as a challenge to the "worship-as-you-please, believe-as-you-please" churches.

> We share with our Anabaptist forefathers the deep conviction that the meaning of history belongs to those who gather unreservedly to Christ, bringing to him, the living head, and to his body, the Church, the whole of life and going with him even when he sets his face to Jerusalem, martyrdom, and death.[51]

Some house churches began spontaneously and functioned without paid leadership. Other house churches were the product of regional conference home mission committee efforts. As renewed efforts at starting new churches began in 1973, the General Conference Commission on Home Ministries adopted the goal of training leaders for house church planting. Regional conferences were encouraged to hire part-time "church planters" to plant and nurture house churches, and David Whitermore became the Home Ministries staff person to investigate possible locations for new churches and coordinate district efforts. About fifty Mennonite-related house churches were started in the 1970s, and in 1977 and 1979, twelve of them joined the General Conference. In 1978 a bimonthly newsletter called *The House Church* was started "to promote and define the concept of the house church and to be a means of communication among existing house churches and fellowships."[52]

The house-church method of home missions served more than one purpose. The house church was a new attempt to apply sixteenth-century Anabaptist principles to twentieth-century North America. It also allowed regional conferences to start more churches simultaneously, since funds for new church buildings were not necessary.

Evangelism Strategies

Funds for starting new churches were in short supply after the adoption of the new General Conference constitution in 1968. The constitutional revision was an effort to reunify evangelism and service. The constitution's primary purpose, in addition to providing a somewhat strengthened General Board, was to combine foreign missions and service under a Commission on Overseas Mission, and North American missions and services under a Commission on Home Ministries. One of the unexpected results of the constitutional change was an immediate decrease in the contributions to Home Ministries from the General Conference churches. Contributions fell from $398,000 in 1969 to $307,000 in 1971.[53] The level of giving built up slowly in the succeeding years, but the number of "home missionaries" and mission churches directly under the Commission on Home Ministries decreased as more responsibility for church extension, or "church planting," as it came to be called, was transferred to regional conferences. The regional conferences— particularly the Conference of Mennonites in Canada, the Western District Conference, and the Central District Conference— built up new programs, added staff, supervised mission projects, and asked for more equal partnership relationships with the General Conference commissions. The increased decentralization was most evident in church planting, where, by 1978, the Commission on Home Ministries had a one-sixth-time staff person who gave general coordination to a number of church planters employed by regional conferences. By the 1970s regional conferences were responsible for all new mission churches, with the General Conference giving subsidies to home mission committees of some of the smaller districts.

The new Commission on Home Ministries, with Palmer Becker as executive secretary, emphasized providing resources for "living, active congregations" in "evangelism that cares." Winning new people to the Mennonite faith was to happen as much through existing congregations as through starting new churches. Throughout the post-World War II period, with Mennonites' increased contact with society at large, the General Conference had had a concern for evangelism, but it was a concern tinged with self-doubt and a lack of models for doing evangelism as an ethnic minority. Although Mennonites found it hard to argue against evangelism in general, evangelism in particular was threatening to the communal spirit. Even where language barriers did not exist, other cultural distinctives existed which were subject to revision if "outsiders" came into the church. Herman W. Enns, city pastor in Hamilton, Ontario, summarized the problems in a 1963 presentation to a conference of mission workers:

> Why do we start churches in certain cities? Is it merely to minister to the Mennonites who have gone there? Evidently some of our own people see this as the only reason why we are here. Someone, after he heard how much money had already been invested in a certain project, suggested that it would be cheaper to fly the few Mennonites that were in the city to other Mennonite churches in the province every Sunday of the year.
>
> In the past we have not been too successful in establishing good inter-Mennonite relations. We have not been successful in winning non-Mennonites to our Fellowship; even though we may be going through the motions of making ecumenical efforts and of seeking to win those of non-Mennonite background. The very fact of locating in a city where there are few Mennonites can be such a motion; in our heart of hearts we are saying that it cannot be done. We have tried it and it didn't work. What is even worse, we may be hoping that it will not work because of the host of problems this might raise. But this attitude is a denial of faith. Through faith it can be done and in obedience [to] Christ's intention and commission it must be done.[54]

Board of Missions staff person Malcolm Wenger asked,

> Has it been easier to send representatives to the frontiers than to work where we are the "sent ones"? Has the ocean been easier to cross than the street?...Perhaps we feared some of the implications for our church if we did win some.[55]

The Board of Missions did not usually address such ethnic issues, but relied on general Protestant evangelism techniques. Its evangelism committee exhorted congregations to do more evangelism, providing brochures, workshops, articles in *The Mennonite* and *Der Bote*, and suggestions for calling on prospective members and keeping a file on them. The year 1962 was suggested as a year of renewed emphasis on evangelism.

The Commission on Home Ministries, after 1969, also introduced General Conference pastors to a number of techniques from evangelical Protestantism: James Kennedy's Clinic on Evangelism, Fort Lauderdale, Florida, and Lay Witness Missions, in particular. The General Conference participated in an inter-Mennonite evangelism conference in Minneapolis in 1972 called "Probe 72" and in the interdenominational Key 73 emphasis on evangelism in the following year. But the effects of Key 73 were minimal. The commission reported to the General Conference in 1974:

> Key 73 was intended to be a fresh approach to help Christians work together in sharing their faith through word/deed ministries. But many congregations and groups simply "tried harder" without asking questions about why persons were in need or why old patterns of evangelism were not effective.[56]

In 1971 the Commission on Home Ministries began promoting the congregational goal-setting program of In-Depth Evangelism Associates, a nondenominational organization which based its strategy on modern business management techniques. The commission, however, soon began modifying the program to fit General Conference theology better. Eventually, In-Depth Evangelism Associates dissolved, and the Commission on Home Ministries again rewrote the materials, now named "Congregational Goals Discovery Plan," to fit the Anabaptist point of view. But more materials were sold to non-Mennonite than to Mennonite churches.

The General Conference also chose to attempt evangelism through the media of radio and television. What had begun as a local daily devotional broadcast on KJRG radio, Newton, Kansas, in 1953 was later expanded into a conferencewide project (first under the Board of Education and Publication, then the Board of Missions, and later the Commission on Home Ministries). The format consisted of hymns and messages by local Mennonite ministers. The early program had two functions: to serve the aged and invalid who could not come to church, and to "present the message of reconciliation with God through Christ and the Christian faith as a living experience to the general public." Beginning in 1967 the General Conference's radio division—now Faith and Life Radio and Television—cooperated with Mennonite Broadcasts, Inc. (an agency of the Mennonite Church), as well as the Mennonite Brethren Church and the Church of the Brethren in producing public service television spots on such subjects as marriage, family life, peacemaking, alienation, and simple lifestyle. The General Conference has also cooperated with Mennonite Broadcasts on "Choice" radio programs, now in sixty-second or ninety-second formats. The radio-television work was intended as a general witness in society, a way to get individuals to think in new ways about some topics of religious importance, rather than an evangelistic tool for congregations. For the latter purpose, a way of measuring was lacking.[57]

Evangelism Evaluation

Most of the external evangelism strategies of the past thirty years have had little measurable effect on church membership—either in the General Conference Mennonite Church or in other denominations. Author Howard Snyder noted that "evangelism will fail if it does not grow out of the integrity and spiritual vitality of the local congregation." In evaluating such Christian mass media campaigns as Key 73, "Here's Life," and Evangelism in Depth, Snyder concluded that, although such efforts produced thousands of "decisions," they produced only a trickle of church members. Evangelism, he said, must be kept in proper relationship to the church's larger work of acknowledging Christ's lordship in every area of society and culture.[58]

The General Conference—in spite of problems it shared with other denominations and its own particular problems—grew in total membership after 1950—from 47,732 in the United States and Canada in 1950 to 58,464 in 1977, an increase of 28 percent, or about 1 percent per year. However, most of this growth came through accepting new congregations into the conference rather than through growth of existing congregations. Leland Harder, in his *Factbook of Congregational Membership,* showed that, although General Conference membership in North America grew 21 percent between 1950 and 1968, the 1950 figure represented 213 churches and the 1968 figure, 295 churches. When Harder looked at 210 churches throughout the eighteen-year period, he found a new gain of only 4 percent.[59]

About half of the seventy-five new churches admitted to the General Conference in 1950-68 were new city churches. The other half consisted of new small-town churches plus older churches deciding to join the conference, such as the ten Bergthaler congregations in Manitoba which were added in 1968. An additional thirty-five churches joined the conference in 1971-79; twenty of these were located in cities of over 9,000. Thus, much of the growth of the General Conference after World War II came not from providing better evangelistic techniques to existing congregations, but from establishing new Mennonite churches where there were none before, particularly in cities.

The city churches started in the post-World War II period were only slightly more successful than their rural and small-town counterparts in attracting people of non-Mennonite background. Although the theology of the city church movement supported outreach to all who needed a church home, regardless of ethnic background, most of the new city churches of the 1950s and 1960s attracted primarily scattered Mennonites. In the Central District Conference, for example, the overall percentage of nonethnic membership (defined as members neither of whose parents were Mennonites) was 17.3 percent in 1970. But rural churches such as North Danvers, Illinois; and Pulaski, Iowa, had as high or higher percentage of nonethnic members as new city churches in Fort Wayne, Indiana; and Columbus, Ohio. The largest percentages of nonethnic members were found in Chicago and the city missions established before World War II.[60] In 1977 urban churches still differed from rural churches most in their greater number of membership transfers from other General Conference churches.

A number of factors affected churches' ability to attract those outside of Mennonite ethnic circles:

1. The smaller the percentage of members who lived on farms, the more likely a church was to have members of other backgrounds. The exceptions to this were the district or provincial conferences which had larger concentrations of churches in a given area, resulting in less intermarriage and the bringing in of fewer spouses of non-Mennonite background.[61]

2. The longer the time since immigration to North America and since the English had been in use, the more likely a church was to have members of other backgrounds. In 1970 the Eastern and Central districts led the way in nonethnic membership with 26.5 percent and 17.3 percent respectively, while the Canadian Conference had 2.1 percent.[62]

3. The shorter the time since immigration to North America, the more likely was nonethnic membership to be concentrated in cities. The longer the time since immigration, the less difference in ethnic makeup between city and country or small-town churches.

Church workers in the 1950s and thereafter searched for ways to cross the ethnic barriers, realizing that many rural Mennonites who moved to the cities were not joining urban Mennonite churches (sometimes because the urban churches were too different from their home churches in size and style). "We can no longer depend on cultural traits or language to identify Mennonites or provide the motivation for them to automatically join another Mennonite church," a Winnipeg study group told the Church and Society Conference in Chicago, October 31 to November 3, 1961. "The growth of our churches will eventually depend as much on non-Mennonites as on Mennonites."[63]

A gathering of General Conference city church workers in 1959 raised questions about how their heritage could be shared with others:

> We are not sure, partly because we ourselves are uncertain as to the dividing line between our religious faith and our ethnic culture. Are we seeking at times to make men and women part of the "Mennonite people" or part of the Mennonite church?
>
> We are therefore often afraid of truly indigenous Mennonite city churches because we do not believe (and perhaps rightly so) that members of such churches could be assimilated into our culture. (Perhaps when barriers of culture prevent the building of true Christian fellowship, these barriers need to be broken down, like all dividing walls of hostility.)[64]

If some pastors complained that a Mennonite nucleus sometimes kept out new church members because of subtle cultural barriers, there was the other side of the coin. Churches which tried to reach out to people of non-Mennonite background but did not have a Mennonite nucleus sometimes could not continue at all. A church in Winnipegosis, Manitoba, tried to minister to people of Ukrainian descent for a brief period in the 1960s. An inter-Mennonite congregation in populous Orange County, California, dissolved in 1977 after attempting for about ten years to start without a Mennonite nucleus other than the pastor's family.

The 1970s and 1980s saw a renewed emphasis on "non-ethnic missions" of the style designed to set up separate, culturally distinctive churches. By 1982, ten Chinese Mennonite congregations were relating to the General Conference. The Conference of Mennonites in Canada became involved in starting Chinese Mennonite churches in Vancouver and Winnipeg. The Pacific District Conference was sponsoring four ethnic Chinese churches. One of these, the Santa Clara (California) Ethnic Chinese Mennonite Church, had as its pastor Adam Liu, a former Mennonite pastor in Taiwan who immigrated to the United States and began work with other Chinese-speaking immigrants. Spanish-speaking congregations also got new attention. In 1979 the Commission on Home Ministries hired Ernst Harder, a former missionary in Uruguay and Paraguay, to oversee and encourage Spanish ministries. In 1978 at least five General Conference congregations in the United States were involved with Spanish-speaking people. The new ethnic churches met a need for people whose first language was neither English nor German. The challenge was whether these churches would be a "foreign" mission at home or whether they would be welcomed into the General Conference family.

The New Anabaptists

Although some congregations had problems accepting people of other ethnic backgrounds (whether black, Indian, or "English"), other congregations were able to "break down the dividing walls." By 1970, over a third of General Conference congregations had at least 10 percent of their members of non-Mennonite parentage.

Among the relatively few Canadian churches with a larger number of ethnic backgrounds represented (one writer counted eleven in 1975) was the Waters Mennonite Church near the mining city of Sudbury, Ontario. The church began in 1946 independent of any mission board and under the leadership of Thomas and Elvina Martin, of Old Order Mennonite background. In the late 1940s the Martins as well as Mahlon and Norma Bast taught children's Sunday schools for Finnish and English-Canadian children. The project was under the Mennonite Church mission board from 1948 to 1955, but joined the General Conference in 1959 because most of the Mennonites who moved to the area were of General Conference background, and the group had not bothered keeping the "details" of Mennonite Church doctrine, particularly the head covering for women.

In 1963 attendance from the non-Mennonite community was still mostly children, so the congregation started to emphasize the need for parents to bring their children. The church grew, but not without struggle. Pastor Menno J. Ediger reported,

> We have come to the conclusion, simply stated, that a mission church such as we are trying to be, demands more of most people than they are willing to give, of themselves and of their things. It is our further conviction that if a choice must be made between the two, in emphasis, that we are here to be a church in the community where any who feel the need of what the church has to offer may come, rather than to a comfortable group of people with similar background who have nice fellowship and good times together. I do not believe that it is a matter of either-or, and we shall continue to strive toward meeting the needs and desires of both groups.[65]

Karen Salo, who had grown up in the congregation, noted in 1975:

> Though the Waters Church is inwardly very Anabaptist, outwardly it is not Mennonite at all (we do not stress the Mennonite culture or history, even though about half of our membership is of Mennonite background).[66]

Another congregation which attracted a number of people of non-Mennonite background was the Arvada Mennonite Church, located in a western Denver suburb. Although the church was begun in 1957 "to gather the nucleus of Mennonites (GCs, both permanent residents and 1-Ws) into a fellowship,"[67] rather than hiding their Mennonitism, the church took an open stand on issues of peace and justice, a stand which was attractive to a number of persons who had dropped out of mainline churches. One such new member, Nancy Williams, in a 1975 presentation to the Consultation of Church Growth, Bluffton, Ohio, noted the parallels between the Arvada church and the early Anabaptists as a diverse city folk.

> Arvada Mennonite is a city church. Once again there are scholars, artisans, and craftsmen. Once again we reach out across ethnic names, food, and language to those not of the Family and offer love and acceptance to all who would draw near with faith. Once again we have diversity of background and belief but affirmation of equality and faith within the Brotherhood. Once again both men and women preach the Word, baptize, and offer the Lord's Supper. We dialog about war and peace with Air Force cadets and Rocky Flats workers; we provide low-income housing; we collect for CROP, etc. We care about each other and the world.
>
> Arvada Mennonite is a radical church, growing from our roots in the cities of the renaissance, nourished in the soil of our tradi-

Table 1
Percentage of members neither of whose parents were Mennonites

	East.	Cent.	West.	North.	Pac.	All U.S.	B.C.	Alta.	Sask.	Man.	Ont.	All Can.	All G.C.
1943						6.1							
1960						11.5						1.6	
1970	26.5	17.3	5.2	6.3	14.9	11.6	1.9	2.8	2.2	1.2	3.2	2.1	8.3

from Leland Harder, *Fact Book of Congregational Membership*

Table 2
Percentage of members of non-Mennonite parentage in U.S. churches

	Country churches	Town churches	City churches
1943	3.1	5.9	17.6
1960	8.2	10.8	17.4
1970	9.3*		20.3

from Leland Harder, *The Quest for Equilibrium in an Established Sect*, p. 319
*Combined figure for town (under 9,000) and country churches

Table 3
General Conference membership in North America

	Eastern	Central	Western	Northern	Pacific	all U.S.	Canadian	all G.C.
1944	3,742	5,550*	12,273	4,534	2,773	28,872	10,216	39,088
1950	4,363	8,594	13,048	5,334	3,441	34,780	10,952	45,757
1959	4,433	8,205	13,477	5,846	3,401	35,362	15,893	51,255
1968	4,579	8,442	14,013	6,102	3,323	36,459	18,823	55,282

1978　4,928　9,085　14,009　5,842　2,911　36,775　23,406　60,181
*Middle District only

Table 4
Urban membership of the General Conference in North America

	1956 percentage in cities over 9,000	1977 percentage in cities over 9,000	1977 percentage in cities over 100,000
Canadian	40	47	34
Eastern	20	16	8
Central	22	25	6
Middle	5		
Western	12	32	17
Northern	1	4	1
Pacific	22	26	13
U.S.		23	7
General Conference	17	32	17

Source: *Handbook of Information 1978/1979*, General Conference Mennonite Church

tion, renewed and flowering once again in our urban society. The
Faith is alive and well in Arvada.[68]

The Waters and Arvada churches were representative of
the new kind of home missions that developed in the General
Conference in the thirty years following World War II. As Mennonites became more urban and more acculturated, they moved
away from the notions of "we" in the country and "they" in the
city, "we" who are German and "they" who are English. When
ethnic Mennonites were no longer as culturally different from
their neighbors, evangelism of their neighbors came more natu-
rally.

In addition, as ethnic separateness grew less important,
General Conference Mennonites felt better able to espouse theological separateness and to say that their theology was worth
sharing with others. As cultural distinctions blurred, rediscovering the Anabaptist vision became more crucial. Mennonites
found in the turmoil of continual wars and social unrest parallels with the sixteenth-century situation of their spiritual forebears.[69] As Mennonite scholars discovered and translated more
Anabaptist documents, the theology of the Anabaptists became
clearer and became a criterion against which to test the modern
church and its mission. If peacemaking and church discipline
were part of the Anabaptists' evangelistic message, should
modern Mennonites see them only as hindrances to church
growth? Home missions had changed. Where once General Conference Mennonites saw city missions as a chance to do their
part in the broader Protestant mission of Christianizing North
America, now home missions was becoming an opportunity to
be salt and light, to proclaim unapologetically the gospel of
peace.

Winnipeg Mennonites welcome Vietnamese refugees

Gerald Loewen

Chapter 11:
An Ethnic Church and Home Missions

You Gentiles by birth—called "the uncircumcised" by the Jews, who call themselves the circumcised (which refers to what men do to their bodies)—remember what you were in the past. At that time you were apart from Christ. You were foreigners and did not belong to God's chosen people. You had no part in the covenants, which were based on God's promises to his people, and you lived in this world without hope and without God. But now, in union with Christ Jesus you, who used to be far away, have been brought near by the death of Christ. For Christ himself has brought us peace by making Jews and Gentiles one people. With his own body he broke down the wall that separated them and kept them enemies. He abolished the Jewish Law with its commandments and rules, in order to create out of the two races one new people in union with himself, in this way making peace. By his death on the cross Christ destroyed their enmity; by means of the cross he united both races into one body and brought them back to God. So Christ came and preached the Good News of peace to all—to you Gentiles, who were far away from God, and to the Jews, who were near to him. It is through Christ that all of us, Jews and Gentiles, are able to come in the one Spirit into the presence of the Father.

So then, you Gentiles are not foreigners or strangers any longer; you are now fellow citizens with God's people and members of the family of God.

—*Ephesians 2:11-19 TEV*

The history of home missions in the General Conference Mennonite Church is the history of the changing definition of what it means to be a Mennonite. Before the beginning of the conference's home mission work, being a Mennonite in North America had not only theological implications, but cultural and ancestral implications as well. Tangled up with particular worship practices and "distinctives" like conscientious objection to war were family ties and the German language and social networks of mutual aid and particular customs. Being a Mennonite meant having a particular ethnic background.

All that tangle, of course, had not been a part of sixteenth-century Anabaptism. The Anabaptists, Mennonites' spiritual ancestors, while having a minority theology, were part of their society, ethnically. Those to whom they witnessed spoke the same language, may often have been of the same socioeconomic class, and may even have been relatives. In spite of a radical theology which the state churches felt threatened the bases of society, Anabaptists had natural contacts for evangelism.

Two factors, however, soon combined to restrict Anabaptist-Mennonite evangelism. The first was widespread persecution by both Catholics and Protestants in Europe. The persecution exterminated many of the best-educated Anabaptists and drove many others from the cities to the farms and to a series of migrations to other countries in search of religious protection. Secondly, Anabaptist—and New Testament—theology contains within it a tension between evangelism and separation, between witness to the world and nonconformity to the world. Christians throughout the ages have found it difficult to be in, but not of, the world. While mainline Christians lessened the tension by emphasizing presence in the world, Mennonites chose to emphasize separation from the world. As a result, early nineteenth-century Mennonites in North America, in Russia, and in Prussia lived relatively isolated from the mainstream of their surrounding societies, although such isolation was never complete. In such situations, Mennonites engaged in little evangelism. In Prussia, Mennonites traded their right to evangelize and to engage in certain occupations for the privilege of exemption from military service.[1] In Russia and North America, too, Mennonites became a separate ethnic and cultural group as well as a separated church. Particular forms of worship, particular patterns of church leadership, and rural residence became the hallmarks of Mennonitism.

Into this stable religious-cultural environment came the influence of the two Great Awakenings in North America and Pietism in Europe with their emphases on missions, higher education, and publications. In North America, the Mennonites who formed the General Conference in 1860 were those who were willing to leave some of the Mennonite traditions—to be less separate. Yet there was a core of Mennonitism which they felt they could retain while adopting the best of the new religious influences around them. They wanted to revitalize Mennonitism with a new evangelical emphasis; they wanted to restore Mennonites' sense of worth, which had suffered through comparison with the pietistic fervor around them. General Conference pioneer Christian Krehbiel (1832-1909) told in his autobiography of a visit to the Berne, Indiana, area in the early days of the General Conference:

> Because the Mennonites were considered a dissolving sect the other churches felt free to proselyte among them. My visit was very welcome, and my first sermon was essentially one of encouragement with special emphasis on Mennonite tradition and the new awakening. Since the doors and windows were open to the summer weather, I gave my voice full rein and was heard by those standing far away. . . . My bold declarations stirred among Mennonites a consciousness of brotherhood and of their own worth, and among their neighbors a respect for Mennonites.[2]

Straddling the wall between tradition and innovation, between Anabaptism and Pietism, between ethnic separateness and ethnic pluralism was sometimes an uncomfortable position for General Conference Mennonites. There was an inevitable tension between the desire to be a missionary church and the desire to preserve the best of Mennonitism, both culturally and theologically. To fulfill the Great Commission would mean bringing into the Mennonite church new people who were culturally different and who might bring in new theological elements as well. To be truly missionary might mean disruption of the Mennonite unity between faith and culture.

The young General Conference's efforts in reaching out to establish churches for Mennonites scattering to other parts of rural North America were the first step in untangling faith and culture. At first, it seemed hard for Mennonites to conceive of a Mennonite church outside the boundaries of a large, close Mennonite settlement. Could those scattering Mennonites really form a Mennonite *church*? The Home Mission Board had faith that these Mennonites could be the church away from the cultural Mennonite enclaves. Conference attempts at intentional colonization never met with great success. But the General Conference Home Mission Board and district and provincial conference mission committees in the United States and Canada followed the scattering Mennonites to scores of rural

areas across the continent and succeeded in forming vital, growing churches.

It was harder yet to take the step of envisioning Mennonites in the city as wanting to be a part of a Mennonite church. If
they had wanted to remain Mennonites, wouldn't they have
stayed on the farm? some rural Mennonites wondered. In the
North American environment, with its increasing urbanism
and technology, fewer Mennonites stayed in the rural Mennonite communities, and more and more migrated to the cities.
The city churches for the scattering Mennonites, were, on the
whole, little different in ethnic composition from the rural
Mennonite churches such people had recently left. Yet the city
Mennonites helped make an important change in the definition
of Mennonitism. They testified to the fact that Mennonite faith
could survive a change in cultural environment. The city did
not automatically destroy Mennonite values. To be sure, social
pressures to conform to Mennonite norms may have been
weaker in the city, and some people of Mennonite origin left the
Mennonite church altogether when they came to the city. But
the neo-Anabaptists in the conference argued that such church
membership because of social pressures was not compatible
with the concept of the believers' church, anyway. City Mennonites adopted urban ways at a faster rate than their rural
counterparts. But, although there were some differences in beliefs, a 1972 survey of five Mennonite groups found little significant difference between rural and urban Mennonites on an
"Anabaptism" scale.[3] The missionary vision was bringing
General Conference Mennonites to untangle faith and place of
residence. Mennonites could form a Mennonite church in
Moundridge, Kansas, or Lowe Farm, Manitoba, or Portland,
Oregon.

While home missions to unaffiliated Mennonite churches
or to scattering Mennonites was changing the definition of
Mennonite, the "foreign missions at home" (the American Indian missions and city missions) also played a part in untangling faith and culture. General Conference Mennonites
undertook "foreign" missions both at home and overseas with a
zeal almost unequaled among North American Protestants in
terms of per capita giving to missions and percentage of the
membership involved in mission and service. Foreign missions
always enjoyed steady contributions, while home missions in
the General Conference hobbled along on less than half the
foreign budget and on more widely fluctuating revenues. Experienced missionaries were sent overseas, while home mission

churches served as training grounds for new workers and safe pastures for those judged not competent enough to serve in the foreign fields.

But while undertaking missions in Oklahoma and India and Chicago with enthusiasm, it was still difficult to think of the converts of these missions as Mennonites. These converts were Christian, but were they *Mennonite*?

Because the Mennonite missionary movement had got its impulse from the widespread Protestant missionary movement, it was easier at first to adopt general Protestant missionary methods and theology than to reformulate a Mennonite missionary theology. Before World War I, Mennonites, who themselves were struggling to become part of the North American mainstream, saw their city and Indian missions as a means of Christianizing and civilizing those of nonwestern European cultures. Mennonite missionaries did not entirely adopt mainstream Protestant theology, but they were hesitant to proclaim too loudly those beliefs which separated Mennonites most sharply from the rest of North American religion. Missionaries were usually cautious about pushing unpopular beliefs such as conscientious objection to all war. In part, they were afraid that people of other backgrounds (who themselves were becoming acculturated to the American environment) would reject the missionaries' entire message if it were connected with pacifism, simplicity, and nonconformity, principles which seemed secondary to issues like the atonement and the deity of Christ, the "fundamentals" of the faith. The missionaries themselves were sometimes not sure how to integrate the Mennonite "distinctives" with the rest of their faith. Neither their training in the Bible institutes nor in the Mennonite colleges before World War II had helped them to do that. Such distinctives were tied in with cultural patterns which the missionaries knew were not an essential part of Christianity, and the successful models of missions which they saw around them did not include such distinctives.

Thus the new churches created by the conference's non-ethnic mission work had few ties with the rest of the General Conference. Even in post-World War II missions, there were difficulties in making Mennonite churches which were not related culturally to the rest of the conference feel a part of the conference. Richard Ratzlaff, pastor of the new Church of the Good Samaritans in the northern suburbs of Philadelphia from 1956 to 1962, told of encouraging church members to attend the annual Eastern District Conference sessions. "After three or four years, it was harder to get them to go," he said. "They told me, 'We do not feel welcome. If the others at the conference can't figure out our relations, they don't have anything to talk to us about.' "[4]

At first glance, the "foreign" missions seemed to offer little threat to the old definitions of who was a Mennonite. The conference could send a missionary to Asia or Africa without fear of disrupting the North American cultural status quo. A "foreign" mission to North American Indians or working-class Chicagoans seemed just as unlikely to produce Christians that would want to join existing Dutch-German-Swiss Mennonite congregations. Foreign missions required financial and personnel support, with relatively few changes in the religious-cultural mix in the home congregations.

Voluntary service programs after World War II, when not connected with a local Mennonite congregation, sometimes unwittingly reinforced the old religious-cultural definitions of being Mennonite. When one black person in North Gulfport, Mississippi, who had witnessed the thirty years of Mennonite work there saw Hubert Brown's black face and heard him identify himself as a Mennonite, the response was "hearty laughter." For North Gulfport residents, Mennonites were a separate people of which others from different ethnic backgrounds could never become a part.[5]

Yet, there was a difference between the foreign missions overseas and the foreign missions at home. While there was little contact between the established congregations in North America and the overseas churches except through the missionaries, the older Mennonite congregations had increasing opportunities for contact with the Indian missions and the city missions, as communication and travel became easier and more Mennonites moved closer to Indian settlements or into the cities. This contact raised the question, Are these mission churches *Mennonite* churches? Gradually, the answer started to be yes, and these "foreign" mission churches began to be included in the Mennonite family.

A third step in changing the definition of Mennonite to include those of other ethnic backgrounds has been the inclusion of members of Mennonite and non-Mennonite backgrounds within the same Mennonite congregation. Most of the early city missions, aimed at people of other backgrounds, failed to attract many Mennonites moving to the city. The city churches established for scattering Mennonites attracted relatively few people of other backgrounds. The claim missions (see pp. 24-25) in Oklahoma around 1890 with both white and Indian members could not remain integrated as Indians were pushed away from areas of white settlement.

But as Mennonites became more acculturated, the barriers of ethnic background and culture began to fall enough that both people of Mennonite and non-Mennonite backgrounds felt comfortable in the same Mennonite congregation.

By 1970, 8.3 percent of General Conference members had had parents who were not Mennonite.[6] However, many of these people were a part of the church family because of marriage ties. Mission workers of the 1960s and 1970s noted the strong ethnic character of the conference. One person traveling for the conference in 1964 commented, "One cannot say Mennonite without somehow inferring German, Swiss, or Russian extraction. Under this arrangement, the Anabaptist vision becomes esoteric and prohibitive to non-Mennonites."[7] A home mission pastor in Oak Point, Manitoba, told the Canadian Board of Missions, "We, too, struggle with the problem of relating ourselves and our faith to non-Mennonite people of our community; it seems that our conservative ways build a wall between us and we do not reach into their lives."[8]

But in other congregations the dividing walls between ethnic and "nonethnic" Mennonites were being broken down. There, one could no longer assume that *Mennonite* implied German descent or a taste for *zwieback* or a familiar family name. There, Smiths and Schmidts, Harts and Harders, could worship together, respect old traditions, create new traditions, and build a new family of God based on a common faith. They could untangle and retie faith and culture in such a way that culture was an invitation to faith rather than a barrier.

Who is a Mennonite? The home mission vision of the General Conference Mennonite Church was changing the answer to that question.

Appendix 1

Churches and Missions Related to the General Conference Mennonite Church

Key: GC = General Conference, R = regional conference, L = local church, MC-
= began as a congregation in the Mennonite Church, d = dissolved,
m = merged, w = withdrew, t = GC mission involvement terminated

Note: This table does not indicate district conference membership. Some
churches listed are members of district conferences but not of the General
Conference

Congregation and location	Work began	Church organized	General Conference member	Received help from	1981 members (or most recent figure)
Conference of Mennonites in Canada: Mennonite Conference of Alberta					
Sunny Slope		1901 (?)	1905	GC	(d-?)
Bergthaler, Didsbury	1900	1901	1938	GC	182
Springridge (Blumenthal) Pincher Creek		1927	1938		59
Coaldale	1926	1928	1929		327
Chinook, Sedalia	1928	1928			(d-1950)
Mennonite (Westheimer), Rosemary	1928	1930	1938	R,GC	200
Lacombe	1930				(d-1944)
Vauxhall	1934	1938	1956	R,GC	32
Tofield (Schoensee)	1927	1936	1938	R	128
First (Scarborough), Calgary	1943	1946 (?)	1947	R,GC	348
Hoffnungsfelder, Wembly	1945			GC	(d-?)
Hoffnungsfelder, Beaverlodge				GC	(d-?)
Hoffnungsfelder, Lymburn	1949				(d-?)
Brooks		1950		L	(d-?)
Hillcrest, Grande Prairie	1955	1963		R	60

Congregation and location	Work began	Church organized	General Conference member	Received help from	1981 members (or most recent figure)
Taber	1949	1964		R	71
Gem	1957			L	(d-?)
First, Edmonton	1949	1959	1959	R, GC	125
Foothills (North Hill), Calgary	1955	1961	1965	R	276
Seven Persons	1955	1963		R	(d-1968)
Hayes	1963(?)			R, GC	(m-1966)
Cardston	1966			R	(t-1967)
Lethbridge					46
Calgary Fellowship	1976	1978	1979	R	47
Faith, Edmonton	1979	1980		L	43
Chinese, Calgary	1981			R	
Vietnamese, Calgary	1981			R	
Camrose Mennonite Fellowship	1981	1982		R	

Conference of Mennonites in Canada: The United Mennonite Churches of British Columbia

Congregation and location	Work began	Church organized	General Conference member	Received help from	1981 members (or most recent figure)
Renata	1909			GC	(d-?)
First, Sardis (Greendale)	1928	1929/30	1938	R, GC	187
Bethel (Coghlan), Aldergrove	1934	1936	1938	L (GC)	279
United, Black Creek	1932	1937		R	66
First United, Vancouver	1935	1937	1938	R, GC	558
West Abbotsford, Abbotsford	1936	1936	1938	L	242
United, Yarrow	1928	1938	1938	R, GC	91
United, Oliver	1933	1938		L, R	28
Cedar Valley (United), Mission	1938	1940	1959	R,GC	261
Cedar Hills, (New Westminster, South Westminster), Surrey	1938	1945	1959	L,R,GC	130
Eden (East Chilliwack, Westheimer), Chilliwack	1945	1945	1959	GC	387
First, Chilliwack		1947		R	(d-1979)
Chilliwack, Mission				R	(m-1969)
First, Kelowna	1946	1947		GC	74
Clearbrook	1951	1952	1953	L	212
Flatrock, Cecil Lake	1951	1954(?)		L	44
Mountainview (Vancouver Mission), Vancouver	1951	1956	1959	R,GC	139
Fort St. John	1958			R	(w-1966)
First, Burns Lake	1953	1959	1980	R,GC	106
Peardonville	1952	1959		R	(d-1968)
Olivet, Clearbrook	1959	1960	1962	R,L	317
South Bank	1960				(m-1967)
Kelowna Gospel, Kelowna	1960	1961		L	154
Eben-Ezer, Clearbrook	1962	1963	1965	L	414
Prince of Peace, Richmond	1959	1964	1965	R	(d-1979)
Kamloops	1967			R	(d-1976)

Congregation and location	Work began	Church organized	General Conference member	Received help from	1981 members (or most recent figure)
Sherbrooke, Vancouver	1965	1968	1971	L	282
Church of the Way, Granisle	1972			L,R	24
Langley	1976			L,R	35
Chinese, Vancouver	1977	1978	1980	L,R	116
Peace, Vancouver (Richmond)	1979	1980		L	162
Vernon	1980	1980		R	15
Indo-Canadian, Mission	1980				
Clearbrook Laotian	1980			L,R	
Emmanuel, Clearbrook	1981	1981		L	138
Chinese Grace Mennonite, Vancouver	1981	1981		R	

Conference of Mennonites in Canada: Conference of Mennonites in Manitoba

(Figures in parentheses under "Church organized" indicate the date that location became a regular church center under the Bergthaler or other larger church organization.)

Congregation and location	Work began	Church organized	General Conference member	Received help from	1981 members (or most recent figure)
Altona Bergthaler (Hochstadt)		1890	1968		747
Bergthaler, Edenburg (Gretna)		(1883)			(m-1954)
Halbstadt (Bergthaler)		(1892) 1937	1968		79
Winkler Bergthaler (Hoffnungsfeld), Winkler		(1895)	1974		895
Bergthaler, Gretna	1889	(1901)	1968		125
Bergthaler, Rosenfeld	1875	(1903)	1968		94
(Bergthaler), Plum Coulee	1875	(1904)		L,GC	286
Bergthaler, Lowe Farm	1900	(1905)	1968		147
Herold, Morden		1920			(m-1934)
Dominion City	1923			R	(d-?)
Stuartburn	1923			R	(d-?)
Steinbach	1923	1923	1945	L,R	414
Blumenorter, Rosetown (Gretna)		1925	1926	GC	254
(Blumenorter), Reinland		1926			(d/m-?)
Lichtenau (St. Elizabeth), Morris		1926	1938		64
Arnaud	1924	1926	1947		95
(Schoenwieser), Starbuck	1925	1926			(d-?)
First (Schoenwieser), Winnipeg	1925	1926	1929	GC	1,390
(Whitewater), Lena		1926			?
Whitewater, Boissevain	1925	1927	1929	GC	285
(Whitewater), Crystal City	1925	(1927)	1929	GC	211
(Schoenwieser), Glenlea	1925	1927	1947	GC,L	79
(Schoenwieser), Springstein	1924	1927	1947		179
(Schoenwieser), Graysville	1926-27	1927			84
Rivers (Whitewater)	1927-28	(1928) 1971	1929	GC	13

Congregation and location	Work began	Church organized	General Conference member	Received help from	1981 members (or most recent figure)
Elim, Grunthal (Spencer)		1927	1929		206
Schoenfelder, Headingly	1925	1928	1945	L	175
(Schoenwieser), Foxwaren	192?				(d-?)
(Schoenwieser), Prairie Rose	1925	1929			(d-?)
(Schoenwieser), Petersfield	1929	1929			(d-?)
Bethel, Winnipeg	1923	1938	1947	R,GC	477
Bergthaler, Morden	1921	(1938)	1968	R	435
(Bergthaler), Steinbach	1937	(1939)			130
Arden	1932	1940 (?)		R,L	(d-?)
(Schoenwieser), Niverville	1927	1944	1953?	GC	158
Bergthaler, Carman	1937	1945	1968	R,GC	138
Gladstone	1932	1947?		R,GC	88
Bergthaler, Graysville	1936	(1947)	1968	L	84
Kane Bergthaler,					(d-1968)
Lowe Farm	1939	1948		L	147
Bergthaler, Morris	1937	1948			(w-1971)
Matheson Island	1948			R	
Pine Dock	1949			R	
Anama Bay	1950			R	(t-1953)
Rabbit Point (Princess Harbour)	1948-50			R	
Sargent Avenue, Winnipeg	1949	1950	1956	L,R,GC	446
(Whitewater), Ninga	1931	1951		L,GC	(d-?)
Grace, Brandon		1954	1962	R	108
Sterling, Winnipeg (St. Vital)	1951	1955		R	47
Loon Straits	1955			R	(t-1966)
Bethel Gospel, Oak Point	1955			L,R	(d-1981)
North Kildonan, Winnipeg	1935	1956	1959	L	474
Home Street, Winnipeg	1955	1958	1968	L	257
Mayfeld	1959?			R	(d-?)
Bagot	1959?			R	(d-?)
Ukrainian Mission, Winnipegosis	1960			R	(d-?)
Nordheim, Winnipegosis	1960			R	88
Burrows Bethel (Elmwood), Winnipeg	1959	1960		L,R,GC	178
Grace, Manigotogan	1957	1960		R	
Killarney	1959	1960			
Bloodvein River	1960			R	
United, Thompson	1960	1961	1977	R	23
Grace, Winkler		1961			227
The Pas	1961			R	(d-1966)
Grace, Steinbach	1961	1961	1965		182
Charleswood, Winnipeg	1962	1963	1965	L	160
Pauingassi	1955	1963		R	35
Altona	1962	1963	1965		113
Springfield Heights, Winnipeg	1964	1964		L	449
Bethel Bergthaler (Hochfeld), Winkler	1963	1965		L	258
Elim, Cross Lake	1956	1967		R	6

Congregation and location	Work began	Church organized	General Conference member	Received help from	1981 members (or most recent figure)
YOU Center, Winnipeg	1965			R	(t-1976)
Bergthaler, MacGregor	1950	(1967)		L,GC	198
Fort Garry, Winnipeg	1967	1968	1971	L	77
Kettle Rapids	1968?				(d-?)
Wingham (Blumenorter), Elm Creek		196?		L	40
Little Grand Rapids	1969			R	
(Whitewater), Mather	1958	1971	(1971)	L,GC	(d-1981)
Trinity, Mather	1976				57
Hole River	1973			R	
Northdale, Winnipeg	1972	1975		L	45
Chinese, Winnipeg	197?	1979?		L,R	91
Riverton	1976			R	
Native, Winnipeg	1979			R	30
Elim, Selkirk	1966	1980		R	50
Pembina, Morden	1974	?		L	20
Douglas, Winnipeg					233
Portage, Portage La Prairie				L	
Bergthaler, Grunthal					95
Homewood					77
Oak Lake					72
Metis, Winnipeg	1981			R	40

Conference of Mennonites in Canada: Conference of the United Mennonite Church of Ontario

Congregation and location	Work began	Church organized	General Conference member	Received help from	1981 members (or most recent figure)
Stirling Avenue, Kitchener		1924	1947	MC	399
Waterloo-Kitchener United		1925	1926		418
Windsor	1926				(d-1942)
United (Essex County), Leamington		1929	1929?		810
United, Vineland		1936	1938	L	419
United, Niagara-on-the-Lake		1938	1938	L,R	717
United, Reesor		1941		GC	(d-?)
United, St. Catharines	1942	1944	1947	R	696
Erie View United, Port Rowan		1947	1947		43
United, Dunnville		1948	1956	R	26
United, Toronto	1942	1948	1956	R,GC	141
Hamilton		1952	1965	R	86
United, Harrow		1953	1953	R	58
Ontario Hebrew Mission, Toronto and Kearney	1954			GC	(t-1961)
Grace, St. Catharines		1956	1959	R	257
Waters, Lively (Sudbury, Copper Cliff)	1946	1959	1959	ind.,R	59
Rockway, Kitchener	1957	1960	1977		77
Faith, Leamington		1961	1962		124
Ottawa	1959	1962		R	81
Bethany, Virgil	1963	1964	1965	L	351
Montreal, Quebec	1969	1981		R	32

Congregation and location	Work began	Church organized	General Conference member	Received help from	1981 members (or most recent figure)
Waterloo-Kitchener Area House Churches	1969	1970			48
St. John's, Newfoundland	1978				
Chinese, Toronto	1979	1980		R	34
Windsor	1980				
North Leamington	1979	1981			480
Mississauga, Oakville	1980			L	56 attending
Welcome Inn Fellowship, Hamilton	1966	1981		R,L	12
St. Catharines Laotian	1980	1982		L,R	100 attending
Guelph	1980	1981		R	14

Conference of Mennonites in Canada: Conference of Mennonites of Saskatchewan
(Figures in parentheses under "Church organized" indicate the date that location became a regular church center under a larger church organization.)

Rosenorter	1894		1908		
Neuanlage Grace, Hague					143
Rosthern		1903	1956	R	414
Eigenheim, Rosthern	1894	1929	1938		176
Aberdeen					99
Laird			1956	L,R	111
Hague		(1909)		R,GC	193
Tiefengrund Rosenort, Laird		(1910)		L,R	149
Osler	1928	(1931)	1956	L,R,GC	144
Herbert		1904	1908	R,GC	128
North Star, Drake		1906	1911	R,GC	276
Zoar, Waldheim	1909	1913	1917	GC	188
Zoar, Langham	1913	1917		GC	183
Bethel, Great Deer		1914?		GC,R	(d-1975?)
Blaine Lake (Kryder)	1915				(d-1922)
Simpson	1915				(d-?)
Rush Lake	1916				(d-?)
Bethany, Lost River	1902?	1917	1926	R	(w-1971)
Jansen and Watson	1918				(d-1925)
Nordheimer		1925	1926		
Dundurn					77
Pleasant Point, Dundurn					70
Elbow					(d-?)
Hanley					117
Ebenfeld		1925	1926		
Herschel					69
Glidden (Kindersley)		(1953)			(d-1972)
Fiske					43
Superb, Kerrobert					44
Carnduff	1921			R	(d-1925?)
Eyebrow (Eyebrow-Tugaski)		1926			(d-1971)
Zion (Emmaus), Swift Current	1913	1928	1941	R,GC	244
Emmaus, Wymark	1913	1928	1941	R,GC	67
Gull Lake					(d-?)

Congregation and location	Work began	Church organized	General Conference member	Received help from	1981 members (or most recent figure)
McMahon					(w-?)
Schoenfeld					(w-?)
Neville					(w-?)
Rheinland					(w-?)
Blumenhof					(w-?)
Carrot River (Hoffnungsfeld)		1929	1953	R	145
Emmanuel					
Barnes Crossing	1929	1929		R,GC	(d-1975)
Daisy Meadow	1929	1929		R,GC	(d-1975)
Compass	1929	1929		R,GC	(d-1978?)
Gouldtown				R	(w-1972)
Garthland		193?			(d-?)
First, Saskatoon	1930	(1932)	1938	GC,R	411
Bethany, Watrous	1924	1932	1947		63
Hoffnungsfeld		1936	1938		
Glenbush					55
Rabbit Lake				GC,R	22
(Rosenort), Hochfeld		1939			(m-1957)
Immanuel, Rapid View					37
Bethesda, Langham					(d-1950?)
Rosenort					
Capasin		(1933)		L,GC	(d-?)
Horse Lake, Duck Lake		(1941)	1956	L,GC	58
Codette	1941			GC	(d-?)
Capeland (Main Centre)	1945?			GC	(d-?)
Nipawin	1945?			GC	(d-?)
Rosenort, Grantland	1945?				(d-?)
Immanuel, Pierceland	1949?			GC,R	(d-1971)
(Grace), Prince Albert	1941	1950	1962	R,GC	44
Bethel, Lake Four	1950			R,GC	(d-?)
Mayfair, Saskatoon	1949	1952	1956	L,R,GC	292
First, Eyebrow		1956	1956		28
Grace, Meadow Lake	1953	1957		R,L	94
Martensville	1954		1971	L	110
Pleasant Hill, Saskatoon	1928	1958		L,R	150
North Battleford	1951	1959	1974	R	21
Pesane	1959?			R	(d-?)
Grace (Victoria), Regina	1940	1960	1962	GC,R	181
Bethel, Park Valley	1964			GC,R	14
Nutana Park, Saskatoon	1961	1964	1968	L	327
Mount Royal, Saskatoon	1961		1965	L	165
Wildwood (College Park), Saskatoon	1975	1976	1977	L,R	66
Covenant, Saskatoon	1980	1981		L	8
Warman					113

Central District Conference: Former Middle District Conference Members

Clarence Center, N.Y.	1824	1824	1880	MC	(d-1916)
(Apostolic), Trenton, Ohio	1825	1825	1866		125

Congregation and location	Work began	Church organized	General Conference member	Received help from	1981 members (or most recent figure)
Niagara Falls, N.Y.	1830	1830	1884	GC,R	(d-1908)
Salem, Haysville, Ohio	1835	1835	1866		(d-1900?)
First, Berne, Indiana	1838	1838	1872		1,176
Ebenezer, Bluffton, Ohio	1835	1846	1893		510
Cleveland, Ohio	1846				(d-1856)
West Point, Lee Co., Iowa	1845	1849	1860		(m-1898)
Franklin, Lee Co., Iowa	1850	1850	1897		(m-1897)
First, Wadsworth, Ohio	1852	1853	1866		129
Zion, Donnellson, Iowa	1853	1853	1860		160
(First), Summerfield, Illinois	1859	1859	1866		20
Polk City, Iowa			1860		(d-?)
Pulaski, Iowa	1861	1861	1892		141
Bethel, Fortuna, Missouri	1867	1867	1881		158
Cleveland	1868				(d-1868)
Hickory, Elkton, Missouri	1868	1868	1884		(d-1896)
Evangelical (Salem), Dayton, Iowa			1869		(d-1878)
Eicher Emmanuel, Wayland, Iowa	1874	1874	1893		87
First, Nappanee, Indiana	1875	1875	1926	Amish	81
Chapel (First Federated), New Stark, Ohio	1876	1876	1929	MC	(w-1940)
Stevensville (Black Creek), Ontario	1880	1880	1884	GC,R	(d-1906)
Salem, Kidron (Dalton), Ohio	1886	1886	1887		248
St. Louis, Missouri	1893			R	(t-1903)
Canton, Ohio	1893	1893	1896	GC,R	(d-1916)
Sterling, Ohio	1900	1900	1902		(t-1919)
Wayland, Iowa	1900	1900	1905	L	271
Woodburn, Indiana	1901	1901	1902		(d-1919)
Grace, Pandora, Ohio	1904	1904	1905		374
Cleveland	1906				(d-1908)
First, Bluffton, Ohio	1906	1918	1920	L	602
Grace, Chicago, Illinois	1917	1920	1941	GC,R,L	87
First, Chicago, Illinois	1914	1921	1923	GC,R	84
St. John, Pandora, Ohio	1889	1923	1923		258
Washington Center, Ashley, Michigan	1924	1924			(d-1933)
First, Sugarcreek, Ohio	1927	1927	1929	MC	277
First, Lima, Ohio	1932	1935	1938	L,R	95
Woodlawn, Chicago, Illinois	1950	1951	1953	GC,R	(d-1972)
Community, Markham, Illinois	1955	1957	1957	R	65
Hively Avenue, Elkhart, Indiana	1957	1958	1959	R	169

Central District Conference: Former Central Conference of Mennonites Members

South Danvers, Danvers, Illinois		1842?			(m-1943)
North Danvers, Danvers, Illinois	1851	1851	1946		193

Congregation and location	Work began	Church organized	General Conference member	Received help from	1981 members (or most recent figure)
Barker Street, Bristol, Indiana (Mottville, Michigan)		1863			(m-1928)
Calvary (East Washington), Washington, Illinois	1866	1866	1946		488
Flanagan, Illinois	1878	1878	1946		94
Belleview, Columbus, Kansas		1880	1946		(d-1972)
Pleasant View, Aurora, Nebraska		1886	1946		(w-1965)
Meadows, Illinois		1891	1946		211
Silver Street, Goshen, Indiana		1892	1946		78
East White Oak, Carlock, Illinois		1892			(w-1934)
Topeka, Indiana		1893	1946	L	131
Anchor Township, Illinois	1884	1894	1946		(d-1952)
South Washington, Washington, Illinois		1895			(m-1937)
Zion, Goodland, Indiana		1895	1946		48
Congerville, Illinois	1891	1896	1946	R	237
Boynton, Hopedale, Illinois		1901	1946		54
Pleasant Oaks (Warren Street), Middlebury, Indiana		1923	1946	MC	125
Twenty-sixth Street, Chicago, Illinois	1906			MC,R	(d-1943)
Bethel, Pekin, Illinois	1897	1907	1946	L	68
South Nampa, Nampa, Idaho		1908			(d-1927)
Sixty-Second Street, Chicago, Illinois	1909				(d-1949)
First, Normal, Illinois (Mennonite Church of Normal)	1910	1912 (m-1976)	1946	R	365
Eighth Street, Goshen, Indiana	1913	1913	1946		322
Carlock, Illinois	1914	1914	1946	L	133
Mennonite Gospel Mission, Peoria, Illinois (United)	1914	1915 (m-1971)	1946	R	78
Tiskilwa, Illinois	1915	1915	1946		40
Kouts, Indiana	1916	1918	1946		(d-1947/48)
Maple Grove, Topeka, Indiana	1924	1924		Amish	(m-1929)
Comins, Michigan	1925	1926	1946	R	96
McKinley, Michigan	1948		1959	R	(d-1966)

Congregation and location	Work began	Church organized	General Conference member	Received help from	1981 members (or most recent figure)

Central District Conference: Members After Middle District-Central Conference Merger

Congregation and location	Work began	Church organized	General Conference member	Received help from	1981 members (or most recent figure)
Crossroads (Wayside), Gulfport, Mississippi	1940			L,GC	(d-1971)
Hope, Columbiana, Ohio	1960	1961	1962	R	6
Neil Avenue, Columbus, Ohio	1957	1962	1965	R	87
Maplewood, Fort Wayne, Indiana	1960	1962	1962	L,R	183
Southside, Elkhart, Indiana	1965	1965	1971		86
First, Champaign-Urbana, Illinois		1966?	1971	R	67
Fairview Park, Cleveland, Ohio	1966			R	(d-1972)
Ann Arbor, Michigan	1967	1967	1968		17
Summit, Akron (Barberton), Ohio		1967?			(w-1973)
Evanston, Illinois			1980	R	29
Fellowship of Hope, Elkhart, Indiana	1971	1971			
The Assembly, Goshen, Indiana			1977		162
Plow Creek Fellowship Tiskilwa, Illinois	1972	1972	1979		26
Oak Grove, Smithville, Ohio			1971		425
Paoli, Indiana	1974				40
Ann Arbor Fellowship, Ann Arbor, Michigan	1974				24
Adelphos, Atlanta, Georgia	1975				19
Detroit, Michigan	1975		1980		21
Michigan State University, East Lansing, Michigan	1969	1975	1977		35
Gulfport, Mississippi	1972			L,GC	
Cincinnati, Ohio	1973	1976	1977	R	24
Muncie, Indiana	1976				
Ames, Iowa	1977		1977		21
Cedar Rapids, Iowa	1977			R	(d-1981)
Harlan, Kentucky	1977		1979		18
Milwaukee, Wisconsin	1974	1977	1979		8
Homestead, Fort Wayne, Indiana	1978			L	(d-1980?)
St. Louis, Missouri	1972	1978	1980	R	42
Lafayette, Indiana					12
K-Dorm, New Carlisle, Indiana					
Whitesburg, Kentucky	1978				
First, Oak Park, Illinois	1979		1981		17
Chinese, Elkhart	1980				
Lexington, Kentucky	1980				15
Cedar Falls, Iowa	1981			R	

Eastern District Conference

Congregation and location	Work began	Church organized	General Conference member	Received help from	1981 members (or most recent figure)
Germantown, Philadelphia		1683	1884	GC,R	38
Lower Skippack, Skippack (Creamery), Pennsylvania		1702		R	227

Congregation and location	Work began	Church organized	General Conference member	Received help from	1981 members (or most recent figure)
West Swamp, Quakertown, Pa.		1725	1866		366
Saucon, Coopersburg (Quakertown), Pennsylvania		1735	1869	R	51
Upper Milford, Zionsville, Pennsylvania		1740	1869		156
Springfield (Pleasant Valley), Quakertown, Pa.		1747	1866		71
East Swamp, Quakertown, Pa.		1771	1866		383
Menno Simons, Boyertown, Pa.		1790			(d-1935)
Flatland, Quakertown, Pa.		1837	1869		
Bertolet, Schwenksville (Frederick), Pa.		1846		L	(d-1923)
Eden, Schwenksville, Pa.		1847 (1818)	1872		159
Hereford, Bally, Pennsylvania		1847 (1725)	1866		173
Deep Run West, Bedminster, Pa.		1848	1869		337
Pine Grove, Bowmansville, Pennsylvania		1852	1872		228
First, Philadelphia (Huntingdon Valley)		1865	1866	L,R,GC	61
New York City	1875				(d-?)
Richfield, Pennsylvania		1883	1941	MC	(w-1972)
Zion, Souderton, Pa.	1887	1893	1893	R	756
First, Pottstown, Pa.		1895		R	(d-1915)
Second, Philadelphia	1894	1899	1899	R,L,GC	38
Bethany, Quakertown, Pa.	1888	1899	1905	R	
First, Allentown, Pa.	1893	1903	1908	R	123
Roaring Spring, Pa.	1898	1912	1914	MC	62
Leidytown, Pennsylvania	1899			L	(d-1907)
Bethel, Perkasie, Pa.	1900	1905	1908	R	(w-1961)
Smith Corner, East Freedom, Pa.		1908	1914	L,GC	31
Napier, Bedford, Pa.		1913	1914	L,R	126
Calvary, Mechanics Grove (Quarryville), Pa.		1914		L,R,GC	(w-1957)
Zion, Mann's Choice, Pa.		1915		L,R	(d-1935)
Upper Poplar Run, Claysburg, Pennsylvania	1920			GC	(d-1933)
Barrville, Lewistown, Pa.		1920	1920	R	(d-1933)
Coupon, Pennsylvania	1921			GC	(d-1926)
Memorial, Altoona, Pa.	1911	1922		L,R,GC	(d-1945)
Yellow Pine and Gadsden, Alabama	1922	1922		GC	(d-?)
Fairfield, Pennsylvania		1927	1941	MC	66
Grace, Lansdale, Pa.	1916	1930	1933	R,GC	268
Men-O-Lan Chapel, Quakertown, Pa.	1935?			R	(d-by 1961)
Springs, Pennsylvania	1935?			R	(d-by 1961)
Emmanuel, Denver (Reinholds), Pa.		1939	1941		79
New York City	1943			GC	(d-?)
Washington, D.C.	1945				(d-?)

Congregation and location	Work began	Church organized	General Conference member	Received help from	1981 members (or most recent figure)
Scripture Memory Mountain Mission, Kentucky	1945			GC,L	(t-1960)
Bethel, Lancaster, Pa.	1944	1947	1947	R	197
Grace, Paint Rock, N.C.	1940	1948		GC,L	(d-1965)
Belva Bible, Marshall N. C.	1940	1948	1962	GC,L	(w-1967)
East Harlem Protestant Parish, New York City	1949			GC	(t-1956)
Children's Bible Mission, Greenville, Tennessee	1949			GC	(t-1970)
Spanish, Lansdale, Pa.	1958	part of Grace Church			
Church of the Good Samaritans, Holland, Pa.	1951	1959?	1959	R,GC	92
Conwego, Manchester, Pa.		1961		R	37
Boston, Massachusetts	1959	1962	1968		26
Kempton, Pennsylvania		1964	1968	R	42
Indian Valley, Harleysville, Pennsylvania		1968	1971	L	221
Akron, Pennsylvania			1974		294
Norriton Community, Norristown, Pa.					(d-1972)
Philadelphia Assembly	1976			R	
Wilkes-Barre, Pa.	1976			R	
Red Hill, Pennsylvania	1978				(d-1982)
Cuerpo de Cristo, Jackson Heights, New York	1979				
Peace, New York City					
Princeton, New Jersey					
First, Hyattsville, Maryland			1979	MC	101
Washington, D.C.	1981				

Northern District Conference

Neu Hutterthal, Bridgewater, South Dakota	1874 in S.D.	in Russia before 1874			117
Salem-Zion, Freeman, S.D.	1874	1874	1881		427
Friedensberg, Avon, S.D.	1874	1874	1899		83
Bethesda, Henderson, Neb.	1875	1875	1893		1,182
Bethesda, Marion, S.D.	1875	1883	1899		204
First, Mountain Lake, Minn.	1878	1878	1917		373
First (Bergthal), Butterfield, Minn.		1878	1923	L	73
Gospel (Bergfelder, Wall's), Mountain Lake, Minn.		1878	1920		197
Bethel, Mountain Lake, Minn.		1889	1890	L	572
Salem, Wisner, Neb.		1889	1902		(d-1954)
Bethel, Marion (Dolton), S.D.		1892	1950		66
(Salem), Butterfield, Minn.		1896	1896	L	86
Menno Simons, Butterfield, Minn.					(m-1934)

Congregation and location	Work began	Church organized	General Conference member	Received help from	1981 members (or most recent figure)
Bethel, Dresden (Langdon), N.D.	1897	1897	1947	R,GC	(d-1978)
Hutterthal, Freeman, S.D.	1877?	1899	1941		246
Salem, Munich, North Dakota		1901	1917	R,GC	147
Swiss, Alsen, North Dakota	1900	1904	1917	R,GC	99
Bethany, Freeman, S.D.	1896	1905	1905	L	348
Hutterthal, Carpenter, S.D.	1877	1906	1962		234
White River Cheyenne, Busby, Montana	1904	1906	1956	GC	64
Salem, Freeman, S.D.	1874	1907	1908		552
Zion, Arena, North Dakota		1908	1929	GC,R	30
Petter Memorial, Lame Deer, Montana	1908	1909	1956	GC	121
Bethlehem, Bloomfield, Montana	1910	1912	1917	R	100
Northern Cheyenne, Birney, Montana	1910	1913	1956	GC	20
Muddy Creek, Montana	1913			GC	(d-1940?)
Upper Rosebud River (Kirby), Montana	1915			GC	(d-1940?)
Christian Fellowship, Ashland, Montana	1917		1956	GC	50
Hydro, Montana			1917		(d-1920)
Yale, South Dakota	1918			GC	(d-?)
New Home, Westbrook, Minn.			1920		(d-1953)
Emmanuel, Doland, S.D.		1921			104
Bethel, Lustre (Frazer), Montana		1924	1926	R	(d-1976)
Bethel, Wolf Point, Mont.		1924	1926	R	48
First, Lost Wood, N.D.			1926		(d-1939)
First, Madrid, Nebraska		1928	1935	L,R,GC	(d-1972)
Pitt, Minnesota	1935?			R	(d-1961?)
Woodland, Warroad, Minn.		1939	1945		(w-1974)
Immanuel (Bergfelder), Delft, Minnesota	1897	1940	1941	L	99
Zion, Bridgewater, S.D.		1940			91
Mount Olivet, Huron, S.D.		1945	1947	R	149
Fairfield-Bethel, Hitchcock (Huron), S.D.			1947		(d-1959)
Community Bible (United), Wolf Point, Montana	1948	1948		GC,R	78
First, Glendive, Montana	1950	1950	1950	R,L	(w-1978)
Good Shepherd, Sioux Falls, S.D.	1957	1959	1959	R	54
Faith, Minneapolis, Minn.	1960		1962	R,L	69
Faith, Geneva, Nebraska	1964?		1968	L,MC	44
Sermon on the Mount, Sioux Falls, S.D.	1975	1977?	1980	R	10
Maranatha, Lincoln, Neb.	1977	1978?	1980	R	(d-1982)
Mankato, Minn.	1979			R	13
Rochester, Minn.	1979				
Casselton, N.D.					64
Billings, Montana	1981				
Fargo, N.D.—Moorhead, Minn.	1979	1981			

Congregation and location	Work began	Church organized	General Conference member	Received help from	1981 members (or most recent figure)
Pacific District Conference					
Menno, Ritzville (Lind), Washington	1888	1888	1902		173
Emmanuel, Salem (Pratum), Oregon	187?	1890	1896	GC	220
Onecho (First), Colfax, Wash.	1886	1893		GC	(w-1962)
Zion, Polk Station, Oregon	1896	1896	1899		(reorganized in 1928)
First, Upland, California	1903	1903	1905		176
Joamosa, California		1903?			(d-?)
San Marcos (Willow Creek), Paso Robles, Calif.	1903	1904	1905		(m-1966)
First, Reedley, Calif.	1903	1906	1908	R	483
First, Aberdeen, Idaho	1906	1907	1917	R	323
Kykotsmovi (Oraibi),Arizona		(1909)			
Arizona	1893	(first baptisms)		GC	56
Moencopi, Arizona	1904			GC	
Salem, Ruff, Wash.	190?	1910	1911		(m-1934)
Emmanuel (Homestead), Aberdeen, Idaho	1912	1912	1917		(d-1929)
Escondido, Calif.	1911	1912	1914	R	(d-1934)
First, Woodlake, Calif.	1915	1915	1917	GC	(d-1929)
Bethel, DuBois, Idaho	1916	1916	1917		(d-1920)
First, Monroe, Wash.	1918	1918	1920	R	(m-1971)
Immanuel (Los Angeles Mission), Downey, Calif.	1908	1918	1920	GC	(w-1978)
First, Shafter, Calif.	1918	1923 & 1935	1923	L	(m-1964)
Minidoka, Idaho	1925			R	(d-?)
Eldon Camp, Flagstaff, Arizona	1926			GC	(d-1929)
Spring Valley, Newport, Wash.	1928	1928	1933	GC,R	74
Grace, Dallas, Oregon	1928	1935	1935	GC,R	212
Dos Palos, Calif.	1930		1931	GC,R	(d-1933)
Peace (Alberta Community), Portland, Oregon	1928	1931	1933	GC,R	74
Grace, Albany, Oregon	1931	1931	1935	R	(d-1968)
First Deer Park, Wash.	1936	1938		R	(d-1944)
United, Atwater, Calif. (Bethel or First, Winton)	1937	1940 & 1966	1945	GC,R	54
Mennonite Country, Monroe, Wash.	1944	1944	1947		(m-1971)
Calvary, Aurora (Barlow), Oregon	1944	1944	1945	MC	265
Glendale, Lynden, Wash.	1944	1945	1945	GC,R	75
First, Caldwell, Idaho	1945	1947	1947	R	(d-1964)
(Community), Sweet Home, Oregon	1948	1951	1953	R	186
Friendly Corner, Eloy, Ariz.	1951			GC	(d-1980)

Congregation and location	Work began	Church organized	General Conference member	Received help from	1981 members (or most recent figure)
Community, Fresno, Calif.	1952	1954	1956	L	113
Faith Memorial, Filer, Idaho	1954	1954	1956	MC	(d-1968)
Bethel Community, Santa Fe Springs, Calif.	1956	1956	1956		26
Warden, Wash.	1954	1956	1962	L,R	47
First, Phoenix, Ariz.	1961	1963	1965	GC,R	90
South Seattle, Seattle, Wash.	1966	1968	1968	GC,R	89
Orange, Calif.	1969			GC,R	(d-1977)
Hotevilla Hopi Gospel Independent, Ariz.	1907	1970		GC	
Community, Monroe, Wash.		1971	1971	merger	(w-1973)
Shalom, Tucson, Ariz.	1973		1979	R	30
Faith, Westminster, Calif.	1973				
Bacavi, Ariz.	1907	197?		GC	
Reno, Nevada	1975?	1975?			(w-1978)
Koinonia, Tempe, Ariz.	1976		1979	R	41
Haight-Ashbury, San Francisco, Calif.	1976				25
Chinese, San Francisco, Calif.	1980			R	23
Ethnic Chinese, Santa Clara, Calif.	1981	1981		R	
Spokane, Wash.	1979	1982			17
Korean, Atwater, Calif.	1981				
Prescott, Ariz.	1981				

Western District Conference

(Figures in parentheses under "Church organized" indicate date congregation moved to North America.)

Grace Hill (Gnadenberg, Michalin), Whitewater, Kans.	1811 (1875)	1881		193
Alexanderwohl, Goessel, Kans.	1821 (1876)	1878		731
Hopefield (Hoffnungsfeld), Moundridge, Kans.	1874	1881		90
Emmanuel (Canton), Canton, (Moundridge), Kans.	1874/75	1896		(w-1978)
First, Halstead, Kans.	1874	1875		357
Brudertal, Hillsboro, Kans.	1874	1878		(m-1966)
First, Newton, Kans.	1875	1881		992
Bergthal, Pawnee Rock, Kans.	1875	1900		172
Bethel, Inman, Kans.	1875	1945		400
Hoffnungsau, Inman, Kans.	1875	1878		308
Emmaus, Whitewater, Kans.	1876	1881		439
First (Wehrlose), Beatrice, Neb.	1877	1896		252
First . . . of Christian, Moundridge, Kans.	1878	1878		265
Hebron, Buhler, Kans.	1879	1917		127

Congregation and location	Work began	Church organized	General Conference member	Received help from	1981 members (or most recent figure)
Darlington, Oklahoma	1880			GC	(d-1902)
Johannestal, Hillsboro, Kans.		1882	1893		(m-1965)
Zion, Elbing, Kans.		1883	1887	L	151
First, Hillsboro, Kans.		1884	1887		421
First, Pretty Prairie, Kans.		1884	1890		564
First, Ransom, Kans.		1886	1923		123
Garden Township, Hesston, Kans.		1887	1893	L	(w-1969)
West Zion, Moundridge, Kans.		1888	1890	L	304
Swiss, Whitewater, Kans.		1890?	1893		(w-1970)
Mennoville, El Reno, Okla.		1891-92	1896	R	(d-1952)
Hanston (Einsiedel), Hanston, Kans.		1892	1902	R	32
Bergthal, Corn, Okla.		1894	1896		(d-1975)
New Hopedale (Neu Hoffnungstal), Meno, Okla.		1895	1905		191
Eden (Hoffungsfeld-Eden), Moundridge, Kans.		1895	1896		863
Dyke, Okla.	1895				(d-1896)
Sichar, Cordell, Okla.		1896?	1896		(d-1947)
Shelly (Washita), Okla.	1889	1896			(d-1896)
Zion (Arapaho), Canton (Cantonment), Okla.	1883	1897	1971	GC	34
First (Red Hills), Geary, Okla.	1892	1897	1905		56
Bethel College, North Newton, Kans.		1897	1899	L	763
Saron, Orienta, Okla.		1897	1905		88
Medford, Okla.		1897	1902		36
Friedensau, Perry, Okla.		1898			(d-1935)
(Cheyenne), Cantonment, Okla.	1884	1898		GC	(m-1926)
Fonda (Mower Chapel), Okla.	1907	1898		GC	(m-1963?)
Longdale, Okla.	1926	1898		GC	(m-1963?)
Koinonia (Haoenaom), Clinton, Okla.	1894	1899	1971	GC	60
Deer Creek, Okla.	1893	1899	1902		92
Herold, Cordell (Bessie), Okla.		1899	1902		156
Central Heights (Friedenstal, North Lehigh), Durham, Kans.		1899	1908		86
Lehigh, Kans.	before 1890	1900	1905	L	162
Zion, Lucien, Okla.		1902			(d-1912)
Friedenstal, Gotebo, Okla.		1903	1905		(d-1921)
Ebenezer, Gotebo, Okla.		1903	1908		(d-1972)
Salem, Cordell, Okla.		1904?			(d-1919)
Caddo (First), Kidder, Okla.		1904?			(d-1910)
Bethanian, Coy, Okla.		1905	1905		(d-1916)
Arlington, Kans.		1905	1908	R	(d-1964)

Congregation and location	Work began	Church organized	General Conference member	Received help from	1981 members (or most recent figure)
Bethel (Red Moon), Hammon, Okla.	1898	1906	1965	GC	50
Bethel, Hydro, Okla.		1906	1933	R	75
Burrton, Kans.	1905	1907	1908	L,R	118
Bethany, Kingman, Kans.		1907	1908		(m-1973)
Turpin (Friedensfeld), Okla.		1907	1908	R	110
Bethlehem, Hooker, Okla.		1907?			(d-1917)
New Friedensburg, Vona, Colo.		1907	1908	R	16
Springfield, Eakly, Okla.		1908?	1908		(d-1919)
Kidron, Taloga, Okla.		1908?			(d-1945)
Ebenflur, Syracuse, Kans.		1908			(d-1914)
Tabor, Newton (Goessel), Kans.		1908	1908	L	369
Zoar, Goltry, Okla.		1909	1914	R	(d-1964)
Sherman County, Goodland, Kans.		1910?			(d-?)
Greenfield (Gruenfeld), Carnegie, Okla.		1914	1917	L,R	29
Eden, Inola, Okla.		1914	1920	R	171
Wheatland, Wyoming	1914			GC	(d-?)
Salem, Weatherford, Okla.		1914			(d-1919)
Palm Lake, Lake Charles, Louisiana	1907	1915		R,GC	(d-1925)
Greensburg, Kans.		1916?		R	(d-1934)
Pleasant Valley (Schoental), Kismet, Kans.		1916?		GC	(m-1959)
Nebo, Meade, Kans.		1917?			(d-1923)
Kirk, Colorado	1919			R	(d-?)
Gospel (Ebenfeld), Montezuma, Kans.	1919	1920	1933	R	(d-1981)
Buhler, Kans.		1920	1920	L	387
Goessel, Kans.		1920	1920	L	219
Inman, Kans.	1909	1921	1923	L	306
Bethel, Perryton (Waka), Texas		1922	1926	R	(d-1964)
First, Hutchinson, Kans.	1913	1922	1923	R,GC	471
Menno, Watova, Okla.		1924?			(d-1927)
(Second), Beatrice, Neb.		1926	1926	L	147
San Juan, Irapuato, Mexico	1927?			GC	(d-1928)
Hoffnungsau, Cuauhtémoc, Mexico		1927?	1941	GC,R	(w-1965)
Deer Creek, Thomas, Okla.	1924	1928		GC	(m-1962)
Christian, Meno, Okla.			1929		(d-1932)
Zion, Kingman, Kans.		1929	1938		(m-1973)
Texline, Texas		1930?		R,GC	(d-1940?)
Plainview, Dalhart, Texas		1930?	1933		(d-1935)
Methodist-Mennonite Sunday School Union, Syracuse, Kans.	1931				(d-?)
Lorraine Avenue, Wichita, Kans.	1929	1932	1933	R	498
Meade, Kans.	193?			R	(d-1923)
Meadow, Mingo (Colby), Kans.		1937	1947	GC,R	(w-1970)

Congregation and location	Work began	Church organized	General Conference member	Received help from	1981 members (or most recent figure)
Grace (Gospel Hall), Enid, Okla.	1935	1938	1941	R	207
First (Bell), Fredonia, Kans.		1939	1947	R,GC	(d-1973)
Southwest Wichita, Kans.	1940			L,R	(d-1955)
Neodesha, Kans.	1930	1941		R,GC	(d-?)
Walton, Kans.		1942	1945	R	85 .
First, Burns, Kans.		1944	1945	L,R	95
First, McPherson, Kans.	1937	1945	1947	R	252
West New Hopedale, Ringwood, Okla.	1895	1947	1947	L	25
Bethel, Enid, Okla.		1947?			(d-1958)
Faith, Greensburg, Kans.		1948			(d-1964)
First, Clinton, Okla.	1950	1951	1953	R	100
Lamar-Wiley, Colo.	1952			R	(d-?)
Indian, Seiling, Okla.	1955	1955?	1971	GC	28
Southern Hills, Topeka, Kans.	1952	1957	1966	R	87
Oklahoma City, Okla.	1956			R	(d-1960)
Rainbow Blvd., Kansas City, Kans.	1954	1957	1959	R,L	179
Faith, Newton, Kans.	1956	1958	1959	R,L	355
Calvary, Liberal, Kans.	1956	1959	1962	R	59
Arvada, Colo.	1957	1961	1965	R	135
Mennonite Church of Mexico Cuauhtémoc, Chihuahua Steinreich, Chihuahua Burwalde, Chihuahua	1945	1963		GC	315
Inter-Mennonite, Hesston, Kans.		1967	1974		157
Houston, Texas	1967	1967	1971	R	47
Trinity, Hillsboro, Kans.		1968		merger	311
Trinity United Mennonite-Presbyterian, Oklahoma City, Okla.	1964	1970	1977	R,GC	(d-1980)
Kingman, Kans.		1973		merger	163
New Creation, Newton, Kans.	1973	1973	1980		23
Ecumenikos, Shawnee Mission (Kansas City), Kans.		1973		R	51
Dallas, Texas	1975	1976		R	30
Servant, Wichita, Kans.	1976	1977	1977	R	20
Jubilee, North Newton, Kans.	1977	1977	1979		9
Manhattan, Kans.	1976	1978	1979	R	35
Covenant, Hesston, Kans.	1976	1978	1979		16
Salina, Kans.	1978	1979		R	25
Oklahoma City, Okla.	1980				
Stillwater, Okla.	1980				
Lawrence, Kans.	1973	1979		R	
Fort Collins, Colo.	1973	1980		R	

Appendix 2

Voluntary Service Units in North America

Location	Dates Summer or Short-Term Volunteers Served	Dates Long-Term Volunteers Served
Aberdeen, Idaho	1958	
Albuquerque, New Mexico		1974-75
Ames, Iowa		1981-
Arvada, Colorado		1969-
Assiniboine Camp, Springstein, Manitoba	1958, '80, '82	
Atlanta, Georgia	1965-66	
Beatrice, Nebraska	1967-75, '79	1975-
Bedminster, Pennsylvania	1981-82	
Blackfoot, Idaho	1967-69	
Bloodvein Indian Reserve, Manitoba	1966-67	
Bloomington, Illinois	1967-74, '76-79	
Bluffton, Ohio	1973, '77	
Bragg Creek, Alberta	1967	
Busby, Ashland, and Lame Deer Montana	1947-66, '68-71, '76	1957, '77-78
Camp Friedenswald, Cassopolis, Michigan	1951-63, '67-71	
Camp Keola, Huntington Lake, California	1973-74	
Camp Koinonia, Boissevain, Manitoba	1979	
Camp Mennoscah, Murdock, Kansas	1956-63, '67, '71-72, '77-78	
Camp Moose Lake, Sprague, Manitoba	1967, '71-72, '77-78	
Camp Palisades, Idaho	1958	
Camp Shalom, Kearney, Ontario	1959-60	
Camp Squeah, Yale, British Columbia	1963	
Camp Valaqua, Water Valley, Alberta	1965, '67	
Canadian Service Team		1972-73
Carbondale, Illinois		1980-82

Location	Dates Summer or Short-Term Volunteers Served	Dates Long-Term Volunteers Served
Champaign-Urbana, Illinois	1973-74	1971-76
Chicago, Artists Communicating Through Service		1975-78
Chicago, Englewood (First Church)	1966, '68, '71	
Chicago, Grace Church	1963, '65	
Chicago, Lakeview		1977-
Chicago, North Chicago		1969-71
Chicago, North of Howard		1982-
Chicago, Pilsen		1981-
Chicago, Woodlawn	1946-68, '70	1965-69
Cincinnati, Ohio		1977-
Colorado Springs, Colorado		1980-
Cuauhtémoc, Mexico	1954, '57, '60-61	1957-69
Dallas, Texas		1982
Denver, Colorado	1971	1972, '76-
Edmonton, Alberta	1967	
Education Team	1961	
Elkhart, Indiana	1959-60, '65, '69-74	1970-75, '82-
Eloy, Arizona	1957-62, '65	
Estes Park, Colorado	1980	
Fort Vermilion and LaCrete, Alberta		1957-61
Fort Wayne, Indiana	1961-77, '79	1966-76
Fresno, California	1956, '58-61, '63-64, '67, '71	1980-
Geary, Oklahoma		1971-73
Goessel, Kansas		1970-73
Grande Prairie, Alberta	1963	
Gulfport and Waveland, Mississippi	1957-72	1957-76
Hamilton, Ontario	1973, '76-77, '79	1966-
Hammon, Clinton, and Seiling, Oklahoma	1950, '54-64, '66 '71-75, '78	1971-75, '76-79, '80-81
Haney, British Columbia	1968	
Houston, Texas	1969	1967-72
Hutchinson, Kansas	1972	1967-68, '71-
Hydro, Oklahoma	1962-63, '65-66	
Illinois Survey Team, Bloomington	1960	
Kamloops, British Columbia	1972	
Kansas City, Kansas	1958-65, '68-72, '75-77, '80	1969-74, '76-
Koinonia Farms, Americus, Georgia	1958, '75-77	
Lancaster, Pennsylvania	1967	
Larkspur, Colorado		1970
Lethbridge, Alberta	1967-68	
Liberal, Kansas		1970-
Lima, Ohio	1967	
Lincoln, Nebraska	1967-70	
Lively, Ontario	1961, '77	
Manigotogan, Manitoba	1965, '67	
Markham, Illinois	1964, '66, '69-70, '72, '75	1965-
Matheson Island, Manitoba	1964-65, '67-68	
Meadow Lake, Saskatchewan	1968-69	
Men-O-Lan, Quakertown, Pennsylvania	1951, '54, '60-63	

Location	Dates Summer or Short-Term Volunteers Served	Dates Long-Term Volunteers Served
Migrant Ministry in Michigan, Minnesota, and New York	1948, '50-52	
Minneapolis, Minnesota	1965-71, '78-80	1968-73
Moses Lake, Washington	1955	
Newton, Kansas	1959, '65, '67, '70, '77	
Newton, Kansas, The Bridge		1971-74
Newton, Kansas, Northview	1966-67	
New York City, East Harlem Protestant Parish	1950-53, '64-65, '68	
New York City, World's Fair Booth	1965	
North Battleford, Saskatchewan	1951, '53-58, '60-64, '66-70	1966-70
Oklahoma City, Oklahoma	1966-71	1965-
Oraibi, Hotevilla, and Moencopi, Arizona	1947-69, '79	1957-
Ottawa, Ontario	1974	
Paint Rock, North Carolina	1951, '53, '57-59	
Peace Team, Canada	1948	
Peace Team, Central U.S.	1971	
People's Teachers of the Word (itineration)		1975-77
Philadelphia, Pennsylvania	1965-66, '68-73	1957-58, '67-82
Philadelphia, Germantown	1972, '80-82	
Phoenix, Arizona	1971, '77-78	1971-74
Pine Lake Camp, Meridian, Mississippi	1971-76, '78-79	1973-75
Pleasant Valley, Woodstock, Illinois		1982-
Portland, Oregon	1960, '62-63, '65, '70-72, '76-82	1972-
Reedley, California	1971	1982
Road Less Traveled (itineration)		1982-
Rockies Backpack, Divide, Colorado	1972-73	
Rosthern, Saskatchewan	1947-56, '58-63, '65-68	1957-70
Roving Reporters	1962	
St. Catharines, Ontario		1980-
St. Louis, Missouri		1973-74, '75-
Salem, Oregon	1967-68	
San Jose, California	1967-69	
Santa Clara, California		1982
Seattle, Washington	1974-79	1971-
Silver Lake Camp, Hepworth, Ontario	1962-63, '72, '77	
Sioux Falls, South Dakota	1964, '67, '71	1965
Swan Lake Camp, Viborg, South Dakota	1957, '64	
Sweet Home, Oregon	1956, '64	
Synapses (itinerating unit)	1979-80	
Thompson, Manitoba	1959-61	
Topeka, Kansas	1952-56, '58	
Toronto, Ontario	1966-68, '74	
Upland, California	1967-72, '74	1969-74
Vancouver, British Columbia	1967-70	
Waldheim, Saskatchewan	1968	

Location	Dates Summer or Short-Term Volunteers Served	Dates Long-Term Volunteers Served
Warden, Washington	1957, '62	
Warroad, Minnesota	1970	
Washington, D.C.	1970	1976-82
Wernersville, Pennsylvania	1967-72	
Wheatridge, Colorado	1964-72, '75-82	1967-69
Wichita, Kansas	1967, '69-70, '78	1968-74, '75-
Wichita, Fairview Mennonite House		1971-74
Winnipeg, Manitoba	1952-58, '60, '67-73	1966-70
Woodlands School, British Columbia	1967-68	
Youth Teams	1947-51, '53, '62-64	

Appendix 3

Organization of North American Mission and Service Work in the General Conference Mennonite Church

Before 1950	1950 Constitution	1968 Constitution
Foreign Mission Board —Indian ministries in Oklahoma, Montana, and Arizona —(overseas missions)	Board of Missions —(overseas missions) —city church committee —rural missions —church building loans —aid to district mission committees —church unity —Indian ministries in U.S. —radio and television work —evangelism	Commission on Overseas Mission —(overseas mission and service) —Mexico churches
Home Mission Board —city missions —migrant and mountain missions —aid to immigrant ministers —church building loans —traveling ministers —orphan fund		Commission on Home Ministries —Indian ministries in U.S. —voluntary service in North America —consultation with and support of local and regional groups on church planting and evangelism —radio and television ministries —Spanish ministries —Chinese ministries —peace and social concerns
Emergency Relief Board —in North America and overseas	Board of Christian Service —voluntary service in North America and abroad —mutual aid —peace and social concerns —Women in Church Vocations —hospitals, homes, and mental health centers —relief in North America and abroad	Division of Administration —Church Extension Service: church building loans —(other administrative and financial matters)
Young People's Union Voluntary Service Committee		
Peace Committee		

Women's Missionary Association
—migrant ministries

Regional Conference Home Mission Work

Mennonite Pioneer Mission and Canadian Conference Foreign Mission Committee
—Indian ministries in northern Manitoba

Amalgamation in 1957-60 as Mennonite Pioneer Mission
—Indian ministries in Canada

Name changed to Native Ministries in 1975

Regional conference mission committees
—starting new churches, urban and rural
—traveling ministers

Regional Conference mission committees

Regional conference mission committees

Notes

Introduction

1. Alfred Habegger, "The Development of the Missionary Interests Among the Members of the General Conference of Mennonites of North America." Unpublished M.A. thesis, Bluffton College and Mennonite Seminary, Bluffton, Ohio, 1917.

2. See Waldemar Janzen, "Foreign Mission Interest of the Mennonites in Russia before World War I," *Mennonite Quarterly Review* 42: no. 1 (January 1968): 57-67.

3. Carl H. A. van der Smissen, "Die innere Mission in den Gemeinden der Taufgesinnten oder Mennoniten," in David Goerz, *Ein Referat ueber innere Mission*, General Conference of Mennonites of North America, 1892, pp. 15-22. See also Edmund George Kaufman, *The Development of the Missionary and Philanthropic Interest Among the Mennonites of North America* (Berne, Ind.: Publication Board of the General Conference of the Mennonite Church of North America, 1931), pp. 38-39.

4. Letter to Canadian Committee for Foreign Mission from missionary John Thiessen, 1953, CMC.

Chapter 1

1. David Goerz, *Ein Referat ueber innere Mission*, General Conference of Mennonites in North America, 1892, p. 12.

2. See especially Minutes, Second Session, General Conference of Mennonites of North America, May 20-23, 1861.

3. For more on this topic, see "Reiseprediger," *Mennonite Encyclopedia*, vol. 4, pp. 280-81.

4. "Seventy-fifth Anniversary of the First Mennonite Church of Philadelphia; The Diamond Jubilee, 1865-1940," Philadelphia, 1940.

5. Minutes, Eastern District Conference, 72nd Session, September 7, 1884; *The Mennonite* 46: no. 18 (April 30, 1931): 15.

6. Samuel Floyd Pannabecker, *Faith in Ferment: A History of the Central District Conference* (Newton, Kans.: Faith and Life Press, 1968), pp. 70ff.

7. H. P. Krehbiel, *The History of the General Conference of the Mennonites of North America* (St. Louis: published by the author, 1898), p. 344.

8. *Ibid.*, p. 345.

9. Krehbiel, *History of the General Conference*, p. 348.

10. Pannabecker, *Faith in Ferment*, p. 127.

11. Krehbiel, *History of the General Conference*, p. 349.

12. Harold Delbert Burkholder, "The Origin and Development of the Congregations of the Pacific District Conference of Mennonites." Unpublished M.A. thesis, George Pepperdine College, 1949.

13. Frank H. Epp, *Mennonites in Canada, 1786-1920* (Toronto: Macmillan of Canada, 1974), p. 295; John A. Toews, *A History of the Mennonite Brethren Church* (Fresno, Calif.: Board of Christian Literature, General Conference of Mennonite Brethren Churches, 1975), pp. 154-56; Henry Gerbrandt, *Adventure in Faith* (Altona, Manitoba: Bergthaler Church of Manitoba, 1970), pp. 86, 103-9. As the "smuggling" was later explained, Toews had bought a pair of shoes for his son in North Dakota, but the customs office was closed when he came back across the border. He meant to return to the customs office the next day to pay the duty on the shoes, but forgot, thus the "smuggling."

14. Krehbiel, *op. cit.*, pp. 344ff.; *The Mennonite* 5: no. 7 (April 1890): 104: Krehbiel, *op. cit.*, p. 223.

15. *The Mennonite* 1: no. 1 (October 1885): 9.

16. General Conference Board of Home Missions correspondence (hereafter referred to as HMB), file 8.

17. *The Mennonite* 2: no. 10 (July 1887): 152-53.

18. *The Mennonite* 5: no. 6 (March 1890): 85.

19. Goerz, *op. cit.*, p. 11.

20. John R. Baergen and John H. Neufeld, eds., "A Summary Report of Home Mission Work in Canada." Unpublished, Canadian Mennonite Bible College, Winnipeg, 1956.

Chapter 2

1. "The Indian Question," *The Mennonite* 1: no. 4 (January 1886): 58.

2. *The Mennonite* 1: no. 4 (January 1886): 59.

3. Virginia Cole Trenholm, *The Arapahoes, Our People* (Norman: University of Oklahoma Press, 1970), p. 263.

4. Before 1881, the U.S. government required denominations to get permission before starting mission work on Indian reservations. Competing church groups were not allowed in the same location. See R. Pierce Beaver, ed., *The Native American Christian Community; A Directory of Indian, Aleut, and Eskimo Churches* (Monrovia, Calif.: MARC, 1979), p. 31.

5. See Donald J. Berthrong, *The Southern Cheyennes* (Norman: University of Oklahoma Press, 1963), pp. 3-26.

6. *Cheyenne Autumn*, by Mari Sandoz (McGraw, 1953), tells this story, as does the movie by the same name.

7. Donald J. Berthrong, *The Cheyenne and Arapaho Ordeal* (Norman: University of Oklahoma Press, 1976), p. 84.

8. H. R. Voth, *The Mennonite* 1: no. 1 (October 1885): 10.

9. Berthrong, *Cheyenne and Arapaho Ordeal*, p. 121.

10. Trenholm, *The Arapahoes*, pp. 265-66; *Christlicher Bundesbote* (July 1, 1883): 103.

11. Columbus Delano, Secretary of the Interior Annual Report, in Executive Documents, 1873-74, Washington, D.C.

12. Anna Hirschler (Mrs. G. A.) Linscheid, *Historical Sketch of the General Conference Mission Enterprise in Oklahoma, 1880-1930*. Unpublished manuscript, 1930, pp. 11-12, MLA.

13. *Christlicher Bundesbote* 2: no. 2 (January 15, 1883): 15.

14. Bergthrong, *Cheyenne and Arapaho Ordeal*, p. 107.

15. Linscheid, p. 12, quoting a letter from Susanna Haury.

16. J. M. Lee to S. S. Haury, August 30, 1881, file 8, Foreign Mission Board (FMB); S. S. Haury to J. Moser, U.S. Indian Agent, August 31, 1885, and S. S. Haury to D. B. Dyer, U.S. Indian Agent, June 2, 1885, Oklahoma State Archives; Berthrong, *Cheyenne and Arapaho Ordeal,* pp. 100, 121.

17. Berthrong, *Cheyenne and Arapaho Ordeal,* p. 128.

18. D. L. Atkins to S. S. Haury, June 13, 1885; S. S. Haury to D. L. Atkins, June 18 and 19, 1885, file 8, 1885-87, FMB.

19. Linscheid, *Historical Sketch,* pp. 15-16; Berthrong, *Cheyenne and Arapaho Ordeal,* pp. 100-2.

20. The identity of the woman involved cannot be determined from any of the written records either of the mission or of the Indian agency of the period. There is no mention that a woman was asked to resign or was disciplined in any way. If one oral source is correct about the identity of the woman, the reason for this is that she had died soon after childbirth and shortly before Haury's resignation.

21. G. D. Williams, Indian Agent, to J. D. Atkins, Commissioner of Indian Affairs, August 10, 1887, Cheyenne and Arapaho Letter Book, Oklahoma State Historical Library. See also Berthrong, *Cheyenne and Arapaho Ordeal,* pp. 144-45, citing G. D. Williams to H. R. Voth, August 25, 1887, Voth Collection, Mennonite Library and Archives, (MLA).

22. "Accounts of Various Experiences in Life; A Diary Begun in the Year 1839 by Johann Jantzen, Beatrice, Nebraska," November 13, 1889, entry, MLA.

23. Linscheid, *Historical Sketch,* p. 22.

24. *The Mennonite* 2: no. 7 (April 1887): 104.

25. See Fred Ringelman, "A Brief History of the Mennonite Church of Geary, Oklahoma," *The Mennonite* 44: no. 12 (March 21, 1929): 1-2; and 44: no. 13 (March 28, 1929): 4-5.

26. The Geary church still had one Indian member in the 1960s, according to Malcolm Wenger (1981).

27. For a history of the early Hammon mission, see Ruth C. Linscheid, *Red Moon* (Newton, Kans.: published by the author, 1973).

28. Modern Cheyenne spelling will be placed in parenthesis.

29. *The Mennonite* 51: no. 44 (November 10, 1936): 7.

30. *Ibid.*

31. *Ibid.*

32. Heinrich T. Neufeld to Rodolphe Petter, Mar. 21, 1921, file 29, Petter Collection, MLA.

33. Linscheid, *Historical Sketch,* p. 78.

34. *Ibid.*

35. "Ich will sie mehren und nicht mindern," *Evangelische Missionsverlag,* 1936, pp. 43-44.

36. Rodolphe Petter, "Some Reminiscences of Past Years in My Mission Service Among the Cheyenne," *The Mennonite* 51: no. 44 (November 10, 1936): 16. Petter's "Reminiscences" were also printed in a separate pamphlet.

37. General Conference minutes, 1911, Appendix I.

38. Rodolphe Petter to Bertha Petter, July 7, 1941, file 8, Petter Collection, MLA.

39. Petter, "Reminiscences," pp. 13-14.

40. *The Mennonite* (May 22), 1902): 4.

41. The graves of the two Cheyenne have been found at St. Seabold Church, near Strawberry Point, Iowa, according to Malcolm Wenger (interview, 1981).

42. Petter, "Reminiscences," p. 14.

43. A. Linscheid, *Historical Sketch,* pp. 9-10.

44. A Letter from a Cheyenne Christian to a Crow "Jesus Man," February 4, year unknown, file "Montana—Historical—IM," CHM.

45. H. P. Krehbiel, *The History of the General Conference of the Mennonite Church of North America,* vol. 2 (Newton, Kans.: by the author, 1938), p. 586.

Chapter 3

1. Russell Hiebert, "J. B. Frey, Missionary to the Hopis." Unpublished paper, Bethel College, 1967.

2. The government records of Lololma's visit to Washington, D.C., in 1890 show no evidence of meetings with the denominational groups listed below. See Gene C. Miller to Malcolm Wenger, Dec. 16, 1976, citing Hopi Agency Letter 23269, Thomas Keam to Morgan, Commissioner of Indian Affairs, July 24, 1890, Letters Received Indian Office; and Letter 19797, Transcription of Moquies Chief's Conference, June 27, 1890, with the commissioner of Indian Affairs, National Archives. Neither do the General Conference Mennonite Church archives record any such meeting with Lololma in Washington.

3. J. B. Frey to General Conference Board of Missions, n.d., Frey Collection, MLA, quoted in Russell Hiebert, "J. B. Frey, Missionary to the Hopis." Unpublished paper, Bethel College, 1967, Appendix A. The story is repeated in abbreviated form in Frank Waters, *Book of the Hopi* (New York: Ballentine Books, 1963) p. 355.

4. P. Staufer to N. B. Grubb, Mar. 8, 1891, quoted in "Keam's Canyon, Arizona," *The Mennonite* 6: no. 8 (May 1891): 118-19.

5. Frederick J. Dockstader, *The Katchina and the White Man* (Cranbrook Institute of Science) p. 83.

6. Charles F. Lummis, *Bullying the Moqui,* (Flagstaff, Ariz.: Prescott College Press, 1968); originally published in the magazine *Out West,* Apr.-Oct. 1903.

7. "Bright Arizona Prospects," *The Mennonite* 27: no. 20 (April 24, 1902): 5-6.

8. *The Mennonite* 27: no. 10 (February 13, 1902): 1.

9. *Science,* February 8, 1901, p. 219.

10. *Ibid.*

11. *The Mennonite* (September 1900): 93.

12. A. B. Shelly to H. R. Voth, March 6, 1899, file 53, Voth Collection, MLA.

13. Thomas V. Keam to Rev. Christian Schowalter, January 16, 1899; quoted in letter from A. B. Shelly to H. R. Voth, March 6, 1899, file 53, Voth Collection, MLA.

14. Timothy Voth, "H. R. Voth." Unpublished paper, Bethel College, 1975, p. 21.

15. Leo W. Simmons, ed., *Sun Chief: The Autobiography of a Hopi Indian* (New Haven: Yale University Press, 1942), p. 100.

16. Interview with Homer Cooyama, April 18, 1978.

17. Interview with Willard Sakiestewa, Sr., April 1978.

18. *The Mennonite* (March 6, 1902), p. 6.

19. Interview with Willard Sakiestewa, Sr.

20. *The Mennonite* (May 13, 1941), p. 2.

21. "The Oraibi Mesa Chapel," *The Mennonite* 56: no. 11 (March 18, 1941): 10. Harry C. James, *Pages from Hopi History* (Tucson: University of Arizona Press, 1974), p. 157, cites Voth's journal in support of the view that the original plan for the building would have put one corner over the path of the kachinas. Upon protest of the Hopi religious leaders, Voth willingly changed the plan for the chapel so that the path of the kachinas remained unobstructed.

22. Mrs. J. Ernest Cline, *Missionary News and Notes,* March 1935.

23. See Matilda K. Voth, "Mother of Hopi Orphans," *Missions Today* 42: no. 12 (August 1968): 6-9, and 43: no. 1 (September 1968): 14-15.

24. Henry C. Thiessen, *The Concordant Version of the Sacred Scriptures; How*

Should We Regard It? (New York: Loizeaux Brothers, Bible Truth Depot, n.d.), is a careful refutation of Knoch's version from an evangelical point of view. It was used by the Arizona missionaries against Frey in the 1940s.

25. Hiebert, "J. B. Frey, Missionary." p. 6.

26. J. B. Frey to Foreign Mission Board, n.d., pp. 11-12, Frey Collection, MLA, cited in Hiebert, "J. B. Frey, Missionary," Appendix A.

27. Interview with Fred Johnson, April 19, 1978.

28. August 11, 1929, Foreign Mission Board, MLA.

29. February 20, 1945, Foreign Mission Board, MLA.

30. July 4, 1945, Foreign Mission Board, MLA.

31. Johnson to Foreign Mission Board, September 1, 1945, Foreign Mission Board, MLA.

32. Johnson to Foreign Mission Board, October 11, 1945, Foreign Mission Board, MLA.

33. July 3, 1953, in file "New Outburst—re J. B. Frey in Our Mission Churches," Board of Missions, MLA.

34. April 28, 1953, file "New Outburst," Board of Missions, MLA.

35. John and Helene A. Janzen, Report, January 8, 1961, Moencopi, Board of Missions.

36. See file "Arizona—Hopi Mission School—IM," Board of Missions; see also William Rayburn, "Hopi Report," unpublished manuscript, 1960.

37. Albert L. Jantzen, "The Hopi Mission School, A Reality," *The Mennonite* (November 20, 1951): 733.

38. Rayburn, "Hopi Report," p. 4.

39. Rayburn, "Hopi Report," p. 8.

Chapter 4

1. Dale Suderman to the Commission on Home Ministries, 1977, CHM.

2. 1974 Indian Ministries report to CHM.

3. *Ibid.*

4. General Conference minutes, 1941, p. 111.

5. Ruth Linscheid, *Red Moon* (Newton, Kans.: published by the author, 1973), p. 126.

6. Harold W. Turner, "Old and New Religions Among North American Indians; Missiological Impressions and Reflections," *Missiology* 1:2 (April 1973): 47.

7. *Ibid.,* p. 54.

8. Mrs. Henry T. Neufeld, file "Montana, historical—Indian Ministries," CHM.

9. Menno Wiebe, "A Stove, a Pulpit, and an Organ," *The Mennonite* 93: no. 32 (September 12, 1978): 514-15.

10. Lois R. Habegger, *Cheyenne Trails* (Newton, Kans.: Mennonite Publication Office, 1959), pp. 40-41; Anna G. Stauffer, *Mennonite Mission Study Course, Part III, Cheyenne Mission Field* (Berne, Ind.: Mennonite Book Concern, 1928), p. 49; file 27, Petter Collection, MLA.

11. Petter to Foreign Mission Board, January 28, 1919, file 27, Petter Collection, MLA.

12. Rodolphe Petter to Bertha Petter, August 6, 1923, file 8, Petter Collection, MLA.

13. January 1, 1919, file 27, Petter Collection, MLA.

14. Circular to the Indians, May 8, 1919, file 26, Petter Collection, MLA.

15. H. P. Krehbiel, *The History of the General Conference of the Mennonite Church of North America*, vol. 2 (Newton, Kans.: by the author, 1938), p. 446.

16. Mrs. A. (Barbara) Habegger, 1932, file 1933, Foreign Mission Board, MLA.

17. George W. Hinman to Commissioner Rhoads, May 23, 1932, Classified Files, 1907-1939, Tongue River, 15687-32-059, Records of the Bureau of Indian Affairs, National Archives—Microfilm No. 209, MLA.

18. James Mooney, *The Ghost-Dance Religion and the Sioux Outbreak of 1890* (Chicago: University of Chicago Press, 1965), p. 19; first published in 1896.

19. Donald J. Berthrong, *The Cheyenne and Arapaho Ordeal* (Norman: University of Oklahoma Press, 1976), p. 138.

20. *The Mennonite* 6: no. 3 (December 1890): 42.

21. *The Mennonite* 6: no. 10 (July 1891): 154-55.

22. Rodolphe Petter, "Some Reminiscences of Past Years in My Mission Service Among the Cheyenne," *The Mennonite* 51: no. 44 (November 10, 1936): 3. Also in pamphlet.

23. Trenholm, p. 294; J. S. Slotkin, *The Peyote Religion; A Study in Indian-White Relations* (Glencoe, Ill.: The Free Press, 1956).

24. Minute Book No. 1 of the Cheyenne and Arapaho Missionary Union, pp. 5-6, MLA.

25. Minute book, January 18, 1922, Conference of Indian Missionary Workers in Western Oklahoma, MLA.

26. H. J. Kliewer, "Prayer and Praise," *The Mennonite* 34: (February 20, 1919): 1-2.

27. February 14-16, 1961, file "Oklahoma, Notes on Visits," Board of Missions.

28. Petter, "Reminiscences," (pamphlet), p. 33.

29. Malcolm Wenger to David Braun, February 12, 1965, quoted in David W. Braun, "Along the Peyote Road; Peyote and the Native American Church." Unpublished paper, Bethel College, 1965, p. 22.

30. Herman and Alice Walde to Board of Missions, April 1, 1960, Board of Missions; David Habegger, "As I See It," *The Mennonite* (February 27, 1951): 137.

31. Braun, *ibid.*

32. Bertha K. Petter to readers of *The Mennonite* (March 13, 1919); "Disclosures at Lame Deer and What Became of Them," p. 4, CHM.

33. Arthur Sutton, file "Oklahoma, Notes on Visits," 1976, CHM.

34. Turner, "Old and New Religions," p. 63.

35. Published by Faith and Life Press, Newton, Kans., in 1982.

36. Frank Waters, *Book of the Hopi* (New York: Ballentine Books, 1963), pp. 381-82; John P. Suderman, "A Hopi Indian Finds Christ; The Experience of Mr. K. T. Johnson and His Judgment on Idolatry," (by the author, Oraibi, Ariz.: n.d.).

37. See file "Hotevilla," CHM.

38. Interview with Malcolm Wenger, 1981.

39. *Cheyenne Transporter,* June 25, 1881, p. 2.

40. *Cheyenne Transporter,* December 24, 1880, p. 2.

41. A. B. Shelly to Rev. Roe, September 5, 1906, file 55, FMB.

42. J. B. Ediger to Malcolm Wenger, February 11, 1946, cited in Judy Voth, "Biography of Jacob B. Ediger." Unpublished paper, Bethel College, 1961, p. 7.

43. Quoted in R. Petter to Foreign Mission Board, February 22, 1929, file 37, Petter Collection, MLA.

44. Rodolphe Petter to Foreign Mission Board, May 23, 1928, file 36, Petter Collection, MLA.

45. Undated note, C. J. Rhoads (1932?), Records of the Bureau of Indian Affairs, Classified files, 1907-1939, 15687-32-059, Tongue River, Record Group 75, National Archives; microfilm 209 in MLA.

46. *Taeglicher Bericht,* 1908 General Conference sessions.

47. Nadenia F. Myron, "The Early Mennonite Missionary's Approach and Atti-

tude to the Hopi Indians and the Effects upon the Mission Work." Unpublished paper, Bethel College, 1979, pp. 7-8.

48. R. Pierce Beaver, ed., *The Native American Christian Community; A Directory of Indian, Aleut, and Eskimo Churches,* (Monrovia, Calif.: MARC, 1976), p. 31.

49. Turner, "Old and New Religions," pp. 56-57.

50. J. B. and Agnes Frey, "Arizona: Mission Work Among the Hopis," *Mission Quarterly* 1:1 (November 1924) English ed., pp. 11-12.

51. Kenneth R. Philp, *John Collier's Crusade for Indian Reform* (Tucson: University of Arizona Press, 1977).

52. Harold L. Ickes to Valdo Petter, May 2, 1934, Records of the Office of the Secretary of the Interior, Central Files, 1907-1936, 5-1. Tongue River, Mission, National Archives; microfilm 209, MLA.

53. Rodolphe Petter to G. A. Linscheid, Nov. 6, 1936, file 45, Petter Collection, MLA.

54. R. Petter to P. H. Richert, July 9, 1936, file 45, Petter Collection, MLA.

55. Milton Whiteman, "Flight of Time Among the Cheyenne Indians in Montana," *The Mennonite* 68: no. 34 (Sept. 1, 1953): 537.

56. Turner, p. 58.

57. A Hopi New Testament was eventually completed by Wycliffe Translators in the 1970s. Voth's early work, a typewritten Hopi dictionary, was to be included in a comprehensive Hopi linguistic file at the University of Northern Arizona, Flagstaff. The original is in the Mennonite Library and Archives, North Newton, Kansas.

58. August Schmidt, Canton, Okla., July 6, 1962, file "Oklahoma, Notes on Visits," Commission on Home Ministries; there is uncertainty, however, whether these Bible portions were actually translated by Funk, or whether Funk's translations exist.

59. Two Oklahoma Indian churches were admitted into the General Conference at the 1935 session, but the applications for admission were withdrawn at the next session with only the notation that it had been a misunderstanding. See General Conference minutes, 1938, p. 17.

60. Elizabeth Q. White (Polingaysi Qoyawayma) as told to Vada F. Carlson, *No Turning Back* (Albuquerque: The University of New Mexico Press, 1964), pp. 81-82.

61. See Lawrence Hart, "Cheyenne Peace Tradition," *Mennonite Life* 36: no. 2 (June 1981): 4-7.

62. Interview with Malcolm Wenger, 1977.

63. Frank Waters, *Pumpkin Seed Point* (Chicago: The Swallow Press, Inc., 1969), p. 51.

64. Interviews with Malcolm Wenger, 1977, 1981.

65. Lawrence H. Hart. "Why the Doctrine of Non-Resistance Has Failed to Appeal to the Cheyenne Indian." Unpublished paper, Bethel College, 1961, pp. 17-18.

66. See *The Mennonite* 27: no. 45 (October 23, 1902): 2; Anna G. Stauffer, *Mennonite Mission Study Course, Part I, Hopi Mission Pamphlet* (Newton, Kans.: Herald Publishing Co., 1926), pp. 42-43.

67. *The Mennonite* 5: no. 12 (September 1890): 180.

68. Petter, "Reminiscences," (pamphlet), p. 23.

69. 1946, FMB.

70. Mrs. Rodolphe Petter, "Hasseoveo, a Beloved Christian," *The Mennonite* (November 25, 1947), pp. 3-4.

71. H. P. Krehbiel, *The History of the General Conference,* vol. 2, (Newton, Kans.: by the author, 1938), p. 451.

72. He and Frank Littlewolf were ordained as ministers in 1942.

73. Malcolm Wenger, "How Long Are You Staying?" *The Mennonite* (June 27, 1950), p. 444.

74. Alice and Herman Walde, Clinton, to Board of Missions, January 4, 1961, Board of Missions.

75. Interview with Calvin Flickinger, November 1, 1977.

76. *Missionary Methods; St. Paul's or Ours?* (London: World Dominion Press, 1960), first published in 1912; *The Spontaneous Expansion of the Church and the Causes Which Hinder It,* (London: World Dominion Press), first edition in 1927.

77. Interview with Malcolm Wenger, December 12, 1977.

78. Malcolm Wenger, "Thoughts on a Strategy for Indian Missions." *Missions Today* 44: no. 7 (March 1970): 8.

79. File "Oklahoma, Notes on Visits," about 1976, CHM.

80. Interview with Malcolm Wenger, 1981.

Chapter 5

1. HMB (Board of Home Missions), file 16, January 15, 1914, Anna Penner.

2. *Taeglicher Bericht der 18. Allgemeinen Konferenz der Mennoniten von Nord Amerika,* Beatrice, Nebraska, September 9, 1908.

3. *Memories of J. W. Kliewer* (North Newton, Kans.: Bethel College, 1943), p. 62.

4. H. H. Van Meter, *Christian Evangel* 1: no. 3 (September 1910): 13.

5. *The Mennonite* 22: no. 10 (March 7, 1907): 4.

6. HMB, file 10, July 26, 1906, and February 14, 1907, John C. Mehl.

7. The long transition to the paid ministry was to cause some friction. As late as the 1950s, Alberta churches were irked when the pastor of the new mission church in Edmonton was the first full-time, professionally trained pastor in the provincial conference. (Source: Anne Harder, First Mennonite Church, Edmonton, Alberta, correspondence with author, 1978.)

8. John T. Neufeld, *Mennonite Work in Chicago Prior to 1960,* unpublished; H. P. Krehbiel, *The History of the General Conference of the Mennonite Church of North America,* vol. 2 (Newton, Kans.: published by the author, 1938), p. 46.

9. *Jubilaeums-Fest der Allgemeinen Konferenz der Mennoniten von Nord-Amerika* (Berne, Ind.: Mennonite Book Concern, 1909).

10. HMB, file 60.

11. HMB, file 13, June 30, 1911, E. F. Grubb.

12. HMB, file 12, July 16, 1909, E. F. Grubb to J. J. Balzer; HMB, file 12, November 24, 1909, E. F. Grubb to J. J. Balzer.

13. HMB, file 13, June 30, 1910, E. F. Grubb to J. J. Balzer.

14. HMB, file 53, September 30, 1914, H. P. Krehbiel; HMB, file 16, April 28, 1914, J. J. Balzer.

15. HMB, file 58, December 31, 1915, F. J. Isaac.

16. HMB, file 59, January 5, 1916, H. P. Krehbiel; file 55, February 16, 1915, E. F. Grubb; file 60, April 8, 1916; file 66, April 14, 1917, David Toews.

17. HMB, file 13, April 6, 1910, W. S. Gottschall; April 18, 1910, J. C. Mehl.

18. HMB, file 62, July 12, 1916, H. Teichrieb; Harold Delbert Burkholder, *The Origin and Development of the Congregations of the Pacific District Conference of Mennonites.* Unpublished M.A. thesis, George Pepperdine College, 1949, p. 99; HMB, file 72, 1918, M. M. Horsch.

19. HMB, file 28, November 1, 1922, Lavina Burkhalter.

20. HMB, file 28, January 2, 1923.

21. HMB, file 48, July 27, 1926, Lavina Burkhalter.

22. HMB, file 24, March 18, 1947, J. M. Regier to A. J. Neuenschwander; file 54,

September 29, 194?, J. M. Regier; General Conference Reports and Minutes, 1950, p. 76; Board of Trustees correspondence, General Conference vault.

23. HMB, file 15, June 21, 1913, W. S. Gottschall.

24. HMB, file 15, June 21, 1913.

25. Krehbiel, *op. cit.,* vol. 2, p. 49; John T. Neufeld, *op. cit.*

26. HMB, file 16, February 16, 1914.

27. HMB, file 19, October 27, 1922, W. S. Gottschall.

28. HMB, file 33, April 12, 1921, W. W. Miller.

29. HMB, file 16, January 13, 1914.

30. HMB, file 65, January 10, 1917, Catherine Niswander; HMB, file 33, April 12, 1921, W. W. Miller.

31. Catherine Niswander, interview with author, January 17-18, 1978.

32. Leland Harder, *Seventy-third and Laflin* (Chicago: First Mennonite Church, 1952), pp. 12-13. See also *The Mennonite* 37: no. 10 (March 9, 1922).

33. HMB, file 50, January 23, 1928, C. Niswander; HMB, file 33, August 26, 1934, P. P. Sprunger to J. M. Regier; C. Niswander, interview with author, January 17-18, 1978; J. Winfield Fretz, "A Study of Mennonite Religious Institutions in Chicago." Unpublished B.D. thesis, Chicago Theological Seminary, 1940, p. 51.

34. As Rhea left First Mennonite Church, he destroyed all local church records. In addition, most of the Home Mission Board's correspondence for 1928-42 is missing. So records of attendance and membership during that period are nonexistent. In 1940, some church members told J. Winfield Fretz that membership had been as high as 200.

35. HMB, file 33, July 10, 1939, J. Winfield Fretz to J. M. Regier; John T. Neufeld, *op. cit.,* with added notes by Esther Neufeld Kressly.

36. C. Niswander, interview with author, January 17-18, 1978; HMB, file 62, August 25, 1916, H. P. Krehbiel to W. W. Miller; HMB, miscellaneous file, February 15, 1940.

37. HMB, file 82a, August 27, 1939, John Warkentin.

38. William T. Snyder, interview with author, May 10, 1979; *The Mennonite* 44: no. 3 (January 17, 1929): 3.

39. HMB, file 39, April 3, 1922, G. M. Baergen.

40. HMB, file 18, May 17, 1921, Jacob Snyder.

41. *The Mennonite* 45: no. 40 (October 9, 1930): 3-5. See also Russell E. Kauffman, *God's Messenger to Red Hook,* published by Elizabeth Foth in Zanesville, Ohio, n.d. This biography focuses on Foth's work in Brooklyn.

42. Eva F. Sprunger, *The First Hundred Years, Adams County, Indiana, 1838-1938,* Berne, Indiana.

43. HMB, file 45, May 4, 1925.

44. HMB, file 92, April 13, 1942, A. J. Neuenschwander to Delbert Welty.

45. HMB, file 61, May 30, 1916, W. S. Gottschall; file 74, October 7, 1918.

46. HMB, file 49, September 13, 1926, L. H. Glass to A. S. Shelly; file 49, December 13, 1927, A. S. Shelly to W. S. Gottschall. Little else is known about the influence of the Klan in Altoona. It was evidently not common knowledge in the conference.

47. HMB, file 44, August 17, 1927, Daniel Gerig to A. S. Shelly; file 49, December 10, 1927, W. S. Gottschall.

48. Miriam Snyder Miller, interview with author, May 13, 1979.

49. HMB, file 139, October 12, 1946; Gordon R. Dyck, *The United States General Conference Extinct Churches (1847-1959).* Unpublished research paper, Mennonite Biblical Seminary, Elkhart, Indiana, 1959, No. 9.

50. HMB, file 62, August 16, 1916, Jacob Snyder; file 39, January 4, 1923, A. S. Shelly.

51. HMB, file 6, February 26, 1917, H. P. Krehbiel.

52. HMB, file 70, January 18, 1918, H. T. Unruh; also Henry A. Fast interview, 1978; John M. Ediger, "History of the First Mennonite Church, Hutchinson, Kansas," unpublished, 1972. This article may be found in the congregation's files in Hutchinson; Richard Ratzlaff correspondence with author, May 1979.

53. See HMB files 69, 70, and 71 for an account of Dickmann's activities in the General Conference and the Home Mission Board's negative attitude toward him. *Christlicher Bundesbote* (26: no. 43 [November 1, 1917]: 1) reported that P. P. Hilty of Donnellson, Iowa (probably a Mennonite), was serving as a treasurer for Dickmann's mission in Brooklyn.

54. This was not the first contact of General Conference Mennonites with the Chicago Hebrew Mission. Mathilde Lehman of Berne, Indiana, had worked there sometime before 1916. (See Mathilde Lehman, "Eine Skizze ueber die Chicago Hebrew Mission und ihre Arbeit unter den Juden," *Christlicher Bundesbote* 35: no. 34 [August 31, 1916]: 5.)

55. Henry J. Gerbrandt correspondence with the author, July 4, 1979.

56. Home missions correspondence, Conference of Mennonites in Canada, file 2, Andrew Shelly, 1957; file "Manitoba, Ontario, Saskatchewan." See also MLA-I-1, file 263.

57. John T. Neufeld, *op. cit.*, has a short history of almost every Mennonite church or mission attempted in Chicago.

58. Betty Hochstetler, interview with author, April 1978.

59. Mary Wiens Toews, "The True to Life Story of the Wiens Family of the Mennonite Bible Mission, now Grace Mennonite Church, of Chicago." Published by the author, n.d., p. 17; John T. Neufeld, "A Brief Story of the Grace Mennonite Church (Mennonite Bible Mission)," unpublished, 1952.

60. HMB, file 57, August 11, 1915, W. S. Gottschall; John T. Neufeld, "Forty Years in City Mission Work," *Missionary News and Notes* 35: no. 7 (March 1961): 15; HMB, file 94, October-December 1941 report, John T. Neufeld.

61. HMB, file 94, October 1942. Both the Neufelds were involved in the civil defense program, Catherine as air warden, and John as chairman of protection for the community.

62. Mary Wiens Toews, *op. cit.*

63. John T. Neufeld, "Forty Years in City Mission Work," original manuscript, unpublished.

64. Amos M. Eash, *After Ten Years: A Brief Report of the First Ten Years of Work of the Twenty-sixth Street Mennonite Mission, 1906-16* (Chicago: published by the author), p. 40.

65. William B. Weaver, *History of the Central Conference Mennonite Church* (Danvers, Illinois: published by the author, 1926), pp. 139ff.

66. A. M. Eash, "The City as a Field for Missionary Work," *Central Conference Yearbook,* 1933.

67. Correspondence, Central Conference home mission committee, October 14, 1936, A. M. Eash to I. R. Detweiler, and October 20, 1936, Detweiler to Eash.

68. Fretz, *op. cit.,* p. 81.

69. Correspondence, Central Conference home mission committee, November 2, 1933; May 3, 1934; July 2, 1934; July 10, 1934; Fretz, *op. cit.,* pp. 102-4.

70. Pannabecker, *Faith in Ferment* (Newton: Faith and Life Press, 1968), pp. 266-67; Minutes, Central Conference home mission committee, 1947.

71. Central Conference Yearbook, 1940. At least one brewery gave Peoria a distinct smell.

72. HMB, file 60, March 31, 1916, E. F. Grubb; file 15, March 31, 1913(?), E. F. Grubb.

73. Fretz, *op. cit.,* pp. 73-76, 130-31.

74. HMB, file 66, May 4, 1917, H. P. Krehbiel to Lena Smith; HMB, file 17, H. P. Krehbiel to Lavina Burkhalter, August 3, 1920.

75. Before World War I, Bethel College did have a Home Mission Band as well as a Student Volunteer Band for foreign missionary candidates.

76. Krehbiel, *op. cit.,* vol. 2, p. 133.

77. HMB, file 19, May 4, 1920, W. S. Gottschall.

78. HMB, file 19, October 27, 1922.

79. Krehbiel, *op. cit.,* vol. 2, pp. 151-52.

80. HMB, file 50, September 3, 1927; file 21, report to 1935 General Conference.

81. Fretz, *op. cit.,* p. 136.

82. Betty Hochstetler, interview with author, April 1978.

83. HMB, file 82A, August 27, 1939, John Warkentin.

84. HMB, file 15, June 30, 1913, E. F. Grubb.

85. HMB, file 76, January 10, 1919, Ina M. Feighner; HMB, file 18, July 6, 1921, P. W. Penner.

86. Eash, *op. cit.,* p. 97; Minutes, Central Conference home mission committee, May 3, 1934; Ernest Neufeld correspondence with author, July 1979.

87. HMB, file 61, April 20, 1916, E. F. Grubb.

88. HMB, file 63, October 10, 1916.

89. HMB, file 55, February 3, 1915; file 61, June 30, 1916.

90. Edmund George Kaufman, *The Development of the Missionary and Philanthropic Interest among the Mennonites of North America* (Berne, Ind.: Publication Board of the General Conference of the Mennonite Church of North America, 1931), p. 176.

91. W. S. Gottschall, "What Shall the Home Mission Board Do?" *The Mennonite* 45: no. 40 (October 9, 1930): 2; Editorial, *The Mennonite* 46: no. 50 (December 17, 1931): 1-2; Conference of Mennonites in Canada, II. T. Vol. 302, Folder: F. F. Enns, 1926-33, April 23, 1932, David Toews to F. F. Enns.

92. HMB, file 83, October 29, 1942.

93. See Fretz, *op. cit.*

94. Among the sources giving this point of view are *Christian Evangel* 2: no. 1 (January 1912): 24-25; HMB, file 58, October 21, 1915, W. S. Gottschall; Weaver, *op. cit.,* p. 134; S. M. Grubb, editorial, *The Mennonite* 45: no. 34 (August 28, 1930): 1-2; Kaufman, *op. cit.,* p. 306; A. J. Neuenschwander, "Our General Conference and a Decreasing Rural Population," *The Mennonite* 46: no. 13 (March 26, 1931), 6-7.

95. Fretz, *op. cit.,* p. 166.

96. John T. Neufeld, unpublished writings; Catherine Niswander, interview, January 17-18, 1978.

97. Pannabecker, *Faith in Ferment,* p. 278.

98. HMB, file 55.

Chapter 6

1. HMB, file 58, October-December 1915, H. P. Krehbiel to H. J. Krehbiel.

2. HMB, file 11, November 14, December 8, and December 14, 1908; board member W. S. Gottschall responded, "She ought to know that many Mennonites are fit subjects for mission work"; see HMB, file 11, December 11, 1908.

3. HMB, file 58, October 21, 1915.

4. P. P. Wedel, "Notes on My Trip to Pennsylvania," *The Mennonite* 45: no. 30 (July 31, 1930): 2-4.

5. J. G. Rempel, *Fuenfzig Jahre Konferenzbestrebungen, 1902-1952,* Konferenz der Mennoniten in Canada, 1954, p. 77; author's translation.

6. P. 36.

7. Report of the 21st Western District Conference, 1910, p. 31; David Haury, *Prairie People: A History of the Western District Conference* (Newton: Faith and Life, 1981).

8. Krehbiel, *The History of the General Conference, vol. II,* (Newton Kans.: by the author, 1938), pp. 165-66.

9. Edward D. Schmidt, "A Short History of the Zoar Mennonite Congregation at Waldheim, Saskatchewan, Canada." Unpublished, located in congregation's files.

10. HMB, file 56, March 31, 1915, John M. Franz.

11. Benjamin Ewert correspondence, Box 1 (Vol. 542), file 16, Conference of Mennonites in Canada Archives (hereafter referred to as CMC); see also J. G. Rempel, *op. cit.,* pp. 13-14, 45.

12. J. G. Rempel, *op. cit.* p. 92; see also HMB, file 15, July 30, 1913, Benjamin Ewert to HMB; file 15, September 12, 1913, M. Horsch.

13. HMB, file 16, August 1914, Johann Gerbrandt, Gerhard Epp, and Benjamin Ewert.

14. HMB, file 20, February 24, 1923, D. J. Unruh.

15. Lee Price Campbell, "Seventy-five Years on the Shores of the Peaceful Sea; A History of the Pacific District Conference of the General Conference Mennonite Church of North America." Unpublished M.Div. thesis, Western Evangelical Seminary, 1973, pp. 26-27; records of the Woodlake church are held by the First Mennonite Church in Reedley, California.

16. Gordon R. Dyck, "The United States General Conference Extinct Churches (1847-1959)." Unpublished, Elkhart, Indiana: Mennonite Biblical Seminary, 1959, No. 14.

17. Campbell, *op. cit.,* p. 26.

18. "Report of the Evangelization Committee of the Pacific District Conference, 1930," *The Mennonite* 45: no. 34 (August 28, 1930): 6.

19. "A Brief History of the Mennonite Church of Geary, Oklahoma," *The Mennonite* 44: no. 12 (March 21, 1929): 1-2; also see Krehbiel, *op. cit.,* vol. 2, p. 15.

20. P. P. Wedel correspondence, file 23, June 14, 1922, Mennonite Library and Archives (MLA).

21. Krehbiel, *op. cit.,* vol. 2, pp. 147-48; Dyck, *op. cit.,* No. 45.

22. HMB, file 31, October 5, 1922, A. S. Shelly; see also Krehbiel, *op. cit.,* vol. 2, p. 147.

23. General Conference Reports and Minutes, 1938, p. 24.

24. HMB, file 21, July 26, 1932, J. M. Regier.

25. Rempel, *op. cit.,* includes biographies of these as well as about 200 other people who figured in Canadian Conference history before 1954.

26. Jacob Rempel, *Sargent Avenue Mennonitengemeinde,* Winnipeg, 1971.

27. HMB, file 47, June 8, 1925, N. W. Bahnmann; see also Krehbiel, *op. cit.,* vol. 2, p. 385.

28. HMB, file 25, April 8, 1949, Cornelius Boldt.

29. Interviews with General Conference missionaries near Cuauhtémoc, Mexico, May 1977.

30. Dale R. Schrag, "The Founding of the Lorraine Avenue Mennonite Church." Unpublished paper, Wichita State University, 1978, pp. 5-11; see also David Haury, *A People of the City: The Lorraine Avenue Mennonite Church* (Wichita: Lorraine Avenue Mennonite Church, 1982).

31. Krehbiel, *op. cit.* vol. 2, p. 138.

32. William B. Weaver, *History of the Central Conference Mennonite Church* (Danvers, Illinois; published by the author, 1926), p. 105.

33. Benjamin Ewert correspondence, XX-1(2), vol. 543, file 34, CMC; author's translation.

34. S. M. Grubb, editorial, *The Mennonite* 45: no. 34 (August 28, 1930): 1-2.

35. Benjamin Ewert correspondence, XX-1(2), vol 543, file 34, April 17, 1939.

36. Henry A. Fast, correspondence with author, July 11, 1979.

37. General Conference Minutes, 1926, pp. 249ff.

38. General Conference Minutes, 1926, pp. 262ff.

39. Henry A. Fast, "An Evaluation of Our Home Mission Work," *The Mennonite* 44: no. 35 (September 5, 1929): 1-3.

40. J. M. Regier, "Statement Concerning the Work of the Home Mission Board," *The Mennonite* 47: no. 30 (August 4, 1932): 2-3. Regier probably had sided against city missions at the 1926 conference only for the sake of debate.

41. HMB, file 51, October 19, 1926, Jacob H. Janzen.

42. The story of the North Kildonan settlement is told in *Fiftieth Anniversary of the Mennonite Settlement in North Kildonan,* Winnipeg, 1978. Text is in both English and German. North Kildonan, established in 1924 as a rural municipality north of Winnipeg, is now a part of the city. About 5,000 Mennonites lived there in 1979, and seven Mennonite churches were located there. The story of the Schoenwieser congregations is told in J. Enns, Abr. Vogt, Joh. Klassen, and Is. Klassen, *Dem Herrn die Ehre; Schoenwieser Mennoniten Gemeinde von Manitoba, 1924-1968* (Altona, Manitoba, 1969).

43. HMB, file 41, January 29, 1926, David Toews.

44. Ronald J. Dueck, "The Development of Canadian City Missions." Unpublished, Canadian Mennonite Bible College, Winnipeg, 1966.

45. J. J. and Katherine Thiessen, "The Mennonite Girls' Home in Saskatoon, Saskatchewan, Canada," *The Mennonite* and *The Christian Evangel* 2: no. 21 (November 5, 1935).

46. J. J. Thiessen, "Forty Years with the First Mennonite Church, Saskatoon, Saskatchewan," compiled for the Wayfarers Club, March 1972.

47. J. J. and Katherine Thiessen, *loc. cit.*

48. John R. Baergen and John H. Neufeld, eds., "A Summary Report of Home Mission Work in Canada." Unpublished, Canadian Mennonite Bible College, Winnipeg, 1956.

49. Henry Harder, "A Short History of the Origins of the First United Mennonite Church, Vancouver, British Columbia." Unpublished, Canadian Mennonite Bible College, Winnipeg, 1976.

50. Baergen and Neufeld, *op. cit.*

51. David Toews correspondence, file (2) II.T., letter from John P. Vogt to General Conference Home Mission Board and David Toews.

52. Henry J. Gerbrandt, *Adventure in Faith* (Altona, Manitoba: Bergthaler Church of Manitoba, 1970), p. 212.

53. Rempel, *op. cit.* p. 113.

54. Gerbrandt, *op. cit.* pp. 213ff.

55. HMB, file 89, April 30, 1942, Benjamin Ewert.

56. G. G. Epp correspondence, vol. 578 (Box 5), David Schroeder file, August 27, 1951, CMC.

57. HMB, file 89, April 30, 1942, Benjamin Ewert.

58. See David Haury, *A People of the City,* and Western District home mission committee correspondence (hereafter referred to as WD), Wichita file, MLA.

59. WD, August 19, 1943, J. M. Regier to Ben C. Frey.

60. See Harold Delbert Burkholder, "The Origin and Development of the Congregations of the Pacific District Conference of Mennonites." Unpublished M.A.

thesis, George Pepperdine College, 1949, pp. 56ff; Catherine Niswander interview, January 1978.

61. W. S. Gottschall, "Home Mission Notes," *The Mennonite* 48: no. 32 (August 17, 1933): 3.

62. Osmund R. Fretz, "Introducing Grace Mennonite Church," *The Messenger of the Eastern District Conference* 19: no. 4 (July-August 1976): 8, and *The Mennonite*, January 23, 1930, and April 30, 1931. Facts about congregational membership and percentage of members from Mennonite parentage here and following are from Leland Harder, *General Conference Mennonite Church: Fact Book of Congregational Membership,* 1971.

63. See Carolyn Neufeld, "First Mennonite Church in Lima: The Beginnings to the Present." Unpublished, Bluffton College, Bluffton, Ohio, 1970.

64. Middle District home mission committee correspondence, January 17, 1943, Victor E. Swartzendruver to D. W. Bixler, Bluffton College Historical Library.

65. WD, October 20, 1935, B. H. Koehn and twenty-nine other signators to P. H. Unruh; March 19, 1936, Frieda Ann Merk to J. M. Suderman, also 1936 anonymous letter; April 8, 1940, H. N. Harder; September 1940, H. N. Harder.

66. HMB, file 148, February 10, 1948, Albert Claassen.

67. HMB, file 11, January 1908.

68. *Pacific District Conference Minutes, 1896-1926,* English translation published by PDC Education Committee, 1977, pp. 71-72.

69. David Toews correspondence, file (2), II.T., Calgary home mission work, July 25, 1944, John P. Vogt to General Conference Home Mission Board and David Toews, CMC.

70. HMB, file 72, no date, H. P. Krehbiel to W. S. Shelly.

71. A. J. Fast, "Home Mission News," *The Mennonite* 46: no. 21 (May 21, 1931): 3.

72. David L. Habegger, "A Study of the Mission of the First Mennonite Church of Upland, Historically, Currently, and Prospectively." Unpublished dissertation, School of Theology, Claremont, California, 1967, p. 40.

73. "Jottings," *The Mennonite* 46: no. 49 (December 10, 1931): 15; no. 50 (December 17, 1931): 15.

74. WD, Ed and Ella Schmidt reports, 1940, 1941, 1942; WD, October 29, 1941; WD, home mission committee report to annual sessions, October 1943.

75. HMB, file 61, May 27, 1916, H. P. Krehbiel.

76. HMB minutes, August 3, 1938.

77. David Toews correspondence, file (2), II.T., Calgary home mission work, John P. Vogt to General Conference Home Mission Board and David Toews, CMC.

78. P. P. Wedel correspondence, file 53, September 27, 1927, and October 4, 1927.

79. Fern Ruth, "Lorraine Avenue Mennonite Church," in *Our Continuing Mission: A Brief History of Western District Conference Home Missions Churches,* published by Western District Home Missions Committee, October 1969.

80. "Grace Mennonite Church, Enid, Oklahoma," in *Our Continuing Mission.*

Chapter 7

1. John D. Unruh, *In the Name of Christ: A History of the Mennonite Central Committee and Its Service, 1920-1951* (Scottdale, Pa.: Herald Press, 1952), p. 286. In addition at least forty Mennonites were imprisoned for violations of draft law (p. 262).

2. For further information on Civilian Public Service, see Guy F. Hershberger, *The Mennonite Church in the Second World War* (Scottdale, Pa.: Mennonite Publish-

ing House, 1951) and Melvin Gingerich, *Service for Peace* (Akron, Pa.: Mennonite Central Committee, 1949).

3. HMB, file 94, Oct. 16, 1942, J. H. Enns.

4. John A. Toews, *A History of the Mennonite Brethren Church: Pilgrims and Pioneers* (Fresno, Calif.: Board of Christian Literature, General Conference of Mennonite Brethren Churches, 1975), p. 356.

5. J. G. Rempel correspondence, Nov. 29, 1951, MLA-I-4 (S), 1-8.

6. HMB, file 57, Aug. 11, 1915, W. S. Gottschall.

7. See Pannabecker, *Faith in Ferment* (Newton: Faith and Life Press, 1968), pp. 227-39.

8. HMB, file, Apr. 21, 1942, Arnold J. Regier to A. J. Neuenschwander.

9. HMB, file 89, Apr. 27, 1942, A. J. Neuenschwander to J. J. Plenert.

10. HMB, file 92, Aug. 3, 1942, Clyde H. Dirks.

11. John T. Neufeld, "Forty Years of City Mission Work." Unpublished manuscript.

12. *Official Minutes and Reports*, 1926, General Conference Mennonite Church, p. 95.

13. Silas M. Grubb, "Germans or Mennonites, Which?" *The Mennonite* (February 1900), p. 37, quoted in Leland David Harder, "The Quest for Equilibrium in an Established Sect." Unpublished Ph.D. dissertation, Northwestern University, Evanston, Illinois, 1962, p. 316.

14. *Official Minutes and Reports*, 1945, General Conference of the Mennonite Church of North America, p. 23.

15. Quoted in S. F. Pannabecker, *Open Doors* (Newton, Kans.: Faith and Life Press, 1975), p. 174.

16. The typewritten history, written in German, is located in the congregational files of the Sargent Avenue Mennonite Church, 926 Garfield St., Winnipeg, Manitoba R3E 2N6.

17. *Official Minutes and Reports*, 1947, General Conference of the Mennonite Church of North America, p. 90.

18. *Official Minutes and Reports*, 1945, General Conference of the Mennonite Church of North America, p. 57.

19. HMB, file 83, Oct. 23, 1942, Jacob H. Janzen. See also John R. Baergen and John H. Neufeld, eds., "A Summary Report of Home Mission Work in Canada." Unpublished paper, Canadian Mennonite Bible College, Winnipeg, 1956.

20. Baergen and Neufeld, *op. cit.*

21. William Dyck and John Sawatzky, "Psycho-Social Changes Within a Metropolitan Religious Minority," in *Mennonite Life* 23: no. 4 (Oct. 1968): 172-76.

22. CMC, Vol. 326, II. T., Toronto file.

23. HMB, file 89, May 20, 1942, D. H. Koop.

24. Henry P. Epp correspondence with the author, Nov. 28, 1977.

25. CMC, G. G. Epp correspondence, Vol. 576, Box 3, Prince Albert file.

26. Anne Harder correspondence with the author, 1977.

27. HMB, file 125, Sept. 14, 1945.

28. A. J. Neuenschwander, "Our General Conference and a Decreasing Rural Population," *The Mennonite* 46: no. 13 (Mar. 26, 1931): 6-7.

29. Quoted in Pannabecker, *Faith in Ferment,* p. 280.

30. Central Conference mission board minutes, May 21, 1940.

31. HMB, file 89, May 19, 1942, Elmer Basinger to A. J. Neuenschwander.

32. CHM, David Toews correspondence, II. T. (2), Calgary file, John P. Vogt to General Conference Home Mission Board and David Toews, July 25, 1944.

33. J. Winfield Fretz, *Mennonite Colonization* (Akron, Pa.: Mennonite Central Committee, 1944), pp. 25-26.

34. *Official Minutes and Reports,* 1938, General Conference of the Mennonite Church of North America, p. 134.

35. William H. Stauffer, "A Study of General Conference Problems; Annual Report of Year's Work of the General Conference." Unpublished manuscript presented at Newton, Kansas, Apr. 1944.

36. *Official Minutes and Reports,* 1947, General Conference of the Mennonite Church of North America, pp. 174ff.

37. HMB, file 85, c. 1942.

38. A. J. Neuenschwander, quoted in Baergen and Neufeld, *op. cit.*

39. Quoted in Pannabecker, *Faith in Ferment,* p. 182.

40. Harder, *Fact Book of Congregational Membership,* p. B-6.

41. Comins report by Florence and Frank Mitchell, *Central Conference Yearbook,* 1937.

42. For a recent history of the Sweet Home church, see Frank McCubbins, "The Hippie Church," *The Mennonite* 91: no. 28 (August 3, 1976): 474-75.

43. More information on the Eldon Camp mission is available in Krehbiel, *The History of the General Conference* (Newton, Kans.: by the author, 1938), vol. 2, pp. 380-81; *The Mennonite* 42: no. 41 (October 20, 1927): 1; and W. Harley King, "Rural Missionary," *The Mennonite* 43: no. 24 (June 14, 1928): 5. The Eldon Camp property now serves as campground for the Southwest Indian Leaders Conference.

44. HMB, file 111, February 1, 1944, J. J. Plenert.

45. S. F. Pannabecker, ed., *The Christian Mission of the General Conference Mennonite Church* (Newton, Kans.: Faith and Life Press, 1961), p. 13.

46. Middle District home mission committee treasurer's report, April 15, 1952.

47. Pannabecker, *The Christian Mission, loc. cit.*

48. *Board of Missions Minutes,* 1946-1956, p. 353 (December 1954).

49. Naomi Lehman, correspondence with author, August 21, 1979.

50. "Migrant Work," *Mennonite Encyclopedia,* vol. 3, p. 684; see also HMB, file 92, Aug. 3, 1942, John B. Jantzen.

51. Glen Habegger, "The Ministry at Friendly Corner in Its Beginnings." Unpublished manuscript, 1978.

52. Florence and Frank Mitchell, *Central Conference Yearbook,* 1937.

53. Published in 1955-59 by Mennonite Publishing House, Scottdale, Pennsylvania; Mennonite Publication Office, Newton, Kansas; and Mennonite Brethren Publishing House, Hillsboro, Kansas.

54. Published in *Church History,* 13:3-34 (Mar. 1944), and in *Mennonite Quarterly Review* (April 1944): 67-68.

55. Erland Waltner, "Whitherbound?" in Cornelius Krahn and John F. Schmidt, *A Century of Witness; the General Conference Mennonite Church* (Newton, Kans.: Mennonite Publication Office, 1959).

Chapter 8

1. James C. Juhnke, *A People of Mission* (Newton, Kans.: Faith and Life Press, 1979), p. 10; see also Chapter 2.

2. David Goerz, *Ein Referat ueber innere Mission,* General Conference of the Mennonite Church of North America, 1892, pp. 2, 8-10.

3. Harold S. Bender, "Mennonite Board of Guardians," *Mennonite Encyclopedia,* vol. 3, pp. 591-92.

4. Krehbiel, *The History of the General Conference,* vol. 2 (Newton, Kans.: by the author, 1938), p. 7; p. 57.

5. *Official Minutes and Reports,* 1938, General Conference of the Mennonite Church, p. 133.

6. See H. J. Andres, "Hospitals," *Mennonite Encyclopedia,* vol. 2, pp. 817-18.

7. See A. R. Shelly, "Homes for the Aged," *Mennonite Encyclopedia*, vol. 2, pp. 797-99.

8. *Official Minutes and Reports*, 1941, General Conference of the Mennonite Church.

9. See also Cornelius Krahn, "Leisy Orphan Aid Society," *Mennonite Encyclopedia*, vol. 3, p. 318; Pannabecker, *The Christian Mission of the General Conference Mennonite Church*, p. 10; and Pannabecker, *Open Doors*, pp. 204-5.

10. See H. A. Fast, "Mental Hospitals, Mennonite," *Mennonite Encyclopedia*, vol. 3, pp. 653-54.

11. See Vernon H. Neufeld, editor, *If We Can Love: The Mennonite Mental Health Story* (Newton, Kans.: Faith and Life Press, 1982).

12. See Julie Mergner, *The Deaconess and Her Work*, trans. by Harriet R. Spaeth (Philadelphia: General Council Publication House, 1911).

13. See E. Theodore Bachman, editor, *Church and Social Welfare*, vol. 1 (*The Activating Concern, Historical and Theological Bases*) (New York: National Council of Churches of Christ in the U.S.A., 1955), pp. 58-59. The first four deaconesses came from Kaiserwerth to Pittsburgh in 1849 to serve as nurses in a Lutheran hospital.

14. See *The Mennonite* 3: no. 11 (August 1888): 161-62. There A. B. Shelly tells of meeting the Meyers on a trip through Chicago and of Shelly's regret that "such able and active workers are obliged to go outside of our church organization for a field of labor of the kind." In 1885 Lucy Rider Meyer started the Chicago Training School, an institution to train young women in urban and foreign missions. She and nine of her pupils became the first Methodist deaconesses, working among the poor of Chicago. Their story is told in Frederick A. Norwood, *From Dawn to Midday at Garrett*, (Evanston, Ill.: Garrett-Evangelical Theological Seminary, 1978).

15. Pannabecker, *Open Doors*, pp. 203-4; C. Goldner *History of the Deaconess Movement in the Christian Church*, New York, 1903, quoted in John T. Neufeld writings.

16. David Goerz, "Zur Diakonissensache; Ein Beitrag zur Kenntnis der Weiblichen Diakonie mit besonderer Beruecksichtigung der Stellung der Mennoniten zu derselben," Part I. Reprinted from *Monatsblaettern*, Newton, Kansas: Bethel College, 1904.

17. "Silver Anniversary Memorial; The Bethel Deaconess Home and Hospital, 1908-1933," Newton, Kansas, 1933, p. 2.

18. See Goerz, "Zur Diakonissensache"; also Marilyn Bartel, "Sister Frieda Kaufman; Builder of Institutions and Lives." Unpublished paper, Bethel College, North Newton, Kansas, 1966, p. 2.

19. Bartel, *op. cit.*, p. 14; "Silver Anniversary Memorial," pp. 2-4; Frank Stucky, "The Western District Conference; A Comparative Analysis of 1892-1920 and 1950-1970." Unpublished paper, Bethel College, North Newton, Kansas, 1971, pp. 25-27.

20. HMB, file 217, March 29, 1950, Daniel J. Unruh.

21. Personal interview with the author, Sister Lena Mae Smith and Sister Dora Richert, January 1976.

22. Bartel, *op. cit.*, pp. 18-25; see also Lena Mae Smith, "Sister Frieda Marie Kaufman," *Mennonite Encyclopedia*, vol. 3, p. 158.

23. Lois Barrett, "Looking at the Deaconess Movement Again," *The Mennonite* 91: no. 16 (April 20, 1976): 278.

24. "Mennonitisches Bethel Diakonissenstift und Hospital," Newton, Kansas: Bethel Diakonissenstift und Hospitalgesellschaft, 1911.

25. Conversation with author, January 1976.

26. HMB, file 217, March 29, 1950, Daniel J. Unruh.

27. *Reports and Official Minutes,* 1950, General Conference Mennonite Church, p. 41.

28. Albert Gaeddert papers, file 124, Board of Christian Service, Minutes and Report, 1952, MLA.

29. *Reports and Official Minutes,* 1956, General Conference Mennonite Church, p. 201.

30. *The General Conference Mennonite Church Report,* 1959, p. 35.

31. Board of Christian Service annual report, 1961.

32. See Frank H. Epp, *Mennonites in Canada, 1786-1920* (Toronto: Macmillan of Canada, 1974), pp. 391-410.

33. See James Juhnke, "Conflicts and Compromises of Mennonites and the Draft; An Interpretive Essay." Unpublished manuscript, 1969.

34. *Official Minutes and Reports,* 1938, General Conference of the Mennonite Church, pp. 131-36.

35. Paul Classen, "Statistics on Mennonite Central Committee Personnel," *Mennonite Quarterly Review* 44: no. 3 (July 1970): 324-29.

36. Henry A. Fast, "The Spiritual Values of Contributing to Relief," *Town and Country Church* No. 33 (March 1947): 12-13.

37. The General Conference Mennonite Church *Report,* 1959, p. 29. For a readable history and description of Mennonite Disaster Service, see Katie Funk Wiebe, *Day of Disaster* (Scottdale, Pa.: Herald Press, 1976).

38. Amos M. Eash, *After Ten Years* (Chicago: published by author, n.d.), p. 59.

39. Mary Hoxie Jones, *Swords into Ploughshares; An Account of the American Friends Service Committee, 1917-1937* (New York: The Macmillan Company, 1937), pp. 204-5.

40. Wilfred J. Unruh, *A Study of Mennonite Service Program* (Elkhart, Ind.: Institute of Mennonite Studies, 1965), p. A-52; see also David S. Richie, *Memories and Meditations of a Workcamper* (Wallingford, Pa.: Pendle Hill Publications, 1973); Elva May Schrock Roth, "Work Camp, Chicago, July 1938," August 1975, unpublished manuscript in the files of Robert S. Kreider.

41. For more information on the 1939 Chicago work camp, see Central Conference Minutes, 1938; letter from Elva May Schrock Roth to Robert S. Kreider and copies of *Plowshare,* the work camp publication, located in Kreider files.

42. Donovan Smucker letter, July 3, 1976, Robert S. Kreider files.

43. Personal interview of Elmer Ediger with the author, July 16, 1979.

44. Wilfred Unruh, *op. cit.,* pp. 48-49.

45. John Unruh, *In the Name of Christ* (Scottdale, Pa.: Herald Press, 1952), p. 309.

46. John Unruh, *op. cit.,* p. 296.

47. MLA-I-4(S), 2-17; also in the mid-1940s other church and secular groups were organizing for service, particularly in reconstruction in Europe. Through the initiative of the American Friends Service Committee, a group of about a dozen agencies formed the Commission on Youth Service Projects in December 1945, of which other peace churches as well as Mennonites were a part. That group, later called the *Commission on Voluntary Service and Action,* grew to include over 150 agencies, but dissolved in 1977. A continuing committee still publishes an annual listing of service opportunities called *Invest Yourself.*

48. *Reports and Official Minutes,* 1956, General Conference Mennonite Church, p. 59.

49. See "Senior Volunteers Sought," *The Mennonite* 80: no. 13 (March 30, 1965): 214.

50. *Report,* 1965, General Conference of the Mennonite Church, p. 65.

51. Board of Christian Service annual report, December 1968.

52. Commission on Home Ministries annual report, December 1969.

53. Camp Landon assistant director, Harold Regier, took part in a sympathy march after the death of James Reeb at Selma, Alabama, in March 1965.

54. David A. Haury, *The Quiet Demonstration; The Mennonite Mission in Gulfport, Mississippi* (Newton, Kans.: Faith and Life Press, 1979), was a major source for this description of the Gulfport project. The quotation is from page 78.

55. *Ibid.,* pp. 50-51.

56. *Ibid.,* p. 124.

57. Canadian Board of Christian Service, minutes, 1956-61, MLA-I-4(S), 2-17.

58. Lois Barrett Janzen, "New Church Schools—for the Very Young," *The Mennonite* 89: no. 25 (June 18, 1974): 398-99.

59. *Report,* 1968, General Conference of the Mennonite Church, p. 18; Commission on Home Ministries annual report, 1970, p. G-1.

60. *Reports and Official Minutes,* 1950, General Conference of the Mennonite Church, p. 271.

61. MLA-I-4(S), 1-7, Board of Christian Service.

62. Albert Gaeddert Papers, file 123, Executive Committee of Board of Christian Service, Minutes and Reports, 1951.

63. *The Church, the Gospel, and War; A Report of the General Conference Peace Study Conference,* April 10-11, 1953, Newton, Kans.: Board of Christian Service, p. F-3.

64. *Ibid.,* p. D-112.

65. "The Gospel, Discipleship, and Nonresistance," *The Mennonite* 69: no. 19 (May 11, 1954): 204-5.

66. Scottdale, Pa.: Herald Press, 1959, pp. 204-5.

67. *Reports and Official Minutes,* 1956, General Conference Mennonite Church, p. 55.

68. Edgar Metzler, "Is Alternative Service a Witness for Peace?" n.d. (c. 1962), MLA-I-4(S), 1-7.

69. *Catalog, 1957, 1-W Service Openings,* Akron, Pennsylvania: 1-W Service Office, Mennonite Central Committee.

70. MLA-I-4(S), 1-7, Board of Christian Service.

71. Albert Gaeddert Papers, file 126, Board of Christian Service Executive Committee Minutes, April 30, 1954.

72. *Ibid.,* Minutes and Reports, 1954.

73. 1-W Program Review Committee Report, 1963.

74. Jeri Engh, "In Denver To Serve Their Country," *The Mennonite* 81: no. 9 (March 1, 1966): 148-51.

75. Metzler, *op. cit.*

76. Wilfred Unruh, *op. cit.,* pp. 212-13.

77. Board of Christian Service annual report, 1968, p. B-11.

78. Commission on Home Ministries annual report, 1972, pp. B-4-5.

79. Board of Christian Service annual report, 1965, p. B-9.

80. Commission on Home Ministries annual report, 1969, p. G-7.

81. *Ibid.*

82. Wilfred Unruh, *op. cit.,* p. B-34.

83. Richard D. Krause, "Peace Through Service," May 15, 1969, Fort Wayne permanent file, MVS office, Newton, Kansas.

84. *Ibid.*

85. See General Conference News Service, July 18, 1974.

86. Kaye Lehman, February 7, 1969, Hamilton permanent file, MVS office.

87. MLA-I-4-48, file 1170.

88. Lois Barrett Janzen, "VS Becomes Life Style for Kansas Groups," *The Mennonite* 87: no. 13 (March 28, 1972): 220-21.

89. Commission on Home Ministries annual report, 1973, pp. A-6-7.

90. Robert Kreider, "The Impact of MCC Service on American Mennonites," *Mennonite Quarterly Review* 44: no. 3 (July 1970): 245-61.

91. Peter J. Dyck, "A Theology of Service," *Mennonite Quarterly Review* 44: no. 3 (July 1970): 262-80; Walter Paetkau, "When Work Is Freely Given," 80: no. 15 (April 13, 1965): 257-59; Elmer Ediger, "Our Colleges and the VS Program in the Present Crisis," MLA-I-4(S), 9-116.

92. *The Mennonite* 80: no. 45 (December 7, 1965): 765; 94: no. 10 (March 6, 1979): 189.

93. Wilfred Unruh, *op. cit.,* p. A-20.

94. *Report,* 1965, General Conference Mennonite Church, p. 64.

95. Leonard Wiebe to George Lehman and Judi Janzen, April 3, 1973, Fort Wayne permanent file, MVS office, Newton, Kansas.

96. Wilfred Unruh, *op. cit.,* p. B-87.

97. *Report,* 1968, General Conference Mennonite Church, p. 22.

98. Listings of agencies which recruit volunteers include *Invest Yourself,* Haddonfield, New Jersey: The Commission on Voluntary Service and Action, published annually; *Directory of Christian Work Opportunities,* U.S. and International edition, Seattle, Washington: Intercristo, published semiannually; and *The Response,* Washington, D.C.; International Liaison, U.S. Catholic Coordinating Center for Lay Volunteer Ministries, published annually.

Chapter 9

1. Menno Wiebe, "Intersection," in Wiebe, "Indians' Talk Back—Churches' Backtrack?" Unpublished presentation to Home Ministries Council of Mennonite and Brethren in Christ Churches, May 16, 1972, p. 1.

2. The experience of Mennonite Pioneer Mission in Mexico is documented in Henry J. Gerbrandt's book *Adventure in Faith* (Altona, Man.: The Bergthaler Mennonite Church of Manitoba, 1970), pp. 330-38; and in Lynne Derksen's unpublished paper "Mennonite Pioneer Mission: To the Tarahumara Indians (Mexico)," (Winnipeg: Canadian Mennonite Bible College, 1977).

3. *Mennonite Pioneer Mission Quarterly* 2: no. 3 (1946): 9.

4. Gerbrandt, *Adventure,* p. 340.

5. Peter D. Fast, "The Mennonite Pioneer Mission: A Venture of Faith." Unpublished paper, Mennonite Biblical Seminary, Elkhart, Ind., 1960, p. 18.

6. Fast, "The Mennonite Pioneer Mission," p. 6.

7. Grace Braun and Edna Enns, "The Mennonite Pioneer Mission in Matheson Island and Pine Dock." Unpublished paper, Elim Bible School, Altona, Man., 1968.

8. Otto Hamm at Cross Lake reported using *Cree Witness,* a periodical of the Northern Canada Evangelical Mission; *Young Ambassador,* published by the Back to the Bible Broadcast; *Junior Messenger,* a children's paper published by the General Conference Mennonite Church; Scripture Press Sunday school literature; and home Bible study courses sent out by the Mennonite Hour radio broadcast. Cited in Otto Hamm, *The Mennonite Pioneer Mission in Cross Lake* (Winnipeg: The Conference of Mennonites in Canada, 1961), p. 13.

9. Interview with Jake Unrau, July 28, 1981.

10. Population figures are those of 1958, taken from *The People of Indian Ancestry in Manitoba; A Social and Economic Study,* vol. 1 (Winnipeg: The Department of Agriculture and Immigration, 1959), pp. 32, 34, 35, 50.

11. Fast, "The Mennonite Pioneer Mission," p. 9.

12. Henry Neufeld, "Pauingassi," *The Canadian Mennonite* 7: no. 16 (April 24, 1959): 6-7.

13. *Bulletin* Conference of Mennonites in Canada 7: no. 3 (May 18, 1971):3.

14. Interview with Henry Neufeld, July 28, 1981.

15. Willms later served in Taiwan under the General Conference Mennonite Commission on Overseas Mission.

16. See "Testimony of Jeremiah Ross" as told to Roger Buechert and interpreted by Madeline McKay, *Totemak* 7: no. 3 (November-December 1978): 6; First Indian Ordained by MPM," *The Canadian Mennonite* 16: no. 6 (February 6, 1968): 1.

17. Ernie Sawatsky, "How to Clothe the Gospel Message in the Cultural Garb of Their Society," *The Canadian Mennonite* 11: no. 11 (March 15, 1963): 8.

18. Hamm, *The Mennonite Pioneer Mission,* p. 6.

19. Fraser Symington, *The Canadian Indian* (Toronto: McClelland and Stewart Limited, 1969), p. 140.

20. Fast, "The Mennonite Pioneer Mission," p. 11.

21. David Adrian, "A Brief History of the Bloodvein Indian Reservation." Unpublished paper, Vauxhall, Alta. 1966, p. 5.

22. Dave Kroeker, "Mennonite Pioneer Mission: Working with and for the Indians," *The Church and the Original Canadians* (Winnipeg: The Canadian Mennonite Publishing Association, the Conference of Mennonites in Canada, and Mennonite Central Committee [Canada], n.d., about 1970), p. 19.

23. Sawatsky, "How to Clothe the Gospel Message," p. 5.

24. 1960 Mennonite Pioneer Mission report, p. 96; 1961 report, p. 97.

25. Adrian, "A Brief History," p. 5.

26. Kroeker, "Mennonite Pioneer Mission," p. 19.

27. Fast, "The Mennonite Pioneer Mission," pp. 18-19.

28. 1965 minutes, Conference of Mennonites in Canada.

29. 1963 report of conference, Mennonite Pioneer Mission, p. 86.

30. Quoted in Kroeker, "The Mennonite Pioneer Mission."

31. "The Responsibility of the Church in the North," *The Canadian Mennonite* 7: no. 16 (April 24, 1959): 5.

32. Interview, July 28, 1981.

33. *Bulletin* 7: no. 4 (June 11, 1971): 27-28.

34. Report, Peter and Anne Marie Warkentin, December 1970, Matheson Island, vol. 2, Mennonite Pioneer Mission Reports.

35. *Bulletin* 7: no. 4 (June 11, 1971): 28.

36. *Bulletin* 7: no. 3 (May 28, 1971): 7-8.

37. Minutes, Canadian Board of Missions, July 9, 1969.

38. 1975 Conference of Mennonites in Canada Report, p. 17.

39. Lois Barrett Janzen, "MPM Sorts, Integrates Religion-Culture Issues," *The Mennonite* 88: no. 39 (October 30, 1973): 623.

40. Wiebe, "Indians Talk Back," p. 9.

41. "Mennonite Communities—MPM—Indian and Métis Communities," *Mennonite Reporter* 3: no. 4 (February 19, 1973): 14-15.

42. *The Star-Phoenix,* July 8, 1969, quoted in Wiebe, p. 7.

43. 1968 Conference of Mennonites in Canada Report.

44. *The Canadian Mennonite* 11: no. 35 (September 3, 1963): 3. Estimates of the combined Indian and Métis population of Winnipeg range to as low as 20,000, according to a 1980 study of the University of Winnipeg's Institute of Urban Studies, commissioned by Employment and Immigration Canada. (See "Native Population 20,000," *Winnipeg Free Press,* November 22, 1980.) The Manitoba Métis Federation puts the Métis population of Winnipeg at 40,000. Others put the figure

even higher. Larry Krotz ("The Bus People: A Silent Migration," *Winnipeg Magazine*, September 1980, p. 22) writes, "In the last ten years the Indian or native population of Winnipeg has exploded by 600 percent to the point where estimates of the number now living in the city range from a low of 25,000 to a high of 60,000. Generally accepted numbers hover around the 40,000 to 60,000 mark of just slightly less than 10 percent of Winnipeg's 600,000 population."

45. *Bulletin* 4: no. 1 (February 20, 1968).

46. See Leonard Doell, "Walhalla Trail." Unpublished paper written for the Conference of Mennonites in Canada, 1978.

47. *Totemak* 1: no. 1 (1972).

48. *Mennonite Reporter* 3:12 (June 11, 1973): 10.

49. Menno Wiebe, executive secretary's report for Mennonite Pioneer Mission, *Bulletin* 3: no. 4 (May 15, 1967): 30.

50. See *The Canadian Mennonite* 2: no. 24 (June 11, 1954): 5.

51. Fast, "The Mennonite Pioneer Mission," p. 19.

52. Minutes, Conference of Mennonites in Canada, 1967, p. 10.

53. 1980 Council of Boards report, Conference of Mennonites in Canada, p. NM-2.

Chapter 10

1. Cornelius Krahn, "The Anabaptist-Mennonites and the Biblical Church," in *Proceedings of the Study Conference on the Believers' Church, Chicago, Ill., August 23-25, 1955,* Newton, Kans.: General Conference Mennonite Church, p. 94.

2. Robert S. Kreider, "Vocations of Swiss and South German Anabaptists," *Mennonite Life* 8: no. 1 (Jan. 1953): 39-42.

3. Paul Peachey, "Some Theological Reflections on the City," *Mennonite Life* 19: no. 1 (Jan. 1964): 26-31.

4. Paul Peachey, *The Church in the City* (Newton, Kans.: Faith and Life Press, 1963), p. 72. (Institute of Mennonite Studies Series, No. 2)

5. Leland Harder, "Mennonite Mobility and the Christian Calling," *Mennonite Life* 19: no. 1 (Jan. 1964): 7-12.

6. *The Mennonite Church in the City,* No. 6 (Aug. 15, 1957), p. 5.

7. *Ibid.,* No. 1 (Sept. 1, 1956), pp. 4-5.

8. "I-W Service and the Urban Trend," *The Mennonite Church in the City,* No. 6 (Aug. 15, 1957), p. 5.

9. "The Church, the Gospel, and War," A Report of the General Conference Peace Study Conference, Eden Mennonite Church, Moundridge, Kans., Apr. 10-11, 1953, p. E-19.

10. Present at the Winnipeg meeting were Floyd and Pearl Bartel, Topeka, Kansas; Peter and Marjorie Ediger, Fresno, California; Ronald and Cynthia Krehbiel, Markham, Illinois; Richard Ratzlaff, suburban Philadelphia; John Thiessen, executive secretary of the GC Board of Missions, Newton, Kansas; Mr. and Mrs. Wilfred Ulrich, Kitchener, Ontario; and Delton and Marian Franz, Bob and Vernette Regier, Elmer Neufeld, and Leland and Bertha Harder, all of Chicago. See *The Mennonite Church in the City,* No. 1 (Sept. 1, 1956), for a fuller account of the meeting.

11. *Minutes,* 1956, General Conference Mennonite Church, p. 207.

12. *The Mennonite Church in the City,* No. 12 (May 15, 1959).

13. *Report,* 1959, General Conference Mennonite Church, pp. 40-49.

14. *Ibid.,* p. 12.

15. Leland Harder, "The General Conference City Church Movement," *The Mennonite Church in the City,* No. 24 (Aug. 1, 1962).

16. Peter J. Ediger, *The Mennonite Church in the City,* No. 32 (Apr., 1964).

17. Harder, *The Mennonite Church in the City,* No. 33 (June 1964).
18. John Esau, "Mennonite Strategy in the City," *The Mennonite Church in the City,* June 15, 1962.
19. Letter, Delton Franz to Elmer Neufeld, Sept. 14, 1959, Committee on City Churches, General Conference vault.
20. Edgar Epp and Max Miller, Minutes of the Committee on City Churches, July 11-13, 1960, General Conference vault.
21. *The Mennonite Church in the City,* No. 7 (Nov. 1, 1957).
22. *Ibid.,* No. 4 (Apr. 1, 1957), pp. 3-4.
23. Editorial, *Pulpit Digest,* Nov. 1963, quoted by Peter Ediger in 1963 report of the Committee on City Churches.
24. Ed Riddick, "Mennonites and Community Organization: A Possibility," in *Addresses, Urban Pastors Seminar, Kitchener, Ontario, June 21, 22, 1966,* Elkhart, Ind.: Mennonite Board of Missions and Charities, p. 39.
25. Delton Franz, "Survey of the General Conference City Church on the Local Level," *The Mennonite Church in the City,* No. 17 (Sept. 15, 1960).
26. Leland Harder, "Stage 4 in Church Planting; What Shape Will It Take?" *The Mennonite* 89 (Apr. 30, 1974): 282-84.
27. Report to Eastern District Conference, 1957.
28. Executive committee of Board of Christian Service, Minutes and Reports, 1951, file 123, Albert Gaeddert Collection, MLA.
29. *Minutes,* 1959, General Conference Mennonite Church, pp. 23-24.
30. Theron Schlabach, in *Mission Focus,* Mar. 1978, pp. 6-12.
31. Two Oklahoma Indian churches were admitted to the General Conference in 1935, but the 1938 conference was told there had been a mistake, and so the churches were no longer listed as members. *Minutes and Reports,* General Conference Mennonite Church, 1938, p. 17.
32. Summaries of General Conference involvement in the East Harlem Protestant Parish may be found in Delton Franz, "The Inner City Protestant Parish Movement," *The Mennonite Church in the City,* No. 26 (Jan. 15, 1963); and in S. F. Pannabecker, ed., *The Christian Mission of the General Conference Mennonite Church* (Newton, Kans: Faith and Life Press, 1961), p. 11.
33. *The Mennonite Church in the City,* No. 3 (Feb. 1, 1957).
34. Curtis E. Burrell, Jr., "A Black People's Interpretation of Religion," *Chicago Daily Defender,* August 5, 1970 (?).
35. Jacob T. Friesen, memo to pastors and congregations, August 12, 1970; Jacob T. Friesen to Curtis Burrell, May 7, 1971; Jack Goering, "Conflicts, Promise Surround the Future of Woodlawn," General Conference News Service, August 31, 1971, with added notes by Malcolm Wenger, CHM.
36. *The Mennonite Church in the City,* No. 30 (Nov. 15, 1963).
37. David Ewert, interview with author, May 9, 1978.
38. E. Stanley Bohn, correspondence with author, September 1979.
39. *Minutes,* 1968, General Conference Mennonite Church, pp. 15, 26-27.
40. *Report,* 1971, General Conference Mennonite Church, p. 39.
41. *Minutes,* 1965, General Conference Mennonite Church. The conference peace and social concerns office also got involved in controversy over whether the conference could send funds to North Vietnam to rebuild hospitals which had been bombed.
42. Minutes of the Committee on City Churches, February 18, 1966.
43. See *The Way of Peace,* General Conference 1971 statement (Newton, Kans.: Faith and Life Press, 1972).
44. *Minutes,* 1959, General Conference Mennonite Church, p. 13.
45. See *The Mennonite* 94: no. 9 (Feb. 27, 1979): 138-141.

46. See *The Mennonite* 97: no. 8 (April 13, 1982): 178.

47. "The Mennonite Church, Columbus, Ohio, 1957-1977," compiled by Mary E. Harshbarger, unpublished manuscript.

48. *Concern*, No. 5, Scottdale, Pa: Mennonite Publishing House; John W. Miller, "A Brief History of the House Church," *The House Church* 1: no. 2 (Dec. 1978): 1-2.

49. David Habegger, interview with author, August 6, 1979.

50. See Arthur L. Foster, "The House Church: Context and Form," *The Chicago Theological Seminary Register*, 61: no. 2 (Dec. 1970): 25.

51. *The Mennonite Church in the City*, No. 8 (May 1, 1958).

52. "A New Newsletter," *The House Church* 1: no. 1 (Oct. 1978): 1.

53. *Report*, 1974, General Conference Mennonite Church, p. 50.

54. Herman W. Enns, "Mission Strategy in the Twentieth Century," presented to Conference of Mission Workers, July 17, 1963.

55. Malcolm Wenger, "Emphasis on Judea and Jerusalem," reprinted from *Missions Today*, n.d. (c. 1967).

56. *Report*, 1974, General Conference Mennonite Church, p. 55.

57. Proceedings of Consultation on Mission Policy and Strategy, 1967; for further information on inter-Mennonite media programs, see Hubert R. Pellman, *Mennonite Broadcasts; The First 25 Years* (Harrisonburg, Va.: Mennonite Broadcasts, Inc., 1979).

58. Howard Snyder, "An Evangelistic Lifestyle in the Church," *Pastoral Renewal* 4: no. 1 (July 1979): 4-8.

59. P. 4.

60. Based on raw data from Harder, *Fact Book of Congregational Membership*, by the author, 1971.

61. Eastern District with 6.3 percent living on farms had 26.5 percent of its members of non-Mennonite parentage. Central with 26.5, had 17.3, Pacific with 26.3 had 14.9, Western with 37.4 had 5.2, Northern with 46.6 had 6.3. In Canada Ontario with 22.2 had 3.2, Alberta with 28.5 had 2.8, B.C. with 29.0 had 1.9, Manitoba with 28.9 had 1.2, and Saskatchewan with 33.0 had 2.2. (Source: Leland Harder, *Fact Book*, p. 91).

62. *Ibid.*, p. 9.

63. Winnipeg Study Group, "The Christian Church and Urbanization."

64. "Concerns and Proposals of City Church Workers," Board of Missions Minutes, General Conference vault.

65. II. T., Vol 340, Canadian Board of Missions, CMC archives.

66. Karen Salo, "A History of the Waters Mennonite Congregation." Unpublished paper, Canadian Mennonite Bible College, Winnipeg, 1976.

67. Ben Rahn to Don Wismer, May 8, 1957, Western District Home Mission Committee.

68. Nancy Williams, "Rooted in History." Unpublished manuscript.

69. For a broad perspective on this issue, see Art Gish, *The New Left and Christian Radicalism* (Grand Rapids: Wm. B. Eerdmans, 1970).

Chapter 11

1. Conversion of some people—particularly spouses of Mennonites—from the surrounding society did happen, however, by the subterfuge of sending them first to the Netherlands to become members of a Mennonite church. At least one Lutheran woman who had married a Mennonite was granted special permission by the West Prussian government to become a Mennonite. For details, see P. M. Friesen, *The Mennonite Brotherhood in Russia (1789-1910)*, trans. by J. B. Toews *et. al.*, (Fresno, Calif.: Board of Christian Literature, General Conference of Mennonite Brethren Churches, 1978), pp. 59-60.

2. Christian Krehbiel, *Autobiography,* manuscript, p. 51.

3. J. Howard Kauffman and Leland Harder, *Anabaptists Four Centuries Later; A Profile of Five Mennonite and Brethren in Christ Denominations* (Scottdale, Pa.: Herald Press, 1975), pp. 290-93.

4. Interview with Richard Ratzlaff, August 1979.

5. David A. Haury, *The Quiet Demonstration; The Mennonite Mission in Gulfport, Mississippi* (Newton, Kans.: Faith and Life Press, 1979).

6. Leland Harder, *Fact Book of Congregational Membership,* by the author, 1971, p. 10.

7. Warren Moore, "Mennonites in June," Race Education Project Report, Board of Christian Service Report, Dec. 1964, p. A-26.

8. Report to Canadian Board of Missions, Jan. 1968.

A Guide to Selected Historical Sources

Unpublished Sources

The boards, committees, and commissions of the General Conference Mennonite Church kept files of their correspondence, most of which are located in the central archives of the conference, the Mennonite Library and Archives, on the Bethel College campus, North Newton, Kansas (referred to in the Notes as MLA). The materials include the Home Mission Board (HMB) files up until the 1950 reorganization (most of the correspondence from 1928 to 1942 is missing, however), the Foreign Mission Board (FMB) until 1950, the Board of Missions and the Board of Christian Service, 1950-68, and the Commission on Home Ministries (CHM) from 1968 to the present.

In addition, MLA holds the collected papers of a number of individuals prominent in General Conference home mission and service work. The Western (WD) and Pacific District (PD) conferences use MLA as a depository also. Other materials at MLA include minutes of General Conference sessions and board reports in printed form; a large number of Mennonite periodicals; microfilm of government documents related to Mennonite missions on the Cheyenne-Arapaho, Tongue River, and Hopi reservations; photographs and artifacts collected by Rodolphe Petter, H. R. Voth, and others among the Cheyenne and Hopi; Sunday bulletins from many General Conference congregations; and Bethel College student papers on congregational and Indian mission histories.

Although most of the General Conference historical materials have been sent to MLA, some legally significant materials have been kept in a vault at the General Conference central offices, 722 Main Street, Newton, Kansas.

The archives of the Conference of Mennonites in Canada are located on the campus of Canadian Mennonite Bible College, 600 Shaftesbury Boulevard, Winnipeg, Manitoba (referred to as CMC). These include correspondence of the home mission committee and Mennonite Pioneer Mission-Native Ministries as well as some newsletters and periodicals related to these. Some committee files are with the personal files of committee members.

The library at Bluffton College, Bluffton, Ohio, has the archives of the Central District Conference and its predecessors, the Middle District Conference and the Central Illinois Conference of Mennonites. Some student papers on congregational histories are located here also. The papers of Nathaniel B. Grubb are located here.

The archives of the Eastern District Conference are located at Christopher Dock High School, Lansdale, Pennsylvania.

The Oklahoma State Historical Library in Oklahoma City has correspondence to and from Indian agents on the Cheyenne and Arapaho reservation.

Helpful unpublished materials include:

Baergen, John R., and John N. Neufeld. "A Summary Report of Home Mission Work in Canada." CMBC, 1956.
Burkholder, Harold Deckert. "The Origin and Development of the Congregations of the Pacific District Conference of Mennonites." George Pepperdine College, 1949. Copy at MLA.
Campbell, Lee Price. "Seventy-five Years on the Shores of the Peaceful Sea; A History of the Pacific District Conference of the General Conference Mennonite Church of North America." Western Evangelical Seminary, 1973. Copy at MLA.
Dueck, Ronald J. "The Development of Canadian City Missions." CMC, 1966.
Dyck, Gordon R. "The United States General Conference Extinct Churches (1847-1959)." Mennonite Biblical Seminary, Elkhart, Indiana, 1959. Copy at MLA.
Fretz, J. Winfield. "A Study of Mennonite Religious Institutions in Chicago." Chicago Theological Seminary, 1940. Copy at MLA.
Habegger, Alfred. "The Development of the Missionary Interests Among Members of the General Conference of Mennonites of North America." Bluffton College and Mennonite Seminary, 1917. Copy at MLA.
Hart, Lawrence H. "Why the Doctrine of Non-Resistance Has Failed to Appeal to the Cheyenne Indian." Bethel College, 1961. MLA.
Hiebert, Russell. "J. B. Frey, Missionary to the Hopis." Bethel College, 1967. MLA.

Linscheid, Anna Hirschler (Mrs. G. A.). "Historical Sketch of the General Conference Mission Enterprise in Oklahoma, 1880-1930." 1930. MLA.

Myron, Nadenia F. "The Early Mennonite Missionary's Approach and Attitude to the Hopi Indianns and the Effects upon the Mission Work." Bethel College, 1979. MLA.

Neufeld, John T., with additions by Catherine Neufeld and Esther Neufeld Kressly. "Mennonite Work in Chicago Prior to 1960." MLA.

Published Sources

On the Cheyenne, Arapaho, and Hopi:

Berthong, Donald J. *The Cheyenne and Arapaho Ordeal.* Norman: University of Oklahoma Press, 1976.

_____. *The Southern Cheyenne.* Norman: University of Oklahoma Press, 1963.

Habegger, Lois R. *Cheyenne Trails.* Newton, Kansas: Mennonite Publication Office, 1959.

James, Harry C. *Pages from Hopi History.* Tucson: University of Arizona Press, 1974.

Linscheid, Ruth C. *Red Moon.* Newton, Kansas: By the author, 1973.

Simmons, Leo W., ed. *Sun Chief: The Autobiography of a Hopi Indian.* New Haven: Yale University Press, 1942.

Stauffer, Anna G. *Mennonite Mission Study Course; Part I: Hopi Mission Pamphlet.* Newton, Kansas: Herald Publishing Co., 1926.

_____. *Mennonite Mission Study Course; Part III: Cheyenne Mission Field.* Berne, Indiana: Mennonite Book Concern, 1928.

Trenholm, Virginia Cole. *The Arapahoes, Our People.* Norman: University of Oklahoma Press, 1970.

Waters, Frank. *Book of the Hopi.* New York: Ballentine Books, 1963.

_____. *Pumpkin Seed Point.* Chicago: The Swallow Press, Inc., 1969.

White, Elizabeth Q. (Polingaysi Qoyawayma) as told to Vada F. Carlson. *No Turning Back.* Albuquerque: The University of New Mexico Press, 1964.

On City Missions:

Eash, A. M. *After Ten Years; A Brief Report of the First Ten Years of Work of the Twenty-sixth Street Mennonite Mission, 1906-1916.* Chicago: By the author.

Harder, Leland, *Seventy-Third and Laflin; The Story of a City Mission of the General Confernce Mennonite Church.* Chicago: The First Mennonite Church, 1952.

Mennonite Life, City Church Issue, January 1964.

"Mennonites in Urban Canada; Proceedings of the 1968 Conference on Urbanization of Mennonites in Canada, University of Manitoba, Winnipeg." Reprinted from *Mennonite Life*, October 1968.

Our Continuing Mission in the City; A Brief History of Western District Conference Home Mission Churches. Home Missions Committee, October 1969.

Peachey, Paul. *The Church in the City.* Institute of Mennonite Studies, Series No. 2. Newton, Kansas: Faith and Life Press, 1963.

On Various Home Mission and Service Topics:

Driedger, N. N. *The Leamington United Mennonite Church, Establishment and Development, 1925-1972.* Leamington, Ontario: 1972.

Enns, J., Abr. Vogt, Joh. Klassen, and Is. Klassen. *Dem Herrn die Ehre; Schoenwieser Mennoniten Gemeinde von Manitoba, 1924-1968.* Altona, Manitoba: 1969.

Gerbrandt, Henry J. *Adventure in Faith.* Altona, Manitoba: Bergthaler Church of Manitoba, 1970.

Haury, David. *Prairie People; A History of the Western District Conference.* Newton, Kansas: Faith and Life Press, 1981.

_____. *The Quiet Demonstration; The Mennonite Mission in Gulfport, Mississippi.* Newton, Kansas: Faith and Life Press, 1979.

Kaufman, Edmund George. *The Development of the Missionary and Philanthropic Interest Among the Mennonites of North America.* Berne, Indiana: Publication Board of the General Conference of the Mennonite Church of North America, 1931.

Krahn, Cornelius, and John F. Schmidt, eds. *A Century of Witness; The General Conference Mennonite Church.* Newton, Kansas: Mennonite Publication Office, 1959.

Krehbiel, H. P. *The History of the General Conference of the Mennonites of North America.* St. Louis, Missouri: By the author, 1898.

_____. *The History of the General Conference of the Mennonites of North America,* Vol. 2. Newton, Kansas: By the author, 1938.

Neufeld, G. G. *Die Geschichte der Whitewater Mennoniten Gemeinde in Manitoba, Canada, 1925-1965.* 1967.

Pannabecker, Samuel Floyd. *Faith in Ferment: A History of the Central District Conference.* Newton, Kansas: Faith and Life Press, 1968.

Rempel, J. G. *Fuenzig Jahre Konferenzbestrebungen, 1902-1952.* Konferenz der Mennoniten in Canada, 1954.

Tilitzky, Jake, ed. *Churches in Profile.* Conference of Mennonites in British Columbia, 1978.

Unruh, Wilfred J. *A Study of Mennonite Service Programs.* Elkhart, Indiana: Institute of Mennonite Studies, 1965.

Weaver, William B. *History of the Central Conference Mennonite Church.* Danvers, Illinois: By the author, 1926.

Index

329